J MP
GIBSON'S
BOOKSTORE
$ 19.95

MICHIGAN POLITICS AND GOVERNMENT

D1039109

*Politics and Governments
of the American States*

General Editor

John Kincaid
U.S. Advisory Commission on
Intergovernmental Relations
and the University of North Texas

Founding Editor

Daniel J. Elazar
Temple University

Editorial Advisory Board

Thad L. Beyle
University of North Carolina
at Chapel Hill

Diane D. Blair
University of Arkansas

Ellis Katz
Temple University

Charles Press
Michigan State University

Stephen L. Schechter
Russell Sage College

Published by the University of
Nebraska Press in association
with the Center for the Study
of Federalism

WILLIAM P. BROWNE AND KENNETH VERBURG

Michigan Politics & Government

FACING CHANGE IN A COMPLEX STATE

UNIVERSITY CF NEBRASKA PRESS
LINCOLN & LONDON

© 1995 by the
University of Nebraska Press
All rights reserved
Manufactured in the
United States of America

The paper in this book
meets the minimum requirements of
American National Standard
for Information Sciences – Permanence of
Paper for Printed Library Materials,
ANSI Z39.48-1984.

Library of Congress
Cataloging-in-Publication Data
Browne, William Paul, 1945-
Michigan politics & government :
facing change in a complex state
/ William P. Browne and Kenneth VerBurg.
p. cm.—(Politics and governments
of the American states)
Includes bibliographical
references and index.
ISBN 0-8032-1209-7 (cl)
1. Michigan—Politics and government—1951-
I. VerBurg, Kenneth.
II. Title. III. Series.
JK5816.B76   1994
320.9774—dc20
94-18928   CIP

The authors dedicate
this book to
national cancer research

CONTENTS

TABLES, MAP, AND FIGURES

MAP

FIGURES

JOHN KINCAID

Series Preface

The purpose of this series is to provide informative and interesting books on the politics and governments of the fifty American states, books that are of value not only to the student of government but also to the general citizens who want greater insight into the past and present civic life of their own states and of other states in the federal union. The role of the states in governing America is among the least well known of all the 83,217 governments in the United States. The national media focus attention on the federal government in Washington, D.C., and local media focus attention on local government. Meanwhile, except when there is a scandal or a proposed tax increase, the workings of state government remain something of a mystery to many citizens – out of sight, out of mind.

In many respects, however, the states have been, and continue to be, the most important governments in the American political system. They are the main building blocks and chief organizing governments of the whole system. The states are the constituent governments of the federal union, and it is through the states that citizens gain representation in the national government. The national government is one of limited, delegated powers; all other powers are possessed by the states and their citizens. At the same time, the states are the empowering governments for the nation's 84,955 local governments – counties, municipalities, townships, school districts, and special districts. As such, states provide for one of the most essential and ancient elements of freedom and democracy, the right of local self-government.

Although, for many citizens, the most visible aspects of state government are state universities, some of which are the most prestigious in the world, and state highway patrol officers, with their radar guns and handy ticket books, state governments provide for nearly all domestic public services.

Whether elements of those services are enacted or partly funded by the federal government and actually carried out by local governments, it is state government that has the ultimate responsibility for ensuring that Americans are well served by all their governments. In so doing, all of the American states are more democratic, more prosperous, and better governed than most of the world's nation-states.

This is a particularly timely period in which to publish a series of books on the governments and politics of each of the fifty states. Once viewed as the "fallen arches" of the federal system, states today are increasingly seen as energetic, innovative, and fiscally responsible. Some states, of course, perform better than others, but that is to be expected in a federal system. Each state is unique in its own right. It is our hope that this series will shed light on the public life of each state and that, taken together, the books will contribute to a better, more informed understanding of the states themselves and of their often pivotal roles in the world's first and oldest continental-sized federal democracy.

DANIEL J. ELAZAR

Series Introduction

The more than continental stretch of the American domain is given form and character as a federal union of fifty different states whose institutions order the American landscape. The existence of these states made possible the emergence of a continental nation where liberty, not despotism, reigns and self-government is the first principle of order. The great American republic was born in its states, as its very name signifies. America's first founding was repeated on thirteen separate occasions over 125 years, from Virginia in 1607 to Georgia in 1732, each giving birth to a colony which became a self-governing commonwealth. Its revolution and second founding was made by those commonwealths, now states, acting in congress, and its constitution was written together and adopted separately. As the American tide rolled westward from the Atlantic coast, it absorbed new territories by organizing thirty-seven more states over the next 169 years.

Most of the American states are larger and better developed than most of the world's nations. Michigan is a middle-sized state in land area (nearly double in size if its territorial waters in four of the five Great Lakes are included), but in terms of its population and its gross domestic product, it ranks with the larger nations of the world and now would be a small power in its own right. Michigan is located just above the mainstream paths of east-west movement in the United States. As a state, it is part of the Old Northwest, but the first of the northern tier of those states. Most of its people are concentrated in the strip just north of the Indiana border at the northernmost edge of that east-west path, while most of its territory lies considerably to the north. Moreover, because of the compromise in the 1830s that gave Michigan its Upper Peninsula and left Ohio with Toledo and its harbor and the land to the west, the westernmost parts of Michigan are nearly as close to Omaha, Nebraska, as they are to Detroit.

In the nineteenth century, Michigan benefited from the northward extensions of the east-west migration, first from New England Yankees and their descendants and then Scandinavians and Dutch. At the end of the nineteenth century its expanding industrial base, particularly the rapidly growing automobile industry, brought in many eastern and southern Europeans, while from World War I onward it was the destination for many tens of thousands of Southerners, white and black, seeking work in the automobile and related industries. Its political culture was originally Yankee and was then reinforced by the Scandinavians. The political culture in its cities began to shift when the eastern and southern Europeans arrived, yet it remained well within the moralistic Yankee frame. It was radically changed by the arrival of the Southerners, so today it is divided.

The American states exist because each is a unique civil society within their common American culture. They were first given political form and then acquired their other characteristics. Each has its own constitution, its own political culture, its own relationship to the federal union and to its section. These in turn have given each its own law and history; the longer that history, the more distinctive the state. It is in and through the states, no less than the nation, that the great themes of American life play themselves out. The advancing frontier and the continuing experience of Americans as a frontier people, the drama of American ethnic blending, the tragedy of slavery and racial discrimination, the political struggle for expanding the right to vote – all found, and find, their expression in the states.

The changing character of government, from an all-embracing concern with every aspect of civil and religious behavior to a limited concern with maintaining law and order to a concern with providing the social benefits of the contemporary welfare state, has been felt in the states even more than in the federal government. Some states began as commonwealths devoted to establishing model societies based on a religiously informed vision (Massachusetts – less so in its Maine district – Connecticut, Rhode Island). At the other end of the spectrum, Hawaii is a transformed pagan monarchy. At least three were independent for a significant period of time (Hawaii, Texas, and Vermont). Others were created from nothing by hardly more than a stroke of the pen (the Dakotas, Idaho, Nevada). Several are permanently bilingual (California, Louisiana, and New Mexico).

Each has its own landscape and geographic configuration that time and history transform into a specific geo-historical location. In short, the diversity of the American people is expressed in no small measure through their states, with the politics and government each state having its own fascination.

Michigan Government and Politics is the thirteenth book in the Politics and Governments of the American States series of the Center for the Study of Federalism and University of Nebraska Press. The aim of the series is to provide books on the politics and government of the individual states of the United States that will appeal to three audiences: political scientists, their students, and the wider public in each state. Each volume in the series examines the specific character of one of the fifty states, looking at the state as a polity – its political culture, traditions and practices, constituencies and interest groups, constitutional and institutional frameworks.

Each book in the series reviews the political development of the state to demonstrate how the state's political institutions and characteristics have evolved from the first settlement to the present, presenting the state in the context of the nation and section of which it is a part, and reviewing the roles and relations of the state vis-à-vis its sister states and the federal government. The state's constitutional history, and its traditions of constitution making and constitutional change, are examined and related to the workings of the state's political institutions and processes. State-local relations, local government, and community politics are studied. Finally, each volume reviews the state's policy concerns and their implementation from the budgetary process to particular substantive policies. Each book concludes by summarizing the principal themes and findings to draw conclusions about the current state of the state, its continuing traditions, and emerging issues. Each volume also contains a bibliographic survey of the existing literature on the state and a guide to the use of that literature and state government documents in learning more about the state and political system.

Although the books in the series are not expected to be uniform, they do focus on the common themes of federalism, constitutionalism, political culture, and the continuing American frontier to provide a framework within which to consider the institutions, routines, and processes of state government and politics.

FEDERALISM

Both the greatest conflicts of American history and the day-to-day operations of American government are closely intertwined with American federalism – the form of American government (in the eighteenth-century sense of the term, which includes both structure and process). American federalism has been characterized by several basic tensions. One is between state sovereignty – the view that in a proper federal system, authority and power over most domestic affairs should be in the hands of the states – and national supremacy – the view that the federal government has a significant role to play in domestic matters affecting the national interest. The other tension is between dual federalism – the idea that a federal system functions best when the federal government and the states function as separately as possible, each in its own sphere – and cooperative federalism – the view that federalism works best when the federal government and the states, while preserving their own institutions, cooperate closely on the implementation of joint or shared programs.

Carved out of the public domain of the Old Northwest and shaped by the Northwest Ordinance of 1787, Michigan expectedly was most influenced by the federal government at the time of the state's settlement and founding. Perhaps even more than the states to the south of it, Michigan followed the spirit as well as the letter of the Northwest Ordinance, successfully utilizing the nineteenth-century federal land grants to develop its educational system and other federal grants and contracts to build its basic governmental and transportation infrastructure. It has not done as well with federal assistance in the twentieth century, although its large urban populations do receive substantial federal aid in matters of social welfare and urban redevelopment. After the boom of World War II its industries declined in relation to those of California, Texas, and other states with regard to federal contracts. Politically, as a state its national role has been limited, featuring individual leaders of stature which Michigan has provided since its earliest days without any clear state pattern, although its military contribution to the Civil War and its political contribution to the expansion of Midwest Progressivism at the turn of the century are both notable.

CONSTITUTIONALISM

American constitutionalism had its beginning in New England. Representatives of the Connecticut River valley towns of Hartford, Windsor, and Wethersfield met in January 1639 to draft a constitution. That document, the Fundamental Orders, established a federal union to be known as Connecticut and inaugurated the American practice of constitution making as a popular act and responsibility, ushering in the era of modern constitutionalism.

The American constitutional tradition grows out of the Whig understanding that civil societies are founded by political covenant, entered into by the first founders and reaffirmed by subsequent generations, through which the powers of government are delineated and limited and the rights of the constituting members are clearly proclaimed in such a way as to provide moral and practical restraints on governmental institutions. That constitutional tradition was modified by the federalists, who accepted its fundamental principals but strengthened the institutional framework designed to provide energy in government while maintaining the checks and balances that they saw as needed to preserve liberty and republican government. At the same time, they turned nonbinding declarations of rights into enforceable constitutional articles.

American state constitutions reflect a melding of these two traditions. Under the U.S. Constitution, each state is free to adopt its own constitution, provided that it establishes a republican form of government. Some states have adopted highly succinct constitutions like the Vermont Constitution of 1793, with 6,600 words, that is still in effect with only fifty-two amendments. Others are just the opposite, for example, Georgia's Ninth Constitution, adopted in 1976, which has 583,000 words.

State constitutions are potentially far more comprehensive than the federal constitution, which is one of limited, delegated powers. Because states are plenary governments, they automatically possess all powers not specifically denied them by the U.S. Constitution or their citizens. Consequently, a state constitution must be explicit about limiting and defining the scope of governmental powers, especially on behalf of individual liberty. So state constitutions normally include an explicit declaration of rights, almost invariably broader than the first ten amendments to the U.S. Constitution.

The detailed specificity of state constitutions affects the way in which they shape each state's governmental system and patterns of political behavior. Unlike the open-endedness and ambiguity of many portions of the U.S. Constitution, which allow for considerable interpretative development, state organs, including state supreme courts, generally must hew closely to the letter of their constitutions because they must. This means that formal change of the constitutional document occurs more frequently through constitutional amendment, whether initiated by the legislature, special constitutional commissions, constitutional conventions, or direct action by the voters, and, in a number of states, the periodic writing of new constitutions. As a result, state constitutions have come to reflect quite explicitly the changing conceptions of government which have developed over the course of American history.

Overall, six different state constitutional patterns have developed. One is the commonwealth pattern, developed in New England, which emphasizes Whig ideas of the constitution as a philosophic document designed first and foremost to set a direction for civil society and to express and institutionalize a theory of republican government. A second is the constitutional pattern of the commercial republic. The constitutions fitting this pattern reflect a series of compromises required by the conflict of many strong ethnic groups and commercial interests generated by the flow of heterogeneous streams of migrants into particular states and the early development of large commercial and industrial cities in those states.

The third is that found in the South and which can be described as the southern contractual pattern. Southern state constitutions are used as instruments to set explicit terms governing the relationship between polity and society, such as those that protected slavery or racial segregation, or those that sought to diffuse the formal allocation of authority in order to accommodate the swings between oligarchy and factionalism characteristic of southern state politics. Of all the southern states, only Louisiana stands somewhat outside this pattern, since its legal system was founded on the French civil code. Its constitutions have been codes – long, highly explicit documents that form a fourth pattern in and of themselves.

A fifth pattern is that found frequently in the states of the Far West, where the state constitution is first and foremost a frame of government explicitly reflecting the republican and democratic principles dominant in the nation in the late nineteenth century, but emphasizing the structure of state government and the distribution of powers within that structure in a direct, businesslike manner. Finally, the two newest states, Alaska and Hawaii, have adopted constitutions following the managerial pattern developed and promoted by twentieth-century constitutional reform movements in the United States. Those constitutions are characterized by conciseness, broad grants of power to the executive branch, and relatively few structural restrictions on the legislature. They emphasize natural resource conservation and social legislation.

Michigan's constitutions have been of the modified commonwealth pattern, the first on our list. While its first constitution was more manifestly a product of Jacksonian democracy, the New England touch was upon it. Its present constitution more or less continues in that pattern, modified by changing times. Its initiator, George Romney, was himself an heir to that culture. The leaders and dominant public opinion in the state when the constitution was adopted thought to introduce the most current elements of the pattern into their revised document. The deliberations of that constitutional convention are themselves interesting as reflections of the discussion regarding what was to be retained and what new items were to be introduced. The end result was a modernized commonwealth constitution that incorporated the ideas of American constitutional reformers of the post–World War II period, as this volume well describes.

THE CONTINUING AMERICAN FRONTIER

For Americans, the very word *frontier* conjures up images of the rural-land frontier of yesteryear – of explorers and mountain men, of cowboys and Indians, of brave pioneers pushing their way west in the face of natural obstacles. Later, Americans' picture of the frontier was expanded to include the inventors, the railroad builders, and the captains of industry who created the urban-industrial frontier. Recently, television has begun to celebrate the entrepreneurial ventures of the automobile and oil industries, portraying the magnates of those industries and their families in the same larger-than-life frame as once was done for the heroes of that first frontier.

As is so often the case, the media responsible for determining and catering to popular taste tell us a great deal about ourselves. The United States was founded with a rural-land frontier that persisted until World War I, more or less, spreading farms, ranches, mines, and towns across the land. Early in the nineteenth century, the rural-land frontier generated the urban frontier based on industrial development. The creation of new wealth through industrialization transformed cities from mere regional service centers into generators of wealth in their own right. That frontier persisted for more than one hundred years as a major force in American society as a whole and perhaps another sixty years as a major force in various parts of the country. The population movements and attendant growth on the urban-industrial frontier brought about the effective settlement of the United States in freestanding cities from coast to coast.

Between the world wars, the urban-industrial frontier gave birth in turn to a third frontier stage, one based on the new technologies of electronic communication, the internal combustion engine, the airplane, synthetics, and petrochemicals. These new technologies transformed every aspect of life and turned urbanization into metropolitanization. This third frontier stage generated a third settlement of the United States, this time in metropolitan regions from coast to coast, involving a mass migration of tens of millions of Americans in search of opportunity on the suburban frontier.

In the 1970s, the first post–World War II generation came to a close.

Many Americans were speaking of the "limits of growth." Yet despite that anti-frontier rhetoric, there was every sign that a fourth frontier stage was beginning in the form of the rurban, or citybelt-cybernetic, frontier generated by the metropolitan-technological frontier just as the latter had been generated by its predecessor.

The rurban-cybernetic frontier first emerged in the Northeast, as did its predecessors, along the Atlantic Coast metropolitan regions merged into one another to form a six-hundred-mile-long megalopolis (the term in this usage is Jean Gottman's) – a matrix of urban and suburban settlements in which the older central cities came to yield importance if not prominence to smaller ones. It was a sign of the times that the computer was conceived at MIT in Cambridge, first built at the University of Illinois in Urbana, and developed at IBM in White Plains, three medium-sized cities that have become special centers in their own right. This in itself is a reflection of the two primary characteristics of the new frontier. The new locus of settlement is in medium-sized and small cities and in the rural interstices of the megalopolis.

The spreading use of computer technology was the most direct manifestation of the cybernetic tools that have made such citybelts possible. In 1979, the newspapers in the Northeast published frequent reports of the revival of the small cities of the first industrial revolution particularly in New England, as the new frontier engulfed them. Countrywide the media focused on the shifting of population growth into rural areas. Both phenomena are as much a product of direct dialing as they are of the older American longing for small-town or country living. Both reflect the urbanization of the American way of life no matter what lifestyle is practiced, or where.

Although the Northeast was first, the new rurban-cybernetic frontier, like its predecessors, is finding its true form in the South and West, where these citybelt matrices are not being built on the collapse of earlier forms, but are developing as an original form. The present sunbelt frontier – strung out along the Gulf Coast, the southwestern desert, and the fringes of the California mountains – is classically megalopolitan in citybelt form and cybernetic with its aerospace-related industries and sunbelt living made possible by air conditioning and the new telecommunications.

The continuing American frontier has all the characteristics of a chain reaction. In a land of great opportunity, each frontier, once opened, has generated its successor and, in turn, has been replaced by it. Each frontier has created a new America with new opportunities, new patterns of settlement, new occupations, new challenges, and new problems. As a result, the central political problem of growth is not simply how to handle the physical changes

brought by each frontier, real as they are. It is how to accommodate new-
ness, population turnover, and transience as a way of life. That is the American frontier situation.

Despite its location off the mainstream, Michigan has actively participated in all four frontier stages, each of which has changed the state pro-
foundly. Its pre-American beginnings, first under the French and then under
the British, saw Michigan as adjoining the main water transportation routes
of both of those imperial powers westward into the interior of the continent,
and the few tiny settlements in Michigan were essentially service stops for
the westward-moving explorers, fur traders, and hunters. The arrival of the
Americans, who did not take control of the territory until some two decades
after the United States had declared its independence, brought with it serious
settlement in the mode of the rural land frontier of an energetic and ingenious
population, principally from New England and its extensions into New York
and northern Pennsylvania. They settled the land, covered it with many local
governments, and established a diverse industrial base that led the state onto
the urban industrial frontier with a diversified economy. They also provided
the many Michigan troops who fought the Civil War on behalf of the Union
and in opposition to slavery.

The urban-industrial frontier in Michigan at its beginning developed a diversified base of small- and medium-sized cities to accompany and encompass its diverse industrial base, but with the invention of the automobile and
the location of what was then the major automobile industry of the world in
southeastern Michigan, the urban-industrial frontier was transformed to
make Michigan for all intents and purposes a one-industry state (even though
its industrial diversity survived, it remained on a much smaller scale than the
huge and burgeoning automobile industry) and brought in whole new populations from different cultures, different ethnic and racial groups, especially
to the southeastern part of the state.

The political struggle in Michigan came to revolve around the automobile
industry. After the automobile workers succeeded with the help of the federal government in organizing unions a generation after the industry itself
began to develop in the state, politics in Michigan settled down to a continuing snarling battle between big industry and big labor, which continued well
into the 1960s. That struggle brought the state to a crisis with regard to its
economic future as the internal fights interfered with Michigan's ability to
adapt properly to changes in the countrywide and world markets.

In the 1960s, a period of rapprochement was begun, but the other weaknesses in the automobile industry led to the rise of foreign competition and a

substantial decline in Michigan's place worldwide and countrywide. Nevertheless, the rurban-cybernetic frontier developed in due course along the southern tier of the state both in southeastern Michigan and in the belt stretching from Detroit to Chicago, restoring some of the diversity which had characterized Michigan's economy in the previous century.

THE PERSISTENCE OF SECTIONALISM

Sectionalism – the expression of social, economic, and especially political differences along geographic lines – is part and parcel of American political life. The more or less permanent political ties that link groups of contiguous states together as sections reflect the ways in which local conditions and differences in political culture modify the impact of the frontier. This overall sectional pattern reflects the interaction of the three basic factors. The original sections were produced by the variations in the impact of the rural-land frontier on different geographic segments of the country. They, in turn, have been modified by the pressures generated by the first and subsequent frontier stages. As a result, sectionalism is not the same as regionalism. The latter is essentially a phenomenon – often transient – that brings adjacent state, substate, or interstate areas together because of immediate and specific common interests. The sections are not homogeneous socioeconomic units sharing a common character across state lines, but complex entities combining highly diverse states and communities with common political interests that generally complement one another socially and economically.

Intrasectional conflicts often exist, but they do not detract from the long-term sectional community of interest. More important for our purposes, certain common sectional bonds give the states of each section a special relationship to national politics. This is particularly true in connection with those specific political issues that are of sectional importance, such as race issue in the South, the problems of the megalopolis in the Northeast, and the problems of agriculture and agribusiness in the Northwest.

The nation's sectional alignments are rooted in the three great historical, cultural, and economic spheres into which the country is divided: the greater Northeast, the greater South, and the greater West. Following state lines, the greater Northeast includes all those states north of the Ohio and Potomac rivers and east of Lake Michigan. The greater South includes the states below that line but east of the Mississippi, plus Missouri, Arkansas, Louisiana, Oklahoma, and Texas. All the rest of the states compose the greater West. Within that framework, there are eight sections: New England, Middle Atlantic, Near West, Upper South, Lower South, Western South, Northwest, and Far West.

From the New Deal years through the 1960s, Americans' understanding of sectionalism was submerged by their concern with urban-oriented socioeconomic categories, such as the struggle between labor and management or between the haves and have-nots in the big cities. Even the racial issue, once the hallmark of the greater South, began to be perceived in nonsectional terms as a result of black migration northward. This is not to say that sectionalism ceased to exist as a vital force, only that it was little noted in those years.

Beginning in the 1970s, however, there was a resurgence of sectional feeling as socioeconomic cleavages increasingly came to follow sectional lines. The sunbelt-frostbelt contribution is the prime example of this new sectionalism. "Sunbelt" is the new code word for the Lower South, Western South, and Far West; "frostbelt," later replaced by "rustbelt," is the code word for the New England, Middle Atlantic, and Great Lakes (Near Western) states. Sectionalism promises to be a major force in national politics, closely linked to the rurban-cybernetic frontier.

As part of the Old Northwest, Michigan is one of the five states of the Near West, not among the original thirteen but not exactly Western either. However, because of its more northerly position, much of Michigan remained unsettled or sparsely settled for many years after states like Ohio, Indiana, and Illinois were fully populated. It was well after the Civil War before the line of settlement of the rural-land frontier advanced northward beyond Saginaw and Bay City, with the exceptions of Sault Ste. Marie, and the Upper Peninsula was essentially vacant until mining began in earnest in its western sections. The common denominator of both the northern two-thirds of the lower peninsula and the Upper Peninsula was lumbering, with the timber harvested used to feed markets in the lower Midwest.

When the Near West industrialized, so, too, did Michigan, acquiring that mixture of industry and agriculture which characterizes the section. Michigan has gone through all of the special sectional expressions of the American frontier and American politics including the economic problems of recent decades which have made it part of the rustbelt. Thus the problems of economic survival are a major feature of this book because Michigan, even more than other states, has had to learn to pull together in order to maintain its economy.

A perennial problem of the states, hardly less important than that of direct federal-state relationships, is how to bend sectional and regional demands to fit their own needs for self-maintenance as political systems. One of the ways in which the states are able to overcome this problem is through the use of their formal political institutions, since no problems can be handled governmentally without making use of those formal institutions.

Some would argue that the use of formal political institutions to deflect sectional patterns on behalf of the states is "artificial" interference with the "natural" flow of the nation's social and economic system. Partisans of the states would respond not only by questioning the naturalness of a socio-economic system that was created by people who migrated freely across the landscape as individuals in search of opportunity, but by arguing that the history of civilization is the record of human efforts to harness their environment by means of inventions, all artificial in the literal and real sense of the term. It need not be pointed out that political institutions are among the foremost of those inventions.

THE VITAL ROLE OF POLITICAL CULTURE

The United States as a whole shares a general political culture that is rooted in two contrasting conceptions of the American political order that can be traced back to the earliest settlement of the country. In the first, the polity is conceived as a marketplace in which the primary public relationships are products of bargaining among individuals and groups acting out of self-interest. In the second, the political order is conceived to be a commonwealth – a polity in which the whole people have an undivided interest – in which the citizens cooperate in an effort to create and maintain the best government in order to implement certain shared moral principles. These two conceptions have exercised an influence on government and politics throughout American history, sometimes in conflict and sometimes complementing each other.

The national political culture is a synthesis of three major political subcultures. All three are of nationwide proportions, having spread, in the course of time, from coast to coast. At the same time each subculture is strongly tied to specific sections of the country, reflecting the streams and currents of migration that have carried people of different origins and backgrounds across the continent in more or less orderly patterns. Considering their central characteristics, the three may be called individualistic, moralistic, and traditionalistic. Each of the three reflects its own particular synthesis of the marketplace and the commonwealth.

The individualistic political culture emphasizes the democratic order as a marketplace in which government is instituted for strictly utilitarian reasons, to handle those functions demanded by the people whom it is created to serve. Beyond the commitment to an open market, a government need not have any direct concern with questions of the good society, except insofar as it may be used to advance some common view formulated outside the political arena, just as it serves other functions. Since the individualistic political culture emphasizes the centrality of private concerns, it places a premium on limiting community intervention – whether governmental or nongovernmental – into private activities to the minimum necessary to keep the marketplace in proper working order.

The character of political participation in the individualistic political culture reflects this outlook. Politics is just another means by which individuals may improve themselves socially and economically. In this sense politics is a business like any other, competing for talent and offering rewards to those who take it up as a career. Those individuals who choose political careers may rise by providing the governmental services demanded of them and, in return, may expect to be adequately compensated for their efforts. Interpretations of officeholders' obligations under this arrangement vary. Where the norms are high, such people are expected to provide high-quality public services in return for appropriate rewards. In other cases, the officeholders' primary responsibility is to serve themselves and those who have supported them directly, favoring supporters even at the expense of the public.

Political life within the individualistic political culture is based on a system of mutual obligations rooted in personal relationships. In the United States, political parties serve as the vehicles for maintaining the obligational network. Party regularity is indispensable in this individualistic political culture because it is the means for coordinating individual enterprise in the political arena and is the one way of preventing individualism in politics from running wild. Such a political culture encourages the maintenance of a party system that is competitive, but not overly so, in the pursuit of office.

Since the individualistic political culture eschews ideological concerns in its businesslike conception of politics, both politicians and citizens look upon political activity as a specialized one, essentially the province of professionals, of minimum and passing concern to the lay public, and with no place for amateurs to play an active role. Furthermore, there is a strong tendency among the public to believe that politics is a dirty – if necessary – business, better left to those who are willing to soil themselves by engaging in it. In practice, then, where the individualistic political culture is dominant, there is likely to be an easy attitude toward the limits of the professionals' perquisites. Because a fair amount of corruption is expected in the normal course of things, there is relatively little popular excitement when any is found, unless it is of an extraordinary character. It is as if the public is willing to pay a surcharge for services rendered and rebels only when it feels the surcharge has become too heavy. (Of course, the judgments as to what is normal and what is extraordinary are themselves subjective and culturally conditioned.)

Public officials, committed to giving the public what it wants, normally will initiate new programs only when they perceive an overwhelming public demand for them to act. The individualistic political culture is ambivalent about the place of bureaucracy in the political order. Bureaucratic methods of operation fly in the face of the favor system, yet organizational efficiency can be used by those seeking to master the market.

To the extent that the marketplace provides the model for public relationships in American civil society, all Americans share some of the attitudes that are of first importance in the individualistic political culture. At the same time, substantial segments of the American people operate politically within the framework of two political cultures.

The moralistic political culture emphasizes the commonwealth conception as the basis for democratic government. Politics, in the moralistic political culture, is considered one of the great activities of humanity in its search for the good society – a struggle for power, it is true, but also an effort to exercise power for the betterment of the commonwealth. Consequently, both the general public and the politicians conceive of politics as a public activity centered on some notion of the public good and properly devoted to the advancement of the public interest. In the moralistic political culture, there is a general commitment to utilizing communal – preferably nongovernmental, but governmental if necessary – power to intervene in the sphere of private activities when it is considered necessary to do so for the public good or the well-being of the community. Accordingly, issues have an important place in the moralistic style of politics, functioning to set the tone for political concern. Government is considered a positive instrument with a responsibility to promote the general welfare, though definitions of what its positive role should be may vary considerably from era to era.

Politics is ideally a matter of concern for every citizen. Government service is public service, placing moral obligations on those who serve in government more demanding than those of the marketplace. Politics is not considered a legitimate realm for private economic enrichment. A politician is not expected to profit from political activity and in fact is held suspect if he or she does.

The concept of serving the commonwealth is at the core of all political relationships, and politicians are expected to adhere to it even at the expense of individual loyalties and political friendships. Political parties are considered useful political devices but are not valued for their own sakes. Regular party ties can be abandoned with relative impunity for third parties, special local parties, nonpartisan systems, or the opposition party if such changes are believed helpful in gaining larger political goals.

In practice, where the moralistic political culture is dominant today, there is considerably more amateur participation in politics. There is also much less of what Americans consider corruption in government and less tolerance of those actions that are considered corrupt, so politics does not have the taint that it so often bears in the individualistic environment.

By virtue of its fundamental outlook, the moralistic political culture creates a greater commitment to active government intervention in the economic and social life of the community. At the same time, its strong commitment to communitarianism tends to keep government intervention local wherever possible. Public officials will themselves initiate new government activities in an effort to come to grips with problems as yet unperceived by a majority of the citizenry.

The moralistic political culture's major difficulty with bureaucracy lies in the potential conflict between communitarian principles and large-scale organization. Otherwise, the notion of a politically neutral administrative system is attractive. Where merit systems are instituted, they tend to be rigidly maintained.

The traditionalistic political culture is rooted in an ambivalent attitude toward the marketplace, coupled with a paternalistic and elitist conception of the commonwealth. It reflects an older, precommercial attitude that accepts a substantially hierarchical society as part of the ordered nature of things, authorizing and expecting those at the top of the social structure to take a special and dominant role in government. Like its moralistic counterpart, the traditionalistic political culture accepts government as an actor with a positive role in the community, but it tries to limit that role to securing the continued maintenance of the existing social order. To do so, it functions to confine real political power to a relatively small and self-perpetuating group drawn from an established elite who often inherit their right to govern through family ties or social position. Social and family ties are even more important in a traditionalistic political culture than personal ties in the individualistic culture, where, after all is said and done, one's first responsibility is to oneself. At the same time, those who do not have a definite role to play in politics are not expected to be even minimally active as citizens. In many cases, they are not even expected to vote. As in the individualistic political culture, those active in politics are expected to benefit personally from their activity, although not necessarily by direct pecuniary gain.

Political parties are not important in traditionalistic political cultures because they encourage a degree of openness that goes against the grain of an elitist political order. Political competition is expressed through factions, an extension of the personal politics characteristic of the system. Hence, political systems within the culture tend to have loose one-party systems if they have political parties at all. Political leaders play conservative and custodial, rather than initiatory, roles unless pressed strongly from the outside. Traditionalistic political cultures tend to be anti-bureaucratic. Bureaucracy by its very nature interferes with the fine web of social relationships that lies at the root of the political system. Where bureaucracy is introduced, it is generally confined to ministerial functions under the aegis of the established power-holders.

Until relatively recently, Michigan's political culture was resolutely moralistic. The New Englanders and Scandinavians came with a moralistic political culture, but even after the influx of others from different political cultures, the state, including Detroit, remained moralistic in its political culture well into the 1960s. There simply were accepted standards of behavior, and the political leadership maintained and enforced them. Truth to tell, nobody really challenged them. Only in the late 1960s did Detroit's political culture shift as a result of changes in political control to introduce a strong individualistic dimension. This, of course, deepened Detroit's isolation from the rest of the state, even from its suburban areas. That is where the situation is today. Detroit is a major concentration of the individualistic political culture, while the rest of Michigan remains its old moralistic self.

MICHIGAN: FROM YANKEE COMMONWEALTH TO CLASS WARFARE TO RECONCILIATION

On the surface, Michigan's politics seem to be those of a typical northern industrial state. Actually, the Wolverine State has passed through several stages in a political history that remains as unique as that of any state. Its Yankee origins made it part of greater New England and gave it an appropriate political personality to match. This Yankee influence predominated through the Progressive era at the end of the nineteenth and beginning of the twentieth centuries and gave the state its progressive foundations and heritage. Indeed, it was the Yankees that overwhelmed an earlier and much smaller beginning, giving the state a combination of individualistic and traditionalistic elements, and the Yankee influence was indeed overwhelming until it, too, was in part overwhelmed. During the nineteenth century large Scandinavian and Dutch migrations reenforced the moralistic politics of Michigan's Yankeedom. Southwestern Michigan to this day has one of the two major concentrations of Dutch-Americans in the United States.

The coming of the automobile age not only gave Michigan its greatest economic boom, but also introduced a politics of class conflict in as intense a form as it was ever found in the United States. This politics of class conflict was intense enough to virtually paralyze the state's development, as big industry and big labor fought their battles without quarter in a struggle that included the use of violent means from time to time. It was only in the 1960s that George Romney brought the state into a politics of reconciliation with a degree of success. By that time Michigan's major industrial base was in trouble, so the reconciliation of adversaries in the state, while surely beneficial, had to be carried out in an era of economic decline that has not yet ended.

With the possible exception of its earliest pre-state days and the period of unionization from the late 1930s to the late 1940s, Michigan's politics have rarely been headline-catching. Rather, they have been decent and moderate, a pattern that continues to the present. In English, the state's motto says it all: "If you seek a pleasant peninsula, look about you." Politically, Michigan has been that pleasant peninsula even in its times of trouble.

Preface

The Michigan motto commands, *Si quaeris peninsulam amoenam, circumspice* – If you seek a pleasant peninsula, look about you. True, of course. When in Michigan, whether in its southern or northern reaches, you are on one of two peninsulas and not far from some point of renowned beauty.

Unlike that of many other states, Michigan's beauty is not linked predominantly either to urban attractions or to the awesome emptiness of remote regions. It remains a usable beauty in contrast to the buttes and mesas of the Southwest or the Badlands of the Dakotas. There, indeed, lies the crux of Michigan's dilemma. Should the state value these resources for their exploitive value or relish them for their natural attractiveness?

These resources have been an inextricable part of the state's economy and politics. The waters bordering Michigan provided a path of transportation for the European discoverers of the state. These waters were focal points for the French and Native American trade in animal pelts and served as a means of transporting this produce to Montreal. Later, ships plied these waters carrying millions of board feet of virgin pine and other species of wood to the East and then to the West. Ships carried the copper and iron ore mined from the Upper Peninsula.

Vessels still operate on these waters, ferrying the vestiges of the region's iron-ore industry to the steel mills and then on to auto plants. Other vessels from around the world traverse these waters to pick up grain and manufactured goods as well as to deliver manufactured products from Europe and Japan. Commerce and manufacturing, however, have not been the only competitors for natural resources. Tourism, too, has demanded extensive development of wilderness areas.

As critical as these waters were to the blossoming and then fading economies associated with pelts, lumber, and ore, they were always incidental. Michigan was too much out of the mainstream of American commerce to become a major trading and shipping center. Its heyday soon passed as commerce shifted to Chicago and ocean ports. Only relatively recently have the Great Lakes and the state's rivers become something more, a valuable resource needing protection. The prevailing state view, reflected even in the posturing of the most callous developers, is that the waters should no longer be exploited and then forgotten like Michigan's other natural resources. The residents of Michigan, along with those of the other Great Lakes states, are beginning to understand that this source of fresh water, the world's largest, is likely to be more than incidental to their future livelihood. Accordingly, the politics of the environment now influences Michigan politics in ways not previously possible.

Environmental politics, though, does not dominate Michigan. No politically astute Michiganian would claim that management of water and the state's other natural resources forms the core of Michigan's numerous and regionally fragmented political contests. Most would assert that the key issue throughout Michigan is how to bring growth and stability to its declining economy in the face of a worldwide restructuring of manufacturing, which Michigan and its neighboring states once dominated. In the halcyon days of automobile manufacturing, it seemed impossible that this part of Michigan's economic base would ever erode as had the pelts, lumber, copper, and iron-ore industries. The state's automobile industry once enjoyed incredible growth, even as it periodically experienced deep recessions. In each recession, laid-off workers were confident that the state would recover and that they would be called back to work. However, the economic drop of the early 1980s was swift, different, and enduring. The recession of 1990–91 proved no better. Recovery was not complete. Both periods raised questions about whether Michigan can, as it so often has, provide for its own economic recovery.

The main theme of this book, therefore, is Michigan's need to cope with a declining economy. What makes coping difficult is the state's regional, ethnic, racial, and socioeconomic diversity, since these components are affected differently by the forces of change. As this diversity increases, and as historically important interests decline in economic influence, Michigan becomes politically a much more complex state. Part of that complexity results from the activism and intensity of government itself. Federal, state, and local governments all struggle with Michigan's economic changes and its future in ways that exacerbate conflict and diversity. As new programs emerge, new interests follow and accommodation falters. Michigan, then, is a contentious state where the struggle to respond to its economy confounds taxpayers and policymakers.

Those who have contributed to the various chapters of this book are not all of like mind on these points, nor are all Michigan policymakers. Nevertheless, the state's struggle for economic renewal provides the appropriate theme for bringing together the disparate pieces of Michigan's political jigsaw puzzle. It is with that purpose that we set about producing a book that consists of systematic data, factual evidence, illustrations, anecdotes, interpretations, and judgments about Michigan's politics. This book emphasizes present governing conditions and problems, but also provides a historical context to show how these conditions developed, especially in recent decades.

To organize this book, we frame our examination of Michigan politics with five types of chapters. Chapters one and two are an introductory look at the state and its regional interests. In chapters three through nine, we look at the institutions of Michigan politics: the constitution, branches of government, and sources of influence. Chapters ten through twelve turn to the dominant issues of state politics: the economy, the environment, and local government relations. Chapter thirteen wraps up our interpretation of the state. Chapter fourteen offers a brief guide to Michigan resources for further study.

We are grateful to the contributors to the various chapters for their efforts. We especially thank them for their tolerance of our suggestions for revisions and for bearing with us as we added our own materials to each chapter. We continually asked for more information and then found more ourselves. We felt especially bad in deleting some points in our contributors' works that seemed extraneous to what we wanted to see in an integrated volume. To further our goal of bringing together a comprehensive analysis, we rewrote nearly every line of what others had contributed at our initial suggestion. We also merged the thoughts and ideas of many of our contributors. We hope that we have achieved the delicate balance of having the chapters remain the meaningful contribution of several individuals while also constituting a single product. As this work evolved, our resolve was to produce a coherent and unified book built on the evidence and insights provided by some of the state's more knowledgeable political observers. John Kincaid, Daniel J. Elazar, Charles Press, and Carol Weissert prompted us on as reviewers. John W. Smith provided the same help and used his students as a testing ground. We thank all of them.

Producing a book that taps into the great amount of specialized expertise used here is a time-consuming task and one that requires a great degree of perseverance. Both of us, having authored and edited several other books, were initially aware of only some of the costs in a venture of the unusual type that we have here, as were our families. Still, these family members permitted us the time to concentrate on this work, and quietly and uncomplainingly gave up some activities that they would have preferred to do. We thank them again. We also thank Debra Ervin and John Kincaid, who helped us delete material from an overly long manuscript, for working miracles in getting this book into its final form.

MICHIGAN POLITICS AND GOVERNMENT

CHAPTER ONE

The Setting for Michigan Politics

A BOOM-AND-BUST ECONOMY

In Michigan today we could exist as an isolated empire while the people enjoyed all the reasonable comforts and luxuries of life. The state with its inland lakes possesses the beauty of the famed Scottish lake district, the Black Forest of Germany, and the clean countryside of rural England. Our network of superior highways and improved country roads makes all parts easily accessible in Michigan-made cars powered by our own oil products. Summer resorts attract people from the entire nation. Tourists come in increasing numbers to enjoy the natural beauty of our state. Michigan is a leading industrial state. Michigan leads in the furniture industry and is the largest producer of such manufactured products as automobiles, refrigerators, and breakfast cereals. Agricultural products are plentiful and varied. Through the development of farm livestock we have produced superior breeds. Many other states buy seed grown on our farms, recognizing their value. People have been attracted here in increasing numbers to work and live, until now we rank seventh in population among the 50 states.

This was how Floyd C. Fischer portrayed the state in a 1966 civics textbook.[1] Had Fischer discovered either Utopia or Camelot? Or was his an accurate description of Michigan? As with all myths, there were threads of both accuracy and falsehood in his commentary. Perhaps most accurate in Fischer's confident representation was its reflection of the heady times of the early 1950s through the mid-1960s.

Indeed, there was a time when Michigan's economy and its politics were judged as Herculean. From many a perspective, the first half of the 1950s was Michigan's "golden age." Like other gilded periods, this period set mythically heroic records by which the contemporary period sometimes is judged. The automotive industry opened the decade of the 1950s with a record production of 6.7 million automobiles. At the midpoint of the decade, production rose to nearly 8 million. Not all these automobiles were assembled in Michigan factories, but most of the parts were. Michigan was home to more than half the workers employed directly in U.S. automobile manufacturing. In 1955, for the first time ever for any American corporation, General Motors reported a profit of more than $1 billion.

The remainder of the decade took a downturn, as automobile production began to slip. By 1958, as the national recession deepened, more than 16 percent of Michigan's workers were unemployed. The following year, automobile production rose, but unemployment did not drop proportionately. Unemployment, at 11 percent, was still nearly twice the national rate.

Michiganians, though, were philosophical. With their golden age in so recent memory, Michigan residents saw periodic economic upheaval as the price they paid for the state's strong reliance on the manufacture of durable goods. Whenever the national economy went into a short-term recession, they suffered. The philosophy was captured in the resigned cliché, "Whenever the nation sneezes, Michigan catches pneumonia." Confidence that good times would return when the national economy recovered was endemic.[2]

By the 1960s, the seeds of change had already been sown and, indeed, were beginning to grow. The Michigan-based auto industry was starting its decentralization. By the end of the decade, eighteen other states, including California, Missouri, and Wisconsin, had automotive assembly plants. Imports, especially from Germany, were beginning to make their mark. By 1958, imported small cars constituted 12 percent of the automobiles sold in the United States, and only one manufacturer, American Motors, responded by beginning to produce smaller cars to counter the "gas guzzlers" of Detroit. Two years later, Ford and General Motors unveiled models that looked smaller but that weighed about the same as earlier products. In addition, with the introduction of automation, the auto industry began to grow more efficient and less dependent on human laborers. By 1960, one-fifth of the state's population was below the poverty line, as defined by federal officials. The downward spiral in economic activity during the late 1950s was the first of seven recessions – some would call them depressions for this state – to plague Michigan over the next three decades.

This rapid shift, and Michiganians' reaction to it, was no anomaly. The Michigan economy, far from being one of utopian stability, has long surged and declined with waves of economic growth and recession. Each of the economic downturns since 1950 lasting a year or longer has cost Michigan residents a permanent share of their personal income compared to the national average. Personal income, however, has not been the only loss. Economics alters politics, and in no place more directly than Michigan. The state developed a recurring pattern. Free-falling revenues and skyrocketing costs of growing welfare and unemployment caseloads land their blows on the state treasury. Governors and legislators typically respond by cutting programs, postponing payments to creditors and local governments, and regularly enacting what have come to be known jocularly at the state capitol as "negative supplements." Such supplements are a bittersweet reference to the annual legislative ritual, in the good years, of adding to current agency appropriations. Negative supplements take already appropriated funds away from agencies, services, and program beneficiaries.

The Habit of Prodigal Waste

This roller coaster of boom and bust is not solely a creation of Michigan's dependence on the manufacture of automobiles and other durable goods. The state has depended for two centuries on dominant industries subject to great vacillation.[3] With abundant natural resources, the state has long practiced what Michigan's laureate historian, Bruce Catton, called "prodigal wastage."[4] By this term, Catton referred to an industry that emerges around a natural resource. The industry then exploits the resource until it is depleted or market demand dissipates. The state has always been poorer for such losses, both socially and environmentally. In the past, however, still able to compensate despite its losses, Michigan always moved on to greater prosperity. Eventually, as state interests adjusted economically, another industry emerged to exploit a different resource. For example, trapping, hunting, fishing, lumbering, and copper and iron-ore mining each generated extraction, transportation, and conversion industries that depleted nearly every useful element of their key resource bases. Nonetheless, wealth and experience created by success in lumbering, for example, provided the impetus for success in producing automobiles.

The furniture industry in western Michigan illustrates prodigal wastage and subsequent adjustment. Grand Rapids became the "furniture capital" of the United States in part because of the rich supply of hardwoods. The industry attracted skilled craftsmen and thrived until the forests could no longer produce large quantities of inexpensive hardwoods. That industry also was hit by new techniques that produced less expensive products. Many plants closed and were abandoned or sold for less productive uses. Much of the furniture industry went elsewhere, contributing to the economies of other states. But, out of the remains, major office-supply manufacturers, such as the aptly named Steelcase, emerged and channeled their furniture expertise into use for new technologies and nonwood components.

Contemporary prodigal wastage manifested itself in the automotive industry as well. Nowhere are the effects of lasting change more evident than in the older cities of Detroit, Flint, and Highland Park, where the industry was founded and once thrived. Vacant multistory plants testify to labor-intensive manufacturing processes of yesteryear, decentralized production, and a declining need for steel suppliers to be located midway between the iron-ore mines of the Upper Peninsula and the coal fields of Pennsylvania and West Virginia.

Prodigal waste in the heavy manufacturing industry left its scars on the lives of people, too. Attracted by high-paying jobs and the economic security assured by generous union contracts, workers streamed to auto plants from all parts of the country. Although many were unskilled and uneducated, they found jobs that opened the door to the American dream of middle-class incomes and homeownership. Even the children of these workers disparaged educational opportunity for factory jobs that promised wages greater than those of college professors with doctorates. They were to find that shifts in manufacturing location, practice, and technique ravaged laborers who were latecomers to this industry. These changes – joined by international competition in trade – created more havoc. Economists, for example, talked of "structural unemployment" when they meant wasted, undereducated, and unskilled former autoworkers. So the people, the vacant lots where they once worked, and the abandoned plants have become public wards – the newest symbols of prodigal wastage.[5] By the criterion of the number of units produced, Detroit lost its claim as the automobile capital of the United States, let alone of the world. However, it still retains that reputation because of corporations that keep their headquarters and technology in the area. Michigan, especially with the rise in job creations in 1993, is still the site of some concentrated growth because of both its resource base and the corporations that are clustered here. New automobile technology has given rise to new research and production centers throughout southeastern Michigan. Even Japanese auto firms have invested there because of unique industry advantages.

RENEWED SEARCH FOR BALANCE AND DIVERSITY

Economics has always pushed state politics because the uncertainty of each decline hastened the search for assistance. The marketplace never seemed to respond fast enough. States such as Iowa have developed more patience and less reliance on public policy initiatives because, even as single-industry places, they recovered from national recessions more quickly and with lower unemployment. In Michigan, however, each recession began a renewed clamor to diversify the state's economic base. Once again, a generalized pattern recurred. With each succeeding national recession, the governor and legislators recited the need to reduce dependence on the manufacture of automobiles and other durable goods. Following each recovery, attention commonly turned to other issues. The auto industry was in some ways just too good for the state's economy when the economy was itself very good.

The economic downturn of the early 1980s was deep, pervasive, and different from any of its predecessors, however. It produced something unlike any of Michigan's prior industrial declines, namely, permanent loss uncompensated by the rise of new industries that were solid economic contributors. Michigan's share of national employment had dropped steadily during the 1970s. From 1979 to 1982, though, employment in Michigan plummeted by some 333,000, a decline of more than 9 percent. Unemployment peaked in December 1982 at 17.3 percent; 750,000 people were out of work. Average unemployment from 1980 to 1984 was more than 10.5 percent.

The free-falling economy was magnified by the crisis facing state government. Governor William G. Milliken, finishing his third full term, began dealing with the crisis as governors before had dealt with economic downturns—as though they were temporary and short-lived. The constitutional requirement for a balanced state budget forced him to call for hiring freezes, tightened agency budgets, delays in paying bills, and other short-term funding adjustments. The crisis, though, continued and deepened; operating loans became more costly as bond-rating agencies downgraded Michigan's ability to meet its obligations. People, in a sudden reversal of trends, began leaving the state in search of employment and new lives elsewhere. Milliken achieved a temporary income-tax increase, but he kept cutting the state work force, ultimately reducing it by nearly 20 percent.

It was not until James J. Blanchard became governor in 1983 that the full extent of the state's fiscal crisis and economic condition became clear to most policymakers. A 38 percent increase in the personal income-tax rate provided temporary relief, and with it came a renewed dedication to enhance the diversity of Michigan's economic base. Policies to make the state's business climate more attractive were addressed; several were adopted. State and local programs to provide infrastructure, worker retraining, and other aids were touted literally throughout the world. Blanchard renewed the goal of seeking a new balance in the state's economic base, pointing especially to high technology as the hope for a replacement industry.

These efforts had limited impact. The 1979 and 1981 recessions were different in ways other than their severity. These were but part of a structural shift that began on the heels of twenty years of steady decline in the state's share of national employment. Moreover, it marked, if it did not exactly produce, a fundamental restructuring of Michigan's economy. After this bust, subsequent booms were guaranteed to leave the state poorer than even previous declines. Given fundamental changes in the state's economic base, and the paucity of replacement industries, these two recessions did not produce merely a lull in a pattern of steady growth. The state still has not recovered from the 1979 and 1981 recessions. Michigan's unemployment rate remained above the national rate for all but one year of the 1980s. For the first time since the Great Depression of the 1930s, the personal income of Michigan residents fell below the national average. The state lost population during most of the decade. Michigan's 1990 official count was 9,295,297, a gain of less than 0.7 percent over 1980 and well below the national growth rate of 10.2 percent.

Defenders of Michigan argue, nonetheless, that the state made significant economic gains after the recessions of 1979 and 1981. They have a point, one that illustrates Michigan's continuing boom-and-bust cycle as well as its pervasive sense of adjustment. Personal income in the mid-1980s, as can be seen in figure 1, attained a level slightly greater than the national average before falling below the average again in 1989. Indices such as investment in manufacturing construction, manufacturing equipment, general construction, and job growth signaled at least some degree of recovery. Michigan's share of national employment rose from 1982 to 1989. By 1993, with a fall to 7 percent, Michigan's unemployment rate briefly stood below the national average for only the second time in decades.

The recessionary periods of the 1980s, nonetheless, were indisputably different in that they led to a more diversified economy, one somewhat less dependent on automobiles and on manufacturing generally. Even with gains during the later 1980s, the state ended 1989 with some 254,000 fewer manufacturing jobs, while jobs in the nonmanufacturing sector increased (see figure 2). The trend continued in the 1990s, with some new manufacturing jobs

Figure 1: Michigan Personal Income as a Percentage of the Average U.S. Personal Income, 1970–91

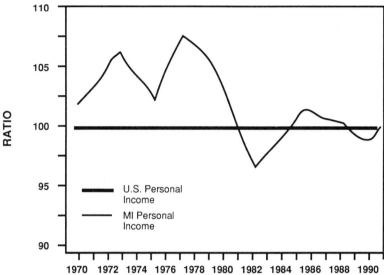

Source: House Fiscal Agency calculations from U.S. Bureau of Economic Analysis.

also being added in 1993. Trade and service jobs increased a bit more rapidly (+14,000) than the decline in manufacturing jobs; however, as primarily nonunion jobs, they also paid less: on average about $15,000 less per year. More than 90 percent of the jobs created in the 1980s were medium- and low-wage jobs, with annual salaries of less than $34,000. The price of greater diversity, in consequence, has been lower personal income for state residents and a diminished capacity of state government to fund programs and services.

The vulnerability of the Michigan economy, however, was again evident during the national recession of 1990–91. By mid-1991, another 62,000 manufacturing jobs were lost, with other losses continuing monthly throughout 1992. As Republican John M. Engler assumed the duties of governor in 1991, the transition was reminiscent of the early Blanchard years of 1987–88. But the realization of a fundamental economic shift downward was even more apparent than earlier. No one missed the message, though not all believed that things had changed permanently. Budgets were slashed and massive state employee layoffs were ordered to adjust spending to falling revenues. Engler also pursued major cuts in property-tax levies in an effort to make the state more competitive for economic recovery.

This type and scale of economic restructuring has strong implications for Michigan politics and state policies. The key element is that Michiganians,

Figure 2: Michigan Employment Mix: Manufacturing versus Service Jobs, 1978–93

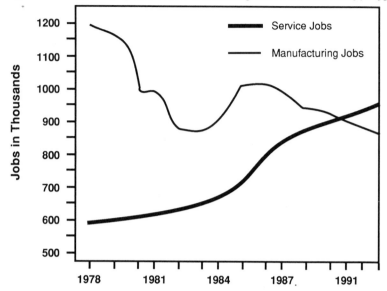

Source: Michigan House of Representatives Fiscal Agency calculations from Research Seminar in Quantitative Economics database.

without tax increases that might well trigger further business losses, can no longer expect the highest level of public service programs from their state government. The state has not become poor. After all, if measured by its gross state product, as compared to gross national products, Michigan in the 1980s ranked fifteenth among the world's national economies. However, Michigan no longer exceeds the average on measures of national prosperity by strong margins, and it sometimes falls below the average. The drop has been from seventh wealthiest state in the nation in the 1960s to eighteenth in the 1980s.

The recognition of likely busts to an economy that is less likely to boom with higher standards of living at the end of each cycle has changed political expectations as much as it has limited political responses and budget appropriations. The election of longtime tax-opponent Engler to the governorship in 1990 marked what appeared to be a broadened awareness of the need for a new balance between state programs and Michigan's fiscal capacity. To attract new jobs and investments, Engler argued, the costs of doing business and living in Michigan need to be reduced. The politics of the early years of the 1990s certainly suggest a widespread understanding of a need for a new set of rules governing how much will be spent and on whom. This represents a profound change for Michigan and its politics.

There are other constants about Michigan politics. Most important is the search for a balance between the declining state economy and its well-developed governmental structure. The state's politics historically has been a persistent, though imperfect, search for policies that favor everyone yet no one. The idea, as played out by policymakers who respond to economic and social adjustment, is that no one loses: not workers over employers, environmentalists over industrialists, renters over homeowners, hunters over animal lovers, north over south, African Americans over whites, urban citizens over rural residents, the insurers over the insured, welfare recipients over taxpayers, physicians over chiropractors, and not state government over local governments. All of these constituents have experienced major accommodations in recent policy decisions.

Certainly there have been advocates of specific constituents, and some win more than others. Yet, in stark contrast to the state's extremes of economic feast or famine, Michigan's political leaders have been engaged in a continuing quest for a politics of balanced attention to the state's diverse and heterogeneous constituencies. Formerly, political leaders pursued balance just by spending more of the state's wealth on those who felt disadvantaged by government or market decisions. That legacy of trying to serve everyone still persists, partly driven by idealism and partly by practical politics. Even in downsizing state government and attacking welfare programs, Governor Engler's staff wrestled with the differences between the truly needy, as they saw them, and General Assistance recipients who had possible options other than public support. They knew full well that the poor had strong proponents who would argue that "the safety net for the needy is disintegrating." The reasons for this search for balance and for the emergence of a new shift in attention are the first subjects that must be addressed in analyzing why Michigan does what it does.

We are not suggesting that a politically satisfactory equilibrium, or perfect balance, was ever reached in all or even many of the issues cited above. Nor do we mean that everyone got all they wanted or found absolute fairness. Certainly, racism and the economic problems of African Americans have been as severe as in any state. Moreover, Detroit, as a predominantly African-American city, is often singled out for harsh criticism in the state's regional battles. But until fundamental economic adjustment was evident, there was a well-understood view that "benefits for all" was a nonnegotiable first principle of Michigan politics. Present was a policy middle ground of doing something for all, well supported by entrenched institutions and aimed at serving the whole of the state's diverse population, economic sectors, and places. Public officials and interest groups tinkered incessantly with resulting programs and legal guarantees.

Many factors that create demands on state government explain this policy environment. Five of these demand factors are especially important: the state's political culture, its interest-group structure, outside influences on the state, Michigan's tendency toward excessiveness, and the state's heterogeneity. Subsequent chapters explore these factors in greater detail.

Michigan's Political Culture

We start with culture because it sets the ideals and expectations of state residents. Michigan's political culture, its collective beliefs as to what state politics should be about, stems from its historical experience and its ethnic heritage. While Americans generally believe in the right of individuals to pursue personal values, states vary in the way in which their citizens reconcile the competing values of individualism and egalitarianism. A state's political culture or cultural mix helps to determine the responses to such questions as: How should politics be conducted? Who should be the principal participants in the political process? What should be the ultimate goals of the political process?

Three major variations in political culture have been identified in the United States: traditionalistic, individualistic, and moralistic.[6] For the most part, two of these subcultures, moralistic and individualistic, combined to give rise to Michigan's political culture. Traditionalistic subcultures, with their elite-maintaining behavior, have not been prominent in Michigan. The possible exception, and one that seems more individualistic, is the present African-American and previously white-only governing network of Detroit.[7]

Michigan's political culture is predominantly moralistic. The state's citizens generally share a view that *emphasizes their own political participation* as an exercise in strengthening the commonwealth's ability to act on behalf of each part of the public. The moral right to be involved is the idealistic dimension of Michigan politics. Politics is seen as everyone's business, and there are few opportunities for closed doors in public policymaking.

Even the posh and industry-responsive government of the 1920s was regularly encouraged to intervene in the private affairs of specific business interests. Michigan added significantly to its progressive reputation during that era, often limiting the political excesses of the rich in order to promote or safeguard the general welfare. Even earlier, interventionist social activists checked laissez-faire interests when they became especially bold and neglected what the public saw as obvious problems.

Today, following the same traditions, citizen groups are notable antagonists to school-district boards and administrators who want to increase millages or pass bonding issues. Party and group loyalties have also been strong bases for encouraging citizen involvement in government, but ironically the institutions built around these loyalties seldom have restrained either the personal political views or the issue positions of their members. Even the United Auto Workers, with that union's strong ties to the state Democratic party, commonly suffered a degree of frustrating inability to deliver the votes of its members for party candidates.[8]

Michigan's general policymaking behavior is as moralistic as its citizens' expectations, and it is here that substantive decisions to reward everyone come into play. Michigan government – through the interactions of its parties, organized interests, and policymaking professionals – embraces the obligation to look after the general welfare of its citizens. What state government does provide is the means to create a multitude of generous programs to help those in need or those who can argue that assistance for them helps the state as a whole. Compared to the programs of nearby individualistic states, such as Indiana, Ohio, and Illinois, Michigan has customarily provided high levels of welfare and unemployment support. Welfare payments in 1991 averaged 29 percent higher than in those other states. Average weekly unemployment benefits were the highest of all populous states, 26 percent above the national average. Until recently, these benefits were maintained even under heavy pressure to make budget cuts.

During the recession of the early 1980s, the governor and legislature gave welfare and basic health programs top priority; by the end of the decade, though, declining revenues made Michigan's welfare assistance lag behind the rate of inflation.[9] Continued budget deficits in the early 1990s led the Engler administration to propose major cuts in welfare programs. As the opposition threatened an unsolvable logjam in budget negotiations, Governor Engler backed away somewhat and then countered with cuts for cultural affairs, science centers, conservation efforts, and selected education programs as well as welfare in order to fit government to revenues rather than let program requests determine tax needs.

In Elazar's terms, however, the state's political culture has individualistic overtones as well. In particular, interest-group and regional conflicts have made individualistic politics important in policymaking. Because legislators are moved by their group and regional ties, the state house of representatives and senate are centers of individualistic bargains and deals. Citizen expectations are now a factor in advancing this part of Michigan's political culture. Residents expect politicians to act on behalf of the public, but much of that public, not just the affected group, is angered when the state ignores the demands of the visibly active interests with which they identify. They become angry about benefits for anyone else when these benefits are seen as having been gained at their own expense. State elected officials, as an example, are accorded a professional status and are then expected to use their best and most informed judgment in making decisions. At the same time, officials who fail to respond to the demands of important state interests or to the general views of the public are taken to task quickly and forcefully by organized movements with quite specific and narrow visions of proper policy. Hence, Michigan's political leaders take a routine buffeting from affected constituents and the press who listen to them. Governor Engler, for example, encountered a noisy recall drive in 1991, organized primarily by low-income residents and public employees who worked with the poor. He received equally vehement support from many middle-class voters who responded to raging newspaper and radio talk-show debates.

As a result of this blending of cultural perspectives, political contests and policy battles have been waged within a limited band of issues generally acceptable to the values of a moralistic culture. Michiganians want to do for all, at least in the sense that none is excluded. Within such a band of negotiable details, however, individualistic values demand a continuing search to satisfy each special case. Policy battles are not waged, for example, over questions of whether the state will assist the poor with housing, health care, or financial assistance. Those answers become givens, even as some opponents of social programs complain about them. The moralistic culture assumes that such assistance will be provided to the less fortunate, although policymakers will debate vigorously the level of support to be given to recipients.

During the 1991 budget-cutting battles, for example, Engler sought to eliminate General Assistance, the basic state-funded aid for the poor who do not qualify for Aid to Families with Dependent Children (AFDC), which is partially funded by the federal government. General Assistance was the most vulnerable program, one that would evoke the least sympathies. However, legislative appropriations committees rejected Engler's plan despite its popular appeal. They opted instead for an across-the-board cut in state spending that, in keeping with traditions, would be shared by all. It was only during the 1992 budget battle, when Democrats sought to protect their priorities elsewhere and the legislative process nearly came to a halt, that General Assistance payments were eliminated for more than 82,600 recipients. The remaining 20,000 or so recipients were moved to one of two programs: family emergency or disability assistance. Even then, for most policymakers, calls for cuts were couched in terms of specific characteristics of recipients: only "able-bodied non-working adults without children" were to be losers.

Other examples of political hairsplitting exist in the state's most time-consuming policy matters. Broad access to higher education is an unassailable hallmark of Michigan public policy. Yet debate is intense as public officials search for a balance between what has become the hotly contested and annual debate between the appropriate level of general public assistance for universities and personal tuition costs to students. The need for aid to students unable to pay for education on their own enters the equation as well. Questions are raised as to whether Michigan funds too many educational frills or whether students justifiably can be charged extra, for example, to use a recreation facility or an auditorium.

Nor does the state seriously debate the need to have an effective means for educating its younger children. Disagreements are over whether the means are to be the public school system or a combination of public and private schools, and whether options include home classes or freedom of choice in school selection. The tendency is to open some doors to all, saying no to neither the public school teacher, the Christian fundamentalist with special education priorities, nor the parent who wants home-schooling options. Also at issue are such questions as the division of state and local responsibility for funding public schools, the employment status of teachers and their accountability, the extent to which private schools will benefit from public expenditures, and how state aid will be allocated among the state's 542 public school districts and 57 intermediate school districts. In essence, there can be no simple definition of the state's central education needs. Demands are too diffuse.

The moralistic culture thus defines broad dimensions of Michigan's public policies as a kind of social contract with the broadest array of constituents. At the same time, individualist values give rise to the unsettled dimensions of the state's public policies. Individualism, by pointing to specific groups and regions that can be portrayed as less deserving of support or best able to get along without support, allows for, or forces, policy adjustments.

In earlier, more prosperous years, individualism called attention to questions of who had the greatest need for additional policy shares. This produced spurts of policy attention to selected issues, such as welfare or state parks and recreation. In contrast, moralistic values, by emphasizing social responsibility to all, always made changes in policy direction exceedingly difficult.

Interest-Group Structure

Highly organized interest groups keep most of this culturally driven action in motion. They can be relied on to keep those policy details of conflict over resources and systematic defense of rights before the eyes of policymakers. Thus, the state has no forgotten issues, even though the legislature may not have enacted solutions to all problems. Economic and social groups in Michigan are well organized and well financed. In a highly developed industrial state with great diversity, such as Michigan, we would expect interest groups to be active and competitive. Under those circumstances, the United Auto Workers (UAW) emerged as an active and well-organized balance to the organized power of the auto companies, giving the state its reputation as a good home for unions. The strong sense of individualism coupled with the recognition of all groups adds to the acceptance of organized interests, even if their appeals are often chastened as those of "selfish special interests." Typically, interest-group representatives, like the people they confront in the state legislature and bureaucracy, are professional and well respected. Lobbyists are accepted actors in the policymaking process because of their demonstrated ability to bring forward, in a cumbersome political process, the state's many different interests and points of view.

All Michigan lobbyists serve as watchdogs over policy initiatives that may affect their own employers. Given the interventionist style of Michigan politics, most are also engaged in proposing policy modifications whenever their sponsors seek a new advantage or attempt to counter the success of an opposition group. Whether they represent labor or management, public employees (e.g., teachers or municipal workers), or public agencies (e.g., school boards, road commissions, municipalities, or counties), lobbyists continually seek to tip the scales in their favor or to prevent others from disadvantaging them. This touches every institutional facet of state politics, even constitution making. It also keeps political tensions high.

Being well represented by a lobby is appreciated because no gotten gain is too small to protect, and with an activist state government since the 1950s, the base of well-used public policies is extensive. Turf wars over even the smallest issue may generate enough attention to attract regional and state-wide interests to the conflict, eventually making it a partisan battle. Policies in question, for example, have been as specialized and technical as rules governing medical malpractice and a physician's or hospital's liability for an injury or death. Trial lawyers want to minimize the statutory and judicial protections; physicians and hospitals seek at least more protection from the law than may be the case at a given point. Involved interests battle over the issues from a variety of informed perspectives: the likely implications of rising costs of medical malpractice insurance, the human costs of closing hospital emergency rooms, or the service consequences of declining numbers of obstetricians. Attorney groups present horror stories of parents or children irreparably damaged by medical carelessness. Insurance company executives and large employers who, through employee benefit programs, end up financing a large portion of the health-care expenditures, also enter the fray. As a legislator who heard these arguments repeated during several sessions said: "Just a typical day of opposing views in Michigan, no rights and no wrongs, just lots of points to ponder. This job is a lot harder than I ever thought possible."

The reasons for such micropolitics, which sometimes lead to neglect of more nationally prominent issues, should not be surprising. Many interest groups are tied directly to the distribution of economic influence in the state. Those interests, no matter how moralistic the polity, do not get the same treatment when they contest with each other. Some gain advantages as they manipulate their images in the eyes of political leaders and the public. When it became necessary to diversify the Michigan economy away from durable goods manufacturing, for example, lobbyists from other industries found renewed attention. They merited, so their logic went, greater concern because the state had to help them upgrade their ability to compete. Also, the decline of labor, both in numbers and in percentage of support for Democratic candidates, reduced the influence of unions and their ability to protect certain policies, such as workers' compensation. The balance was tipped against labor as technology and the economy created intense political pressures to revitalize the state. In the process the poor, who benefited from labor's political intervention on their behalf, were accordingly left vulnerable to cuts in their budget share. Faced with choices about what to protect, labor leaders could not spend scarce political capital and their members' good will in working for the unemployed when political battles for the employed union member still loomed. This type of shift in advocacy exemplifies the growth of individualism in the state's political culture.

Outside Influences

Not all influences on the state's political balance come from Michigan. The economic productivity of Michigan is significant, even in a world setting, and so it is constantly subject to external intervention. Although automobile manufacturing remains central to this economic base, the state's economy is complex and highly interdependent with the national and global economies. Outside factors are always likely to threaten previously settled policies, creating in the process a catalyst for renewed state politics around one or several issues.

Nowhere is this more evident than federalism. The federal government initiates numerous demands that affect many targets in the state. A change in federal income-tax laws affects state revenues, thus giving rise to new debates about how to spend the increase or, if a decrease, how to cut programs. To illustrate, the $10 billion that the state lost in federal-aid revenue from 1981 to 1990 led to cuts in aid to the poor as well as cuts in other state services. When the federal Nuclear Regulatory Commission established new rules for nuclear power plants, it set off a debate over whether ratepayers or stockholders should bear the costs as state regulators review utility rates and company profits.

A federal judge, in another instance, added to the complexity of state politics through interpretations of agreements with Native Americans that allowed fishing rights not accorded to other state residents. This generated over a decade of intense conflict with sportfishers beginning in the mid-1970s. Confrontations took place in court as Native Americans sued for their rights, in local communities as residents fought to keep Native Americans from using marine facilities, and even in parking lots where individuals assaulted one another. Federal action, in this case, played an important role in ensuring balance in state politics. Native Americans represent only 0.6 percent of the state's population, and they are concentrated in small numbers in the far north, central Michigan, and the Detroit metro area. Because of this, they were generally ignored by state policymakers before the court action.

An unsettling influence may also come from nationally organized interest groups that never think specifically of Michigan. For example, when the Natural Resources Defense Council campaigned in the media against growers across the nation who were applying the chemical Alar to their apples, Michigan growers and merchants lost sales income because of the adverse publicity. Larger policy questions were raised as well about the proper role of the state agriculture department. Should it monitor and promote state agriculture to assist producers or to protect consumers? That question brought a new point of balance to agricultural politics in Michigan by suddenly turning the attention of consumers to an agency that previously attracted little citizen interest.

The politics of other states enter in as well. Adjacent states, for example, have historically paid welfare recipients less than did Michigan. The in-migration of welfare clients to Michigan was a form of outside influence that gave rise to demands for policy adjustments, motivated largely by demands for fairness in dealing with what many saw as an exploitive group entering the state for financial gain. Similarly, out-migration of industry frequently sets off other debates about tax policies and unemployment taxes or workers' compensation benefits. Or, as conflict in the Middle East changes the price of oil, economic gains made in U.S. oil states such as Oklahoma are met by losses in Michigan's tourist businesses as well as state revenues generated by auto sales. These often bring on rolling recessions nationally, more regional in impact at any one time and more likely to inspire hotly debated state political responses. These examples have one thing in common. Each such influence, beyond state control, is likely to tip the scale in one direction or the other and generate a call for some kind of policy adjustment by an interest group or the public.

Tendencies toward Excess

Moralism, individualism, interest-group politics, historic wealth, and political responsiveness have combined to produce another characteristic that moved the state toward balance and sometimes – especially in the face of serious revenue declines – difficult readjustment. Michigan, quite simply, has a frequent penchant for excess in policy choices. Michigan – as a state government – has attempted to do everything, still wants to, and, of course, cannot do so. As a result, it often gets caught in high levels of policy demands and rapidly escalating state expenditures for some policies. Then policymakers are forced reluctantly and under difficult circumstances to retrench and search for a new equilibrium. There is almost always an example of this recurring inability to say "no." In 1992 and 1993, for example, three brand-new prisons were mothballed temporarily because revenue shortfalls made it impossible for legislators to agree on how to reallocate funding for them. "These are bankrupting the state," said one senator. As crime became a major issue again in 1994, however, some were thinking about more prisons.

This excess has been evident not only in the state's prodigal wastage of natural resources but also in providing for public services. Michigan has ranked high in comparative per capita expenditures for some time: fifth in 1970 and in 1980 and nineteenth in 1990. In generating revenues, the state and its local units ranked twelfth in 1990. However, the state capacity to provide services and expenditures at that level is much lower. A tax capacity index developed by the U.S. Advisory Commission on Intergovernmental Relations placed Michigan sixteenth in 1967 and in 1977. During the 1980s, Michigan's capacity generally declined, placing it twenty-sixth among the fifty states by 1991.[10] Individual services show this excess more vividly. In the mid-1980s, for example, the state launched a program to expand its prison system from 7,000 beds to 34,500, the largest prison expansion in the nation's history. The program was coupled with an effort to impose stiffer criminal penalties, especially for drug dealing. By 1993, Michigan's reputation for being tough on crime was secure.

There are numerous other examples of overzealous action. Michigan has fifteen public institutions of higher education, placed throughout the state on the basis of regional politics rather than need. When two universities faced shortages in facilities in 1993, state legislators parlayed that demand into a new building committed for each of the fifteen campuses: "Things just snowballed." The state also ranks first in the nation in aid to private colleges. As a second example, Michigan has 1,821 miles of limited-access highways, a number that can be compared most favorably to the federal government's announced goal of 41,000 miles for the National Defense and Interstate Highway Act of 1956. This led to Michigan's building two east-west highways within a short distance of each other and three north-south routes pointing eventually to the Upper Peninsula, or UP. There is a huge number of greatly independent local units of government (see chapter 12). Finally, high salaries paid to state officials rankle the public. At the close of 1990, for example, the State Officers Compensation Commission (SOCC) ordered the salaries of ranking public officials to be increased by 16.2 percent. SOCC also proposed to raise the annual salary of legislators to $52,800, the governor's salary to $120,500, and supreme court justices' salaries to $120,000. Only under pressure from the media and the public during a period of severe budget cutting did the legislature reluctantly reject the proposed increases. It was the first such rejection in twenty years of SOCC recommendations. The increases would have placed the pay of Michigan's elected officials among the top five states nationally.

The salary issue was unique. Most examples of excess came in periods of economic prosperity when the state appeared able to afford generous programs. Given the need for future budget allocations, however, these increased expenditures were not without problems. In times of economic downturn, public officials repeatedly discover that the state can ill afford recent additions. Little was left to do but to adopt a general belt-tightening for all of state government. Accordingly, citizens frequently are angered and policymakers frustrated by the requirements of their fiscal crisis. During those times, Michigan experiences policy drifts that are excessive in their own right.

Excesses and drifts have taken on numerous forms. Some were operational. For instance, the fixed operating costs of programs associated with such capital-intensive facilities as prisons, state universities, highways, and recreational areas always stretched the state's fiscal resources. This led unavoidably to program adjustments elsewhere, especially in more easily adjustable but popular and useful services. These, such as increased welfare caseloads for social workers in the 1970s, often created hardships for recipients.

Other drifts have been political reactions to operational adjustments, sometimes to protect a few nearly sacrosanct programs, such as those for natural resource use that had the greatest statewide constituencies and economic vitality. Citizens also asked, for example, whether the state could keep its commitments to higher education when it was found to be lagging in facility maintenance. As popular or needed programs for individualistic interests were slashed, pockets of anger escalated, leading to taxpayers' referenda and protests during the 1970s and early 1980s. Faced with no options for restoring cuts, policymakers responded by identifying culprits on whom to place blame. Resulting political posturing created endless cycles of blame directed at the nonworking poor, the auto industry, highly paid teachers, industrialists who had previously wasted natural resources, taxpayers who were in revolt, or any other momentarily handy source. This rhetoric, of course, further committed its targets to defensive interest-group politics and even more unsettling offensive actions to prepare for later restoration of losses. Excesses, in brief, have escalated the overall amount of activism in the state by giving residents more to fight over.

State Diversity

The state's geographic characteristics compound that high level of activism, creating intense regional politics. In Michigan, regions are interests. As much as any of the other four factors, the state's unique diversity leads both to a search for balance and to unsettled policies. Michigan's longstanding divisions have forced a pluralism of interests upon state officials. Recent efforts to further diversify the state's economy continue a century-long practice of facilitating job creation in different parts of the state through government intervention. Historically, each of the extractive industries benefited from policies that turned natural resources and land over to them. The state also assisted in building transportation facilities that linked the "outstate" areas of northern and coastal nonurban parts of Michigan to Detroit. Detroit soon became a center of commerce and banking, both supported by other state policy decisions. By the mid-nineteenth century, outstate and Detroit interests were feuding over symbols of influence, such as where to locate the state capital – a compromise made in favor of Lansing, which was neither too close to Detroit nor too far outstate.

Even when Detroit became a center of manufacturing after 1904, other cities with different economic bases competed for attention. Grand Rapids, with its furniture industry, and Battle Creek, growing into a cereal-processing center, were notable sources of diverse demands on state government. So, too, were the boat-building, chemical, and food-processing industries based in smaller communities, such as Muskegon and Midland. As Detroit became more noted for post–World War II racial differences in its work force and population, its urban identity was separated even more – many say divorced – from its own region and the rest of the state. Poverty, which struck hardest at African Americans in a segregated and gentrified Detroit, sharpened the distinction between that central city and the rest of Michigan. Separation worsened with the race riots of 1967. White residents began a decades-long exodus from the city. Michigan's most populous city and the outstate centers, as a result, developed as significant sources of contrasting diversity and as objects of policy balancing.

Race is certainly the state's deepest divide. Indeed, it is one factor that continues to push Michigan further toward two political cultures. From numerous perspectives, individualism rules on racial issues as Michiganians seek both to protect their own status and to gain a larger share of the total economic pie. Most of the time, this translates into white-versus-black conflicts and the resolution of grudged political bargains that rarely satisfy all claimants. Neither the division into two political cultures nor the continuing tensions should be surprising. Michigan was alone among the moralistic states of the upper Midwest in attracting large numbers of African Americans to its already ethnically diverse population. Most moralistic states of the Northeast were spared such racial divisions, and none of them, including New York and Massachusetts, encountered racial diversity at such an economically critical time in their development.

Rural Michigan, where agriculture and tourism dominate, constitutes another source of diversity. Part of that diversity is tied to distinctions that are based on those economic sectors. Agriculture, which has recently varied in ranking from second to third in terms of economic importance to the state, produces over fifty different cash crops, making Michigan the third most varied agricultural state in the nation. Producers of beans, cherries, grains, livestock, and other products are regionally distinct; yet all look for larger export markets. All, as did two competing dairy cooperatives in 1992, place demands on state government for financial and other forms of assistance as well as protective policies. Without supplements to federal policy, Michigan farmers argue, jobs will be lost. Thus, the state's Farmland Protection Act, which took effect in the 1980s, became critical to state producers. By 1990, with federal payments to Michigan farmers falling to $168 million, from a 1987 level of $391 million, state tax credits under the act provided $53 million in farm revenues.[11] Moreover, further accommodations were made to agriculture in the massive 1994 property tax reform act.

Similarly, the tourist industry, which shares the rotation from second to third in overall importance to the state economy, imposes its own policy demands on state government. As a four-season industry, tourist interests insist, for example, on professional management of the state deer herd and on the development of superior sportfishing in the Great Lakes as well as in the state's many inland lakes and rivers. They also demand marinas and loading ramps for boaters, to say nothing of other infrastructure facilities required for winter skiing and snowmobiling and summer golf and touring.

The diversity is complicated further by intense competition among different rural regions for state attention. Upper Peninsula residents often ask whether anyone in Lansing knows that they are part of Michigan. Physical and social distances from the state capital and other major population centers are so great that many UP residents have a closer affinity to the interests of Wisconsin than those of southern Michigan. As sports fans, most root for the Green Bay Packers and Milwaukee Brewers. Periodically, as voters, they propose to secede to form the state of Superior. The "Yoopers," though relatively small in number, successfully demand from most governors that they make annual State-of-the-UP visits. From the legislature, largely through seniority and pork-barrelling, the UP has extracted a disproportionate share of state-financed projects. Under the old long ballot, those responsible for balancing the ticket of state office holders usually made certain to include someone from the northern peninsula in an office of statewide importance. The legislature, at least prior to 1993, has done the same in the modern era. As distinct as the UP's regional demands are, they are only slightly better articulated and more visible than the similar sectional battles between the eastern and western halves of the northern lower peninsula. While the West calls itself the "Gold Coast" and looks for state environmental and planning assistance, the east coast is underdeveloped and wants state-assisted growth.

PROGRESSIVE, REFORMIST, AND PROFESSIONAL GOVERNMENT

The state electorate, as might be expected in the context of these five high-demand factors, can be volatile, even quick-tempered, in its effort to place political blame or identify a villain. Voters are not alone in doing so, however. Two additional factors inherent in state policymaking lend complexity and balance to state government: the emphasis on citizen involvement in Michigan institutions and the professional nature of Michigan government.

Michigan's citizenry has a tradition of being attentive to policy events and following them from a variety of perspectives. When sizable minorities believe that state officials are unresponsive to their needs, or simply to their preferences, they often raise havoc in Lansing. The upheaval may be exhibited in acts that nearly turn politicians on their heads by ousting incumbents, recalling errant legislators, or adopting reforms that change the rules or impose new restrictions on political practitioners. This paradox of extensive citizen involvement in an otherwise professionalized state government is another recurring theme throughout this book. Some highlights of these traditions are the subject of this section.

Partisan Diversity

With an active and involved citizenry, Michigan's political parties have been strong mechanisms for organizing and aligning diverse opinions into electoral coalitions. This partisanship has been instrumental in shaping state government and politics. Not unexpectedly, then, parties have also been in flux. The Democratic party first dominated the state as an almost necessary response after Jacksonian values about popular control of government by common citizens became prevalent in the 1830s. Someone had to organize the electorate to help people make sense of their new choices about candidates and control of government. Even with the statewide conversion to the Republican party after the Civil War, Democrats retained a following and periodically helped to elect Republican governors who identified more with popular reforms than with business interests.

Republican control generally reflected conservative economic values coupled with the need to provide important business interests with ports, roads, and bridges essential to commerce. Exceptions were important. Outstate, or rural, concerns and other divisions within the party were evident but were often muted by public policies that minimized interference with local business interests. Those in the North who wanted unlimited use of natural resources and those in the South who desired inexpensive labor were able to satisfy their wants until abuse and exploitation became too visible. When such greed, or the economic problems created by greed, racked the state, either populists or progressives mobilized citizens to prove that the Republican party could not be dominated by a single group of leaders. Electoral forces would rectify imbalances.

Democratic party ascendance, short-lived as it was, proved the same point. Democrats won the governorship and both houses of the legislature during Franklin D. Roosevelt's national landslide presidential election in 1932. However, all statewide elective offices and the legislative branch returned to Republican control in 1934. Only the auto-dominated southeast lower peninsula and the western and central upper peninsula failed to follow outstate areas back into Republican ranks. This was, in large part, because of the influx of new residents into the area, a migration that began in the 1920s and lasted through the 1950s. Both southern African Americans and whites from Appalachia moved to industrial areas, bringing their Democratic loyalties plus the new beginnings of an individualistic culture. This sectional division between the parties has been a permanent fixture of Michigan's electoral politics since the Great Depression.

Entrenched regional sectionalism by itself, though, does not explain the relationship between Michigan's independent electorate and its relatively strong, but in some ways waning, parties. Partisanship remains relatively fluid. For example, a 1990 survey of likely voters reported that respondents were nearly equally divided in party preference: 26 percent Republican, 30 percent Democratic, and 33 percent independent.[12] In the same survey, 26 percent of the respondents said they were liberal, 26 percent conservative, and 35 percent middle-of-the-road. Partisan cleavage is not evenly distributed throughout the state, however. It has been dispersed in similar patterns for at least the past forty years. Democrats, at least through party identification, dominate in heavily populated Wayne County, and they are a major force in nearby Macomb. But other southeastern counties are high in Republican party identifiers. Most Upper Peninsula counties, though lightly populated, also are Democratic.

This pattern does not quite produce the simple regional split in state politics that it might suggest, however. Things might well be easier in state politics if it did. While labor represents the core of the modern Democratic party, and many other southeastern Michigan residents are among the party's other regular followers, Democrats become competitive only when they employ a delicate outstate balancing strategy to win votes and legislative seats. The Republican party, when it is most successful, wins by following a similar strategy of courting urban voters and even targeting traditionally Democratic voting blocs. Macomb County, as an example, has become a key battleground with its shifting electorate. The movement of older Michiganians, after retirement, to northern Michigan also brings some instability to the electorate of the lower peninsula.

As a result, control of state government is volatile and shifting, affected as much by voter ticket-splitting as by their partisan attachment.[13] Public officials, attempting to exercise policy leadership and balance programs, shift back and forth accordingly on the middle ground between bipartisan cooperation and partisan conflict. In both instances, they remain aware that one way or another, parties are still a major – yet not the only – practical vehicle for seeking policy balance and organizing Michigan's diverse electorate.

Reforms and Professional Government.

Various political reforms provide an additional vehicle for bringing about policy equilibrium or preventing major policy imbalance. Michiganians, for example, were quick to adopt concepts of municipal home rule to avoid undue interference by state officials over local affairs. Home-rule provisions relating to cities and villages were incorporated by the 1908 constitutional convention.

Similarly, citizen reformers promoted the Progressive reforms of initiative, referendum, and recall and in 1913 celebrated their success with new amendments to the state constitution.[14] These reserved the rights of citizens to participate directly in state policymaking and to remove elected officials from office. Citizens have used these provisions on numerous occasions to impose limits on taxing and spending, on sharing state revenues with local governments, and to push other reforms.

Modern management techniques were established by 1941 as civil service was brought to an administration that had already been practicing executive budgeting since the reforms of the 1920s. George W. Romney, before he was elected governor in the early 1960s, mobilized a citizen movement to reform state government against partisan control. Through the revised 1963 constitution, this movement brought about a consolidation of many agencies, greater accountability to the governor, openness to citizens and groups, and improved reporting of agency performance to the legislature and public.

Such professionalism has been extended to all facets of state government. The postconstitutional legislature of 148 members (38 senators and 110 representatives), except for its particularly strong leadership, operates much like the professionalized U.S. Congress. A fully staffed Legislative Service Bureau to research issues, draft bills, and provide other policy assistance has been in existence since 1941. Legislative services have expanded gradually to include individual offices with personal aides for each legislator, additional staff and offices provided under the direction of the majority and minority leaders in both houses, research staffs that serve committees, and fiscal agencies to generate independent budget analyses for members of both houses. These provide assistance to ensure legislative responsiveness to all sources of policy demand, even as the legislature suffers low public esteem in yet another parallel with the Congress.

Legislators have more than ample reasons and time to act. They serve full-time, are in Lansing throughout the year, and are afforded incentives to continue service by a health-and-retirement benefits plan that vests them after a five-year tenure. As a result, this state is governed by a well-supported chief executive, a competently managed bureaucracy, and legislators who are persistent in their personal involvement in state government.[15] The only irony in that status was the imposition by constitutional referendum of six-year and eight-year term limitations for house and senate members in 1992.

Professionalism in state government has greatly facilitated the creation of a highly professional lobby from among the state's plentiful interests. Interest-group representation of issues cuts across partisanship, often muting it, and sometimes causing numerous minor issues to divide both Democrats and Republicans among themselves. Complex government and public officials with strong beliefs about their own competency, in the view of many who want something from the state, are perhaps best dealt with by well-informed lobbyists who understand what makes the state capitol and other state policy centers work. While citizens are seen as having many buttons to push for legislative attention, they are not thought to be effective in clearing away the obstacles to legislation.

SOME CLOSING THOUGHTS

Michigan's political and economic environment has produced a complex mixture of public policy and values. Many of these elements became juxtaposed as citizens, professional administrators, and state policymakers sought their own satisfying place in a balance of policy needs and wants. Yet, no matter how technically skillful the state bureaucracy becomes or how proficient its officials are in operating government, the solution to Michigan's problem of cyclical prosperity and economic decline eludes state policy managers. Severe distortions in the auto-dependent economy still happen, and a large reserve of unemployed workers remains.

The diversity of the state presents a continuing challenge for any public official who seeks to satisfy the majority of the electorate. "Have" versus "have-not" tensions inevitably exist, often spurred by the clamor of regional, ethnic and racial, economic, and social interests. Friends and partners on one issue quickly become adversaries on another. Professionalism is challenged repeatedly by populist traditionalists who complain about lack of responsiveness and by fiscal conservatives who believe that big government and annual legislative sessions serve only to bring about higher taxes.

The claims of those proposing deceptively simple solutions to Michigan's problems unleash new pressures for reform in the unending search for political balance. In the midst of befuddling complexity, Michiganians want easy answers and thus find rhetoric as appealing as the idealism with which they were raised. This mix of deceptively simple answers, rhetoric, and ideals surfaces so routinely that a final uncertainty is created, producing continual tensions between professionalized government and amateur political activism.

CHAPTER TWO

Geopolitics and the Federal System

*Debra S. Brand and James D. Slack also contributed
to this chapter*

THE GEOPOLITICAL LANDSCAPE

To a great extent, Michigan is driven by the politics of place, creating more significant and enduring factions here than in most states. These carry over to involvement with the federal government as well. The state possesses distinctive physical characteristics, many of which are regionally based, and it has a somewhat isolated location. Few travelers come to Michigan on the way to somewhere else, unless driving from Toledo to Duluth. Moreover, the regional distinctions in the state encompass ethnic and racial differences along with those of geography.

All this greatly affects the state's social and economic integration. The geography of the state must be given the same detailed attention as its public officials and its most important policy issues, even before looking specifically at the behavior of state legislators or the importance of environmental demands.[1] Geographical conflicts in Michigan affect nearly all its battles, making it almost impossible to see – or represent in Washington, D.C. – the interests of the state as a whole.

With its 58,527 square miles, Michigan ranks twenty-third among the fifty states in land mass; its 9,430,000 residents rank it eighth in population after a 1.5 percent growth from 1990 to 1992. This large state has two peninsulas, the lower and the upper, connected to each other by a five-mile suspension bridge over the Straits of Mackinac. Although the Mackinac Bridge, completed in 1957, now connects the two land masses, it has not led to the melding of the social and economic character of the two areas.

The Upper Peninsula has little in common with much of the lower peninsula. It consists of vast wilderness areas; its population centers are few, most being of the small crossroads variety. Marquette is the only city of more than 20,000 people. The UP is well populated with Scandinavians because of mining, lumbering, and some farming migration patterns that also spread west across Minnesota. However, unlike northern Wisconsin and Minnesota, Cornish and Eastern Europeans also settled in the UP to work the mines. The region today reflects a hearty peasant tradition that, like areas to the west, never escaped the burdens of limited education and economic underdevelopment.[2] What holds the UP together is its remoteness. It remains a place left alone to contend with a harsh environment that provides few opportunities except for resource extraction and tourism. Educated young people rarely go home to jobs. The federal government occasionally finds this remoteness attractive – for a miles-wide defense communications grid or a proposed nuclear dump site. State dollars, UP legislators note, "basically come to us if we extort them, certainly not through a spirit of cooperation."

The lower peninsula also has extensive natural areas, but is more developed; it has 70 percent of the state's land mass and contains 91 percent of its population. Most residents live in the southern third of the lower peninsula. This settlement pattern intensifies the contest between the urban interests of the lower peninsula, especially Detroit and the southeast region, and outstate or rural Michigan, including the UP. Space and density differences are as pronounced as anywhere in the country. Hence, vastly different public service needs exist from region to region. Even simple differences, such as population density, divide rural parts of the peninsulas. While federal and state income transfers do much to sustain the economies of both regions, the larger population of the lower peninsula counties brings far more of those revenues. As a result, more stores and businesses are supported there than in the UP. Some contests over who gets what from state politics see UP forces aligned with the rural areas of the lower peninsula north of Lansing for such reasons as encouraging income transfers. On other issues, such as looking for supplements to income transfers through jobs programs, the independent-minded UP charges into battle without allies, seeing its own lack of development as a case for special treatment from the federal and state governments.

These shifting alliances and suspicions can only be understood by noting the varied history of the lower peninsula. Even when Michigan first began developing a major lumber industry beyond the limited commerce of Detroit in the 1830s, the emerging lumber economy was bifurcated between eastern and western Michigan coasts. Although white pine covered two-thirds of the peninsula, towns on Lake Huron served the eastern United States while Lake

Michigan ports shipped pine west to Chicago and, via railroad links, off to the frontier. When a recession stalled timbering in 1837, lumber cities evolved into their own unique places as local economies shifted in different ways. Saginaw saw an influx of German farmers, attracted by open spaces and lumber roads. Bay City, only a few miles north, grew more slowly as a fishing village until lumbering boomed again in 1859. During this period, Muskegon made inroads as a mercantile home to those servicing inland Michigan from Chicago. Yet the industries attracted different ethnic groups, with Poles eventually dominating Bay City while the Dutch moved first onto the southern Lake Michigan shoreline and then east to Grand Rapids.[3]

By the time lumbering declined in the early twentieth century, Michigan had developed local and regional economies that were homes to their own ethnic groups, evolving industries, and political styles.[4] Parts of the lower peninsula variously came to be known as Dutch country or the German region, farm communities or furniture towns, reform city governments or entrenched islands of ward politics. Detroit initially came to be identified with its Irish residents. Out of lumber mills, cities like Manistee grew to be stoutly Democratic, Polish and German, and Catholic. Only thirty miles south on the same Lake Michigan shoreline, Ludington was solidly Republican, Scandinavian, and Protestant. Yet both cities, like nearly all the rest of the lower peninsula, housed other ethnic groups and occupations that were less recognized, but that still divided local and regional politics.

Only one factor gave common purpose to state business, even in its own diversity of products. Manufacturing, as vital to supporting lumbering, was spread throughout the state and provided the artisans and workers needed for further industrialization. When Detroit and the surrounding Wayne County prospered years later, Michigan's labor base supplied the auto industry until, from the 1920s to the 1950s, low-paid southerners flocked to the state for high auto wages. These even less educated whites and African Americans, never comfortable with one another, brought the last fragmenting waves of population and regionalism to Michigan. Hispanics, sometimes brought by auto jobs but far more often by migrant farm work, only trickled into the state, representing just over two percent of the population.

THE EFFECT ON STATE AND FEDERAL EXPECTATIONS

Michigan's geopolitical character is not just about instate differences, however. The location of the state also affects Michigan's relationships with neighboring states and the federal government (see map 1). These relation-

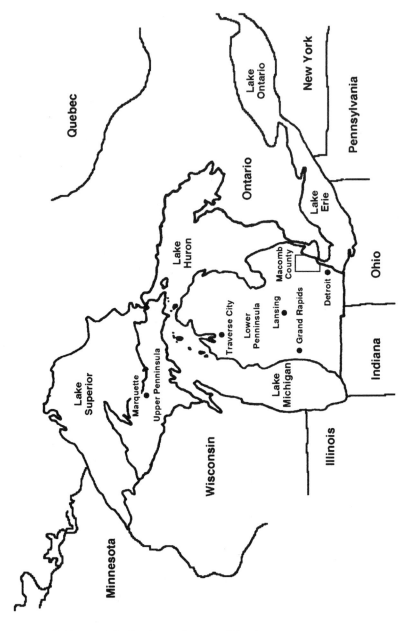

Map 1. Michigan and the Contiguous States and Provinces.

ships both respond to and create instate stresses that are important in determining policy demands and responses. This can most clearly be seen in Great Lakes issues. The Great Lakes water system largely surrounding each peninsula also has shoreline in Indiana, Ohio, Wisconsin, Illinois, Minnesota, Pennsylvania, and New York. International, federal, and multistate agreements each result from that shared interest. The eight states on the Great Lakes share extensive ecological concerns about water quality and management. This concern is crucial because the Great Lakes contain one-fifth of the fresh water supply in the world and one-half of North America's supply. The fact that two Canadian provinces, Ontario and Quebec, also share Great Lakes shoreline brings international issues directly to Michigan government, often via federal actions.

Although the Great Lakes bring about a natural alliance among the shoreline states and provinces, they also introduce conflict. Thus, no other factor in the state provides more of an impetus for federal cooperation. The states are not just caretakers of these waterways as scenic wonders. Externalities, or third-party effects of state and provincial use, are major policy concerns in the Great Lakes basin. Examples abound. Some Michigan residents and policymakers become especially piqued at other jurisdictions that allow commercial fishers to net what the state plants for the catch of sportfishers. In turn, the water and chemical runoff from Michigan's major industries irritates its neighbors. The distinctiveness of each state or province, in fact, causes problems in defining appropriate use of the lakes because each seeks to gain advantage or limit losses in any new agreements.

Yet there are commonalities within these differences that help facilitate interstate and federal cooperation. All of the basin states are also either rustbelt states or states otherwise affected by problems associated with the decline of durable goods manufacturing. Southern Canada in the lakes region has similar problems. In fact, the conditions of the term "rustbelt" link the entire region, describing the huge number of empty, decaying, and rusty factories and warehouses that dot each state and province. So, for the entire basin, renewal and redefinition of the economic base is of prime importance. The onerous nature of that task can be seen in the major changes that any economic shift would entail for both state business practices and multistate interdependence. These states, aided by Great Lakes ties, depend heavily on each other for raw materials and manufactured parts for their assembly plants. Coal from Ohio and iron ore from Minnesota and the U P are essential to steel production in the lower lake ports of Indiana, Illinois, and Pennsylvania. Steel products, in turn, are fundamental to automobiles made in

Table 1: Great Lakes Bulk Commerce, 1986–89

Commodity (in millions of metric tons)	1986	1987	1988	1989
Iron Ore	51.0	61.7	68.3	66.7
Coal	36.3	37.7	40.5	39.5
Stone	26.3	33.2	35.5	35.1
Cement	4.1	3.8	4.2	4.5
Potash	1.6	1.7	1.7	1.4
Petroleum	12.0	11.5	12.0	11.2
Grain	20.2	22.3	19.1	15.0

Source: Lake Carriers' Association, "1989 Annual Report" (Cleveland OH), p.44.

Michigan and elsewhere. If automobile manufacturers in Michigan do well, then component, assembly, and service plants in New York, Ohio, and Wisconsin thrive. A breakdown of Great Lakes bulk commerce is presented in table 1.

Similarly, these states and provinces share the 2,342-mile-long St. Lawrence Seaway. This shipping channel has two faces, each with its own problems. It extends the multistate and provincial neighborhood for trade and mutual dependence, and thus it mandates more Michigan involvement in use and trade agreements. In 1990, 41 percent of the more than 36 million metric tons of goods shipped through the seaway was intended for domestic use in either the United States or Canada. Only 3.45 percent of that total volume left U.S. ports, however; so Michigan gained relatively little from export trade at the eastern end of the shipping zone. This has made Michiganians take a more active interest in making the lakes and their trading lanes more viable to the state. Trade initiatives by state officials have emphasized use of the lakes and development of facilities, ships, and personnel.

This brings up the seaway's second face. The St. Lawrence opens up the manufacturing and agricultural interests of the basin to worldwide markets while, of course, making them vulnerable to competition. The trading advantage seems clear: 12.6 percent of traffic volume is imports from overseas, 15.7 percent is U.S.-originated goods being exported overseas, and 26.7 percent is for goods with Canadian origins being exported overseas. Yet the principal export is grain, little of which comes from Michigan. Most of the grain is shipped from west of the Great Lakes. The primary imports, though, are iron and steel, which compete heavily with Michigan products as well as those of basin states and provinces. Both Michigan and the other Great Lakes units face added seaway export problems from oceanside competitor ports, events such as increased overseas trade subsidies that often disrupt traffic stability, and the width of canal locks, which limits the size and efficiency of transport vessels. For example, automobile exports are impossible through the lakes. Even parts, which are shipped more economically on larger ships, are generally excluded. None of these problems can be resolved by Michigan alone.

Obviously, these common problems require political attention from Michigan's public officials before they can be brought elsewhere. Their attention is not easily gained, though. Even the problems of industrial transformation are not viewed as important by all Michigan residents. The idea of the Great Lakes as an expanded transportation network is hotly contested in the north, pitting commercial and development interests against environmentalists and recreation interests. Michigan, however, suffers from many other continuing policy debates about how the state should invest its remaining resources and seek reallocated ones from the federal government. Michigan residents have difficulty seeing their state as one entity for trade and commerce, and find it nearly impossible to view the Great Lakes as a whole. Some states, as does Iowa with farming, contain a unifying factor that makes for a well-integrated statewide economy. Others, like Alaska, unite because they deviate from national norms.[5] Michigan, as a large state rich in natural resources and geographical fragmentation, does not unite.

Many different contributors to the state economy grow or decline largely on their own, somewhat free of trends experienced by other economic segments. Only national recessions bind them together. The state economy of the 1990s, as it affects the state budget, is still much like that of past decades. It remains largely dependent on the auto industry, but most residents of most of the state's regions think of themselves as more dependent on local economies than being tied to auto manufacturing. Moreover, auto manufacturing is seen by most as distinct from other manufacturing, even of the durable goods type. The problem is that most of the jobs provided by the auto industry are located in or near urban centers in the southern part of the lower peninsula. The rest of the state relies on a uneven mix of agriculture, tourism, mining, other manufacturing, auto supplier firms, services, and government income transfers. These divisions have long produced tensions among the state's different policy interests and those who represent them. As such, they contribute to a dynamic, yet fragmented, policy process as legislators deal with the competing claims of both regions and economic sectors.

This very much affects, in mostly negative ways, the state's ability to work cooperatively with the federal government on multistate problems. To the surprise of many federal officials, however, these differences also lead to conflicts and a lack of cooperation on jobs and economic development programs. As one federal administrator observed, "Even after we gained gubernatorial support on federal rural development initiatives, others dragged their feet, complaining that such actions were controversial and unlikely to produce results." Under such conditions, the problems of the Great Lakes, the multistate economy, the auto industry, state development plans, and international trade are relegated to secondary status. Local and regional politics takes over, bringing with it frequent chaos and sometimes ugly animosity.

Population changes illustrate additional reasons for tensions between regions. Michigan's population increased by only 0.7 percent from 1980 to 1990, compared to a national growth rate of 10.2 percent. Only two regions actually experienced significant population growth.[6] Western Michigan, with the Grand Rapids metropolitan area, the state's second largest urban complex, experienced a 13 percent growth rate. While still considerably smaller than the southeast region surrounding Detroit, West Michigan is a growing competitor. The thirty northern counties of the lower peninsula grew at an average annual rate of 9.4 percent from 1980 to 1990. Growth was nearly double that in the counties surrounding Traverse City. Moreover, population growth in this region is expected to continue, according to the most optimistic estimate, by an additional 20 percent by the year 2000.

People settling in most northern Michigan counties have been and are projected to be retirees as well as residents employed in highly paid professions and industries linked to technology. A smaller percentage are younger workers, with few job skills, who want rural lifestyles. This mix also creates development problems. Retirees rely on costly public services, and the younger workers frequently need welfare and other public assistance. The region typically falls behind the state in employment, with an unemployment rate of 9.3 percent in late 1993 compared to the overall state rate of 6.5 percent. This diversity creates two problems in the planning and use of state and federal funds and programs: first, some communities need such services far more than others; second, determining those needs is ponderous. Local communities have great problems accepting uneven growth and want to be like their more prosperous neighbors. Yet, for state and federal agencies to invest in the most needy communities is often wasteful. "The outstate parts of the state are so variable," said one grant administrator, "that the best investments are those in communities that probably don't need them. Others will invest there. In many other places, no infusion of money can help. We should probably be discouraging people from living in many of those places."

Despite that perspective, population change is usually less of a problem for outstate communities than is the retention of old expectations as to what should be emphasized there for the local economy. These have turned into unwieldy biases that make adaptation and diversification harder. While those in areas presently or formerly dependent on manufacturing perceive increased heavy industry as a positive development, that view is not widely held beyond southeastern Michigan. Only a few other older, blue-collar cities of the north have sizable numbers of residents who share such a vision for their future: Alpena, Manistee, Muskegon. In those cities, longtime residents complain about grants that bring recreation development projects such as marinas and river walks. What they want first are industrial parks. Saginaw and Bay City, on the northern rim of the auto-belt corridor that extends through southeastern Michigan, want the same, but with more of a realization that manufacturing is deserting them. Other small rural towns with mixed economies, of which there are many throughout the state, only sometimes see a new plant as a plus.

Recreation communities may totally disagree on plants unless new jobs bring high technology and low pollution. In nearly all cases, however, the residents of each type of community have become divided over the environmental price to be paid when rural and open lands are converted to industrial, commercial, or closed recreational use. Some outstate residents, both long-term and recent in-migrants, oppose increased population and development of even a recreational sort. The belief remains among many that any new growth erodes their small-town values and quality of life. The resulting local problems for economic and community development have spread throughout outstate Michigan, even around Grand Rapids. The phenomenon has been characterized as a "politics of escapism," where residents want service amenities but not the new businesses and citizens needed to pay for them.[7] In the wake of such conflicts, little attention is directed to doing what seems best for Michigan's overall economy. The most visible response is a flurry of project-specific local government grants from state and federal agencies. These are prized because local officials can get what citizens either want or can be led to accept. Most communities like capital improvement projects. These have become so important in many redeveloping, low-income communities outstate that between 80 and 98 percent of their project expenditures over the past three decades have come from such sources.

No such uncertainty exists for residents of southeastern Michigan, but neither are their plans directed statewide. Residents of economically stalled urban centers, such as Detroit, Pontiac, and Flint, plus rapid growth areas, such as Oakland County, want large amounts of state money to resolve their problems. They also want the bulk of state investments, except for environmental protection, to come to them rather than to the escapists. They have two reasons, held constant even across the divide of a central-city/suburban split. First, urban residents see themselves as entitled to state funds because they constitute a majority of the population and serve as major generators of the state's fiscal resources. Second, they consider themselves as a population group to be in need, one to which the state's other regions are morally obligated.

Poverty in Detroit and some nearby suburbs motivates some of those beliefs. The high population density in the urban center of southeastern Michigan and the political pressures to serve the large minority populations residing there have led to the establishment of large state and federally supported programs for the urban poor.[8] Forty percent of the state's welfare caseload has been generated in Detroit, which has less than 12 percent of the state's population.[9] Residents of Detroit and its older suburbs have become the state's most vocal political forces behind the federal government's shifting reallocation of intergovernmental aid, which now goes more to persons than places. Intergovernmental federal aid to persons stood at 31.8 percent nationally in 1978, which left considerable funding still available for the grants valued by outstate communities. However, by 1992, 62.9 percent of all federal aid to state and local governments was through payments to individuals, for such programs as Medicaid and Aid to Families with Dependent Children.[10] While those communities would also like redevelopment assistance, the sheer momentum of their demands for support payments overwhelms policymakers who must decide between the two priorities.

Another factor influencing intergovernmental policy is suburban in origin, but in this case from newer and more prosperous places. These are rapidly expanding new cities on the metropolitan fringe. Residents articulate the contrary belief that the state and federal governments should take every initiative to foster their growth, because that growth is the most likely source of future state wealth and prosperity. These are the Michiganians most likely to raise political arguments about reasserting the economic strengths of the state and the Great Lakes basin. They also want – but often fail to vote for – property-tax relief and caps on intergovernmental entitlement programs, which they see as anti-growth.

Southeasterners, though, receive little sympathy from the rest of the state. Outstate regions, with fewer recipients, gain fewer state and federal dollars than does the Detroit metropolitan region. Hence, outstaters are distressed by feelings of inequity. They believe that Detroit, in particular, benefits disproportionately from state and federal outlays and that these are too great a burden for the remainder of Michigan's taxpayers. This attitude toward what many residents see as minority-directed welfare is exacerbated by the recognition that public services and income transfers are needed to alleviate both extensive rural poverty and accelerating infrastructure problems outstate. The declining number of jobs, and the remaining poor left behind when the educated and skilled move out, necessitate outside assistance to sustain many rural residents and to bring in state dollars to shore up small communities.[11]

The Detroit area in general and the city in particular are seen as having little in common with the rest of Michigan. Sometimes the city is seen as a competitive threat to Copper Harbor, West Branch, and any number of other small Michigan towns. At other times, metro Detroit is seen as the source of demand for a more intrusive federal role, bringing not just costly federal programs but regulations that make environmental use difficult or that extend state resources, such as fish, to Native Americans. The contrast most often drawn is between the woods of the Upper Peninsula and the concrete of Detroit. Stories about their differences have become symbolic of the state's lack of common purpose and understanding. In the UP, residents insist that they seldom see state officials other than game wardens, as they would say, of the Department of Natural Resources. Providing services over such a large space indeed is a problem, both financially and logistically. But in Detroit, where offices can serve numerous clients, state officials seem ubiquitous. This perception of relative neglect facilitates the frequently expressed desire of some UP residents to join with parts of Wisconsin in forming a new state that need not balance such starkly different needs.

This contrast in peninsulas also contributes to prescriptions about how to govern effectively for only regional needs, forgetting the interests of the state. Extensive demands for specific types of assistance that relate to unique UP features are made routinely in Lansing and oftentimes passed on to Washington. As state officials have attempted to serve as many northern groups as possible, these complaints have resulted in blatant pork-barrel politics that allocate many state program benefits disproportionately to the Upper Peninsula. Tensions and antagonisms in the UP, nonetheless, remain so high that many state officials feel pork-barrel efforts are still needed to keep other perceived inequities from boiling over, and to keep UP lawmakers from being total obstructionists in the legislature. To facilitate cooperation, some recent governors have opened offices and placed staff in the UP, even elevating the chief staff member to cabinet status under Governor James Blanchard. When asked to justify their unwieldy politics, UP officials argue that they are only countering mayoral bossism, racial favoritism, abuse of power in Detroit, and a federal government that returns state dollars only to Wayne County residents. As such, regionalism in Michigan, at its extreme, often plays out in acrimonious charges, racial spite, and just plain envy.[12] Michigan lacks intrastate cohesion, thus keeping the state focused more on its parts than its totality.

THE MULTISTATE NEIGHBORHOOD

Despite this often chaotic regionalism and localism, many aspects of state and intergovernmental politics result from multistate commonalities. In fact, the importance of federalism has been largely defined by the cooperation among sovereign states. Even if they are too easily forgotten, location and natural resources tie Michigan's neighboring jurisdictions inseparably together. Michigan and the contiguous states and provinces share many cultural and resource features that cannot be overlooked; they also have important differences that need be sorted out. This affects cohesion and governing relationships that force several multistate Great Lakes basin issues to the fore, but only sometimes for resolution. The federal government is only partially a facilitator when it comes to neighborly cooperation. Often it fails to bring cooperation, as it has in dealing with the seemingly unavoidable issue of low-level nuclear waste. As noted in chapter 1, Michigan's culture is touched heavily by individualism within its dominant concern for moralism. At times, the pursuit of individualism is unavoidable. A dual culture, simply to keep government operational, is to be expected in a divided state where economic opportunities are often seen as being distributed inequitably and even illegitimately.

The sharing of geopolitical space with so many other states, not all alike, also influences culture. This leads to perceptions of local needs, such as transportation problems in the UP, being at least partially defined through generalized beliefs. Michigan, particularly in its southeastern urban areas, shares the individualistic political subculture that dominates basin neighbors to the south: Ohio, Indiana, and Illinois.[13] Individualism came to Michigan as white and later African-American southerners brought traditional values to moralistic Detroit and the auto assembly lines. Later, as a result of conflicts in values and the lack of support for an elite governing structure, traditional-ism gave way to individualism as a large metro Detroit blue-collar work force challenged the rest of the state. Still later, as statewide conflicts spread, individualistic expectations colored all of state politics. In terms of beliefs, therefore, regional self-interest is seen as a legitimate and necessary pursuit.

Michigan, however, does not share the dimension of individualism that permits the patronage system once found in Indiana or the machine politics of Chicago, probably because historically independent outstate voters would not allow it. Even Detroit is governed more through an interlocking network of African Americans who cooperate with one another, rather than through a more traditional boss system with centralized authority. Mayor Coleman Young did not govern primarily by the patronage and service methods of New York's legendary Boss Tweed and Chicago's original Richard Daley. Young managed, for twenty years, more through bargaining with state offi-cials and appeals to racial solidarity. It is that kind of cultural individualism, so often linked to spatial location and settlement patterns, that characterizes Michigan as well as its demands on the federal government. Yet Michigan, like Ohio, restrains individualistic tendencies by creating its professional-ized check: state agency officials who are well rewarded for their work and guaranteed public service autonomy. Bureaucracies of this sort are not ma-nipulated easily for special interests or regional favoritism. As a result of such independent professionals, strong tendencies exist in state agencies to do things for the good of the state, not just specific locales. These expecta-tions carry over in the way federal allocations are managed by state agencies, especially in determining the distribution of housing and infrastructure awards.

The moralistic political culture that provides for professionalism and public service is shared with Minnesota and Wisconsin.[14] It also has mod-erating effects on state politics. These three states tend to emphasize what is best for the whole of their polity, even if some potential economic gains are lost. Final political agreements in these states tend to center on doing what is best for the general citizenry, rather than what seems best for only some fac-tions. Michigan, though, has a difficult time achieving this, in part because old industry interests and emergent public interests are not easily reconciled. Also, conflicts are strongly regionalized, and special interests are tenacious in seeking their goals. Hence, despite articulated goals to the contrary, polit-ical bargains made ostensibly for the public as a whole often allocate benefits piecemeal to various groups, regions, and sectors. Nonetheless, there exists the generalized belief that all state interests deserve to be served, at least as long as they agree to coexist.

The important feature of this dual culture, beyond just rewarding select policy claimants, is the symbolic appearance of evenhanded and farsighted policy, and the preparation that goes into appearing fair-minded and farsighted. Moral agreement, especially in articulating important future policy initiatives that will benefit as many as possible, such as economic redevelopment, is extraordinarily important to policy debates. It goes far in preventing the state from permanently splintering into unworkable factions inside the legislature and among the citizenry. The agreement also keeps policy disputes from getting too far removed from those essential matters of statewide economic and environmental needs that reflect basin and rustbelt problems.

For Michigan, in uneven degrees then, two variations of the American political culture coexist uneasily. As an upper Great Lakes state, Michigan works regularly with Minnesota and Wisconsin. The three states share, for example, a strong environmental and conservation ethic. All also have strong social service programs, with Minnesota even going through the same turmoil in cutting welfare rolls as Michigan in the early 1990s. But Michigan officials must also work and compete with the lower Great Lakes states that favor more relaxed approaches to the common good and more willingly sacrifice even the image of public interest for competitive economic gains. Many Michigan officials, because they live with it, both understand and value the politically pragmatic give-and-take of an individualistic culture. Not surprisingly, these are the very political leaders who, with assistance from agency personnel, often arrange the deals that overcome in the short term the difficult obstacles of determining mutually acceptable solutions to policy disagreements. However, these deals also escalate instate political tensions between regions, so they have long-term costs. Differences over how federal clean air legislation would affect instate regions constitute a case in point. Officials in both Lansing and Washington representing industrial areas opposed strict auto emission and acid rain standards that are costly to state industries. Many outstaters, charging favoritism to Detroit and citing the conservation ethic of the outstate, remain outraged over the weakened compromises finally adopted.

These sorts of conflicts certainly affect how the state is able to deal with its neighbors and federal officials on common problems. In other words, the abstractions of political culture come to life in the way in which specific issues arise and are handled. Interstate tensions are even more severe than instate disagreements for those same reasons, but also because there is no single federal mechanism to force accommodation. The example of the Great Lakes makes that point well. The Great Lakes complicate multistate relationships, mostly because of the large number of jurisdictions involved. Each of the American states, along with Ontario and Quebec, is concerned with the comprehensive management of the lakes, both for economic and environmental reasons.

Regional cooperation for Great Lakes management began in 1952 when Michigan's attorney general proposed an interstate compact. In 1954 the Michigan legislature authorized the governor to participate. Participants in that compact then formed the Great Lakes Commission. Membership included the eight Great Lakes basin states and Ontario. The purpose of the commission was to study all problems involving the Great Lakes and to devise agreeable solutions.

The commission, of course, was not quick to come up with results. Significant evidence of regional cooperation did not appear until 1985, when each of the original participants and the province of Quebec signed the Great Lakes Charter. The charter is a good-faith agreement that provides for "undertaking Great Lakes basin management activities in a spirit of cooperation and for following a watershed management approach that respects the hydrologic unity of the Great Lakes system."[15] The states agreed to sign the charter mainly because the entire region took seriously the much discussed threats to divert large quantities of water to the Great Plains and to southwestern states that are outgrowing their supplies of fresh water. It was plain self-interest. Nearly all Michiganians, regardless of region, saw this diversion as a major blow to the state if ever allowed. Four small diversion projects already were operational as precedents to further water losses.

Participating political units had many reasons for cooperating against diversion. The immediate reasons were and remain economic and statewide in their impact. Commercial navigation benefits from higher water levels because ships can carry heavier loads. Decreased shiploads affect the winter stockpiles of ore, limestone, and coal. Without these stockpiles, steel mills and other dependent industries in the region cannot maintain normal production.

Hydroelectric generating capabilities also are reduced with the lower water levels. Moreover, municipalities and industries that depend on the Great Lakes for their water supply would find pumping from the lakes more expensive. The higher cost of doing business would create even more difficulty in retaining and attracting industry.

Both Great Lakes water levels and quality affect tourism. Marinas and other recreation facilities are less functional when lake levels fall. Reduced levels threaten fishery programs and depress both sportfishing and fish production. The collective loss for such industries could be staggering for Michigan. A diversion of Great Lakes water averaging 5,000 cubic feet per second would cost Great Lakes users approximately $53 million annually.[16] Perhaps most important are the concerns that Great Lakes diversion would strengthen the commercial and industrial capacities of sunbelt states with which the Great Lakes states already compete rather unsuccessfully.

Powerful incentives to rally around the lakes have had one other positive effect: encouraging other efforts for state and provincial cooperation. Congressional delegations from Great Lakes states now caucus regularly in Washington. The caucus not only reviews the effects of pending legislation, but it also gives focus to Great Lakes needs by representing them to the administration and to federal agencies. Yet the lessons of Great Lakes cooperation are the same geopolitical constraints that characterize instate relations. No state has been willing to view the interests of the region, on any issue, as having a higher order than its own interests. Arguments invariably get down to temporary winners and losers. For example, a bitter disagreement took place during the severe drought of 1988. The Great Lakes Charter prohibits increased diversion from the Great Lakes unless supported by all the signers. Illinois Governor James Thompson, under political pressure to raise water levels and thereby assist shipping on the Mississippi River, requested the U.S. Army Corps of Engineers to increase water diversion through Chicago's Lake Michigan diversion system. Seeing little gain for themselves and further encouragement of a dangerous precedent, most states and the Canadian provinces opposed this increased diversion. Illinois, of course, charged that commission members were only adept at saying no to crisis assistance, showing once more that individual state interests were of higher priority than neighborly relations.

That charge of self-interest, even in questions of Great Lakes quality, is hardly a surprise to federal officials who deal with Michigan and its neighbors. They point to the federal clean air and clean water acts as the most important institutions protecting the lakes and ensuring their wise use. Controls over point- and nonpoint-source water pollution, regulation of air emissions that fouled the lakes, and provisions for required sewage and water treatment facilities were strengthened under these acts. Not only did the states of the basin exhibit laxity in protecting the lakes throughout much of their history, but their congressional delegations mobilized against stronger regulation, such as the Clean Air Act Amendments of 1990. Federal officials, accordingly, view multistate compacts and the congressional caucus with suspicion: "Much like a brigade of foxes being formed to protect the proverbial chicken house."

A more recent illustration, having even more self-interested results, concerns a combination of some Great Lakes states and other Midwest states in implementing the Midwest Interstate Low-Level Radioactive Waste Compact. The compact, consisting of Michigan, Iowa, Missouri, Wisconsin, Minnesota, Indiana, and Ohio, has the common goal and federal mandate of building a facility for long-term storage of low-level radioactive waste. Illinois was an early member and then withdrew. A group decision required the state that produced the greatest volume of waste to build the region's first facility. After Illinois left the compact, and another state fell below Michigan's increasing production of waste, politics shifted. Michigan, by default, became the leading candidate, something for which state officials were totally unprepared, given the initial bargain and production rankings.

Despite an extensive search for a Michigan site and action by the state legislature to raise the minimum site standards, a suitable site was not found. It was another of those issues that all instate regions sought to avoid, despite statewide incentives to devise a solution. Disposal sites in South Carolina and elsewhere, in an effort to pressure Michigan for a decision, closed their facilities to materials from the Midwest compact members. Compact members complained that Michigan officials, by raising environmental and safety standards, made it impossible to find a suitable site. Governor James Blanchard, bowing to outstate pressures, threatened to pull Michigan out of the compact; Governor John Engler subsequently questioned whether a facility was needed at all. While wastes accumulated at hospitals, research labs, and university sites where they are produced, the issue remained both critical and unresolvable. What remains important about this issue, as well as ones that come to the Great Lakes Commission, is the tenacity with which moralistic expectations keep them on the policy agenda. In less resolute states, such as Indiana, efforts to keep issues quiet are frequent.

Problems of acid rain have created the greatest tensions within the Great Lakes states, in no small part because Michiganians were not split on the issue. Acid rain, a byproduct of coal burned by the smokestack industries found in the basin's southern states, defoliates forests and destroys the water habitat in northern states and the provinces. In a heated exchange in 1988, Michigan Governor Blanchard and New York Governor Mario Cuomo called for Ohio Governor Richard Celeste to limit the amount of coal burned in his state's factories. Because of prior fuel and equipment conversions in

Michigan, the proposed restrictions would have given Michigan's industries a distinct advantage. Ohioans, already charged with pirating Michigan industries through tax incentives, accused Blanchard and Cuomo of protectionism and political grandstanding, especially because Michigan officials had not advocated strong federal regulations in earlier contests over air quality. Michiganians responded with a stern moral outrage that kept Ohio interests in trouble throughout Clean Air Act debates in 1990: "Our position is that this remains the right thing to do."

RELUCTANT DEPENDENCY AND A HALF-HEARTED FEDERAL ROLE

The acid rain example and the state's otherwise reluctant position on clean air legislation show Michigan's dependent yet suspect relationships with federal officials, relationships that are an outgrowth of the state's geopolitics and mixed political culture. As with all states, Michigan depends on the federal government for the defense of its borders. Even with federal cuts, the state relies on federal financial assistance to maintain its social and employment programs. It also depends on Washington to enrich a variety of infrastructure and other programs: roads, bridges, airports, ports on the Great Lakes, river and harbor dredging, municipal facilities, parks, recreation facilities, water plants, sewage treatment facilities, and myriad others.

Total federal transfer dollars to the state for 1990 were estimated at $19.1 billion, up from the $14.3 billion of 1983. But, as mentioned, only about 40 percent of this went to these place-specific projects. The state-federal relationship, even before the shift from places to persons, has not been not altogether a happy one. Hence, when they have a choice, Michigan officials seldom permit the U.S. government to do much of anything by itself in the state. Often Michigan officials choose an independent course of action. One reason is the view that more can be done, at least in terms of reflecting the state's interests. While the federal government establishes and maintains diplomatic relations with foreign governments, for example, Michigan officials dealt directly with Canada on the issues of the Great Lakes and, to a lesser extent, acid rain.

Macroeconomic policies of the federal government disproportionately affect heavy manufacturing and auto jobs in the state. Federal tax, spending, and energy legislation have all been viewed negatively by many Michiganians. Michigan officials, however, have persisted in attempting to mitigate the negative effects of national economic policy shifts. To bolster slipping exports and overcome a troubled economy, the state in the 1980s was exceptional in venturing into its own foreign affairs beyond the Great Lakes Commission. Michigan cities were encouraged by the state's commerce department to promote trust and international trade with foreign countries through sister-city relationships.[17]

Michigan also made pioneering efforts to establish trade offices overseas, operate trade fairs in foreign countries, support local economic development officials on short-term exchanges abroad, and educate and otherwise assist state firms in export and international sales.[18] The Michigan attitude has been simple: the federal government cannot and will not work for everything that state residents want, nor can it meet the diversity of instate demands. As one state senate leader said: "We can't be content with what the federal government does; they aim for the average and we are much more than an average state."[19] The state must also perform unique balancing acts. Trade officials marketed Detroit autos with no less vigor than tart cherries from the Traverse City region and plastic components for refrigeration units from Cadillac.

Much of what Michigan's leaders aim for in federal relationships seems bound to fail, largely because satisfying regional balance while assisting the state's changing economy is hard for federal officials to accomplish. This is a second reason for state independence in dealing with the federal government. One factor is Congress. It is extremely difficult for Michigan's Washington delegation, especially in the Senate, to reflect the diverse regional and special-interest expectations that occupy the state at home. In addition, House members often represent more than one set of regional problems but seldom enough of them to reflect a common Michigan perspective. Members also represent districts that are geopolitically divided. For example, most outstate districts are a blend of prosperous and disadvantaged communities. The sprawling tenth district merged environmentally focused northwest Michigan with corn and bean farmers of middle Michigan and the chemical workers and executives of Midland. UP residents were dismayed to learn that they had to share the eleventh district with the northeastern lower peninsula. Also, prior to 1992 reapportionment, only two of the six congressional districts that clustered around Detroit had majority African-American populations. The others divided sometimes small percentages of African-American residents into majority white districts, creating charges of underrepresentation.

The problems of congressional representation are often misunderstood. The state's two senators and sixteen representatives (eighteen before 1992 reapportionment) certainly vote along with the most generalizable economic

Table 2: Voting Patterns of the Michigan Congressional Delegation, 1983–88

Delegation	Ratings (in percent)			
	Liberal	Conservative	Pro-Union	Pro-Business
Senators	91	5.9	94.3	25.5
All House Members	62	33	67	46
Republican House Members	21	70	29	81

Source: Ratings are group averages based on voting records and range from 0, no support, to 100, total support. Liberal ratings provided by Americans for Democratic Action (ADA); Conservative ratings provided by the American Conservative Union (ACU); pro-union ratings provided by AFL-CIO's Committee on Political Education (COPE); pro-business ratings provided by U.S. Chamber of Commerce (COC).

interests of the state. On average, as expected in a state with the second highest percentage of unionized workers, the congressional delegation is more liberal than conservative and more pro-union than pro-business (see table 2). However, voting patterns on matters of ideology and on the economic concerns of unions and business vary across party lines. Voting patterns in Michigan also differ as a result of dramatic partisan differences between various regions of the state. Michigan's seven Republican House members of the 1980s represented outstate and white-collar suburban districts. Hence, they did not share the values of their Democratic colleagues when it came to liberal, pro-union issues.

Without instate regional cooperation, the Michigan congressional delegation is not as well integrated as delegations of many other states, even diverse ones like California that have a longer tradition of cooperation as they grew from underdeveloped economies. Factionalism has reduced the ability of Michigan's delegation to secure federal benefits for the state. With a long history of resource richness and auto dependence, Michigan's members of Congress did not feel the need to compete for federal spending on such projects as military bases, defense contracts, and water improvements. As a former congressman acknowledged: "Michigan didn't have to pursue growth and, as a result, its members of Congress didn't have to work together." At least, downstate legislators did not; outstate rural Republicans were not fans of big government anyway. Battles within the state, rather than needs of the state economy, have long set the delegation's congressional agenda. The loss of three northern Michigan Air Force bases has only reinforced the view that members of Congress from one region do not watch out for members from another. Residents were surprised when Kinchloe in the eastern UP closed, badly startled when Wurtsmith in eastern Michigan shut, and vocally outraged when Marquette's K. I. Sawyer was announced for closure. This left the state with no major defense bases.

Cooperation is a relatively new and difficult endeavor for the delegation. To satisfy diverse constituencies, members still defend issues that divide the parties and factions in the delegation. Many members worry more about how much federal money goes where, a rough measure that can be used to assuage those from home who complain that they missed out in obtaining federal grants. The suburban twelfth and eighteenth districts, for example, got only 4.5 and 4.3 percent of transfer dollars to the state in 1990, but those shares were up from 3.9 and 3.7 percent in 1983. Meanwhile, the Democratic Detroit first district got 5.5 percent in 1980, while the Republican eleventh district of the UP got 6.1 percent. But both have lost since 1983, when each had 6.3 percent shares.[20] House members also dislike that the lion's share of federal dollars goes to direct payment programs shared by the state rather than to their communities. They also complain about direct expenditures to the state. This meant that 12.2 percent of federal dollars went to the third district, mostly to Lansing on its eastern fringe.

None of these revenue problems exists because the delegation lacks representation on key committees or legislative power. Members are well distributed on all committees of stature. Moreover, prior to the 1992 elections in which one-third of the members resigned, the delegation averaged about nineteen years of seniority per member. Michigan also has two House committee chairs whose committees in 1990–91 claimed jurisdiction over roughly 60 percent of the legislation considered by Congress. Even these two, Representative William Ford (D-Taylor) of Education and Labor and John Dingell (D-Treaton) of Energy and Commerce, must – or at least feel they must – fight national and partisan issues more than they play the part of statewide representative. When they do engage the Congress on Michigan's behalf, they are usually fighting an uphill battle against the further decline of key industries and labor unions rather than working on legislation for new facilities or federal dollars. That frustration was part of Ford's reason for not seeking election in 1994. Despite his power in Congress and the extent of his support for the auto industry on such key policies as the Clean Air Act of 1990, Dingell has not been able to halt the erosion of auto manufacturing jobs in the state, because decisions are made by corporations more often on the basis of economics than politics.

As a result, despite a powerful delegation, Michigan suffers the disadvan-

Table 3: Federal Expenditures Allocated in the Great Lakes Basin States, 1990

State	Per Capita Amount	National Rank
Ohio	$3,495	37
Minnesota	3,445	40
Illinois	3,210	44
Michigan	3,141	47
Wisconsin	3,051	48
Indiana	3,050	49
U.S. Average	3,974	——

Source: Federal Expenditures by State for Fiscal Year 1990 (Washington, DC: Department of Commerce, Bureau of the Census, March 1991), pp.27, 44.

tages of declining state economics and regional politics in Congress. The perception, as one veteran Senate staff member explained, is that, beyond Ford and Dingell, "much of the Michigan delegation seems too distracted to concentrate on real lawmaking, the nuts and bolts of preparing legislation." So Michigan's members of Congress have reputations in the state and in Washington for being more partisan, more ideological, and more contentious than they are skilled at manipulating programs to the entire state's advantage. House Assistant Majority Leader David E. Bonior (D-Mt. Clemens) was the member most frequently criticized on those grounds, with such publicity leading to declining popular support and stronger political challenges in his district. As Dingell observed in commenting on the Republican 1992 plan to reapportion the delegation's districts: the plan was typically "pick the word . . . outrageous, egregious, ruthless, overreacting, self-serving, or myopic." What he meant was that the plan failed to protect many very senior incumbents, such as Ford, and their political power. With a lack of statewide support enforcing cooperation, members indeed reflect the state's geopolitics and their own regional origins. This should hardly be surprising, because fifteen of the eighteen incumbents in the pre-reapportionment delegation of 1992 came from the Michigan legislature, a training ground for teaching divisive regional politics and depending on others for leadership.[21]

Because of partisan and regional politics within the delegation, blaming the federal government is a handy excuse for inaction. As a result, negative attitudes about the federal government are reinforced by what appears as general federal neglect of Michigan. As Governor John Engler contemplated the state's fiscal problems, he said: "Given the track record, for whatever reason, we can't count very much on federal policy to help us through prob-

Table 4: General Revenue of State and Local Governments Originating from the Federal Government, as a Percentage of Expenditures

Year	Michigan	All Other States
1963–64	12.9	14.6
1973–74	18.8	20.1
1983–84	15.8	17.9
Average	15.8	17.5

Source: Federal Expenditures by State for Fiscal Year 1990 (Washington, DC: Department of Commerce, Bureau of the Census, March 1991).

lems."[22] His adversary, Governor James Blanchard, often voiced the same concerns even though he, as a member of Congress, had negotiated a $1.2 billion federal loan to save Chrysler Motors from bankruptcy. The public also speaks on this issue. In the 1992 primary election campaign, thirteen-term Representative Guy Vander Jagt (R-Luther) was forced by attacks from opponents to apologize to his constituents for neglecting his district while chairing the National Republican Congressional Committee. Despite his apology, the electorate turned Vander Jagt out in favor of a never-before-elected candidate who biked through the district promising a local approach to his congressional work.

Such successes as the Chrysler bailout notwithstanding, the governor and the public seem correct in their assessments. The federal government spent less per capita in Michigan in the late 1980s than it did in all but two states, Wisconsin and North Carolina. By that time, in comparison to 1975–76, federal revenues fell from a 27.2 percent share of the state budget to 23.4 percent. Between 1981 and 1986, the proportion of federal expenditures allocated in Michigan fell by nearly one-quarter, decreasing from 3.7 to 2.8 percent. For the entire decade, despite overall growth in federal revenues, $10 billion in federal payments to the state were lost from individual agency and program accounts. Within the state, this problem is often discussed, even among anti-tax crusaders who also want more for their investment. Michiganians are chagrined that they have to pay approximately four percent of the federal tax burden, the ninth largest share of all states, and yet receive such a small return in federal spending. As is evident in tables 3 and 4, the federal government returns funds to Michigan at rates well below those for most other states in the region and, certainly, for the nation as a whole.[23]

This low ranking cannot be blamed solely on the congressional delegation or federal bureaucrats. Federal spending in Michigan is low for several reasons. Unlike states such as New Mexico (ranked fourth in per capita federal spending), comparatively few Michigan residents are employed by the federal government. Unlike Virginia or Maryland (ranked second and third), Michigan has few federal civilian and military installations within its borders. Unlike Florida (ranked nineteenth in federal spending), Michigan lacks a large elderly population and, therefore, receives comparatively less in Social Security payments.

Even so, the federal presence in Michigan is significant, a point frequently forgotten by critics until cuts are made. Approximately 58,000 federal employees live in Michigan, a number that has grown by 36 percent since the 1950s. The expansion of federal programs and the direction of many federal programs throughout the state, in turn, have stimulated an increase in the number of state government workers, with over 60,000 employed in state agencies and some 85,000 more working in state universities. Some of the 379,000 public employees in schools and other local units also have been hired to participate in federally funded programs.[24] Federal transfer dollars pay for social programs particularly vital to Michigan. These reflect the industrial nature of the state and the periodic economic swings that especially beset durable goods manufacturing. All these employees, programs, and dollars bring along requirements and regulations that limit the independence of state policymaking, bringing also a reassuring stability to an otherwise tumultuous politics. "Luckily, there are some necessary issues that we just don't have to decide. We also can blame unpopular decisions on the feds," explained a state senator. Federal equal-opportunity and worker safety complaints, in particular, have forced the legislature to act on deadlocked issues.

Sometimes federal officials and the clout of the congressional delegation produce important results. For instance, the state had to borrow more than $1 billion from federal agencies to finance its unemployment obligations in the mid-1980s. Most of that is still owed to the federal agencies. Another example is the Federal Loan Guarantee Act – Blanchard's highly successful Chrysler bailout – through which the federal government lent operating revenue directly in the state. Grants and infrastructure support are important to the state's tourist and travel industry and the 200,000 to 300,000 workers it employs. The U.S. Department of Agriculture's commodity programs provide the hedge that keeps many Michigan farmers in business. When Michigan's farm sector was troubled financially in 1987, government payments equaled $391 million and provided unexpected stability. Table 4 also shows the total federal assistance to Michigan state and local governments, despite the state's relative disadvantage, as an impressive percentage of total revenue.

What Washington does not do provokes state residents and officials. The basis of distrust exists. Because of Michigan's northeastern rustbelt problems and the generally neglected development needs of rural regions, Michigan needs federal funds beyond those allocated for social welfare and other direct payment programs. State leaders and policymakers have been especially disturbed by the lack of federal initiatives in economic development and job retraining, both high items on the state's agenda. The state, accordingly, has had to assume much of the responsibility itself, a factor that helped define the policy thrust of the Blanchard administration. Precipitating this emphasis was the massive drop in jobs, especially in the automotive industry, during the 1980s. While Michigan's economy improved during the late 1980s, the state's unemployment rate remained above the national average until 1993. Moreover, the restructuring and changing technology of the auto industry led to the layoff of some 30,000 more people in 1987, despite a year of good auto sales. These persons had little chance of being rehired anywhere without being retrained.[25] The federal government offered little support other than the temporary relief of income transfers to the state work force, a large segment of which ranks low in education. These examples illustrate a key point about Michigan politics, even when reduced to its most common denominators: widespread complaints exist that big government will not take care of the most pressing problems.

The politics of federal funding is not the only area of contention. Control over state resources, many joke, has been a problem since the nearly bloodless Toledo War. When disputes arose over the Michigan-Ohio border in 1834, Michiganians felt that sending the militia under Governor Stevens T. Mason was necessary to retain control. Although Michigan forces routed a survey crew from Ohio, the state was not allowed by Congress to enter the Union unless it gave up claims to that territory. Although the events of statehood in 1836 are now distant, fears of the federal government linger in Michigan. Disputes over acid rain and Great Lakes water use are sustained by a belief that the state loses when it takes an issue to Washington.

Two notable examples of recent losses produced major state controversies. Both deal with Michigan's relations with its small Native American population, residents who gained state influence initially through federal courts and officials. In 1988, federal legislation allowed tribal casino and gambling operations to continue in Michigan without state oversight. However, the state and tribes were mandated to reach agreement on gambling practices, something they were unable to do until 1993. Gambling disputes followed a decade of courtroom debate over another bitter issue, Native American fishing rights as guaranteed by federal treaty. In the state's eyes, as well as those of major state conservation groups, federal officials sided with the tribes to the detriment of Great Lakes fishing and conservation interests. As late as 1993, state policymakers tried to tie state gambling agreements to Native American concessions on fishing.

Of course, as with all states, Michigan has prevailed in some federal conflicts. The U.S. Environmental Protection Agency, for example, almost always defers to rules of the Michigan Environmental Protection Act. Even victories, however, only harden the view that federal officials cannot govern state resources to Michigan's advantage. The U.S. Bureau of Commercial Fisheries managed the Great Lakes fishery until the mid-1960s. After a bitter intergovernmental dispute over development of the Great Lakes, the Michigan Department of Natural Resources won control and began establishing a Great Lakes fish-management program by introducing salmon into surrounding waters. The dispute over federal or state control was resolved only after Michigan emphasized the vast economic potential of the Great Lakes as a recreation and tourist haven for itself and adjacent states. For the most part, federal officials eventually acquiesced to the state's view that the economic value of recreational fishing in the Great Lakes would overshadow that of commercial fishing. As a result of that sweeping redefinition of purpose, federal fisheries officers and generations of non–Native American commercial fishing families were practically eliminated from Michigan's Great Lakes waters.[26] Twenty years later, Michigan's Great Lakes fishery had grown into a $750 million sports industry. The optimism of state officials, even with fluctuating conditions in the fishery, was well rewarded.[27]

Despite that success, state officials asked what could have been accomplished earlier had they not been saddled with this cumbersome federal partner. To many Michiganians, the state's drive to control its Great Lakes fishery was another example of Michigan officials planning for a miracle while federal workers, at best, hoped for a holding action. To others, it was just shortsighted action that failed to see the potential for regional growth. For many, this case exemplified why the state, when possible, would be better off depending on its own valuable but uncertain resources rather than waiting for limited external support. This belief, especially beyond the Detroit metropolitan region, has an ideological tone derived from outstate beliefs that local and regional politics best take care of local needs. This view has geopolitical origins that make ideas of limited government popular in much of outstate Michigan. While calls for such limits have inconsistencies, given the state's level of government activism since the 1950s, they have very real origins. Such roots lie in the difficulties that each region has with appreciating and understanding actions taken by the state government for its local places. Once again, geopolitics explains why Michiganians see and expect things as they do, even if they appear to outside observers as shortsighted.

SOME CLOSING THOUGHTS

The geographical composition and location of Michigan have significant impacts on state and intergovernmental politics. Both factors create circumstances where state-federal relationships are far from cooperative. Michigan is part of, but not always a willing partner to, the federal system. The division of the territory between two peninsulas, the remoteness of the upper peninsula from the rest of the state, and the concentration of the industrial sectors in the state's southern counties are only three among many geopolitical factors that give rise to a variety of claims in Lansing and in Washington. For example, northerners argue that the vast state and federal ownership of forest land works to keep local tax revenues low; Detroiters contend that people from the entire state benefit from the city's major cultural facilities and that Detroit is therefore entitled to state and federal support.

Similarly, Michigan's geographical position in the center of the Great Lakes, midway between great reservoirs of natural resources, has contributed to sometimes contentious relations with other governments. The claims of neighboring states, Canadian provinces, and the federal government occasionally run contrary to the state's interest or those of one or more of its regions, at least as Michiganians perceive them. The positive effects of federalism, in contrast, are simply expected as the state's due – money back for federal taxes paid. The result is that only some things get done or pursued, not always the most urgent ones at that. This perspective and understanding is important because, as later chapters will clarify, Michigan's problem solving is far from being perfectly responsible and accommodating.

CHAPTER THREE

The Michigan Constitution

Susan Fino is a principal author of this chapter

A CONTRACT AMONG STATE INTERESTS

Michigan voters, along with those in fourteen other states, have the opportunity to call a constitutional convention periodically. The state constitution of 1963 requires that every sixteen years voters decide whether to redraft that document. The provision gives citizens a chance to vent any dissatisfaction that they might have with state government or state policy without having to marshall the signatures necessary to request constitutional change on their own. Despite the ongoing appeal of reform, the first such referendum was defeated in 1980.

One of the arguments that citizens and policymakers often make for this and likely future defeats is that constitutional conventions are costly. Others add that because of their right of initiative and referendum, Michiganians can bring about desired changes in this basic law by individual amendments. It is not so much that people think that the constitution is just fine; rather, they prefer not to risk rights and privileges that they now have vested in the document. Avoidance of reform exists because Michigan's constitution is very much a detailed contract among highly diverse interests. If a constitutional convention were called, all of the state's social and economic forces would assemble on center stage. In order to "cut a deal," much of what nearly every state interest uses to its present political advantage would be open to renegotiated claims. This would include rights now explicitly defined in the constitution, those implicitly protected, and presently unstated rights represented by interests that would like to stake a claim in the constitution, such as, for example, pro-life and pro-choice groups. All legislative statutes could be brought forward for reconsideration by conventioneers. No point other than this often expressed fear of constitutional reform better illustrates how central and basic is this underlying set of institutional rules as to who gets what in Michigan.

The importance of vested rights in the state constitution suggests much about its nature, specifically the idea that all interests share in this mutual contract.[1] Despite a general "We, the people" introduction, the current and other most recent Michigan constitutions have been detailed social contracts between citizens and the government. This is because the emphasis has been on provisions that allocate specific rights rather than on general popular sovereignty. The intent of these constitutions was more to resolve specific disputes than to serve as a generic covenant or simple pledge toward democratic governance as found in many other states of the upper Midwest. As such, Michigan's constitution does much to specify the explicit terms that provide various interests with potential opportunities to exercise their own rights within the context of the rights of others. The detail helps soften political conflict in the legislature and with the governor. Who can make statutory law? Under what circumstances? What officials will the public elect? What limits will the legislature face in taxing citizens? Under what circumstances can the state assume control over private property or, indeed, over the life of a citizen? The answers to these questions are greatly determined by the state's constitution and, through interpretation, by state supreme court justices, who apply the words in the constitution to specific situations.

One might have expected in this moralistic state a constitution that, as a more generic covenant, idealistically and generally emphasizes the positive role of government for bettering the state as a whole. Rather, Michigan's contract provides limits on government for such specific purposes as mandating a regressive income tax and preventing local governments from raising other taxes to meet their own determined needs. Yet, for logical reasons, it performs not only that purpose. The diversity of interests in Michigan, coupled with the practical need to resolve disputes, also requires that such generalities focus first on creating an environment for a workable state politics. The resulting document, therefore, reflects the state's moralistic concerns quite adequately, even as many criticize it for not doing more to encourage the state's communal life and sense of common purpose. A broad spectrum of citizens is now included in the contract; much is done to ensure the rights of all citizens; government is given an activist role; and governing powers are clearly divided to ensure access by numerous claimants.[2] Unlike the constitutions of many southern states, this contract is not elitist.

All these features have been brought forward by the Michigan constitutional process from its predecessors. One constitution after another – first in 1837, then in 1850, and again in 1908 and 1963 – was built upon the work crafted by the moralistic views of early Michigan settlers from New England. The young state began with a tradition of local government and state guarantees of rights and liberties, and its growth led to the inclusion of many new policy concerns. Some clearly outmoded provisions were dropped during constitutional reforms. The process of change, though, has been one in which divided and contending interests negotiated settlements to preserve vestiges of the old and, at the same time, to add provisions for those who had more recently acquired power in the state. The 1963 constitution, for example, established a state Department of Civil Rights, reflecting not only Michigan's moralistic commitment to all, but also recognizing the emerging power of African Americans and Hispanics. Later, the department's powers were also directed to the goals of feminist and disability rights movements. It is at such points that the state's individualistic culture merges with the moralistic.

Specifying a particular department in a state constitution, as is done in Michigan, is the type of provision that reformers often criticize. They argue that a constitution should include only fundamental policies. But, scholastic ideals aside, remembering that state constitutions are first and foremost political documents is fundamental to understanding them, at least in Michigan.[3] Details such as whether a state government will include an agency called the Department of Civil Rights, some reformers argue, should be a matter of legislation as long as guarantees exist that some authority enforce minority rights laws. Other reformers, however, argue the opposite, citing the possibilities of both neglect and undue interference if the office lacks constitutional status. An automatic funding provision for the Civil Service Commission, for example, such as Michigan's constitution provides, is so basic to the operation and independence of merit-system employment that its proponents fear funding cannot be left to the whims of the governor or legislators.

State constitutions, then, are documents by which interest groups can solidify their stakes for decades, simply because these fundamental laws are more difficult to change than ordinary statutes. As such, constitutions reflect the conditions and issues of the times and the society in which they were written. Judicial interpretation of these basic provisions of law provides one means for keeping a constitution current. Initiatives and referenda for specific amendments are used frequently as well. Between 1964 and 1993, Michigan voters approved sixteen of fifty-one proposed amendments. If the future holds true to form, they can expect to face at least one or two proposed amendments in each biennial election.

Amendments, of course, give state constitutions a growth and weight problem. Amendments often change existing provisions rather than add new sections. Hence, more words are usually required in the amendments than the framers used initially to deal with a particular matter. This problem is only a moderate one for Michigan. The several constitutions have been rather tightly written, and voters accept only one in three proposals. The constitution contains about 20,000 words. Compared to other states, it is about average in length. It is well below the estimated 174,000 words that comprise Alabama's fundamental law and about twice the length of the brief documents of Connecticut, New Hampshire, and Indiana.

THE MICHIGAN CONSTITUTION

After a heady beginning, the 1950s brought several severe problems to Michigan state government: fiscal difficulties, controversy over legislative apportionment, and an impasse between the legislature and governor. Each set of issues is covered in detail in other chapters, but their combined effects are relevant here. The 1908 constitution, with its many amendments, was widely perceived to be one reason for these compounding problems. As an incremental revision of the 1850 constitution, Michigan's 1908-style governance was widely acknowledged to be rooted in the values of nineteenth-century Jacksonian democracy.[4] George Romney, the chief executive of American Motors Corporation in the early 1960s, and other prominent citizens believed that a complete revision of the state constitution was the only solution to the turmoil created by the 1908 document.

In 1961, a constitutional convention was called to rewrite the constitution for the twentieth century. Delegates to the convention wanted to remove much of the statutory language that had been worked into the 1908 document and to create a constitution more appropriate to an industrialized economy with a rapidly expanding service sector.

One convention delegate was elected from each senate and house district on a partisan basis, a plan that reflected the biases of conservative rural communities that disproportionately ruled in the pre–*Baker* v. *Carr* era, before one person–one vote apportionment. Big business, big labor unions, and farm interests were most commonly represented among the delegates. Persons chosen were mostly white males; "only ten women and a handful of blacks were among its members."[5] The delegates paid considerable attention to the practices of other states, listened to recommendations of political scientists, and seriously considered citizen opinions expressed at hearings. Despite the efforts of the delegates and academic recommendations to keep statutory language to a minimum, the state's numerous and well-organized interests demanded that advantageous provisions in the old constitution be continued in the new document. The resulting document was less than half the size of the 1908 constitution but failed even to approach the sparse, simple framework for government of Michigan's first constitution.[6]

The 1963 document represented a combination of delicately crafted compromises befitting a state whose citizens practice the politics of balance. Three examples of these compromises stand out for their balanced approach. The legislature was permitted to adopt a personal income tax, but only one that did not provide for graduated rates. Candidates for supreme court justice would be elected in nonpartisan elections, but candidates could be nominated at political party conventions if the legislature so desired – as it eventually did. Finally, members serving on the governing boards of the state's three largest institutions of higher education – the University of Michigan, Michigan State University, and Wayne State University – were to be directly elected, and the state legislature and administration would be prohibited from interfering in internal university matters. The governor, however, would appoint governing board members of the smaller institutions, but even for these places, no internal interference was allowed. The battles associated with these compromises did not merely pit conservative against liberal interests. Some involved partisan control versus good-government reform values. Others pitted advocates of legislative authority against those who favored institutional flexibility. All, however, were highly specific battles over the direction of basic state institutions.

The difficulty of crafting balanced constitutional provisions did not rest solely in the need to obtain a majority on the floor of the constitutional convention. Delegates knew that another majority remained to be mobilized: the voters. The conservative rural majority, if it was to achieve anything through the convention, had to incorporate its own views as strongly as possible without inciting opposition from the sizable liberal urban minority. Their fears were well founded. Voters approved the new constitution by a margin of only 7,424 votes, about 0.2 percent of the total ballots cast. The conservative majority of the constitutional convention, no doubt, played the politics of balance nearly perfectly.

Michigan's constitution begins with a Declaration of Rights, many of which were traceable to the Northwest Ordinance of 1787 and the 1850 constitution. Many rights, however, were added to reflect issues of the early 1960s. The declaration contains a number of provisions that differ significantly from the federal Bill of Rights. Article I, Section 2, for example, guarantees the equal protection of the laws but, unlike the U.S. Fourteenth Amendment, also specifies that there shall be no discrimination on account of "religion, race, color, or national origin."

The Michigan constitution is strict on separation of church and state, a tradition dating from 1837. State appropriations or property donations for the benefit of "any religious sect or society" or theological seminary are prohibited. Citizens are guaranteed the right to speak freely and to express and publish views on all subjects, but they are held responsible for the exercise of those rights. Truth, however, may be offered as a defense in all libel cases.

Right of trial by jury was protected; juries must consist of twelve members in criminal trials in courts of record but may consist of fewer than twelve in other courts. In civil proceedings, juries of twelve are permitted, and a vote of ten jurors is sufficient to sustain the claims of the plaintiff.[7] Criminal defendants are also granted a right to appeal. All persons, except those accused of murder or treason, are eligible for bail, and no person can be imprisoned on account of debt.

The Declaration of Rights is also careful to safeguard the rights of all individuals, firms, corporations, and voluntary associations called before legislative and executive investigatory committees. This provision is clearly an outgrowth of concerns over the abuse of the investigatory power of government during the McCarthy era (1953–54).

Despite the important differences between the Michigan Declaration of Rights and the federal Bill of Rights, the Michigan Supreme Court has been inconsistent at best in using the state document to expand the protection of individual rights as urged on the states by U.S. Supreme Court Justice William J. Brennan in 1977.[8] Thus, what scholars commonly call "the new judicial federalism," based on an independent and institutionally adequate state constitution, is only nominally advanced in Michigan. The Michigan constitution is specific on guarantees of religious liberty and separation of church and state. However, in an important decision on state certification of private school teachers, the state's highest court relied exclusively on the First Amendment to the U.S. Constitution.[9]

In criminal cases, the court has acknowledged that Michigan's constitution may provide a higher standard of protection of defendant rights than the U.S. Constitution, but the court has selectively applied the higher state standards.[10] Sometimes criminal defendants receive the benefits of Michigan court decisions that differ from the more prosecution-oriented outcomes of the U.S. Supreme Court. Other times they do not. Again, what we see here is the cumulative effects of political balance, both among interests and in procedures that enhance different interests.

The role of the Michigan Declaration of Rights in providing enhanced protection for civil rights and liberties became important to the debate on state funding of elective abortions after a 1991 legislative ban. The U.S. Supreme Court held that a state's decision not to fund such abortions does not interfere with a woman's right to terminate a pregnancy.[11] Some state supreme courts, however, have held that state funding of elective abortions is required by state constitutional law. That interpretation was then used for litigation in Michigan.[12]

The 1963 constitution goes beyond the Declaration of Rights, but the basic framework for government was not changed. Operational changes, however, were extensive, especially in providing direction and policy goals. The legislative branch (Article IV) consists of a senate, whose members serve a four-year term, and a house of representatives, in which the term is for two years. The legislative article provides much detail on legislative procedure and reapportionment, though the state supreme court threw out the latter provision in a case reviewing legislative redistricting in 1981. Initially, this document also permitted the legislature to set its compensation by law, but a 1968 amendment created the State Officers Compensation Commission to determine salaries for the legislature, governor, and other officials, including supreme court justices.[13]

The 1963 constitution invites legislation in a number of specific areas. The legislature is empowered to enact laws governing working hours and conditions of employment (Section 49) and to regulate and provide safety measures for atomic energy. Section 52 characterizes the conservation and development of natural resources as a matter of "paramount public concern" and directs the state to protect air, water, and other natural resources from "pollution, impairment, and destruction." Section 51 declares that protection of the general welfare and public health are of "primary" importance; the legislature is directed to enact laws to protect both. As a consequence, this section may provide the legislature with constitutional authority to pass regulations for persons with AIDS, subject, of course, to the limitations imposed by the Declaration of Rights. Article IV contains some added limitations on legislative power. Section 41, for example, prohibited lotteries until voters approved an amendment in 1972. Section 46 disallows the death penalty.

Article V vests the executive power of the state in the governor, who is nominated by primary election. Party conventions nominate candidates for lieutenant governor, secretary of state, and attorney general. The governor and lieutenant governor run on the same ticket. In addition to lengthening terms of office for members of the executive branch to four years, the new document eliminated several elected positions: director of highways, superintendent of education, and auditor general. Candidates for governor and lieutenant governor must be at least thirty years of age and registered voters in Michigan for at least four years preceding the election.

Article V also carefully arranges the operation of the executive branch, which is limited to twenty principal departments, each consisting of agencies of similar purposes and each directed, unless otherwise specified by law, by a single executive who is appointed by the governor with the concurrence of the senate. This constitutional limitation consolidated approximately 130 agencies, bureaus, and commissions that had been added to the executive branch under the 1908 constitution. These proliferating units had rendered strong executive management virtually impossible. Most department heads now also serve at the pleasure of the governor in order to ensure policy and administrative responsiveness. The governor may change the organization of the executive branch, but when such a change requires the force of law, the governor must make the change through an executive order and must submit it to the legislature, where it is subject to a two-house legislative veto. The order takes effect within sixty days unless both houses disapprove a proposed reorganization.

The constitution does not vest the governor with complete control over all executive agencies, though. A bipartisan state transportation commission is charged with appointing a state highway director, who serves as the chief executive officer of the department.[14] The partisan-elected state Board of Education supervises public education, except for institutions granting baccalaureate degrees. The board appoints a superintendent of public instruction, who is the principal executive official of the Department of Education.[15] Universities are constitutionally autonomous, with, as noted earlier, elected or gubernatorially appointed governing bodies of each institution supervising the operations, appointing the president, and directing all expenditures.

The executive article also establishes budget procedures. Under Article V, Section 18, the governor submits to the legislature a detailed budget, including proposed expenditures and anticipated revenues. The budget must be balanced; proposed expenditures may not exceed anticipated revenues. The majority of state employees are covered by Article XI. As a carryover from the 1908 document, Article XI provides for a competitive civil service system. The Civil Service Commission selects its director through an open, competitive examination process.

The governor also possesses the item veto for appropriations.[16] Specific budget items, from programs to projects, can be removed by gubernatorial objection unless a two-thirds majority of both the house and senate override. In the event of an item veto, the other parts of the appropriations bill become law. The legislature may override the item veto by a procedure common to U.S. bodies, a two-thirds vote in both of its houses.

The judicial power is vested in a unified court of justice that consists of the state supreme court, a court of appeals, trial courts of general jurisdiction, a probate court, and courts of limited jurisdiction established by legislative action.[17] The 1963 document ordered an end to justices of the peace, who ultimately were replaced by judges of the district courts created by the legislature.

The supreme court has general supervisory authority over lower courts and may issue rules pertaining to the practices and procedures for such courts throughout the state. The Michigan sentencing guidelines are a recent and controversial example of these rule-making powers. The guidelines, developed by the supreme court to help ensure uniformity in criminal sentences, generally require judges to choose a sentence within ranges, based on the nature of the crime and such characteristics of the defendant as prior record. The supreme court also has superintending control over the appellate jurisdiction.

The 1963 constitution continues Michigan's tradition of a democratic judiciary. The seven supreme court justices are elected to eight-year terms. The governor may fill a vacancy by appointment; senate confirmation is not required. The court selects from among its members a chief justice who serves for two years. The eight-year terms, the inapplicability of recall to judicial positions, and the constitutional mandate that justices' salaries may not be reduced except as part of a general salary reduction affecting all branches provide a measure of judicial independence. However, Michigan justices are not as insulated from majority pressure as are their federal counterparts. Not only may Michigan justices be impeached; they may also be removed for causes "insufficient" for impeachment by the governor on a concurrent resolution of two-thirds of the members of both houses of the legislature.[18]

Direct democracy is preserved in the latest constitution. Although most of the statutory language was removed from the sections on the initiative and referendum, they and the recall process operate in much the same way as when they were adopted in 1913. The signature requirement for triggering the legislative (as opposed to the constitutional) initiative and referendum remain the same in the 1963 document, but state law now specifies the rules by which signatures are collected and validated.[19] The state supreme court has scrutinized the implementing legislation for Article II, Section 9, and has ascertained that the procedures and time limits for collecting signatures do not unconstitutionally burden the right of initiative and referendum.[20]

Section 8 of Article II strengthens the power of recall by limiting the ability of critics to use courts to alter requirements or interfere with the process. The constitution explicitly states that the sufficiency of any reason for recall is a political rather than a judicial question.

The Michigan constitution, as before, may be amended through two major mechanisms: by legislative proposal and popular vote, and by citizen petition and popular vote. Under the first mechanism, legislators in either house may propose a constitutional amendment. A two-thirds majority in each house is necessary for passage, after which the issue goes to the people at the next general election. A majority of those voting is required for ratification. Amendments may also be introduced through the constitutional initiative. The procedure is more rigorous than for a statutory initiative.[21] This is consistent with the original framers' idea that it should be more difficult to change the constitution than to propose a statute. Constitutional initiatives that pass the procedural threshold are placed on the ballot for popular vote at the next general election. Adoption requires a majority of those voting on the issue.

Operational and policy changes continued after this constitution went into effect. Amendments limiting state expenditures and thereby affecting the operation of state government came as the result of an initiative petition in 1978. These changes, popularly called the Headlee amendments after Richard Headlee, who led the amendment campaign, came as part of a powerful taxpayers' revolt that previously included attempts at still more restrictive tax and revenue provisions. These amendments limit state and local taxes, including the tax on real and personal property, to specified levels unless a majority of voters authorize a waiver of the limits.[22] The amendments also restrict state government revenues to a formula – what amounts to currently 9.49 percent of total state personal income. They also require the state to maintain the level of its aid to local units at what it was when the amendment took effect, 41.6 percent of total state revenues. Moreover, the state must pay the full cost of all new programs that it requires of local units. The

Headlee amendments are a part of the longtime Michigan tradition of registering public policy in the constitution as a way of placing it beyond the reach of an ever-changing legislature, seen by some state interests as fiscally irresponsible and not entirely trustworthy.

A citizen-petitioned amendment that passed in 1992 raised even more alarm for elected officials by limiting U.S. senators to two more terms in office and members of the House of Representatives to three. Because Congress incumbents can serve only six to eight more years, the seniority of congressional delegations of the twenty-first century will be limited severely if this withstands court challenges. In addition, because similar limits to the terms in office apply to the Michigan house and senate, legislators of the next century will have limited institutional memories. With two terms allowed for elective statewide executives, no one will have the long tenure of Governor William G. Milliken (1969–82), Attorney General Frank J. Kelley (1962–present), or Secretary of State Richard Austin (1971–present).

While the nation in 1989 celebrated the bicentennial of the U.S. Constitution, Michigan and other states are not destined to have such long-lived documents. Despite widespread reluctance to risk changes, the Michigan constitution will be rewritten at some point in the future. One reason is the basic difference in approach between the state and federal documents. The U.S. Constitution is a joint product of the states. Together, the people of the states delegated certain powers to the national government. In addition, the U.S. Constitution reserves specific powers to the states and prohibits both the state and national governments from exercising certain other powers altogether. State constitutions are much more complex because, in theory, a state and its people together can exercise any power not prohibited by the federal document. Bargaining and negotiating these largely unrestricted powers into a satisfactory statement is much more difficult, especially in Michigan with its complexity and diversity. As conditions change, the basis for acceptable deals consequently unravels, costing the constitution legitimacy.

A second reason for the comparatively short life of our state constitutions is that Michigan citizens can amend them much more easily than the U.S. Constitution. Michiganians have used this power rather liberally in the past and are likely to do so in the future. This, too, reflects the goals set in the original bargains, reducing satisfaction with the new political terms of the contract. In addition, many of these very specific amendments deal with structural elements of government and, as a result, are time-bound; that is, they reflect the passions of the moment and, after a period, become outmoded or outdated. For example, in 1968 the Michigan legislature proposed, and voters approved, the amendment changing the way salaries of legislators and other top officials are set. In 1991, after the State Officers Compensation Commission recommended increases amounting to 16.2 percent, citizens immediately began preparing petitions to abolish the commission. Demonstrating the temporal thrust of citizen initiations, the threat to repeal the amendment subsided when legislators rejected the proposed pay hikes because of a fiscal crisis.

The recognition of constitutional change as a constant in state politics leads to one unusual state political event that merits broader recognition than it receives. Surviving delegates to the last constitutional convention gather every two years to renew acquaintances and evaluate how their handiwork has weathered over time. Their views provide yet another context for evaluating the performance of Michigan government. Of course, they have mixed feelings when they consider the addition of a new amendment. Often they recall, for better or worse, that the convention attempted to deal with that issue but could not. Delegates periodically are pleased to see a provision that they opposed finally being modified or a position that they supported eventually being sustained.

What they comment on mostly, though, is the slow-paced dynamics of reform and the unraveling effects of incremental constitutional changes. They see the document, despite its many defenders, as being less stable over time. So, based on the state's record, and taking active resistance to change into account, this 1963 constitution will have a life span of perhaps fifty to sixty years.

MICHIGAN'S OTHER THREE CONSTITUTIONS

Much of the present context of Michigan's constitution has its roots in the state's prior basic document and even the actions of the Continental Congress. Michigan's political and legal history begins with that body's adoption of the Ordinance of 1784, passed at the urging of Thomas Jefferson. This ordinance decreed that ten future states would be carved form the Northwest Territories, roughly the area west of the original colonies, north of the Ohio River and east of the Mississippi River. Jefferson himself provided fanciful names for the future states, one of which was Michigan. This was the first mention of Michigan as a political unit.[23] But the ordinance had a shortcoming: it provided no procedure for the transition from territory to statehood. At the urging of land speculators who held property in the territories, the Confederation Congress passed the Northwest Ordinance of 1787 to govern the territories and provide for a three-stage progression toward statehood, each with an increasing degree of self-governance.[24]

During the first stage, Congress would appoint a governor, three judges, and a secretary. The governor and the judges could not write new laws but were empowered to adopt any laws then in existence in any of the thirteen original states. Congress reserved for itself the right to reject a law so adopted.

A territory could progress to the second stage upon demonstrating that it had 5,000 free, adult male residents. The territory could then convene a general assembly to make its own laws as long as no law repudiated a principle or article in the Ordinance of 1787. The general assembly was to consist of an elected governor, an elected house of representatives, and a legislative council that Congress appointed from among the elected representatives. The territory could also send one delegate to Congress with the right to debate but not vote. Finally, when a territory had 60,000 free adult male residents, it could be admitted to the federal Union as a state.

The Ordinance of 1787 contained several important provisions that have since become part of the fabric of Michigan's constitutions. It guaranteed religious liberty, provided for due process, prohibited cruel and unusual punishment, and banned slavery. Thomas M. Cooley, Michigan's most noted legal scholar, praised the ordinance for its "far seeing statesmanship" and saw it "as the beginning of the end of American slavery."[25] A particularly important provision held that "religion, morality, and knowledge being necessary to good government and the happiness of mankind, schools and the means of education shall forever be encouraged." This statement has been embedded in each of the state's constitutions.

The First Constitution

Governor Stevens T. Mason, as empowered in the Ordinance of 1787, called for a census of the Michigan Territory in 1834. The results demonstrated that Michigan had enough residents for statehood. A state constitutional convention was called, and a document was written for adoption in 1835.[26] This first constitution "was framed quickly by men of modest means."[27] Most of the delegates were farmers, but some merchants were among them. Only ten delegates were trained in the law. A majority were Democrats committed to the ideals of Jacksonian democracy, with its emphasis on political participation. The delegates borrowed freely from other state constitutions, especially those of their previous home states, Connecticut and New York.[28] In this way, moralistic elements of the political culture of New England were injected into Michigan politics and constitutional law at the state's inception.

The first constitution began with a bill of rights that incorporated some guarantees from the Northwest Ordinance, elements of the federal Bill of Rights, and provisions from Connecticut's bill of rights. The government was divided into the present three branches. The governor and members of the state senate were elected to two-year terms. In keeping with Jacksonian values about ensuring public officials' responsiveness to the peoples' wishes, state representatives were given one-year terms. The two houses had the joint responsibility of selecting the state treasurer; supreme court justices were appointed by the governor with approval of the senate. Lower court judges, including county, circuit, and probate judges, were elected – an especially democratic provision at that time.

Michigan also adopted the New England traditions of local government, including townships. Jefferson, enamored with New England town government, advocated surveying the territory into 36-square-mile areas. He saw these townships as developing into "elementary republics." In keeping with the times, officers of all minor subdivisions of the state were subject to popular choice. Judges, sheriffs, county treasurers, coroners, registrars of deeds, and surveyors were all elected. [29] Michigan's still ongoing tradition of having many elected offices and strong county governments can be traced to the constitution of 1835. Jacksonian and Jeffersonian values embedded in the new constitution preserved the emphasis on education. Article X guaranteed the perpetual support of schools, provided for common schools and libraries, and created a fund derived from the sale of lands to create and maintain an institution of higher learning.

State historian George Fuller praised the constitution's dignity and simplicity. Indeed, it was very much a covenant rather than a detailed social contract. Cooley noted that it was carefully restricted to the fundamentals of government, and because it did not contain much statutory language, citizens could regard it as a model constitution. [30] This constitution was Michigan's least specific document but one full of worthy goals for the state. One commentator, writing in 1954, stated those values forthrightly, "The constitution of 1835 was the best one Michigan has had." [31]

However, this broad, flexible document was not without its weaknesses. [32] Scarce attention was paid to what some state interests saw as a need to regulate business. The legislature, it was said, was "beset by an importunate and aggressive lobby" of business interests that influenced the state to push transportation development by road, canal, and navigable waterways.

Business demands for costly projects earned them the reputation for being "intolerable nuisances. They threw suspicions on the honesty of everything they favored."[33]

Under clouds of scandal, charters were granted to railroads and banks without personal liability clauses; when a railroad or bank failed, investors had no recourse for recovering their investments. More important, in a state with imposing geographical obstacles, the Miscellaneous Provisions section of the constitution required the state to encourage internal improvements. "Extravagant application" of this clause, in one of the earliest references to the state's history of political excess, almost bankrupted the state.[34] These difficulties, coupled with the fact that the midwestern states of Ohio, Illinois, Indiana, Iowa, and Wisconsin were engaged in constitution making, led to a new constitutional convention in 1850.

The Second Constitution

The constitutional convention of 1850 was framed even more than the first under the influence of Jacksonian democracy, by then the "prevailing radicalism" of the day.[35] The delegates again were mostly farmers and Democrats. There was no evidence of the influence of corporate wealth or railroad interests, despite their reputation for corruption under the first constitution.[36] Michigan, even then, was showing its diversity and its propensity for controlling dominant interests. Delegates held a number of common sentiments. The Jacksonian impulse led the framers to expand the democratic framework and bring "the exercise of power as near as possible to the people concerned and to make responsibility constant and direct."[37]

These framers also felt that consistent public policy could not be achieved by a legislature whose members changed regularly.[38] Their solution, as representatives of specific state interests, was to include detailed policy measures to assure stability.[39] This desire to place certain areas of policy beyond the reach of the legislature is the source of much of the statutory language in the 1850 document and subsequent constitutions. The result was a constitution more than twice as long as the 1835 document and, according to historians Willis Dunbar and George May, one that "ranks as the worst state constitution" because of its inflexibility.[40]

For reasons not entirely clear, the separate bill of rights disappeared. Instead, the delegates placed contractual guarantees of individual rights throughout the constitution as specific limits on particular branches of government. For example, they placed religious freedom and freedom of the press in the legislative article and the procedural rights of criminal defendants in the judicial article.

All major state offices, including supreme court justices, were subject to election. Delegates also gave considerable attention to finance, taxation, and regulation of corporations. As in the current constitution, concerns were expressed for a balanced state budget. Article XIV required the legislature to provide for an annual tax sufficient to pay the estimated expenses of state government, the interest on the state debt, and any deficiency that might occur in revenues. To curtail abuses of business in state government, the new document prohibited the purchase of stock in any corporation involved in making internal improvements, banking laws could take effect only after voter approval, and government borrowing was limited to a total of $50,000. To prevent any group from gaining special privileges, the constitution forbade the legislature to adopt special acts of incorporation for single firms. Thereafter, corporations could be formed only in compliance with general statutes having broad applicability.

This constitution was not without progressive intent as well. Several progressive elements were scattered among its provisions. Women's political rights were debated at the convention, and although women's suffrage failed, the constitution did recognize and protect the property rights of married women.

The framers established few requirements for state citizenship because they wanted to encourage settlement by Scandinavian and German immigrants who were skilled in farming as well as in the emerging industries of lumbering and mining.[41] The constitution forbade manufacturing by prison inmates and allowed indeterminate criminal sentences in the interest of rehabilitation. Moreover, it demanded that the state establish and maintain institutions for the benefit of the "deaf, dumb, blind, and insane." Libraries were mandated in each city and township. Finally, and prior to the federal Morrill Act that provided grants of federal land to schools, the constitution directed the legislature to establish a university for instruction in agriculture and natural science, the first constitution of any state to do so.[42]

By the turn of the century, however, a new sentiment began to take hold in the state. The Democratic party, which had dominated the constitutional conventions of 1835 and 1850, was in disarray; Republicans controlled the statehouse and the White House. Business interests were growing in influence. It was also a time of reform when Progressive activists believed that government and society could be changed for the better. They argued that an unwieldy nineteenth-century constitution, especially one written by interest groups of another era, was no longer adequate for a state that was making the transition from agriculture to industry.

The Third Constitution

Twice in the years after 1850, Michigan voters defeated moves to revise the constitution. In 1907, Governor Fred M. Warner campaigned successfully for a new constitution; and on October 22, 1907, ninety-six delegates gathered in Lansing to write Michigan's document for the twentieth century. These delegates reflected the dramatic changes that had occurred in Michigan's economy, politics, and society as business took its place alongside extractive industries. All but eight delegates were Republican and only seven were farmers. At least sixty delegates had some legal training, and most represented the new business interests, although representatives of newly emerging labor organizations also were present. Progressives dominated the convention, but conservative Republicans were present as well and actively opposed wholesale changes in the constitution. Consequently, the rewritten document was mostly an expansion of the evolving social contract agreed to in 1850.[43] New interests gained new provisions; old interests generally retained theirs.

The third constitution was a ponderous code of seventeen lengthy articles riddled with statutory language. The framers continued the practice begun in 1850 of embedding policy decisions in the constitution to place them beyond the reach of the legislature. The new constitution went into much more detail on legislative procedure and introduced the gubernational item veto for appropriations. Guarantees of individual rights and liberties were collected and reestablished as a separate declaration of rights. The article on taxation and finance grew in length and detail as did the article on local government. Women's suffrage was again debated and defeated, but women were allowed to vote on bond issues. Voters approved the new constitution by a wide margin, and it went into effect in 1909.

An especially important development came in the form of amendments to this constitution, which substantially redistributed political power within the state. Progressive delegates at the convention argued for including the power of legislative initiative, legislative referendum, and recall of public officials, but conservatives turned them back. In 1912, however, Republicans split their support for William H. Taft and the Progressive Theodore Roosevelt; Democrat Woodrow Wilson won the White House. Democrats and Progressives came to dominate Michigan politics and, working together, led the fight for direct democracy provisions. In 1913, all three provisions were added to the constitution.

Progressives were more successful within the constitutional convention on another issue of citizen control: home rule for local governments. The new constitution directed the legislature to adopt a law providing home rule, or greater governmental self-control, for cities and villages. The convention debated extending the same freedom to counties but ultimately decided against granting these governments a shield against state intervention.

The Balance between Citizens and Public Officials. One feature of the third constitution, with its citizen focus, deserves special attention because of its LaFollette-style Progressive influence on Michigan politics. The powers of initiative, referendum, and recall remain features – and to some, weapons – of Michigan politics. These are used as means to influence and restrain policymakers and to decide policy. Accordingly, the pros and cons of direct initiatives, as debated in constitutional conventions, should be understood by all who want to know state politics. The idea that citizens are capable of the wisest governance was at its zenith during the period of the third constitution. These provisions were the principal reaction to the scandals of business involvement in politics.

For the most part, sympathizers of Progressive politics, such as W. A. Coutts, argued for the reform: *vox populi, vox dei* (the voice of the people is the voice of God).[44] Others, such as Henry M. Campbell, saw direct democracy as a

> crisis as great as any except the Civil War. . . . Direct democracy is not possible in political units of any considerable size; what works in a New England town meeting cannot work in a large, populous state. Fleeting passions may govern the choice of an aroused electorate or uninformed voters may decide on the basis of attractive title to a proposal with nothing more. Propositions are placed before the people in a "take it or leave it" manner and there is no room for discussion, modification, or accommodation as in a representative legislative chamber. The good must go along with the bad.

Campbell warned the people of Michigan about the excesses of the initiative and referendum in other states. In Oregon, in 1908, voters deliberated on 126 pages of amendments and statutes. The next year, the issues had grown to 208 pages of laws and amendments, among them a constitutional amendment of 36 sections that had to be voted on as a single proposition. In South Dakota, in 1910, the ballot was seven feet long, one foot for candidates and six feet for initiatives and referenda. Campbell saw recall as being just as in-advisable: its "natural effect" would be to place every officeholder on the lookout for "every passing whim, the clamor of newspapers, the shouting of agitators."[45]

But it was not the reactionaries who prevailed in Michigan. The sponsors of the initiative, referendum, and recall amendments were careful to attach considerable procedural language to the initiative and referendum so that these provisions would never depend on the legislature for implementation. Initiative, defined as the power to "propose legislative measures, resolu-tions, and laws," required a petition signed by a number of registered voters equal to 8 percent of the total votes cast for governor at the last gubernatorial election.[46] The legislature then, as now, was given a chance to approve or re-ject initiated laws. If the legislature enacted an initiative, it was not placed on the ballot. However, the legislature could reject a proposed law by a three-quarters majority in each house or, alternatively, suggest another measure on the same subject. If it suggested another measure, though, both versions would be presented to the electorate.

Referendum, the power to "approve or reject any act passed by the legis-lature," had a 5 percent signature threshold. To allow for its operation, no legislative act, except appropriations to state institutions and those "imme-diately necessary for the preservation of the public peace, health, or safety," could take effect until ninety days after passage. This period allowed time for citizens to collect signatures to suspend an act and vote on it at the next gen-eral election. A majority vote in the general election was to determine pas-sage or failure of an initiative or referendum. The governor's veto power did not extend to acts so adopted. No initiated act could be repealed or amended by the legislature. Resubmitting the issue to the people through another ref-erendum, as a means of constitutional amendment in this case, was the only means of change.

The 1908 constitution, as amended, limited the initiative and referendum, and these limits remain in place today. The referendum now extends only to laws enacted by the legislature, but does not apply to appropriation acts or to supplemental appropriations to correct shortfalls in state agency accounts. The legislature, with supreme court approval, has used these two exceptions as a technical means of placing changes in tax law beyond the reach of a ref-erendum. The technique works this way: The legislature passes a law to put a "necessary" new surcharge on a service or usable property, places its pro-ceeds in a special fund, and then immediately appropriates the income from that tax to a state institution that needs a supplemental adjustment. The resulting tax increase, therefore, is not subject to referendum.

Significantly, in setting the tone for their use as well as in inspiring constitutional amendments, the Michigan Supreme Court generally allows initiatives of dubious constitutionality to be placed before the people. Citizens try nearly anything. The court reasons that the people may reject the law, but should an initiative succeed at the polls, there will be ample opportunity for judicial review in actual application. In *Detroit Automobile Club* v. *Secretary of State*[47] and again in *Moreton* v. *Secretary of State*,[48] the court not only upheld this practice but, in preaching more of the gospel of balanced attention to state competitors, expanded the number of exemptions as well. State institutions were construed broadly to include "all organized departments of the state to which the legislature has delegated the exercise of state functions."

This effectively unleashed citizens groups and organized interests to advance initiatives for their own narrow purposes. Insurance reform, for example, was placed on the 1992 general election ballot by Michigan Blue Cross and Blue Shield. However, because state law requires a broad representation of petitionary voters from throughout the state, few of Michigan's regional battles are fought out here. Initiatives often reward regions more or less inequitably rather than leading to the resolution of regional conflicts. Auto rates and their impact on Detroit ratepayers, for example, were a factor in defeating insurance reform, but not the only one.

The 1908 constitution contained less detail on the power of recall. All elective officers, except judges of courts of record, were subject to recall.[49] Signatures amounting to 25 percent of the votes cast for governor in the last election, and the same percentage within each electoral district, were required to trigger recall. The legislature was to provide other procedures for its exercise.

PROFESSIONALISM FINDS ITS PLACE: A CLOSING THOUGHT

When the new constitutional convention was called in 1961–62, the 1908 document had been amended seventy times. Not many of these amendments were truly important to the framework and structure of state politics. Amendments addressed issues ranging from veterans' bonuses for service in World War II and the Korean conflict to the operation of public utilities by cities and villages. These and most others were statutory in nature and need not have been enshrined in the constitution.

But there was one important exception, an amendment that provides a balance to direct democracy. Given Michigan's emphasis on amateur politics, it is one of the most significant milestones toward political balance in the constitution. Added in 1940, an amendment established a nonpartisan Civil Service Commission and required a competitive civil service system. It directed that state employee performance be judged "exclusively on the basis of merit, efficiency, and fitness of the qualifications of all candidates." The state civil service reflected Michigan's moralistic abhorrence of the potential for partisan politics to bring about corruption. The civil service section was very progressive for its time, prohibiting any removal from or demotion in the civil service on the basis of "partisan, racial, or religious considerations."

This reform, as a reaction to party bosses, was the forerunner of an emerging but still-to-be-defined professionalism in Michigan government. Although it contrasts greatly with the citizen emphasis of legislative and constitutional initiatives, referenda, and recall, professionalism continued on course in modern Michigan politics from 1940 to the present. Thus, the real legacy of Michigan's constitutions is more than the creation of a diverse and explicit social contract. Also evolving was a specifically stated balance between citizens as amateur watchdogs and government officials as authoritative experts.[50]

CHAPTER FOUR

The Politics of Gubernatorial Leadership

Bernard Klein and Joseph Cepuran also contributed to this chapter

THE GOVERNOR AS CAPTAIN: A TOUGH COURSE WITH AN UNCERTAIN HEADING

The story of Michigan's modern-day governors is one of competition for leadership with boards, commissions, elected executives, other party leaders, and state legislators. The term *governor* originates from the ancient Greek word for steersman, giving rise to the Latin *gubernare*. The job of the governor, then, is to steer the ship of state. Like captains of ships, governors have limited resources to power their way through the waves of public opinion and policymaking. Michigan governors are buffeted by a variety of forces no less perplexing than the wind, current, and sudden storms that plague the surrounding Great Lakes. Things are only somewhat less tempestuous than they were for Michigan's first territorial governor, General William Hull. He found himself sentenced to death, which was later reprieved, for surrendering Detroit to the French in 1812.

Unlike ships enroute, for which the captain usually knows the compass heading and the final port, ships of state are on a continuing journey. Citizens and other public officials certainly expect the governor to chart the course for a time. But both amateurs and professionals reserve the right to intervene when they disagree or question a specific proposal. Indeed, because of the historic strength of both amateurs and professionals, they often attack the governor for being "too tied to Lansing power brokers" or, conversely, "pandering to the public's worst instincts." More often, Michigan's complex governing structure imposes such severe limitations on the governor that plotting a too well planned course for the state seems futile. Because of economic busts and intense political competition, Michigan politics frequently withholds the financial resources needed to achieve those goals. Michigan's governors have had to draw imaginatively on a variety of formal and informal powers to provide leadership and give direction to the state.

Michigan's modern governors have gradually accumulated many of the structural tools essential to leadership; hence, unsuccessful chief executives cannot blame the nature of the Michigan office. The 1963 constitution gives the state's executive power to the governor.[1] It also specifies a four-year term, giving the governor time to build a record of accomplishment, or failure, before having to stand for reelection. Michigan's governors propose the state's annual budgets and can veto bills or individual items of expenditure in the budget passed by the legislature. They have broad power to reorganize agencies of the executive branch and to appoint officials to head many of the state's nineteen executive departments.[2] The constitutional powers of the office, in fact, are sufficient to classify Michigan's governor as relatively strong when compared to other governors.[3]

Measures of relative strength, however, lack meaning unless comparisons are made between actual contestants, not just someone who holds a similar position in another state. In Michigan, the contestants are those who shape the demands that confront the executive and who share the executive's powers. The formal and informal powers of governors are never absolute. The Michigan Constitution, like others, includes a variety of means for checking gubernatorial powers. The framers of the Michigan Constitution, for example, provided for an important degree of independence for several other executive officials. Although party conventions nominate candidates, and voters choose the secretary of state and attorney general, the recent experience is that incumbency is tantamount to lifetime appointment for those willing to serve. Richard Austin (elected in 1971) and his predecessor, James M. Hare (1955–71), held the secretary of state position for nearly forty years with little more than token opposition from Republicans. Branch secretary of state offices, the last bastions of patronage in Michigan, may have accounted for Hare's extended tenure, but under Austin, branch offices were staffed with civil service appointees. Similarly, Frank J. Kelley, who first gained the office in 1962, was the longest serving attorney general of any state by 1993. In some states, the offices of attorney general and secretary of state have functioned as steppingstone positions. This has not been the case in Michigan. No recent occupants of these offices have been able to translate their advantages into victories for gubernatorial or U.S. Senate offices. What these positions have become, however, are offices valued in their own right as sources of power and statewide opinion leadership, especially in being able to critique or embarrass the governor.

The elected members of the state board of education and the governing boards of Michigan's three largest universities, along with the executive departments that have appointed governing boards – agriculture, transportation, natural resources, and corrections – sometimes limit the governor's power by their independent actions. In addition, an independent, constitutionally funded Civil Service Commission establishes the wages and most of the employment conditions for the state's 65,000 employees. Governors appoint the members of these boards and commissions, but it usually takes a few years to appoint a majority of loyalists to a particular board. Occasionally even loyalists may disagree with the governor who appointed them. Governor John Engler appointed a majority of natural resource commissioners who, at their first meeting, ignored his request for a national search for a department director.

Michigan governors most often find their powers being checked by state legislators. Some of this comes about because the legislature possesses formal lawmaking and oversight powers. Legislators are also relatively well staffed and very informed. Appointments to boards and commissions also are subject to the advice and consent of the senate. Although veto overrides are extremely rare, gubernatorial vetoes can be overcome by a two-thirds vote of both houses. Executive reorganization orders and executive budget reductions, as well as proposed administrative rules, require the concurrence of both houses, a condition that opens these areas to negotiation and compromise.

Conditions beyond the structure of government impose equally significant constraints on gubernatorial powers. Michigan voters, for example, often split tickets and provide for divided government. Either the governor is of a different party than the majority of the legislative houses, or the two legislative bodies have different party majorities. The last time one party controlled the executive office and both houses of the legislature was when Governor James Blanchard came to power in 1983. The advantage failed to last the year, however. Following adoption of an increase in the personal income tax, two Democratic senators were recalled and replaced by Republicans. This set the stage for Engler's ascendancy as senate majority leader and, later, his successful campaign for governor.

Citizens have very real formal powers to check those of the governor, especially the power to recall the governor as well as all elected officials except judges. Although no Michigan governor has been recalled, the recall power remains an imposing threat. An unsuccessful recall drive against Governor Blanchard for his leadership in the 1983 tax increase served to remind him and other officials that another boost in tax rates might renew the recall drive. Only four months into his governorship, two groups scheduled hearings to get petitions approved to recall Engler, presumably because of his welfare cuts. The ensuing months of public scrutiny that accompanied signature gathering did much to convince the administration to take a more balanced approach to budget cutting. However, Michigan voters more frequently use their powers of direct democracy not to recall governors or legislators but to move certain public issues to resolution when elected leaders fail to satisfy sufficient public demands. State taxing policies have been common targets for such citizen actions, as have abortion policies.

In this chapter, we examine further how Michigan governors in the modern era have sought to lead the state. The focus is on the six governors who have occupied the office since 1948 (see table 5).

LEADERSHIP IN PUBLIC OPINION

Personally and directly, governors can do little. A governor, for example, uses the work of many people for several months to prepare the annual budget for presentation to the legislature each February. Governors cannot pass laws or run a department. Despite what some of their supporters claim, they cannot create jobs, at least not enough jobs to turn the economy around from a recession. Moreover, they can intervene in the governmental processes only occasionally to emphasize what they think needs to be done. To do otherwise consumes, and may waste, limited political capital and goodwill.

Administration Themes

The key element in each of the six modern governors' careers has been the ability or inability to set a theme. Incumbents usually set their themes by appealing to a public that sees the governor as the personification of state government. Each modern governor has defined the state's needs as he perceived them, charted key goals for his administration, and used his office as a "bully pulpit" for advancing those goals. When successfully articulated, gubernatorial goals have brought a clear and ringing focus to the governor's efforts. Gubernatorial goals have generally reflected the social and economic times in which they were created more than the ideological premises of the person or the balancing of the state's political problems. While the lat-

Table 5: Modern Michigan Governors

Name	Term	Political Affiliation
G. Mennen "Soapy" Williams	1949–60	Democrat
John B. Swainson	1961–62	Democrat
George W. Romney	1963–69	Republican
William G. Milliken	1969–82	Republican
James J. Blanchard	1983–90	Democrat
John M. Engler	1991–present	Republican

ter are important, they are usually added to a message of current statewide urgency. Despite the efforts of recent governors to distinguish themselves and their parties from one another on a wide variety of issues, pandering to a narrow band of regional issues would cost them the attention of too many Michiganians. The governor would become just another Michigan politician, not a respected leader.

Governor G. Mennen "Soapy" Williams, for example, let it be known that his administration, at the end of President Dwight D. Eisenhower's years in the White House, would treat Michigan as a social laboratory for enhancing the lives of its less fortunate citizens. If need be, this was to be done at the expense of the well-off. Williams, who became a liberal icon of Michigan politics, is still remembered for his emphasis on state care for the mentally ill and his focus on civil rights.[4] George Romney, as a proponent of business practices in government, sought to modernize state government and reconcile state interests after a decade of rancorous combat between an old-guard, rural-dominated legislature and two strong-minded governors, Williams and then John B. Swainson. Republican William Milliken, to further the healing process, advocated a broadly active state government administered by a nonpartisan, professional bureaucracy. Democrat Blanchard sought to rebuild the economic prowess of the state after the serious economic recession of the early 1980s. John Engler promised a smaller, tight-fisted government at a time when budgets of the state and nation were in serious deficit.

The Importance of Reaching Out

Because the governor is the state's main political figure, he has no trouble getting media attention. Modern governors have commanded a great deal of press ink and electronic airtime, so much so that many citizens incorrectly see these executives as being in absolute control of all of state government.

With improvements in technology, major television stations in the state have found it much easier to cover state politics. This has expanded even further the ability of media-conscious governors to reach out to the public.

The single most important event for the governor today is the annual State of the State speech, a leadership opportunity required by the constitution.[5] James Blanchard, more than any of his predecessors, used this as a platform to address the people of Michigan and to lay out his agenda. What made his use of this event more notable was its presentation during prime-time evening hours through a public television network that telecast the speech statewide. With the help of media advisers, Blanchard adroitly planted in the audience citizens who had benefited from new state programs, such as job training, business loans, or college assistance. While cameras panned the audience, he called the public's attention to individuals who were personal testimony to the benefits of his administration's efforts. In contrast, Williams and Romney typically – and strategically – delivered their State of the State speeches to a legislative session in the late morning. Although some radio stations would pick up a feed, the main coverage was by reporters who were able to complete their reports in time for what were then predominantly evening newspapers.

Governors use other means of communicating too. Blanchard and Milliken, governing in the age of television, mastered the staging of media events. Each instigated events with good visual displays for evening television news programs. They created opportunities to push a favored project or to be identified with a particular cause. The modern governors also use press conferences to build public support for their programs and to comment on legislative issues or problems in the administration. For a time, Romney used the technique of meeting an hour each week with ordinary citizens. The press then reported on what Romney said he learned from these grass-roots sources. Engler expanded Romney's technique by also requiring his department heads to schedule weekly meetings with citizens. At the first scheduled meetings, television cameras covered Engler wearing a blue cardigan sweater as he greeted his first citizen visitor outside his office.

Governors regularly are invited to address interest-group conventions in Lansing and around the state. No governor accepts all invitations. Rather, they pick and choose in terms of the opportunities important to them as well as, of course, their schedules. Groups turned down by the governor's office are usually offered a member of the governor's staff so that some degree of personal communication can take place. However, interest groups increasingly want the governor, not substitutes, since they consider it a matter of price and prestige to have the governor address them. A visit by a second stringer may make the group look like it plays second fiddle to other interests. Thus, visits are powerful political weapons for governors. That importance led Engler to race frantically to meetings in each Michigan county during his first year in office.

How governors present themselves to the public, as Engler's cardigan suggests, is also an important part of their message. Williams and Romney employed quite different approaches. Noted for his green-and-white polkadot bow tie, Williams "appeared at countless community festivals, crowned queens, made speeches, called square dances, shook hands with millions, and developed a personal popularity rarely matched in political annals."[6] Romney, the former take-charge president of American Motors Corporation (AMC), gave less time to social gatherings than Williams and conveyed the image of being both frugal and hardworking. He often caught up on sleep on the fold-down seat of his AMC Rambler while his state police chauffeur drove him from place to place. Romney was also famous for his hurry-up golf game: hitting three balls for six holes and tallying his score as if he had played eighteen holes. Better to get back on the job, or so state reporters raved.

Recent governors have considered public opinion vitally important to their success as leaders. But have these chief executives simply been dealing with the public as though they were involved in nonstop campaigning for the next election? For Williams, this may have been partially the case. He was governor for twelve years, but he had two-year terms. Moreover, his early victories were very narrow. He carried his first reelection by just 1,154 votes out of two million cast. Also, as a liberal in a pre-liberal era, he faced a contentious and very conservative legislature for his entire tenure. Romney, in contrast, won his election over Governor Swainson with a plurality of about 100,000 votes. Romney was a devout Mormon, however, and his no-nonsense persona was not merely a creation for public consumption. It was in large part, as perhaps is the case with many public figures, who he was and whom he thought state government should emulate.

There are dangers in such actions, of course. Although Romney increased his use of the media when he developed presidential ambitions in the late 1960s, journalists proved to be his downfall as well. During the New Hampshire presidential primary campaign, Romney said that he had been "brainwashed" by the military about the Vietnam War. The comment sidetracked his campaign, dominated press coverage for a time, and finally caused him to be seen as odd and naive rather than coldly efficient. He never recovered his momentum.

But there is more to a governor's image than future election opportunities. Some gubernatorial actions are intended to heal differences or at least disguise partisan divisions generated from the past campaign.[7] Persistent divisions hinder governing. Continuing partisan conflicts are nearly inevitable in Michigan. Only Milliken successfully put them aside by being nonpartisan himself. Nonetheless, conflict between the governor and the legislature, especially when it produces deadlock, usually proves be an embittering experience for this state's population. At such times, it becomes essential for a Michigan governor to continue in conversation with citizens about the relevancy of his or her proposed solutions to the state's problems, even if the other party refuses to move. Engler, while embroiled in legislative politics and the budget in his first year, learned that need firsthand. One year after his election, Michigan pundits were nearly unanimous in charging that the electorate saw the budget-slashing governor as neglectful of the state's traditions of fair treatment for all. This gave Democratic legislators ammunition to use in capturing media attention for their attacks, and eventually in pushing the governor to spread budget cuts over other programs.

Blanchard had suffered a similar fate, even if it took longer for his image to haunt him. The importance of influencing and staying abreast of public opinion was never so apparent as when Blanchard, as a new governor, persuaded the legislature to adopt a temporary increase in the state's personal income tax. During the election campaign, he had promised to ask for a tax increase only "as a last resort." By December 1982, however, before Blanchard even took office, the transition team was releasing data about the size of the state's deficit. The governor-elect, noting the problem to be more severe than he saw it as a candidate, pushed for a tax hike. The legislature's approval of a 38 percent increase in the personal income tax in March 1983 set off an unexpected recall fury in some parts of the state. Two Democratic senators, Philip Mastin of Oakland County and David Serotkin of Macomb County, fell victim to recalls by overwhelming margins. Blanchard also became a target but was saved from a recall election only because the petitions did not meet technical legal requirements. Although a tax increase may have been courageous and the only remedy to the fiscal crisis, it was also a miscalculation. With more nurturing of the citizenry and with greater effort to muffle the open controversy with Republican legislators, the tax hike might not have generated such an intense public reaction.[8]

Milliken's reaction in the 1978 election to the proposed Headlee amendment provides an example of a governor's more successful public relations effort. This was a time of tax revolts nationally. Michiganians had rejected a tax-cutting proposal referred to as Headlee I two years earlier. Milliken, in acting with customary Michigan balance, endorsed the 1978 Headlee proposal, even though its purpose was to restrict the state's taxing and spending powers when the budget was already experiencing stress. However, Headlee II was less damaging than another proposal on the ballot, a harsher amendment backed by Robert Tisch and his supporters. The Headlee amendment passed; the Tisch proposal failed. Milliken's sensitivity to the tax revolt and his reluctant acceptance of the Headlee proposal undoubtedly was instrumental in heading off the more radical approach.

Michigan governors, therefore, try to position their particular image to look like leaders of all the people rather than politicians seeking reelection. The lesson has been that, in a state where proposals are always modified in order to find balance, public opinion is a fuel important to powering gubernatorial clout in policymaking.[9]

Given the importance of public opinion for any governorship, press secretaries and, more recently, communications directors have ranked alongside, or perhaps just below, the chiefs of staff. Williams, in a pre-television era, wrote, "My press secretary was my eyes and ears as well as my voice. He was also no small part of my brain . . . he developed my ideas as I would have liked to do if I had the time."[10] No doubt other modern governors have felt similarly about the people who managed their relations with the press and the public.

George Weeks, Milliken's press secretary and now a columnist for the *Detroit News,* gave insights on the importance of the job. He commented admiringly on Blanchard's management of the stories about his 1989 State of the State speech. For example, a proposal to improve air service in northern parts of the state was released early to the *Traverse City Record-Eagle.* Weeks noted that for a time Milliken had tried to keep his speeches confidential until their presentation. Despite every effort, the governor found secrecy to be virtually impossible because so many staff and agency personnel were involved in putting each speech together. In response to the inevitable, the administration decided to let the various stories filter out, as they would anyway, and then use the leaks to their strategic advantage. Weeks, in explaining how to be popular with the media and get good press in particular communities, acknowledged his own role as a "leakmeister of sorts."[11]

Not all press secretaries have gained such favor. Governor Engler's press secretary, John Truscott, took numerous blows from the media for his perceived lack of empathy for those being hit by cuts in state funding. Several reporters took up the complaint that Truscott's attitude showed the administration to be meanspirited. Of course, the press secretary's image was portrayed as an extension of the media's image of Engler's "heartlessness." By November 1991, only one year after his election and despite 60 percent public approval of his welfare cuts, the governor enjoyed only 39 percent overall approval ratings in a statewide poll.[12]

LEADERSHIP IN THE LEGISLATURE

Despite the immense importance of images for creating leadership advantages, dealing directly with the legislature matters most in determining whether the governor's proposals pass muster. Success and failure depend on personal involvement and negotiation, not popularity alone. Governors have a number of tools to influence actions of the state legislature, especially in seizing the initiative on policy ideas. The power to recommend through the executive budget process, make appointments, and propose programs that will be reported widely is especially important.[13] Supported by favorable public opinion, the power to recommend enables the governor to influence both the legislative and public agendas. For example, one plank of Engler's 1990 campaign for governor was a major tax cut. His later recommendations for dealing with the state's fiscal crisis, therefore, could not include an income or business tax increase, even a temporary one. This was a preemptive strategy. Neither did his outnumbered Democratic opponents in the house of representatives propose a tax increase. Debate raged instead over which programs should be eliminated. Even when the governor proposed increased user fees for some services, a subject that Democrats would not touch, many claimed the tax promise broken: "a fee is a tax."

In addition to public support and policy initiation, the governor has the powers of veto and item veto. These are major weapons even though Michigan governors use them sparingly. The governor also has numerous opportunities, as the state's most visible politician, to extend or withhold favors to legislators. These range from kind words on a legislator's bill or a campaign appearance in the legislator's district to making personal announcements of grants to city and county officials. Blanchard used the latter tactic in numerous districts on a highly publicized boat and helicopter tour of Lake Michigan's western shoreline.

Still, despite such overtures and powers, recent governors have not dominated the legislature. Except for Romney's years in office, Michiganians have perpetuated the politics of balance by electing divided governments. Much of the time, the opposing party controls one or both houses of the legislature. Moreover, since Romney, professionalization and resulting independence have increased in the legislature. The house and senate both operate full-time, officially staying in session throughout the year. This means that Michigan's governors, unlike those in many other states, rarely can exercise the power to call special sessions for action on measures that they have prepared in the legislature's absence. The legislature fights hard to make its own decisions. It also maintains its independence from undue gubernatorial influence by keeping personal staff, committee employees, press offices, and leadership staff on top of issues. To the disadvantage of governors and administrators, legislators are available in Lansing much of the time to oversee departmental programs, question administrators, develop their own initiatives, and even compete for media coverage. Governors, then, are far from the sole source of new policy ideas, even if they get most of the public credit and blame.

Shared Influence

This is not to suggest that governors have been ineffective, just that they have little option but to share power. Michigan's governors do not get all they want from the legislature, nor do they expect it. Rather, governors posture a great deal; then they negotiate and accept compromises on most major issues, only occasionally using a power play that rolls over legislative resolve.

But governors are not ineffective just because legislators pass numerous policies on their own initiative. Governors, by and large, are most effective at agenda setting on the most contentious issues, seldom having the time to intervene where consensus already exists or can easily be reached. In programmatic areas, such as mental health, public education, urban affairs, and tax policies, governors have both led and followed public opinion. G. Mennen Williams, for example, sustained interest in building the Mackinac bridge between upper and lower Michigan when many state observers thought it could never be done. John Swainson, over much public protest, persuaded the legislature to pass a law that gave cities the authority to tax all personal incomes earned in the city. William Milliken shaped state policies to provide financial assistance to Detroit and other major cities. Without gubernatorial leadership, these policies for an unpopular central city would not have been adopted at that time. John Engler's persistence finally led to a massive property tax act in 1994.

Leading over the Long Haul

Gubernatorial support for a personal priority does not guarantee its resolution. As Williams learned, these priorities sometimes produce an extended deadlock.

During the Williams era, the Michigan legislature, like most around the country, was apportioned in favor of rural regions. A 1952 constitutional amendment favored by Williams was an attempt to apportion the districts more fairly as a first step in dealing with neglected issues. The plan called for reapportionment based on population, but allowed district lines still to be based on county boundaries. County boards of supervisors, themselves malapportioned, were to divide a county into several legislative districts whenever one was entitled to more than a single representative. County boards thwarted the governor by structuring legislative district plans dominated by rural regions, small towns, and the big manufacturing interests that dominated many larger Michigan communities. Williams, responding to state labor unions and intellectual followers of New Deal programs, could not get support for his other programs when conservative legislators elected from these locales poured into Lansing. By the end of the decade, Democrats had captured nearly all of the statewide elected posts, and Williams had appointed Democrats to judicial seats and executive boards and commissions. But he could win few policy reforms. Republican legislators prevented Williams from following through on his platform to make Michigan his testing ground for "social democracy."[14]

The ongoing battle came to a head in 1959 when Williams sought an income-based corporate profits tax to finance a proposed record budget for his social programs. Republicans countered with a proposed increase in the sales tax. The governor and the legislature deadlocked over which increase would prevail. As his final tactic, Williams resorted to a last-ditch power play and argued that the state general fund lacked the money necessary to meet the state payroll. Two payless paydays for state employees, and endlessly unfavorable publicity for the governor, came and went before the crisis was resolved. Eventually the legislature approved the temporary use of money in restricted accounts. Later, however, the voters rejected Williams by approving a sales tax increase rather than his proposed corporate tax.

Williams himself understood the root of his problem: "Once you get too far ahead of the people you become ineffective and your legislative and administrative programs then tend to lag."[15] After this loss, he chose not to run for another term. In 1961, he joined President John F. Kennedy's administration as the assistant secretary of state for African affairs. Later he returned to Michigan with his reputation still in disarray. Williams was defeated in a race for the U.S. Senate and, after years as an elder statesman, ended his political career by serving as a Michigan supreme court justice.

This tax controversy, however, set the stage for the campaign for a new constitution, one intended to be better suited for reconciling state differences. Leadership for reform was undertaken by the Citizens for Michigan committee, with George Romney as its chief spokesperson.[16] One of the items at the constitutional convention was allowance of a flat-rate income tax that would in part tax corporate profits; it was urged by none other than Romney. Only five years later, in order to advance his own platform for expanding state government, Romney recommended and battled for adoption of the state's first use of this hard-won but not yet implemented tax. However, in adding to the controversy, Romney's budget needed $1.4 billion, three times the amount proposed by Williams in 1959.[17] Moreover, despite more favorable apportionment, many of the same conservative Republicans who had resisted Williams were still serving in the senate. They were no more enamored with Republican Romney's income tax proposal than they had been with that of Democrat Williams.

Early on, however, Romney had formed a coalition of moderate Republican and Democratic senators. They served him well. Still, on the Monday night in 1964 when the senate was to take up the tax issue, efforts appeared lost. Time ran out because, by law, sessions end at midnight. Majority Leader Frank Beadle, a moderate Republican and Romney supporter, moved for the senate to reconvene at 12:01 A.M. Tuesday following the Monday evening adjournment. The furious Senator Lynn Francis from Midland, realizing what was afoot, invited all "real Republicans" to recess to an anteroom to select a new leader. Although ten Republicans joined him, the effort failed as moderate Republicans and the Democrats voted to sustain Beadle's leadership. The shaky coalition held together through the night until it passed the state income tax. Even to the end, Williams visited the senate chambers frequently to encourage those who were pushing one of the state's longest sought gubernatorial initiatives.

Milliken exercised similar but less extended leadership when, in April 1982, he invested his personal reputation and political debts to push through a temporary tax increase to offset plummeting revenues. Democrats controlled the house and the senate and were willing, in a crisis, to do the unthinkable: adopt a tax increase in an election year. However, they insisted on a strong vote across party lines so that neither Democrats nor Republicans could be blamed. Milliken called Republican legislators into his office one by one to urge them "to give a yes vote. If you do, you won't regret it. If you don't, we will all regret it." A call to Democratic Mayor Coleman Young in Detroit resulted in a promise to help bring African-American legislators into line. Milliken later interrupted a meeting to help House Speaker Bobby Crim keep legislators from leaving the floor. To persuade Midland Republican Representative Michael Hayes to change his vote, Milliken called a top executive at Dow Chemical Company to secure a promise of no retaliation against Hayes if he voted for the tax. During an all-night session, Milliken gave new meaning to "personal leadership" as he went to nearby hotels to rouse legislators who had gone off to bed hoping to avoid voting on the tax.[18]

Dependence on Executive Leadership

Blanchard fostered another bipartisan agreement when he successfully pressed the legislature to adopt and change programs related to economic development. He was unable, however, to take the same initiative on other issues, often because support across state regions was lacking. Blanchard attempted to reform public financing of k–12 education, an issue that had plagued the state since the early 1970s. However, to the chagrin of friendly legislators, Blanchard offered, but did not fight for, his proposal for solving this complex reallocation problem during the waning weeks of the 1988 legislative session. When the new legislature took up the matter in early 1989, Blanchard still seemed content to let legislators struggle on their own to bring a proposal for a two-cent sales tax increase to the voters for constitutional amendment. He argued through the media that his recommendations for improvements in the quality of education needed to be enacted before asking citizens to approve a tax increase. Finally, Blanchard and legislative leaders called for Edgar Harden, the former president of Northern Michigan and Michigan State Universities, to mediate the development of a proposal among key legislators, lobbyists, and administration staff. Again, the effort came to nought as the governor abdicated his expected responsibility.

Blanchard's actions were strategic, in a personal rather than policy sense. He knew that there were limits as to how much gubernatorial intervention would be tolerated, especially on an issue that created real financial losers. He was content to let a broad-based coalition generate a compromise plan on which citizens could vote. If voters approved a tax increase, the governor would not be blamed. If they defeated it, legislators would be back asking for stronger gubernatorial leadership in the future. Although this appeared to be a win-win formula for the governor, it did nothing to resolve the issue. Legislators from both parties accused Blanchard of purposeful neglect of education funding.

Opinions vary as to whether the issue would have been resolved even with Blanchard's leadership. Nonetheless, citing lack of necessary leadership, many Democratic legislators attributed Blanchard's 1990 defeat, at least in part, to his failure to meet constituent expectations about the governor's role in Michigan. In addition, because no action was taken to adjust the state's tax share, the resulting need to finance a greater percentage of K–12 education through local property taxes set him up for Engler's popular campaign promise to support both education funding and a 20 percent property tax cut as his top priorities. By 1993, he was combining these issues with the sales tax increase in a gubernatorially led special election. Even if he did not like the total percentages in some provisions, Engler was not going to be accused of weak leadership.

On the state's most contentious issues, governors need to be out front working because legislators will not do it themselves, and these members can make or break a chief executive's career by their inaction. While legislators usually are not greatly concerned about protecting the prerogatives of the governorship, they do understand that they will sometimes need the governor's personal attention, as in the school finance issue. As such, they do worry about the governor because they worry about the legislature.

That concern for the governor is a function of the diverse expectations about how government should work: the people often elect a governor on the promise that things will change. Accordingly, the public has held the governor accountable for making changes that he could not carry out alone. Legislators, in contrast, are chosen for parochial reasons peculiar to the districts and regions of which they are a part. In their eyes, each legislator must deliver for his or her district because regional constituencies are quite different from one another. Legislators tend to be held less accountable for actions of the legislature as a whole.

Veto Politics

Continuing statewide leadership, not just shared power on an issue, is what matters most for the governor when it comes to legislative affairs. The governor's role as leader can be seen in what the executive does with bills that pass the legislature. Governors have the veto, or the threat of it, as a device for shaping legislation. Yet they use it sparingly, making proactive leadership to initiate legislation especially vital.

In some states, the veto is a used frequently. For example, in 1988, the governor of Maryland used the veto 217 times; in California it was used 417 times; in Illinois, 313; in New York, 91; and in Washington, 121.[19] Governors Blanchard, Milliken, and Williams averaged fewer than 10 vetoes a year, while Romney and Swainson vetoed a little more than 10 times a year. Swainson, averaging 13 vetoes a year for his term, probably saw the veto as necessary to protect his policies from an aggressive legislature. His veto of the Bouman bill, which would have curtailed Detroit's authority to assess a personal income tax on nonresident workers, and of a milk bill, which would have increased the retail price of milk, were considered politically significant items of legislation. Both vetoes, however, made him many enemies and contributed to his status as a one-term governor.

For every state rule of thumb, though, significant deviations are possible. When, as a new governor, Engler faced the need for budget cutbacks in 1991, agreement with the legislature was deadlocked. After weeks of haggling, no solution was evident. Engler presented one plan. The Democratically controlled house proposed and passed another. The Republican senate, working with the governor for strategic advantage, then surprisingly passed the house version. With such a rare opportunity to resolve deadlock, Engler took the unusual action of signing the budget but vetoing many of its items to gain his desired cuts. He did the same the next year in order to balance a budget that Democrats found best to leave unfinished before sending on. Such use of the veto, however, created the same hostile reactions that helped to topple Swainson three decades earlier. Democrats, playing to the press after the initial surprise, helped spread the impression of insensitivity. House Democrats maintained that their 1992 bill was but a vehicle for negotiating a compromise, not a device for the governor to use in making unilateral decisions. Making decisions without further consultation, they claimed, violated rules of fair play and balanced policies as understood in Michigan politics.

The governor's choice, however, was a sound one strategically. Engler knew that veto overrides are less likely to occur in Michigan than in many other states, especially those where vetoes are common. For modern governors, a single override of a Milliken veto is the only instance of the legislature's exercise of this power.

The unique nature of that lone override, however, reveals even more about Michigan government's concern for a proper balance between the executive and legislature. The action against Milliken occurred on a bill that became a key interbranch disagreement over redefining the executive-legislative balance and procedures for establishing administrative rules. Previously, the legislature was allowed sixty days in which to overturn regulations proposed by an executive department. Doing so was difficult because majorities had to be won in both houses. If the legislature did not act during that period, the rules took effect. In 1976, to make rejection easier, the legislature amended the law so as to require a joint house-senate committee to *approve* proposed rules before they could take effect. The new procedure was one more way for the legislature, with its growing concern for asserting its professionalism, to exercise its powers over the executive branch. Democrats and Republicans joined to override Milliken's effort to preserve the old balance and this longstanding tool of executive leverage over the legislature. The override angered the laconic Milliken, who made statewide news by venting his frustrations in public.[20]

In other instances, using the veto can satisfy forces on both sides of an issue. It happens infrequently, but on the question of using public funds to pay for abortions for welfare mothers, both sides won for a number of years. Milliken and later Blanchard repeatedly used the item veto to cut from budgets of the Department of Social Services legislative initiatives to prohibit the use of funds for abortions. The legislature was not able to obtain the necessary two-thirds vote in each house to override the vetoes, in large part because of intervention from pro-choice voters. The predictable item vetoes and failures to override them permitted many legislators to appease either pro-choice or right-to-life constituents by voting for or against the question with the confidence that nothing would change. Finally, in 1987, the game came to an end. Right-to-life groups used the legislative initiative and presented the prohibition to the legislature, which promptly enacted the bill, an action not subject to veto.[21] Pro-choice forces then countered with their own petition to refer the issue to a voter referendum. Voters upheld the prohibition, however.

LEADERSHIP IN THE EXECUTIVE BRANCH

Governors in Michigan are not so directly involved in working things through with bureaucrats as they are with legislators. Distance has been almost a rule of thumb since the introduction of civil service, often to the chief executive's chagrin. Recent governors have been frustrated by bureaucratic opposition to new regulatory priorities, overly stringent enforcement of policies not favored by the executive, and career officials stirring up public opposition to certain gubernatorial proposals.

As explained, the 1963 constitution modernized the executive branch and gave the governor greater authority to provide administrative leadership.

The new organizational structure reduced the number of independent boards and commissions, cut back the number of directly elected department heads, and limited the number of principal departments to no more than twenty. In addition, it extended the governor's term from two years to four. As such, the new constitution set precedents nationwide as twenty-two other states reorganized after watching Michigan set a path for change.[22] That set of changes also ordered the governor and lieutenant governor to be placed on the same ballot, eliminating the possibility of having a governor of one party and the lieutenant governor of another, as was the case during Williams's early terms and Romney's first term.

These reforms addressed political division in an administration but could not altogether solve basic differences. They were prompted in part by political jabbing by Democratic Lieutenant Governor T. John Lesinski at Governor Romney. To the entertainment of reporters and political observers, Acting Governor Lesinski would often call a news conference to report on the "successful" conduct of state business while Romney was away from Michigan. Although such overt partisanship contributed to constitutional reform, reform did not bring an end to strife between the governor and lieutenant governor. Lieutenant governors often chafed under their leader's need for monopolizing media attention. Blanchard certainly discovered that in 1990. Martha Griffiths, who along with Blanchard had been a member of Congress, served two terms as his lieutenant governor. With a pending election and tough opponent, Blanchard decided that because of her age, seventy-eight, and growing frailty, she should not be on the ticket for a third term. Griffiths, however, had already announced her willingness to run again if the governor wanted her. Her bitter public response to Blanchard, "You help some son-of-a-bitch get what he wants and then he dumps you," was enough for some women and senior citizens to withhold their votes or cast them for Engler. In a 1994 press interview, Griffiths revealed that she, too, voted against Blanchard in 1990.

That example apart, the 1963 reforms improved if not solidified relationships within the executive branch. Three constitutional changes represented a rejection of many of the structural reforms of Jacksonian democracy. These had created weak governorships through short terms of office, election of many administrative officers, and election of numerous independent boards and commissions. The new constitution created more executive order in the everyday politics of planning and regulation. It did the same in terms of crises. Instead of creating political gains from being commander-in-chief of the state National Guard (as do some governors), Michigan governors have let their professionals handle natural disasters and, for the most part, even such human crises as the Detroit riots.

The Michigan governorship now is as fundamentally strong with respect to hierarchical control over the executive branch as are those of nearly all other states. Because of stout defenders, however, the constitution continued the offices of attorney general and secretary of state as statewide elective positions and retained many appointed commissions to head several executive departments. These independent offices limit executive control in ways not found in states with the strongest governorships. Hence, Michigan's governor must bargain directly on many executive branch decisions, especially when agencies are controlled by members of the opposite party. For example, in the place of an elected superintendent of education, the new constitution established an elected but part-time Board of Education to set administrative policy for the state's Department of Education. Typically, the governor plays a part only as an *ex officio* member of this board, one that only periodically meets in short sessions. Governor Engler, however, leaned on his partisan allies on the board to dismiss a Blanchard-appointed superintendent and appoint someone more to his liking.

The present organizational arrangement affords Michigan's governors a substantial number of appointments not only to the commissions mentioned above but also to some 260 advisory boards, such as those governing numerous professions. Physicians, dentists, cosmetologists and barbers, urban planners, registered surveyors, and all but three of the state universities gain gubernatorial attention through such boards. Altogether, the number of appointments reached the slightly awesome number of 2,700.[23] These numbers both trivialize and overwhelm gubernatorial involvement, a point Engler emphasized in seeking to downsize. Only some can claim any real attention from the governor, let alone personal intervention, depending on his priorities.

The governor's most important appointments are directors of executive departments, where much of the groundwork is done for legislative proposals and for regulatory change. While many of the other appointments symbolically reward friends, they are more a burden to the governor than a political advantage. Outside the key staff positions in the executive office, the most important appointment is the director of the Department of Management and Budget (DMB), which has the key responsibility of forming the executive budget and administering the budget throughout the year. In addition, the DMB head oversees central administrative service functions, such as purchasing, property management, and information management, as well as numerous retirement plans and a variety of minor boards and commissions.

Because of such responsibilities, the DMB director is the key adviser on fiscal plans for the administration. Not only does this appointee coordinate development of annual budgets; he or she also is the key spokesperson for the governor's spending and revenue proposals. This is the one and only position in Michigan's public bureaucracy that ensures insider status with the governor and his close advisers. Unlike the federal government, there are no other standard "inside" and "outside" cabinet positions. The matter of which department heads are close to the governor and which are not usually revolves around the personal relationship between the individual administrator and the governor. Sometimes, as with the Department of Commerce under Blanchard and Engler, the importance of the subject ensures a close tie to the governor. When Blanchard made rebuilding the state economy a keystone of his administration, the commerce department was delegated a large task. Engler, seeking to downsize the department because of a different leadership agenda and its close ties to Blanchard, appointed a longtime ally to head its reorganization.

At other times, such as with Milliken's director of agriculture during the PCB cattlefeed poisoning crisis of the 1970s, an official may suddenly and temporarily be a part of the governor's inner circle. Even though the Department of Agriculture received much of the blame for a problem that contaminated dairy herds with chemically laced feed, Milliken's office eventually had to bring in the director to help with damage control. Such a sudden elevation seldom means that a new insider becomes a trusted confidant of the governor. Later, in the case of agriculture, Milliken's office complained about constitutional problems that made it impossible to quickly appoint a new director in whom the governor could have more confidence. Over time, as happened in this case, gubernatorial inattention often allows department heads to develop closer ties with legislators and industry spokespersons than with the administration. When it came time for Milliken to be involved with the unfamiliar director of agriculture, G. Dale Ball, there existed little common ground or mutual trust.

Sometimes reliance on one or another office changes radically from one administration to the next. Blanchard, for example, used the office of state treasurer differently than any previous governor. A person appointed to be state treasurer typically gets some public notice at the time of appointment and then is not heard from again. Not only did Robert Bowman, state treasurer during the Blanchard administration, become a visible spokesperson for the governor; he was also a source of numerous policy innovations. M ET (Michigan Education Trust), a program to permit residents to deposit funds now to guarantee availability of college tuition later, and H OST (Home Development Savings Trust), which assisted first-time home buyers in accumulating a down payment, are examples of prominent policies shepherded by Bowman.

The appointment process involves more than just selecting the governor's team and deciding who gets what degree of attention and discretion. Governors employ different styles in making their appointments. Part of the difference may be in changing political circumstances, such as new electoral coalitions that must be rewarded and interest groups that are suddenly successful in electoral and legislative politics. Another, and perhaps more important, part involves the availability of professionals willing to work in state government. All recent administrations have had problems finding people, often leaving numerous appointments vacant for several months.

The unavailability of skilled people can sometimes bring the chief executive and his personal staff new assignments. Blanchard and Engler both found themselves quite unexpectedly in foreign policy roles as an interdependent international economy increasingly affected the state. Nothing comparable to the U.S. Department of State exists in Michigan to provide advice or support. Accordingly, both governors organized their own offices and schedules to promote trade, involve state government with foreign investors, and even travel internationally. Engler found himself in a political near-vacuum where no other state officials could speak forcefully on behalf of Michigan's stake, as a whole, in the proposed North American Free Trade Agreement (N A FT A), although Representative David E. Bonior led much of the charge against N A FT A in Congress.

The same is true for interstate and national political relationships. Since Milliken's forceful leadership on the Great Lakes Commission, governors have found their time consumed by political problems that administrators alone are ill-equipped to handle. For example, in one May week, Engler found himself defending state Medicaid payments with Congress and attempting to reverse the Federal Base Closing Commission's recommended closure of Sawyer Air Force Base. At the same time, his personal staff was still resolving a federal conflict over Superfund environmental costs; plus they were reviewing legislation to ensure the state's conformity with 1990 federal Clean Air Act standards. This escalating conflict, caused by a larger federal regulatory posture, has had the past two governors more involved than their predecessors with both the National Governors' Association and the Council of State Governments. To an important extent, these organizations provide intergovernmental services that cannot be provided by state administrators.

In general, Michigan governors now seek to appoint more professionals or acknowledged experts than political loyalists. Engler was especially interested in people with a background in trade and international matters. However, the supply of willing and politically acceptable experts who also are highly competent and proven administrators is short.[24] Finding those willing to be loyal to the governor compounds the difficulty. Fortunately, professionals come in many forms. Engler found his choice for the director of the Department of Agriculture in a former member of Congress who had served on the house agriculture committee. Each state party also is developing a cadre of professional administrators who work in government while their party is in office.[25] When the other party controls the governorship, these administrators may go to work for the legislature, a lobbying firm, or a think tank. Others may find a job in Washington or perhaps another state. When their party regains control, they return for another stint at helping to run Michigan.

This cadre of supporters is of less help than might be imagined. Oftentimes a trusted and capable person cannot be found for a vacant department headship, or an independent commission will not appoint a particular person. Moreover, appointments, even those important to the governor, are not all prominent ones or necessarily influential in making policy. These positions lack potential officeholders. Indeed, selling the appeal of positions is a special problem for new governors. Although governors appoint a large number of people to public office, by far the large majority of these appointments, except for judicial vacancies, are to nonsalaried positions. Even when people are willing to serve, financial problems may prevent them from doing so.

In addition, an overwhelming array of merit constraints limit many appointments. Because of the way one does business in a moralistic state, Michigan governors have few opportunities to appoint people to technical and policy jobs in the administration. Virtually all positions in the executive branch are part of the classified civil service. The office of governor is limited to only eight unclassified, full-time, salaried positions. The ten department heads that the governor appoints directly are permitted to name only two – and with special permission, three – deputies outside the civil service system.[26]

Blanchard, in particular, chafed under appointment restraints, especially commission appointment of directors. He openly pressured boards and commissions to appoint directors of his choosing. In doing so, Blanchard expressed the governor's most accurate political truism coupled with a plea: that the public holds him responsible for what goes wrong in the administration and that, at the very least, he should have some say in hiring and firing the persons who make or break the departments. Blanchard's comment calls attention to the question of whether merit employment or political control best serves the state.

The governor had a point. The civil service system generally provides the governor with a skilled, professional, and honest bureaucracy. However, it also creates a largely immovable force for the status quo that is insulated from political interference, if not altogether from outside pressure. At times, the bureaucracy is more responsive to its own interests than to those of the governor and his appointees. At other times, it is more responsive to lobbyists who represent agency clients or legislators who have their own agendas and budgeting roles. One of the most telling characteristics of the civil service bureaucracy is that not many recommendations for major changes in state programs come from professional bureaucrats. Many Michiganians, in responding to the conflict over executive control, believe the state's strong civil service system, constitutionally funded at a level of one percent of annual state payroll, diminishes a governor's leadership. Although public complaints about the competence, dedication, and professionalism of the public service are few, a more favorable balance is on the public as well the gubernatorial agenda. Given the state's financial pattern, and what appears to be a repeatedly strapped economy, changes in the administrative branch are more likely than for any other part of Michigan government. Few legislators seem opposed to such changes.

LEADERSHIP IN THE PARTY

Governors play one other important role, albeit one less directly involved in policymaking. Governors become the leaders of their particular party. They must set the party agenda to support their own agenda for the state. Michigan's partisan politics is highly competitive, but voters are "more attracted to the candidate than the party. Ticket-splitting is increasingly common, and when voters find an appealing incumbent, they stick with him or her regardless of party affiliations."[27] To a great extent and where it suits the governor, recent occupants have taken over what are relatively strong parties rather than allowing themselves to be controlled by their parties' traditional priorities. Partisan responsiveness, or lack of it, says a great deal about the energy that governors must invest in building and strengthening their own political goals in balance with the needs of their parties. As Carolyn Stieber observed, even by 1970 candidates were being "sold to the public by repetition and eye appeal, much like any other commercial item."[28] Political parties are not unimportant to claiming the Michigan governorship, but neither are they any longer key to winning. Candidacies, especially gubernatorial ones, are highly individualistic today. Some degree of independence from the party is important, especially in the eyes of likely ticket-splitters. The party, of course, plays an important role in the nominating process, especially in the Democratic party. Yet even there, Michigan's open primary system gives independents ample opportunity to influence primary outcomes.

The party role was quite different for Williams than it is today. He came to Lansing in 1949 as the lone statewide Democratic officeholder and left twelve years later surrounded by Democrats whom he pulled into office. His was a partisan and ideological crusade. Romney emerged on the state scene as the prominent leader of the nonpartisan Citizens for Michigan, who developed the image of being independent of his party's conservative past. He, of course, ran on the Republican ticket, but he won as a crusading reforming moderate, downplaying party affiliation.

Milliken, in his first gubernatorial campaign in 1970, won by carving out a razor-thin majority of the first observable wave of ticket-splitters.[29] Milliken's subsequent campaigns saw his support diminish in West Michigan and his native north and expand in the urban southeast counties. In 1978, he won a majority even in traditionally Democratic Wayne County.[30] Milliken, with his bipartisan views, contributed little to Republican party strength in Lansing.

James Blanchard began his gubernatorial candidacy with a stronger partisan orientation. Running against the conservative insurance executive and tax-cut advocate Richard Headlee, Blanchard captured much of the moderate middle of the electorate. In contrast to Milliken, Blanchard demonstrated greater concern for partisan allegiance of personal staff and department heads as well as of appointees to boards and commissions. Still, many of his policies and programs catered to moderate voters, especially in appealing to business. This thoroughly irritated many veteran Democratic pols. In 1990, for example, in spite of a very stringent budget that was rapidly moving toward a deficit, Blanchard refused to propose a tax increase. He supported little in the way of increases in welfare grants and promised, as Engler eventually got, a program to remove from the rolls young General Assistance recipients who refuse to take job training. His programs to advance economic development and create jobs led him to support moderate reforms in unemployment compensation and workers' compensation laws as well as to support tax-abatement programs for major industries. Moreover, his urban policies, especially as they rewarded Detroit, were less emphasized and less clearly articulated than were those of outstate Republican Milliken. Nonetheless, Blanchard continued those programs and supported aid to the cities.

John Engler's 1990 campaign took on a more focused look: openly conservative but decidedly populist. Only that first part of the image was traditional Michigan Republican. Engler promised large cuts in property taxes, a smaller state government, and one that was less involved in the trappings of power. He promised, for example, to sell the jet-powered helicopter that the state police used to transport Blanchard around the state. As governor, Engler would drive his Oldsmobile even to the executive mansion on Mackinac Island. With help from Democrats and Republicans, Engler surprised most state pundits by defeating Blanchard by fewer than 20,000 votes, less than a half percent of the total vote. He, not surprisingly, carried the same theme over to the 1994 election.

Modern campaign techniques and strategies, together with public funding of gubernatorial campaigns, have made gubernatorial candidates less dependent on the political party. Because of television and skilled public relations and polling assistants, governors are not entirely reliant on partisan responses to promote their leadership image. This is not to suggest, of course, that political parties have lost all relevance. Far from it. Because parties remain important in the nominating process, candidates need support within their respective party organizations. Parties in Michigan play key roles in behind-the-scenes recruiting of candidates for legislative and county offices. They also help to generate funds for campaign coffers, both those of candidates and the parties. At the same time, however, partisan identification among voters has waned in favor of a growing number of independents and ticket-splitters. They give money the same way, across party lines. With an electorate of such moderate views, most candidates cannot appear too doctrinaire about party allegiance. Consequently, governors find that even symbolically leading their particular party can detract from other policymaking goals. All governors since Romney have backed off from party responsibilities that did not prove advantageous to their desired image.

There has been one partisan task that modern Michigan governors have fulfilled because of self-interest. All have been active in national party decisions. They seem to be looking intently at opportunities from Washington. Still, Michigan has produced only one president of the United States. Gerald R. Ford attained that office in 1974 through appointment, not election, first as vice-president when Spiro Agnew (once governor of Maryland) resigned and later as president when Richard Nixon resigned. Ford, in his only national election, lost to a former Georgia governor, Jimmy Carter, in 1976. Nor have any of Michigan's governors gotten their party's presidential nomination. Governors Williams and Romney announced their national ambitions. For reasons mentioned earlier, they were hurt politically and failed under media scrutiny, receiving instead presidential appointments to administrative posts.

SOME CLOSING THOUGHTS

Michigan is a diverse, complex place whose residents remain uninclined to deal with its statewide problems. Those problems get left to the governor. The governor is expected to symbolize the state as a whole, yet be sensitive to the impact of public policies on a variety of human and economic circumstances found there. Citizens look to the governor to bring together enough supportive public opinion to blend their own diversity into a form of unity, an umbrella under which most, if not all, can find a place.

In general, modern Michigan governors have lived up to those charges, but not without being battered severely. Building this sense of unity is difficult, especially when governors come to the executive office with a good measure of provincialism themselves. All come from a specific town and region, often with ties to only one legislative district – although some of this localism breaks down as they travel around the state seeking support for their programs or campaigning for votes.

In the final analysis, modern Michigan governors have been more similar than dissimilar as captains. They succeeded or failed in setting new state policy objectives based partly on public image but mostly on how effectively they worked the legislature. No other jobs were more important. The issues that they emphasized, for the most part, reflected the social, economic, and political environments on the entire ship of state. This is not to say that who becomes governor matters little. On the contrary, how governors read political conditions and how carefully they construct their responses are in no small part the product of their own thoughts and judgments as well as those of their aides.[31] In the end, though, what each recent governor recommended did little more than frame contentious policy discussions and define relevant debates. What they proposed seldom dictated final policy outcomes in this state, where both legislators and citizens remain exceedingly active participants in deciding the course of state government.

CHAPTER FIVE

Legislative Quandary: Leaders or Followers?

Richard McAnaw and Noelle Schiffer also contributed to this chapter

EXPECTATIONS OF A PROFESSIONAL LEGISLATURE

Michigan's policy process is beset by one perplexing phenomenon. As the previous chapter made clear, legislators depend on gubernatorial leadership. Without the governor's intervention, the most divisive issues bog down. This result is not due just to the threat of a veto or to the exercise of other gubernatorial powers. Nor is it due simply to the expectation found in most states that the governor will be the "chief legislator," the initiator of major legislative proposals.[1] No, Michigan's modern governors have had to do more than put the ball in play and await the action. Legislators have truly depended on the chief executive's prodding to enact bills of statewide importance. Jeff McAlvey, legislative liaison for the governor and former legislative aide to both David Stockman and John Engler, explained this dependency: "Part of the governor's job is to put aside the resistance that legislators feel. They want to take the path of least resistance, so they become more comfortable in following the governor as leader rather than jumping out on these big issues on their own."[2]

The irony in this dependency lies in the legislature's seeming capacity to do more. Yet the processes and demands that legislators face keep them from identifying with a statewide interest. Nothing within the legislature overcomes that problem. Michigan has a highly professionalized legislature; consequently, legislators appear to have the means to lead on the most important state policy questions. Moreover, in contrast to most states, Michigan legislators have long had this capacity. Yet they rarely use it for statewide policy leadership. In fact, Michigan legislators are more noted for adding items of interest to the bills of their colleagues than they are for sponsoring their own legislation.

Nearly twenty-five years ago, Michigan's legislature was ranked eighth nationally as a capable policy institution – functional, accountable, informed, independent, and representative.[3] That report found the legislature to be especially good in exercising many of these professional characteristics, but not with respect to its internal organization and external communications. Accountability, or the detailing of why the legislature did what it did, was where the state ranked lowest.[4] Few legislators ever explained for the public record how their efforts addressed state problems. Responsiveness to regions, interests, and personal quirks has always played a part that few legislators were willing to discuss openly.

Since that report, inspired by national efforts to improve state legislatures, Michigan has worked on its strengths but less on its weaknesses. Facilities were built, and even the capitol building was restored to its historic grandeur. Numerous staff were added, but little was done to improve, for example, committee reporting and strained partisan relations.[5] Conference committees, especially on appropriations bills, are still legendary for their lack of accessibility and their frequent middle-of-the-night deliberations. The technically well-respected House Fiscal Agency was locked in scandal in 1993, primarily because house leaders had long ignored their oversight responsibilities while other legislators were left out of agency operations. Staff, since 1986, had been misusing funds and dipping into agency budgets for personal use.

What we see in Michigan is clear: professional arrangements do little to resolve basic conflicts in the policy process, especially in a state where so many factions want something from government. Professionalism lacks the same purpose in politics that it has for management or sports, where we can see increased efficiency or better performance. Skilled Michigan legislators are praised for using their resources effectively in deal making and negotiation, but not for bringing important issues to closure. Meanwhile, the ineffective legislator is most likely criticized for not responding well to a wide variety of constituents or even being aware of their problems.[6] In Michigan, professionalism has contributed mostly to sharpening basic representative instincts, or to ties to constituents and other interests, the very characteristic on which the legislature ranked highest twenty-five years ago.[7] This capacity to be better informed about diverse views and wants has made legislators more cautious, more concerned with fine-tuning programs, and, therefore, more willing to wait for the governor to assume political risks on statewide or highly controversial issues.

Michigan's legislative professionals use the capacity of office to balance off political forces rather than to make them work together. This highly personal emphasis of legislators has always been evident, ever since bickering over where to locate the state capital. Such individualism detracts from an institution-wide focus on common problems. In the early 1990s, the effects of region and interest were readily apparent. Representative David Jaye Jr. (R-Utica) is a good example. A bright and well-educated young legislator, Jaye followed a staunch Republican line on roll-call votes. Yet he never curried the favor of the party's leaders, choosing instead to tweak their noses by a forceful rhetoric that led to charges of personal racism and insensitivity to the disadvantaged. Because of that posture, Jaye was popular in his Macomb County district, home to some of the state's most socially conservative blue-collar voters and home of the 1983 recall drive against tax-hike-supporting state senators. Jaye galvanized bipartisan constituent support in a recessionary era by harping on what the state could not afford but never apologizing, as did most legislators, for the government's failure to raise more revenue for anyone.

Legislators have pursued personal electoral needs because they have been rarely sanctioned in Lansing, at least directly. On the contrary, rewards have been frequent. For example, Senators Gilbert J. DiNello (R-East Detroit, who switched from the Democratic party after the 1992 elections in a reapportioned district that gained five percent more Republican voters) and Joseph S. Mack (D-Ironwood) were cut from the same cloth of personal aspirations. DiNello, as a Democrat from a predominantly white district in a region dominated by African Americans, played on his voters' Democratic but decidedly anti-liberal biases to be a major swing vote in the Republican-controlled Senate. In the process, he gained a committee chairmanship while in the minority party. Yet he also worked hard, even while sometimes sponsoring anti-union bills, to avoid a direct challenge from the United Auto Workers. Mack dealt with regional politics by beating on issues and agencies that his UP constituents found unpopular, particularly the Department of Natural Resources. His efforts in the 1980s halted several environmental initiatives, even as he held back his explosive rhetoric when regulation favored development projects in his district. Otherwise, he voted as a party-line Democrat. In turn, and by currying favor with other UP Democratic legislators, he often built party support for ideas that his colleagues found distasteful. "Hold your nose and vote," they often said. Ultimately, though, he was forced to resign under allegations of cheating on travel vouchers.

This behavior, which often leads to intense credit taking and even misrepresentation of legislative intent, creates public acts that fail to meet some obvious needs. While the passage of the state income tax in 1967 marked a legislative highpoint, its regressive impact was not reversed for even the state's neediest wage earners. The act establishing the state lottery in 1972 had more widespread implications. Legislators, who feared being attacked by churches and other opponents of gambling, claimed that they voted for it only to give schools more money. However, because lottery revenues went to the general fund, legislators actually earmarked little of the money for education. A cynical public raised that point for the next twenty years and more, each time a new tax was proposed. Some local voters expressed their anger by regularly voting against school funding proposals: "The damned lottery was supposed to make this unnecessary."

Even some of the state's most esteemed legislators have shown the strains of trying to balance region, interests, party, and program favorites. When John Engler was senate majority leader, he was described by a staffer as having a "tendency to muck up the process" but being effective in doing it. This was said in the context of praising Engler as one of the state's ten best lawmakers.[8] Senator Vernon Ehlers (R-Grand Rapids), a former physics professor long regarded as one of the legislature's hardest workers and brightest innovators, stayed independent of party and leadership. Before being elected to Congress in a special election in 1993, he carved out an image as a fiscal conservative and as an activist for his growing, river-basin community back home. He liked to be characterized as a bit of all things: "so knowledgeable about environmental issues that legislative committee staff come to him for expert counsel . . . (author) of numerous scientific articles . . . respected for his down-to-earth pragmatism."[9] He also used his clout and seniority for parochial reasons when it suited him – for example, by securing a seat on the appropriations subcommittee on higher education. This allowed him to work on behalf of community and private colleges back home even though it irritated colleagues who felt that such seats should go first to legislators whose districts included state universities.

What these personal aspirations bring forward is a legislative body that is reactive, not proactive. No one pretends that being a legislator means getting out ahead of the governor, voters, or state interests on an issue: "You use your staff and office to find out what others seem to want, whether they really want it, and what the results will be if they get it." There are so many different influential sources to which legislators must respond, and so many crosscutting ones, that no two members share the same perspective. Being, for example, a Republican representative from the UP, with a stake in facilitating economic development and privatizing government services, presented a complex mix for one-termer Stephen Dresch (R-Hancock). Dresch's interests meshed only partially with the Democratic senator from the same region who, despite being a supporter of Republican Governor Engler on several important votes, shared little common ground with Dresch on the key problem of jobs and economic development in the UP. As a consequence, Representative Dresch and Senator Don Koivisto (D-Ironwood) spent none of their overlapping years in office representing the western UP as a team. As a close lobbyist observer of the two commented, "Hey, different people vote for those two guys and they know it. They're pros!"[10]

Yet the professionalization of personal aspirations is not what the public and many Michigan officials have in mind for effective lawmaking.[11] Many want more action from the pros, and with more immediate resolution of the state's problems. Based on public complaints that always place Michigan's legislature considerably lower in polls than the governor, residents seem to want the one thing that state politicians cannot give: easy decisions that satisfy the public as a whole. Michigan's legislature, responsive to so many influences, apparently cannot function in this manner.[12]

Cautious members learn from their colleagues that coalition building is extraordinarily difficult and that the will to make policy is difficult to foster. For that reason, Michigan's best are praised most often for their ability to cut deals. Given the obstacles, not many can do it well. Moreover, legislators find that policymaking is most difficult during Michigan's recurring recessions, which escalate citizen frustrations and tensions between regions, interests, and parties.

But the problems of legislative governance cannot be laid solely on economic circumstances. Legislators have rushed to react to complaints in ways that produced often silly results. One case was the 1980 establishment of the Board of Massage and the labeling of "myomassolgists." After intense complaints about massage parlors and their sexual services, the legislature dealt with the problem by licensing and regulating them for health and safety. Massage parlors have refused to go away, but they may be cleaner places now. The same overreaction occurred in 1992 as the legislature and governor rushed to take credit for a bill banning assisted suicides, a practice by Dr. Jack Kevorkian that gained national publicity. The problem was that Kevorkian kept assisting suicides while waiting for the act to take effect. Then, after it took effect, he promptly aided another patient, was arrested, and was freed after a judge ruled the legislation unconstitutional. Legislators, who had once been vocal, disappeared from media sight, waiting, as one said hopefully, "for court vindication."

Under such conditions, movements to remove many of the professional components of the Michigan legislature preceded by several years national debates on term limitations for officeholders. Beginning in the late 1970s, citizen activists began arguing for a return to part-time, amateur legislators who have "real-world" occupations back home. Criticisms of staffing and office perks were prevalent. Even a few veteran legislators, such as Representative Colleen House Engler (R-Bay City and Mt. Pleasant), became advocates of less professionalism. More than a decade of such critiques eventually gave rise to the citizens' group Campaign to Limit Politicians' Terms, using the amateur's favorite weapon, the referendum. While that group's six- and eight-year term-limitation proposal was approved in the 1992 general election, the fate of the proposal was less important than the battle. Like the state's numerous initiatives and referenda, its popularity provided continuing evidence that Michigan's professional and amateur politicians have enduring suspicions about one another.

In the remainder of this chapter, we explore the operation and policy involvement of the legislature, with an eye on its strengths and limitations. We particularly highlight the competing expectations about the meaning of professionalism and the difficulty of governing effectively in the complex interplay of Michigan politics.

ONE OFFICE, TWO JOBS, NUMEROUS TASKS

Earlier, we referred to the personal aspirations of Michigan's legislators. We did not do so disparagingly. Greed of any sort is hard to satisfy in Michigan politics, with its open participation and close scrutiny by likely opponents. Corruption has not been borne lightly in the legislature, where a single lobbyist's accusation of offering a small bribe – one that could have been seen as a campaign contribution – seriously damaged the reputations of both the donor and the legislator who reported it in the 1980s. As was the case in the 1945 unsolved murder of the state senator, Warren G. Hooper, media and public attention to scandal brings down all participants.[13] Even human failings – the drug bust of a senator, cavorting with Lansing prostitutes, and ethics violations in business transactions – have doomed legislative careers. With the discussions about doing the "right thing" so prevalent in the media and in the electorate, the moralistic tenor of state politics pretty well overcomes any aspirations of legislators who are motivated mostly by self-aggrandizement. Some, in fact, refuse to claim all the expense money to which they are entitled so as not to generate a controversy. In that sense, Michigan's reputation is preserved as a straightforward and honest state, where politicians have "met one another head-on with radically differing approaches to the problems of governing."[14]

What we mean by personal aspirations is simple: each legislator must serve a uniquely complex mix of constituent interests. Serving that mix often sacrifices the well-being of the institution as a whole. In a sense, the individualistic component of the state's political culture has landed full-square on the legislature.

To an extent, the personalization of the legislator's job also reflects changing times. Raymond C. Kehres (D-Monroe) exercised considerable influence on the House Appropriations Committee in the 1960s. During his years in the legislature, his job was simple: serve as a labor Democrat for the state's industrial corridor. In those days, the linkages between region, interest, and party were direct and easily managed. Big labor and the Democratic party were synonymous; party discipline was easy to comprehend and follow.

The modern era, with greater voter and candidate independence, as well as more diversity in the state's urban core, has changed all that. Republicans like David Jaye now win high percentages of labor union votes while blasting public benefits for Detroit as antithetical to the interests of suburban constituents. Of course, Jaye reached out through an electronic medium to explain that view directly to voters, on his own terms. Kehres had to meet the electorate mainly through personal handshaking in labor forums, assisted by watchful labor volunteers.

Changing times and a shifting state economy help explain why personal aspirations make it more difficult for legislators to agree today. The complexity of their tasks is also important in determining why legislators do some things well and depend on the governor for others. Each legislator has personal rather than institution-wide aspirations because, while holding a single office, that person really has two jobs. One is representing the legislative district, and the other is serving on committees that exercise authority over limited sets of state policies. When it comes to legislative work, the standing committees – which still maintain their influence by dividing policy problems into specialized segments – are important in exercising control over what the legislature considers.[15] The job of powerful Morris Hood Jr. (D-Detroit), despite broad personal interests, revolves around two narrow concerns: first, representing African Americans from his district and, second, merging their interests with the technical work he does as higher education subcommittee chair on the House Appropriations Committee. For example, a priority for Hood has been to protect exceptional funding for Wayne

Community College, which receives millions more in state appropriations beyond formulas set for the other twenty-eight Michigan community colleges. Why? The original rationale was the district's inability, or unwillingness, to pass a millage increase.

However, things are even more complex than the "one office, two jobs" idea. The dual jobs entail numerous tasks that keep even the most professional offices so busy that those who run them find it hard to develop either a statewide policy emphasis or a commitment to bills that appear exceptionally difficult to pass. Even a cursory look at jobs and tasks shows why. Sometimes tasks center around a legislator's committee assignments. Oftentimes, especially on constituent matters from the home district, they do not. When committee and constituent tasks do not overlap, legislators are often forced to solicit support from other house and senate members. "The expectation is, if you have a problem, you go to a colleague who sits on the right committee for help. Raising public hell about it would not be right," explained a legislator.

The tasks that bring legislators closest to the governor obviously involve lawmaking, a process that often generates conflict with the governor or administrators. This happens especially when legislators feel that the executive branch has ignored its directives. For example, legislators challenged Governor Engler's cuts in state program allocations and his reorganization of the Department of Natural Resources. The latter challenge temporarily won a court injunction in 1992 just before the reorganization was to take place, dragging the issue on for more than another year.

Legislators won considerable support for that challenge from both the public and interest groups, including some Engler backers. It was not surprising. The same support was given earlier to legislators who resisted administrative changes under Governors Milliken and Blanchard. These examples show a contrast between legislative and gubernatorial interests. Legislators have two tendencies: one, to favor administrative innovations that give an increased voice both to amateur politicians from someone's district and to spokespersons for organized interests; and, two, to intervene in minor problems involving a specific commission, agency, or program. Thus, while the governor emphasizes statewide policy and broad administrative reform, lawmakers are more inclined to play "little-issue" politics. Even the initiative process is affected as legislators react to proposals. "Citizen initiatives," charged one Michigan representative, "are a bane because the framers know nothing of their likely impact. If we see the handwriting on the wall (that the idea behind an initiative is popular), we preempt it ourselves."[16]

Legislators also attend to a myriad of tasks of which the public is little aware. "You would not believe how much my job involves education," explained one legislator. "I have literally to take people to where they ought to be in support of issues. They just don't know how it works." In Michigan, all laws that provide or regulate services require that a legislator introduce a bill, both houses pass it, and the governor signs their joint product. In that context, even a "little-issue" bill to allow free fishing licenses for senior citizens becomes a big issue with regional implications involving tourism in the North and resident use of the Detroit River. Those circumstances also lead to minimal allowances for administrative discretion. Even agency research projects often require authorizing legislation.

Some of this intervention in the executive branch occurs because of the priority attention given appropriations. Programs and state institutions receive funds annually in a complex appropriations process that depends a great deal on decisions made in small subcommittees. Intervention also stems from the legislature's view of what agency oversight should accomplish. Regulations, for example, are reviewed individually and often rewritten under legislative direction. Program oversight is time-consuming but rarely comprehensive because legislators monitor agencies, intervene, correct or expand programs, overhaul statutes, and protect legislative intent only periodically.[17] "We often get involved to see that people from our district are getting something or are treated fairly," is a typical legislator's view.

Thus, when scrutiny of a large number of programs is expected, few legislators know very much about a wide range of issues and public agencies. Specialization, usually through the committee system, is one of the legislature's ways of life and leads to considerable dependence on a single legislator's knowledge. Those like Senators Dan L. DeGrow (R-Port Huron), with his emphasis on policies for K–12 education, and Jack Welborn (R-Kalamazoo), who mixes concerns for family life with prison reform, stand out. Both have used their committee seats effectively to stay involved in their issues. DeGrow gained bipartisan influence and was impossible to ignore when others addressed his issues, but so too was Welborn, a legislator who, on most issues, was regarded as a doctrinaire conservative. He grabbed the abortion issue for his committee, even as many worried about his being too ideological. Representative Mary C. Brown's (D-Kalamazoo) knowledge of insurance and pollution issues was just as impossible for colleagues to ignore, even when business interests from around the state attacked her committee reports.

While committees control the flow of legislative and oversight actions, issue expertise is not always found on the committee having jurisdiction over the bill. When Lt. Governor Connie B. Binsfield (R-Maple City) was a senator, most of her reputation was due to her interests in issues before her Natural Resources and Environmental Affairs Committee. But her most noteworthy success was as sponsor and driving force behind a bill that banned surrogate parenting in the state. She, in her colleagues' view, "learned the issue inside and out, getting enough floor support to overwhelm the committees."

Other legislators specialize in things that seem tangential to specific policymaking. A core of legislators routinely asks other questions regardless of the issue: How does this cut state funding? What are the effects on the poor? Does it enhance administrative performance? What are the racial implications? Does it encourage citizen participation and information? What about labor costs? What of state job loss? In most cases, such legislators are well informed, ask tough questions, and often impose their agendas on various bills and agency operations. Frequently, other legislators come to expect that these individuals will scrutinize all bills for their likely effects on pet subjects. After being embarrassed by a provision in a bill he had sponsored, one legislator complained: "Frankly, Perry [Bullard, D-Ann Arbor] should have caught that and called me weeks ago. He knows all about Freedom of Information requirements. I depended on him."

The perspective of the home district rather than the specialized substance of lawmaking also comes into play in dealing with agency operations. The size of Michigan government, its regulatory emphasis, and the problems of implementing a common policy throughout a diverse state generate volumes of constituent requests. Satisfying them is a major task, one that most staff feel takes up 65 to 85 percent of their office time. Legislators are asked to find for constituents – and many do – everything from temporary lodging to a waterway dredging permit. Requests involve more than personal favors for those plagued by glitches in state services, however. Regional and district interests commonly find their way into the actual authorization and appropriation of policy benefits – for river maintenance, permission to operate a landfill, or research on technology for a farm commodity.

Constituent service leads to charges that the legislature has elbowed its way into things that administrators think should be their prerogative. Exemptions on wetlands rules for development are particularly contentious, with legislators wanting to look at specific local problems and administrators wanting to stick to technical issues. Contracts to design and construct state buildings, as another example, require legislative committee approval. To get a new facility built requires hard work from a legislator who serves the district. Despite the burden of time, legislators have been unyielding in their attempts to retain and acquire powers for determining how laws will be administered and how regulations will be written.

Representation of constituents' problems also affects the drafting of bills and the criteria that legislators apply in allocating who gets what. Most legislators, regardless of party, have a healthy distrust for analytically determined solutions that allocate program benefits through systematic formulas, such as formulas for state aid to universities or local school districts. These take too much discretion away from members, unless, of course, they can be used to pry money or control away from a committee chair. Nor do legislators like to see anyone insist that all state appropriations for programs in a certain issue area, such as education, go into the budget for that department. While that may be technically neat and may promote accountability, it limits legislative discretion. Legislators are especially likely to think of unique features of their own districts that can be served by flexible rules in allocating projects and dollars. This is just part of the unending emphasis on pork-barrel politics – balanced and for everyone. Such pride is taken in being responsive to the district that Senator Joseph Mack once insisted on being taken to the senate by ambulance so he could vote for the UP.

Representative Dominic Jacobetti (D-Negaunee), also of the UP, wore his district and regional pride especially well – at least until House Fiscal Agency problems cost him his power in 1993. As the longest-serving member in the history of the legislature, having been elected continuously since 1954, he used his position as chair of the House Appropriations Committee for eighteen years to move funds and programs quite openly for UP interests. Northern Michigan University enjoyed the benefit of "Jake's" power as he fought formula funding of state universities. His committee position was so significant that drafters of nearly all legislation allocating state services gave specific attention to UP concerns. In a region rich in natural resources, Jacobetti was often proclaimed as its greatest asset. Although Detroit-area legislators lack the seniority accumulated by Mack and Jacobetti, they have long played a similar game. By using the voting power of, at least, a five-person senate cadre and a sixteen-person house group, the "Detroit Delegation" swung numerous votes.[18]

What should not be overlooked about the numerous tasks of the legislature, moreover, is their interconnections. These add to the logistical difficulties of getting action. Constitutional changes, initiating a law, passing a bill, appropriating funds, overseeing agencies, reviewing regulations, serving constituents, and incorporating district needs into pending legislation blur from one to another so easily that even the dual jobs of the legislator – home work and Lansing work – are often impossible to separate. The question most often asked about a problem confronting a legislator, as one said, is "not what legal responsibility I'm meeting here but how, given this job, I can work on things for my constituents, my party, and the groups that support me."

LEGISLATIVE OPERATIONS AND STRUCTURE

Of course, legislators are not left to pursue whatever aspirations they find appealing or necessary. "I never thought this is how I would spend my time here," exclaimed one member, "but these are the issues I need to address to get ahead." The organization of the legislature, while far from authoritarian, is designed to bring some order to two very personalized legislative chambers. Yet the conditions described earlier persist because rational organization exercises few effective controls over the rank-and-file members. Power, if anything, is dispersed. What order exists is mostly dependent on the two house majority leaders who try to manage the legislative flow of the nearly four dozen committee chairs who emphasize policy content.

Except for a few constitutional provisions, the legislature organizes itself. No one tells the legislature much about how to run its business. The state constitution provides for a bicameral (i.e., two-house) legislature, specifies a 38-member senate and a 110-member house of representatives, designates the lieutenant governor to be the presiding officer – or president – of the senate with voting rights only on tie votes, specifies that all legislation shall be by bill and may originate in either house, mandates five days between printing and passage of a bill as well as three readings in each house before a vote, requires a majority of all elected and serving members in each house on identical measures for a bill's passage, and specifies recorded roll-call votes. The constitution also prohibits bills that embrace more than one subject, precluding the kind of unrelated riders that the U.S. Congress frequently attaches to bills. But, in a peculiar feature, bills can be tie-barred. That is, the legislature can require that two bills, even unrelated ones, be enacted before either becomes law. Except for this feature, which facilitates brokering of deals, the Michigan legislature is structured rather typically.

Party Leadership

Much of the in-house rule making of the legislature goes into defining the leadership, namely, who will serve and what positions are available. With a legislature inclined to worry less about rules than representational problems, house leadership is an important means of sorting through the morass. The four party caucuses in the legislature handle some of this, considerably more than found in Congress. A caucus of majority party legislators from each house selects its candidates for leadership positions, as does the minority. Then each chamber elects those leaders by majority vote. Party crossover voting for who shall lead the chamber was needed once during the Romney years to elect a Republican leader, Don R. Pears (R-Berrien County), who then served as speaker from 1959 to 1962. In 1993, another solution was found when the house was again deadlocked with a 55–55 split. The parties divided the speakership, one month at a time, between Curtis Hertel (D-Detroit) and Paul Hillegonds (R-Holland), who became known as the "stereo speakers."

While each caucus selects several legislative leaders, the four most important are the Speaker of the house, majority leader of the senate, and each house's minority leader. The Speaker presides over the house. Both the Speaker and the senate majority leader appoint all committee members and committee chairs and vice chairs, assign bills to committees, and act as chief party spokespersons within the body. Hence, committee members feel beholden to the leadership: "I thank them from the bottom of my heart that I'm not on agriculture, where I would have a much harder time doing things for a wide range of people in my district." The minority leaders assist with committee assignments, including the selection of ranking members, and each acts as the party's spokesperson for that house. These leaders have considerable influence in their caucuses and beyond, much more so than in many states but not as much as in those states where caucus rules bind a member's vote.

The Speaker, however, traditionally has the most power within the respective houses. Because the senate has fewer members and senators serve longer terms, the majority leader is more subject to challenge. A former Speaker once explained: "The senate has 38 prima donnas, and the house, 109 sheep." Given their independent, prima donna status, senate majority leaders frequently count on and gain the support of senators of the other party. Discipline, however, generally reigns in the house. A legislator who ignores the Speaker's concerns will likely find his or her own bills ignored by the Speaker. This stronger sense of discipline explains why the house minority leader ranks as the least powerful and visible of the four leaders. Seldom have they been able to mount bipartisan opposition to issues important to the Speaker. However, Co-speaker Hillegonds became well known as minority leader by persistently advocating more policy research and information gathering. "He worked his way out of a real hole in that job," explained a sympathetic lobbyist, "and did it by crying for more information in a place that oftentimes becomes its own worst enemy by ignoring basic facts."

That lobbyist noted the degree of self-definition in each leadership position. Each leader has an assistant chosen primarily for personal loyalty. In-house popularity is a lesser but still significant factor, especially in the more personal senate. Other positions, only some of real importance to leaders, include the numerous floor leaders of each caucus and their whips. Basically, their job is to shepherd partisan bills through to passage. In so doing, floor leaders traditionally depend on active support from the leadership. This minimizes the floor leaders' actual influence over bills and legislative action. Floor leaders also play a secondary role to the committee chairs.

An important reason for the large number of positions, often over forty in all, not including another forty-five or more committee chairs, is the need for the leaders to accommodate various regions and interests.[19] Balance is the key word for assignments. Characteristics such as liberal, moderate, and conservative also are important, sometimes because of leadership preferences and sometimes because certain types of individuals best satisfy certain interests. Selecting committee chairs is even more complicated. The formal rules state that the Speaker and majority leader are to consider the preferences, seniority, and experience of members in making appointments. Expertise and concern for relevant issues also come into play, but interest-group endorsements usually complement consideration for committee positions. "We have to have people in those posts that lobbyists can work with comfortably," is the explanation.

The appointment process enhances leadership authority because the offices of the house and senate leaders become important centers around which state interests are bargained. "If we let [the leaders] have [chairs] they like," the explanation continues, "at least lobbyists can get our okay on issues they bring to committee." Appointments also strengthen the leadership because each position has perks of staff and office size, and some of the legislators receive an additional stipend for the assignment. Rank-and-file legislators actively solicit appointments and are indebted to the leaders who appoint them.

Nonetheless, the dispersal of influence in a legislature where nearly one-third of the members are partisan leaders, one-third are committee chairs, and one-third are the committees' ranking minority members is extensive. Moreover, organizational structure is not entirely hierarchical. Leaders look at whether bills are acceptable to the caucus or governor as they come from committees, but chairs control their content. Power is shared extensively:

"It's like fine old wine, nobody gets very much." In addition, many appointments cannot be denied to certain members, unless those members have thoroughly insulted the leadership. Some legislators are too bright to overlook, others have too many endorsements to ignore, and still others would be unacceptable in all but a few minor positions. Of course, leaders of the caucuses eventually run out of choices. So, despite the leaders' formal powers, effective leadership through appointments has limits.

Recent Speakers of the house have demonstrated both their power and its limits. Detroit Democrat William Ryan (1969–74), recognized as perhaps the most effective Speaker, ruled the house just as the legislature made the transition from a part-time legislature of amateurs to a full-time body of aspiring professionals. To win supporters, all in the name of legislative reform, Ryan expanded personal staffs, arranged private offices, and added professional staff. Such trades gave him a strong reputation for influence; but, eventually, they also weakened the leadership because the rank-and-file members gained more help in making independent judgments and meeting with a broader circle of informants.

Ryan's success, like that of his successor, Bobby Crim (D-Flint), also had other origins. Both served as Speaker when Republicans held the governorship. As such, they were chief spokespersons for Democratic positions, and the Republican governor had to negotiate solutions with them. This helped each to maintain party solidarity, even in going to the committee chairs with policy requests. More recent Speakers, Gary Owens from Ypsilanti and Lewis Dodak of Birch Run, spent some of their time working alongside fellow Democratic Governor James Blanchard. While still key actors in negotiating issues in the legislature and with the governor, their task was also different. Owens and Dodak, to avoid embarrassing their party, had the not always possible job of delivering house votes on issues important to Blanchard but not to long-term Democratic supporters, such as labor.

Because legislators in this fragmented state also have many unique district reasons to remind them of the old adage that "all politics is local," these leaders could not routinely keep house Democrats in line. Blanchard typically delivered on about half of his ten to twelve annual priority issues during his eight years in office. However, the situation became at once better and worse under Dodak when Engler assumed the governorship. Dodak restored party discipline a bit in order to check the governor, but he had next to no chance of passing a house leader's agenda. Instead, he tried to save certain things. He did, however, become state party leader in public battles with the governor, elevating his own visibility a great deal through the media but also being required to articulate many positions that he might not have otherwise stated in his home district. This visibility, along with a reapportioned district, worked to his demise. Dodak was defeated by a conservative Republican in 1992.

Majority leaders in the senate have managed to create statewide power while working under opposition governors. Engler, who became majority leader in 1984, was Blanchard's chief political nemesis for the remainder of the decade. Presiding over the senate, Engler became the focus of Republican power in state politics and the front-running Republican candidate for governor. He used the political tools at his disposal to elevate the importance of the entire chamber. Often he did the unheard of, trampling on what were thought of as gubernatorial prerogatives. Engler, for example, put the governor on notice by having a committee reject, without a hearing, two gubernatorial nominations that required senate confirmation.

William B. Fitzgerald (D-Detroit) also used his position as majority leader to launch – unsuccessfully – a campaign for governor in 1974. While both Engler and he found their statewide prominence to be the chief advantage of opposition in the senate, they also discovered that their heightened name recognition presented problems. The media tended to present both as contentious individuals and questioned their ability to succeed as governor. That was the price both had to pay because opposition leadership accounts for much of the hostility that characterizes politics when different parties share control. Republican majority leaders during the Milliken years, on the other hand, saw their first job as helping the governor. Hence, few saw them either as controversial or as likely candidates for higher office.

All of these leaders shared one important feature that is distinctly representative of Michigan politics. Since at least the rise of labor in state politics and the conflict created by its emergence, legislative leaders have demonstrated a willingness to play political hardball. Consequently, they consistently and vocally seek credit for themselves or their party's governor on popular decisions, and they try to blame unpopular actions on opponents. To do so, legislative leaders have often hammered hard at committee chairs and the rank and file to keep partisanship pronounced, at least enough to clarify differences to ticket-splitting voters who so easily seem to forget them. The preferred way of doing this is within the caucuses, shaping issues jointly to unify caucus members and secure commitment to a single approach within the party. The inescapable consequence of such strong leadership, even without strong caucus rules that bind the members, was to produce enduring conflicts on key issues, such as tax, education, and labor law policies.

Subtle changes have occurred, however, because colleagues, governors, and private interests increasingly expect house and senate leaders to help pass policy on their own as well as mire it in conflict when necessary. Obstructionist practices that plagued the Williams administration when Republican conservatives such as Midland's Lynn Francis and Coldwater's John R. "Jumpin' Joe" Smeekens, with his hand-painted ties, were in office, seem to be gone. They have been replaced by the need to meet an informed action agenda imposed on the legislature by the dynamics of economic change. Combatants are usually loathe to let a state crisis, such as payless paydays for state employees, suddenly appear and endure in the public's mind.

Unfortunately, despite good intentions and a willingness to compromise, leaders rarely salvage issues that have been exposed to bitter partisan, interest-group, and regional rancor. When legislative leaders help draw statewide attention to issues, such as education finance reform, nearly every affected interest and region gets drawn into the contest. The aspirations of every legislator are touched as well. As a result, when legislative leaders turn to facilitating solutions for one of the state's many problems, their concern brings with it the likelihood of stalemate and, paradoxically, the only chance of success.

The Committees

Committees provide yet another forum for enhancing or curtailing legislators' aspirations. Their means and their effects, however, are quite unlike those of the party caucuses. If leaders can rely on the caucus, they are in a much stronger negotiating position. The committees, in contrast, tend to limit the leadership's coalition building, even in caucus, because the actual marking up of final bills and budget authorizations, which then go to the floor, takes place within their confines. With leadership positions dispersed so broadly across the house and even more so in the senate, committee chairs and members are conscious of the specifics of regional and group accommodation. For recent majority parties, nearly every senator and over half of the members of the house have been chairs. If one chair follows too faithfully a statewide caucus strategy designed by the leaders without respecting other considerations, that individual's own district concerns are likely to be ignored when taken up in bills in other committees. Being a chair, therefore, does not insulate one from collegial demands.

This fragmentation of power helps to explain why, in boom times, policy benefits are distributed widely and why, in periods of economic bust, cuts are made on the basis of balance and shared pain. Fairness, as a moralistic tradition that allocates something for all, plays itself out in extensive committee compromise whenever there are interparty differences. With the views of the other party actively represented in committee but not in caucus, the latter is not a good forum for negotiating accommodations that must cross party lines. Committees have gained strength in this way since the 1950s, when splits within each party were first observed as a regionally inspired and remarkably consistent phenomenon.[20]

The committees are quite effective in rejecting many sponsored bills and in getting their way once they negotiate an agreement. Hence, they are respected as the principal gatekeepers of public policy. For the same reason, Democrats and Republicans agreed on cochair positions when the house divided equally in 1993. As with the Speaker, chairs rotated in positions each month. While lobbyists understand the need to work closely with the leaders, most of their time is spent with the committees.[21] "A lobbyist would have to be nuts not to spend most of his or her time with the proper committee, and most of the rest of it should be spent with your local [district] senator and representative so they know how to work the committee for you," noted a veteran legislator.

The importance of committee gatekeeping has been much in evidence. Over a twenty-three-year period, 1956–78, 318 different legislators sponsored 602 district bills intended to benefit just senior citizens. Those bills were sent to fifteen different standing and special committees. None was passed without a favorable committee report. Less than 3 percent were voted down on the floor after gaining committee support.[22] Roughly the same was true for all legislation from 1965 to 1986. During that period, 25,460 bills were introduced in all legislative sessions, or 1,157 per year. House committees, as can be seen in table 6, reported out 8,631 (34 percent) of these; legislators then passed 7,143 (83 percent) of those on the house floor. A similar pattern existed in the smaller senate, but senators introduced only 675 bills per year. They passed an average of 203 (78 percent) of 260 (39 percent) annually reported out. Clearly, the committees were determining factors in both houses. They kept most – 64 percent – policy ideas out of consideration, and when they approved an idea, it had an excellent – 81 percent – chance of passing its house of origin.

The leaders and the members support committee gatekeeping as the only means of managing so many bills and resolutions. Much of the hard decision making, moreover, falls on the committee chairs. As one chair summarized his years in office: "If something doesn't have my approval, it doesn't hap-

Table 6: Legislation in the Michigan Legislature, 1965–86

	House of Representatives		Senate	
	Number	Average per Year	Number	Average per Year
Bills introduced	25,460	1,157.3	14,853	675.1
Bills reported from committee	8,631	392.3	5,675	260.0
Bills that passed house of origin	7,143	324.8	4,463	202.9
Bills that passed other house	5,109	232.2	2,832	128.7

	House of Representatives	Senate
	(percent)	(percent)
Bills reported from committee	33.9	38.2
Reported bills that passed house of origin	82.8	78.6
Bills that passed other chamber	71.5	63.5
Bills introduced that became law (both houses)	18.9	

	Gubernatorial Action	
	Number	Average Per Year
Bills Submitted to Governor	7,869	357.3
Vetoed	179	8.1
Vetoes overridden	1	0
Number of laws	7,679	349.0

Note: Some discrepancies exist between the number of bills submitted to the governor, number vetoed, and number of public and private acts.

Source: Michigan House and Senate Journals, 1965–86.

pen.'' Chairs control the work of the committees and, by negotiating with their members, establish the agenda for considering bills. If a bill does not get on the agenda, it does not get a hearing. Thus, by controlling the agenda, the chair winnows the number of items for consideration and focuses committee work on those bills deemed personally significant. This, of course, is an exercise of real power over the rest of the house. When chair positions were shared in 1993, some lobbyists feared that Speakers Hertel and Hillegonds would spend all their time, and that of the committee chairs, keeping the other's agenda locked out. To alleviate fears, both publicly announced the need to emphasize aggressive lawmaking, not gatekeeping. While a majority of committee members occasionally overrides the chairperson, to do so has never been considered good form: "That's what you'd call a norm, one inspired by the desire to not get your butt burned." Also, the full chamber, by majority vote, may discharge a bill from a committee. However, this rarely happens because committees perform such important gatekeeping work that even dissenting members act as if they should not be insulted: "It's just not worth the hassle." When a discharge occurs, it is usually a mark of deep disagreement between either the committee chair and the chamber leaders or between the leaders and their caucuses.

Gatekeeping is also effective because the markup process is relatively sophisticated, and conciliatory for those who wish to enhance a bill. "Introducing a bill in this state is like opening a Pandora's box," was how one member described committee work. The distinct stages explain why: review of proposals, screening of proposals as legislators and staff check with both affected state interests and constituents, multiple analyses of the potential impact of popular proposals, careful selection of who will be allowed to testify on a bill, extensive and public hearings to establish the credibility of bills that are likely to go forward, and careful reporting to the leaders of why committee support was forthcoming. Committee members also network widely with legislators whose districts are affected by any bill. The trades necessary to get bills passed are most often made at this point, with the size and weight of a bill increasing as more legislators are consulted.

Goals of the leaders and party, often simply through extensive supplements, get lost more easily than do those of committee members who participate in these negotiations. To prevent such losses, leaders have frequently attempted to control the legislature's research capacity, normally by approving or rejecting policy research or staff assignments to committees. This practice, to which many members object, has been more common than leaders' using their discretion over which committees will get a bill, a choice that is usually limited by housewide understandings of which committees should get what. Less formally, leadership staff sniff out rumors of agreements between members that will change a bill's intent unfavorably.

Committees, however, are more likely than leaders to prevail because the personal aspirations of legislators usually win out over party discipline and the potential for regional neglect. Most frequently, committee members turn to interest groups for information. Most legislative estimates suggest that slightly more than 50 percent of all bills are in substantial part drafted by lobbyists or their agents. To minimize leadership complaints about particular legislators or favored groups unraveling leadership agreements, most legislators retreat to back rooms to negotiate in private. "You don't think I ever let [Speaker] Bobby Crim get wind of deals I was cutting to get special job training in my district, or some money for a waterways or college project," observed one member. "He would have found a way to kill them before they were done, embarrassing me in front of constituents who I'd worked with [throughout the process]." Under such conditions, with committee deliberations as open places for other members to pursue their wants, the leadership is usually able to discipline only the most blatantly recalcitrant members of their caucus.

Over the years, two sets of legislators have quietly used back-room discussions to help change state politics and serve a broader constituency than did the state's combative labor-versus-business political parties of the 1950s. Urban Republicans of the 1960s and 1970s found back-room tactics important to break from the conservative dictates of rural Republican leaders. These efforts were facilitated by getting suburban legislators into chair positions. Democrats from throughout the state found privately negotiated deals even more important than Republicans, though. They used these to break ranks with labor leaders and their liberal allies who had captured the party until mid-way in Milliken's administration. In this case, the back rooms made bipartisan deals especially attractive, hidden as they were from organized labor's demands for accountability.

Exercising leadership in Michigan's legislative committees, for those strategic reasons, is more complicated than what appears to be the case for either the Congress or the legislatures of more accountable states. That complexity can be seen in the unwillingness of Michigan legislators to reform their committee reporting procedures and other mechanisms of accountability: "Screw that, we'd never get a thing accomplished." It behooves them to be able to do things away from the public eye. In essence, committees run on the basis of, first, acquired knowledge about highly particular needs and, second, generalized acceptance of nearly every Michiganian's right to some piece of what the legislature produces. The emphasis of committees, then, is on particular products and how happy the recipients are with them.

That orientation is possible because of the comprehensive structure of Michigan's committee system. The primary workhorse committees are the twenty-nine standing house committees and the eighteen standing senate committees that existed in 1992 (see table 7). They provide a thorough overview of the issues likely to be addressed in members' bills. It seems rela-

Table 7: Standing Committees of the Legislature

House Committees (number of members)

Agriculture, Forestry and Minerals 15	Judiciary 17
Appropriations 24	Labor 13
Civil Rights, Constitution and Women's Rights 7	Liquor Control 11
Colleges and Universities 8	Marine Affairs and Port Development 7
Conservation, Recreation and Environment 19	Mental Health 7
Consumers 10	Military and Veterans Affairs 5
Corporations and Finance 19	Public Health 19
Corrections 7	Public Utilities 13
Economic Development and Energy 14	Senior Citizens and Retirement 10
Education 19	Social Services and Youth 7
Elections 12	State Affairs 9
House Oversight 13	Taxation 19
Housing and Urban Affairs 10	Tourism, Fisheries and Wildlife 15
Insurance 17	Towns and Counties 7
	Transportation 19

Senate Committees (number of members)

Agriculture, Forestry and Minerals 5	Judiciary 5
Appropriations 13	Local Government and Veterans 5
Commerce 4	Mental Health 5
Corporations and Economic Development 5	Natural Resources and Environmental Affairs 5
Education 5	Reapportionments 5
Family Law, Criminal Law and Corrections 6	Regulatory Affairs 5
Finance 5	State Affairs and Military/Veteran Affairs 5
Government Operations 5	Technology and Energy 5
Health Policy 5	Transportation and Tourism 5

Note: The listing of senate committees includes only substantive committees.

Source: Rules of the House, Rules of the Senate (1991).

tively clear, because of committee title, where each bill will go for consideration and markup, even if that means that specific constituents such as senior citizens are served by several committees. However, this system of committees is less stable than one would expect. Unlike the U.S. Congress, where committee jurisdictions are set within rigid rules, the names, functions, and number of members of standing committees vary somewhat with each legislative session. Changing leadership, new personalities, shifting state and regional agendas, and just plain whim drive those changes. For example, Senator Welborn's interest in families and the law led to "Family Law" being added to the title of that body's committee on Criminal Law and Corrections. Republicans in the house, under Engler, have argued for fewer committees to better centralize leadership power with a Republican governor and coordinate policy.

Things are not entirely flexible, though. Long-term chairs and members are difficult for leaders to replace, and these individuals can clamor for jurisdiction over an issue. Nonetheless, as membership turns over, the committees shift as well, often opening unexpected avenues for policy change. A region or interest frequently loses its prime committee defender, as was the case for developers in the UP when Senator Mack retired.

Committee control over legislation is also fluid because of the inherently unstable relationship between the appropriations committees and the other standing committees. The House and Senate Appropriations Committees are the two most important committees in the legislature. These committees routinely start new programs without statutory mandate through back-door enabling acts, merely by appropriating and specifying uses of funds. They also work with open-ended and unspecified "vehicle bills," fleshing out their content at the last minute without following rules that govern introduction or meet research expectations. Other committees can do little to provide back-door appropriations because few Michigan programs run as entitlements or by exact formula.

To facilitate agency critiques and policymaking, the appropriations committees are the only ones to operate under extensive and independent subcommittee rules. There are nineteen house appropriation subcommittees with six to eight members each, and fifteen mostly three-member senate subcommittees. All replicate the responsibilities of other standing committees, making them more than just complementary. To a great extent, they compete. The subcommittees serve as sources of countervailing power, both for legislative leaders and governors who want options for pursuing their goals and for rank-and-file members who seek regional and interest-group favors that they might not get elsewhere. This feature adds to the problems of governing effectively on statewide issues: "It adds a whole layer of trouble." Because much of their work is done later in conference committees, to reconcile house and senate differences and also to unravel many negotiated deals, other members suggest that this process really adds two such layers: "If you are not included in conference, your point has a great chance of just plain getting dropped."

On the Floor

The tendency to make most deals in committee, coupled with the impact of the leadership, leaves floor actions by the rank and file relatively unimportant yet subject to conflict. Many observers miss the point, however, when they suggest, as did one reporter, that Michigan lawmakers "fight very hard with one another over very little." Things are often more important to legislators than they appear to others. Action on the floor provides the last chance to modify a bill to meet a member's personal aspirations. It also is the last and most public place to posture against partisan, regional, and interest-group agreements that legislators feel compelled to attack. "If my constituents are not to be well served by a bill," said a junior legislator, "the floor is the place for me to remind them that it wasn't my fault."

Floor action is relatively unimportant because of both legislative rules and what legislators leave to be done at this stage in the process. The legislature allows amendments that can alter committee reports, but these seldom lead to the reshaping of bills on the floor of either chamber. One reason is because amendments must be tied directly to the subject and purpose of the bill. A second reason is that amendments are infrequent because of leadership pressures. Amendments are common only when committees leave points of contention unresolved in markup. Under such circumstances, floor debate may turn from a quick vote to a discussion of bringing closure to final areas of disagreement.[23] To tie up action in any serious way, a legislator needs what are usually scarce – several floor supporters willing to risk offending the leaders by providing a block of swing votes.

The rules for finalizing a bill into law, other than for the difficulty of amendments, are much like those of other states. A quorum is necessary for a chamber to hold an official meeting and pass bills. Extraordinary majorities are sometimes required: a two-thirds vote to give a bill immediate effect, propose constitutional amendments, and override a gubernatorial veto; and a three-fourths vote to amend or repeal a law initiated through citizen petition. Laws take effect ninety days after the close of the session unless they receive immediate effect. Ordinarily, leaders speed up the legislative process, from floor readings of a bill to recording roll-call votes, in order to expedite many bills in a short time. The norms of the legislature, or the informal rules that members tend to accept as appropriate, favor haste. Members report that haste is the only way to lessen endless haggling.

Beyond the widespread acceptance of hasty floor action, few of the norms that prevailed in the past can now be found in the legislature.[24] Self-restraint, which supports speeding up the process, is one example. Legislators infrequently talk about things that are either beyond their expertise or the interests of their supporters. However, disruptive floor conditions that are allowed today would have been intolerable in the past. First-term legislators now become active and gain influential status on key committees. Many, in fact, say that they were encouraged to "hit the legislature running." Moreover, verbal and sometimes physical floor attacks by one member on the integrity of another are often bitter. An unpopular and inattentive house member of the 1980s, for example, had her microphone switched off when she chose to speak. Some legislators reject the notion that they need to be sociable to colleagues or lobbyists whom they dislike.

The most startling change, at least since the mid-1970s, is the greater distrust of colleagues. "Most of my fellow caucus members," observed one long-term house Democrat, "are as true to their word as the day is long. After a promise on Tuesday, they break ranks on Wednesday." The most accepted norm found in state legislatures of the 1950s was "keeping one's word."[25] Now, legislators are reluctant to commit their word. They note that crosscutting pressures by interest groups, legislative leaders, and district constituents create an unstable situation in which keeping promises is often difficult. When eight members of the Michigan Senate were running for Congress and facing recorded roll-call votes in 1992, unpredictability became nearly a way of life in that chamber: "These guys worried about so many factors that they were figuring things out even as their fingers pushed their vote buttons." The two who were elected to Congress were thought of "as the guys with the slowest button fingers." Frequently, promises are broken or commitments are held back because leaders cannot support proposals that come out of committees in quite different form from the way they were initially drafted. "Because things are so subject to change as legislation progresses," said one legislator, "loyalties are tentatively given."

Legislative contentiousness and lack of trust, however, work against getting on with the business of statewide policy solutions. One result of this is a legislature that, with its many problems of getting majorities together, typically races to finish at least half of its annual business in the final week of each session. Nearly all close observers find this a bitter but hardly unexpected irony of a full-time legislature where members may well stay in session twelve months of the year.

Organizing Districts

One final set of rules, largely beyond the legislature's control, affects legislative relations and their impact on policy leadership. Apportionment of the state by districts helps produce a legislative environment where both strong leaders and effective brokering in committees are necessary, but largely unsuited to controlling members. As we explain, districting also helps create the more independent modern legislator fostered by Speaker William Ryan, at least one less dependent on any single source of influence. Three decades of reapportionment after each decennial census have left the state with legislators from most house and senate districts who have considerable judgments to make about who matters most back home. If legislators respond favorably to their districts, they are rewarded with reelection.

Obviously more than just partisanship determines a legislator's district success, although generalized patterns of party strength have prevailed in Michigan. Democratic legislators, with the exception of those from parts of the UP, tend to come from districts that are predominantly labor, African-American, central-city urban, or liberal university communities. Republicans typically represent districts dominated by commerce, industry, agriculture, small towns, or suburbs. Partisanship enters at these points.

Although there are exceptions, the great majority of districts, including the partisan exceptions, are relatively homogeneous places. Indeed, homogeneity is increasing in many districts. For example, Detroit lost 50 percent of its white population in the 1980s. So, while all legislators get and answer requests from both Democrats and Republicans, most face the need to develop a back-home style that, despite ticket-splitting, is distinctive both from one district to the next and from legislators of the other party. A legislator's most likely voters get attention first. Hence, one often finds differences in policy priorities among legislators from the same region.

Such results complicate the representative role of the legislator and would not have been found often in the 1950s. Legislative districting at that time was understood as inherently unfair and malapportioned, severely disadvantaging urban and labor interests.[26] Democrats, to no avail, used lawsuits, initiatives, and referenda to wrest legislative control from outstate Republicans.

Finally, the U.S. Supreme Court required apportionment of both chambers of state legislatures on the basis of one person, one vote, or equally sized districts. County lines were no longer appropriate, and rural control was broken. *Baker* v. *Carr,* in 1962, was the landmark for mandated reapportionment.[27] The key case was *Reynolds* v. *Sims* in which the Court held that the equal protection clause of the U.S. Constitution requires both houses of a state legislature to be apportioned on a population basis.[28] *Reynolds* was specifically applied to Michigan in *Marshall* v. *Hare,* which directed the state to be reapportioned in time for the 1964 elections.[29]

Michigan responded under its new constitution and carried out its first of now four reapportionments. Article IV provided for a Commission on Legislative Reapportionment to design districts and allocate seats. The commission was equally divided between Democrats and Republicans. If it failed to reach an agreement by majority vote within 180 days, the commission or any of its members could appeal to the state supreme court. The constitution specified that the court would then determine which plan complied most closely with the constitutional requirements and direct the commission to adopt it.

The ensuing struggles have been epic, leading first to renewed partisan interest in winning seats in what are actually nonpartisan supreme court elections. Too much politics, from the justices' perspective, led to strongly partisan reapportionment submissions, court refusals to hear them, court decisions returning the task to legislators and lawmaking, and even the appointment of a special master to decide a final plan.[30] Throughout the saga, one factor prevailed. Democrats, as can be seen in table 8, gained fairer representation.[31] Because of divided party control of state government, however, legislative leaders were not able to dominate reapportionment on behalf of either Democrats or Republicans. They could never generate a plan on which a majority of both houses could agree.

This meant that legislative politics of the 1960s split the state between Democratic urban/labor and Republican business interests. It was the heyday for Michigan's reputation as a progressive, liberal state.[32] This period of a single cleavage between two interest-group titans was short-lived, however. Southeast Michigan and, to a lesser extent, an already diverse outstate were changing considerably by the 1970s. There was no single rural interest, and labor no longer controlled Democrats, especially in new outstate and suburban districts.

Legislators discovered their independence. This recognition hindered the idea of disciplined party politics, as well as hopes for efficient legislative leadership. As can be seen in table 9, legislative districts historically have not been competitive. While the parties fought to seize competitive seats to swing legislative control, a great majority of legislators were winning election by over 20 percent vote margins. Over 40 percent of house districts and 12 percent of senate districts were won by landslides of more than 40 percent margins in 1950. This increased slightly in the house and significantly in the senate by the 1980s. For most legislators, limited competition meant that they were not dependent on party leaders to create winning margins for

Table 8: Percentage of Democratic Votes and Seats in the Michigan Legislature, 1950–88

	House		Senate	
Election Year	Votes	Seats	Votes	Seats
1950	46.3	34.0	46.7	21.9
1962	55.9	47.2	51.7	33.3
After Reapportionment I				
1964	57.3	65.1	58.1	60.5
1966	48.6	50.0	48.7	47.3
1968	52.6	52.7	——	——
1970	55.4	52.7	54.4	50.0
After Reapportionment II				
1972	51.1	55.4	——	——
1974	54.9	60.0	60.1	63.2
1976	55.7	61.8	——	——
1978	57.6	64.5	56.9	63.2
1980	52.6	59.1	——	——
After Reapportionment III				
1982	58.2	58.1	57.7	52.6
1984	47.9	50.9	——	——
1986	55.2	58.2	54.7	47.4
1988	51.2	55.5	——	——

Note: The house was restructured by Article IV, Section 3 of the 1963 constitution from 86 districts with 100 members to 110 single-member districts. The senate was enlarged by Article IV, Section 2 of the 1963 constitution from 32 to 38 single-member districts. At the same time, the senators were given four-year terms, concurrent with the governor's term.

Source: Calculated from *Official Canvass of Votes,* published biennially by the Michigan Department of Management and Budget (formerly the Department of Administration).

them. Noncompetitive and landslide districts, for both parties, were found throughout the state, making legislators organize in their home districts around Michigan's regional geopolitical peculiarities and interests. They did what was necessary to win locally.

It is precisely these safely organized districts in a competitive party state, combined with an equally strong interest-group politics, that facilitate legislative pursuit of personal aspirations. No matter how professionally organized the legislature, each district is unique. A legislator struggles to serve both professional and district interests acceptably in Lansing, but attention

Table 9: Degree of General Election Competitiveness in Michigan Legislative Districts

	Number of Races in House Districts			Number of Races in Senate Districts		
Year	Competitive Races (<61% victory range)	Noncompetitive Races (61% to 70% victory range)	Landslide Races (>70% victory range)	Competitive Races (<61% victory range)	Noncompetitive Races (61% to 70% victory range)	Landslide Races (>70% victory range)
1950	32	29	41	12	16	4
1980	21	37	52	—	—	—
1982	39	25	46	16	13	9
1984	35	25	50	—	—	—
1986	20	42	48	13	13	12
1988	17	42	51	—	—	—
1990	24	36	50	13	14	11

Source: Michigan Bureau of Elections.

to a statewide agenda is far from a priority for most. Hence, legislators depend on their caucus leaders to carry the statewide agenda. Their leaders, in turn, burdened by declining discipline and strong committees, depend on the governor. Under such conditions, professionalization of this complex legislature is not a prescription for good government. Rather, being a professional legislator, at least in Michigan, means being more informed and better equipped to deal personally with divergent expectations: "At home I have one set of expectations from a very pro-business district, but I was elected because a very different group of close friends kept supporting me. In Lansing, though, there are about four interest groups that I need to work with who are irrelevant to either the business interests or my friends in the district. All this needs to be juggled; no, make that handled professionally." That type of juggling meant that when the Michigan house was divided 55–55 for each party after the 1992 elections, leadership elections were very uncertain. Many members were likely to behave as free agents and bolt the party. Only hard work by Democrats prevented Republicans from making gains in that fashion.

LEGISLATORS, THE LEGISLATURE, AND PROFESSIONAL CAPABILITIES

It should be clear that legislative rules, including some important informal norms, evolved within a house and senate whose members increasingly faced many tasks and no clear set of expectations about whom they should serve. This is disconcerting to those who felt that professionalizing the legislature would create more statewide commitment and interest.

Ramifications of Reform

No one should have expected, though, that adding professional features to the legislature would negate representative ties to the constituents and groups that sent legislators to Lansing. The most that many realistic reformers, such as Michigan's own state legislative expert, Charles Press, hoped for was something far more simple: effective evaluation and democratic review of proposals from other branches of government and the private sector.[33] The simplicity of the reformers' hope was rooted in what they saw as the need for greater legislative insight and a break from traditional values. They wanted timeliness in state government, with legislators freed from the traditional values of small-town Michigan.[34] They wanted relief from legislators such as Russell Strange (R-Mt. Pleasant), who delighted constituents with his belief that he was in Lansing for one thing: to teach people in the 1960s how important it was to return to small-town values and a World War II work ethic. Reformers believed that legislators should be active and informed members of communities as diverse as the character of the state, with small-town legislators just another minority.

Reformers appear to have gotten much of what they wished for, especially in attracting capable and ambitious candidates who appreciate politics. There are minimal requirements for service, and barely eligible legislators have gone on to distinguish themselves in office. A legislator must be twenty-one years old and an elector in the district that he or she represents. John Engler was elected just after graduation from Michigan State University in 1970. He and a roommate ran his first house campaign against Strange while the future governor wrote the electoral analysis as a senior paper. Engler then beat each incumbent whom he faced in subsequent elections.

A handful of legislators have found residency no more of a problem after each reapportionment, moving across new district lines to stay eligible. Unless thrown in with another incumbent, most are returned to office. Senator Jack Faxon (D-Farmington Hills), one of the state's most active lawmakers, joked that he had to move five times over the years to stay in office. What each youthful legislator and each redistricted incumbent have shown is precisely what reformers who advocated professionalism sought, the resilience and the capacity to learn and become known, both in a new electoral setting and in the legislature. Michigan's legislators think of themselves as active politicians, and all have belonged to an array of community, religious, fraternal, occupational, and partisan organizations.[35] These people are joiners; in their groups, they are leaders. These are no longer the reluctant legislators or the spectators once criticized by political scientists. "That does not mean that this legislature is without our share of the inattentive when it comes to policy and projects. It *does mean* that there is not a single legislator here who is not trying hard to stay."[36] Contemporary members are mostly self-starters who are readily adaptable. As one senator with several new counties observed of her reapportionment challenge in 1992: "They've made a pencil lady out of me! Go from place to place, can in hand. I'll really have to be out working these new areas to get to know the people and their problems." She, however, was not at all doubtful of her reelection. Joanne G. Emmons had already demonstrated the ability to undertake numerous legislative initiatives important to her constituents.

Salaries, designed not to discourage hardworking officeholders, have become important incentives in purging the spectators, not just in inspiring people to seek office but in motivating legislators to gain recognition from the leadership. So, too, do other benefits and office perks. Salaries range from $45,450 to $68,450, depending on leadership status; pension benefits increase with time in service; major leaders have electoral funds to help loyal lawmakers; and established legislators have ample opportunity to develop reputations that often move careers forward to Congress or to lucrative private-sector jobs.[37] In 1992, thirteen of eighteen Michigan members of Congress came from the legislature. Three of the five newly elected after reapportionment had state legislative experience. Consequently, most legislators fight to stay in office until they find a better political or professional alternative. A total of forty-one, or 9 percent, voluntarily left office to seek other positions in the 1986, 1988, and 1990 elections; only twenty incumbents were defeated for reelection. Six of these were changes repeated from the same districts in 1986 and 1988, in the same three southeast suburban house districts in which movements against Blanchard-led tax increases were most severe. With that type of volatility on a single issue, legislators have every reason to be cautious about how their Lansing activities play back home.

Legislative reforms appear to have produced an eclectic field of candidates and legislators from across the state who reflect their constituents' values. Given district homogeneity in a very heterogenous state, fewer than eighteen districts could elect any one of several sorts of people to office. Michigan has its districts where the next legislators will be a Dutch protestant, a Roman Catholic, a Christian fundamentalist, a WASP liberal, a white professional, a labor leader, an African American, a farmer or rural businessperson, or a specific person having any other of several characteristics that define who lives in those places. This means that minorities are well represented, at least when they dominate a district. In 1991–92, nine African Americans served in the house and three in the senate, somewhat less than the proportion of African Americans in the state. Responsiveness to district and region under these conditions is unavoidable.

Reforms also led to legislators with professional backgrounds in private life. Legislators of pre-reapportionment days were four times as likely to be involved in what Jack R. Van Der Slik called "archaic" pursuits.[38] They also were older then, often owners of small businesses or retirees. Modern legislators are metropolitan, experienced with large organizations, well-educated, and involved in social action. More than three-quarters of legislators have bachelors' degrees; 40 percent have advanced degrees, with only one-third of those in law. The average age has declined to the mid-forties, even though house members have averaged just over ten years in office, and senators – who tend to come from the house – have averaged nearly that long in the upper chamber. While most rely on their state salary, about 20 percent of legislators of the 1980s earned some regular income from jobs held prior to their election as full-time lawmakers.

Citizens want legislators with whom they feel comfortable. They want the person to typify the district but be a bit more qualified than ordinary voters. The good side/bad side of that expectation can be seen in the treatment of women. Women have not fared nearly as well as African Americans. Both Democratic and Republican female legislators maintain that a woman must be clearly better than male contenders to develop a favorable image before district voters. The first woman was elected in the 1920s. The 1993–94 sessions included only twenty-eight women in the house and three in the senate. "Competition for seats is fierce. In a professional environment, you create a situation where many want to be there. And voters are not that responsive [to women]," explained one woman legislator. Another noted that "women incumbents are often targeted as the easiest to defeat." Indeed, of the twenty defeated incumbents from 1986 to 1990, four were women.

Women also face other problems in the legislature. Although they come from both parties and represent a broad spectrum of beliefs, women legislators have coalesced around issues related to children and family problems. "This is a vacuum," explained one. "Men ignore it. If we don't accept this leadership, those vital issues are ignored." These legislators, however, seldom espouse feminist issues. Nor are the efforts of female legislators as strident as those of African-American legislators, who often use their more secure seats to combat racism. "Were any of us to do that," said one, "a woman would first lose the ear of fellow legislators and then lose her seat in the next election. State government is organized to deal with black minority politics, but not women majority politics."

The one woman who has most violated this rule has been Senator Lana Pollack (D-Ann Arbor). For her assertive efforts, she was rated by colleagues and other capitol regulars as one of the ten worst legislators in 1992 – a decided fall from her 1988 ranking of 35th of 147 members.[39] In contrast, Michelle McManus (R-Traverse City) came to the legislature with no intention of being slotted as either a women's or a new generation legislator. A lobbyist noted: "She told me in explicit terms that she was there to represent her whole district. That was it!" McManus told the lobbyist, "Look at me as a farmer."

Staffing

The other professional change in the legislature has been staffing. "Staff are truly legislative people," noted one senator. Until recently, they were not even present. In 1959, the house of representatives added its first professional staff member, Richard Miller, to serve individual members and, more frequently, the leadership. Miller and the lone staffer in the senate, Walter DeVries, were left, as one said, "in charge." Both were high-profile participants, seen widely as agents of the Speaker and majority leader in maintaining political order.

The highly praised Legislative Fiscal Agency and the Legislative Service Bureau had but a half-dozen or fewer professional staff until 1965. Only a pool of five house secretaries assisted all house members when Miller came on board. These, however, provided very impersonal service. When a staffing plan later brought five professionals to the majority caucus and set a goal of one secretary for every two to three representatives, "there was widespread fear that lots of Dick Millers would be wandering around," explained an observer of that era, "giving every good political reason why a thing could or couldn't be done. People wanted to keep the circle of players small."

By 1993, an estimated 1,025 full-time professional and clerical personnel were employed by the legislature.[40] That number reflected a decline since 1990, largely in unfilled positions that could be reinstated. Budget cuts also caused a drop from what may have been as many as 1,500 employees. Not unexpectedly, given the diversity of regions and members as well as the legislature's many leaders and tasks, numerous types of staff are designated to meet various needs. All legislators now have personal staff who serve at will in performing office work and communicating with both constituents and Lansing's many policy participants. Most legislators look for individuals who can handle the most demanding, as opposed to the most routine, responsibilities, oftentimes for clerical jobs. As such, well-educated secretaries often supplement the varying number of legislative aides in each office. Approximately 55 to 60 percent of all legislative employees work in the offices of individual members, either because of normal assignment or because of additional allocation through leadership and committee positions.

Personal staffs are viewed as loyalists, but equally important, many are hired because they know the legislature and how to find solutions. Accordingly, they often cycle from one office to another, and only a small number of aides are brought in from the home district. Knowing the constituents is not enough to deal with their complaints. For example, in the early 1990s, a senator's staff spent much of their time finding a way to clean up an abandoned cement factory so it could be converted to a resort. Development, environmental, and facility construction problems sent the staff searching for answers throughout state government. By managing caucus contacts, doing fundraising, and advising on floor votes, staff serve as adjuncts to the legislators.

Legislative advice, however, is a responsibility shared with committee staff, in large part because personal office staff lack policy experience. But use of committee staff presents problems, especially in improving the quality of advice. Unlike the U.S. Congress, Michigan legislative committees rarely have their own designated staff. They draw talent often on an ad hoc basis from two sources. Assistance comes from personal office employees who are assigned committee responsibilities, usually bringing their inexperience and lack of expertise with them. Because a legislator's staff grows with added leadership and committee responsibilities, this arrangement makes it easier to control staff and ensure that district concerns are dealt with. "These kids have a limited range of interest in lawmaking," observed one veteran committee staffer, "they usually just know whom the legislator likes to listen to and stroke."

The remainder of committee staff, chosen even more for analytical expertise than legislator loyalty, comes on assignment from the three independent staff offices that serve both houses. They are a valuable counterweight to interest-group or district parochialism. These staffers come from the House Bill Analysis Section, its senate counterpart, and the Legislative Service Bureau. Bill Analysis identifies the legislative intent of each bill, charts its legislative history, tracks those who support and oppose the bill, explains fiscal implications, and often shows the potential fallout of a bill's passage or failure. In the senate, the bill analysis office was folded into the Fiscal Agency in the mid-1980s. But that unit still performs much of the same background work as the House Bill Analysis Section. In the case of the northwestern cement factory/development project, bill analysis staff helped convert the local problem into an expanded idea to create special bonding and shield local governments from financial liability on all 300-or-more-acre site developments.

The Legislative Service Bureau drafts legislation, contributes to legislative history, and seeks to avoid loose ends or unintended consequences. Its staff did much of the work in drafting the development/shield plan mentioned above. In addition to in-state research, the bureau exchanges information on similar bills with other states. On the development/shield plan, bureau staff modeled their draft after legislation in Colorado, California, and Florida. Employees of all three offices respond to political and regional inquiries as well as technical ones: "Otherwise we have no rapport with legislators."

Like the third independent staff agency that serves both houses, the civil-service–staffed auditor general office that follows committee meetings and exercises much of the legislature's limited technical oversight of programs, the House Bill Analysis Section, and the Legislative Service Bureau operate as nonpartisan units. Legislative protocol accepts that status, on the basis of past experience only. That understanding about nonpartisanship and the former service role for both houses separates these three staff units from the house and senate fiscal agencies.

The original joint Legislative Fiscal Agency divided as the chambers came under split partisan control. After that, the two fiscal agencies were under considerable pressure to serve both party and committee leaders. This led to a lack of oversight in the house, although this was not the only problem troubling these agencies. Agency projections frequently reflect economic assumptions that serve leadership and committee chair interests. Nonetheless, the fiscal agencies maintain reputations for having the most proficient staff in the legislature. They are financial experts who project state revenues, and they also specialize in specific subjects, such as transportation and mental health, as they forecast program costs. These tasks make them indispensable to the committees and to appropriations subcommittees. Ironically, just as fiscal agency assumptions about the imprecise art of projecting revenues make them vulnerable to pressure from their bosses, the technical responsibility and skills it entails also free these analysts from extreme partisan behavior. This middle ground gives fiscal agency staff considerable status in all policy discussions and on any bill that implies budget costs. That importance led most legislators to address the house scandal by requesting that the two fiscal agencies again be brought under joint leadership control. The desire was to get expert staff quickly back in business and to prosecute malfeasants.

Overt party service is found in another component of legislative staffing. There are four issue-oriented legislative offices, each controlled by the caucus leadership. Each party in each house maintains its own caucus staff for a wide variety of services. Their strength is found in the weakness and limits of the other personal and technical staffs. Caucus employees – divided into policy and legislative counsel units – do much of the staff work on issue background and analysis, sending information to all legislative offices. They also identify goals, redraft bills, attack the legislation of the other party or house, and provide detailed briefs on policy problems. These staffs are also intended to provide a statewide balance to regional concerns, but this is often lost in the need to respond to individual legislators' requests and the limited capacity of the leadership to supervise details of staff work.

Other caucus units operating under different budgets do media and campaign work that enhances constituent communication through newsletters and radio and television messages. Media assistance, as opposed to the direct handling of constituent complaints, is intended to send a carefully constructed image of the legislator back to the home district. Much of this material is picked up directly by local media. This emphasis again reinforces regional concerns in the ongoing tug-of-war with statewide problems.

While staff often handle legislative specifics for many members, they seldom dominate the office agenda.[41] Moreover, they do little to speed the process, identify problems ahead of other observers, resolve disagreements over legislative content, or create a statewide focus on issues. Such tasks are beyond their assignments and capabilities. Despite all their work on the cement plant/development project, for example, the staff could hardly be blamed for its eventual economic collapse. Like the professionalization of legislators themselves, staff only let legislators know more about the problems of governing an extraordinarily complex state. "Collectively, they tell me what I already know, but in more perplexing and scarier terms."

SOME CLOSING THOUGHTS

The Michigan legislature has changed far more than the governorship during the last forty years. When "Soapy" Williams was governor, a conservative rural minority was still able to elect a conservative Republican legislature. But small-town, rural values died not just because legislative districts changed, but also because many districts evolved into something new. The decline and regional concentration of agriculture, the rise of tourist meccas, the continued isolation of the UP, the economic growth of West Michigan, the exodus of whites from Detroit, suburbanization, and many other factors furthered a regional geopolitics that played itself out in the legislature. Regionalism had no better political forum. As a result, legislators could not for long be disciplined by the partisan expectations of the 1950s or by the dictates of organization and knowledge. As legislators learn, what works well for one part of Michigan does not work the same for other places.

The professionalization of the legislature cannot change that simple fate of regional disparity. Professionalism can only make for better informed choices about the few things that the legislature can do, brokered around the ongoing partisan splits in state government. Most modern legislators are more capable, more proficient, more representative, better informed, and – yes – more timely in their values than those of any other era. Moreover, they come to the legislature only rarely as strident ideologists.[42] Still, achieving consensus and agreement is not premised on being well-intentioned. The processes and demands faced by legislators do not lend themselves to easy decisions, even if social and economic problems mandate quick and dramatic action. What will be fascinating is seeing how decision making changes when term limits take effect. In 1999, the new Speaker of the house will have less than six years service, and in 2003, the senate majority leader will have less than eight. Will the less-experienced legislature be less cautious or more ponderous? Certainly, the governor will still be looked to for leadership.

CHAPTER SIX

The Bureaucracy: An Ambiguous Political Legacy

Richard Elling and Peter Kobrak are also authors of this chapter

MIXED VIEWS OF ADMINISTRATION

Any discussion of the governor and legislature would be incomplete without reference to state executive agencies. Within the tug of war between the governor and legislature, state administrators are essential political participants. They have considerable policy expertise, and despite conflicting views of whom they should represent, administrators tend to see the state as a whole. Jeff McAlvey, the legislative liaison to Governor John Engler, summarized state administrative politics well: "The biggest surprise we faced when moving to the governor's office from that of the senate majority leader was in working with the bureaucracy. We now had to recommend programs that could be effectively implemented, and we needed state agency assistance on that. We were surprised at how many really good people were over there, after years of not really working directly with them."[1] McAlvey's comments reveal much about the professionally anonymous involvement of most state administrators in state politics. As a twenty-year veteran of the legislature remarked in discussing limited agency oversight, "We do not really work with administrators over here. Actually, legislators talk to them in committee hearings to set the ground rules, and staff yell at them over the phone to keep their attention. Then we just depend on them to go on about their business, mostly with the governor's blessing."

This relative isolation – from more than just the legislature – usually leaves Michiganians judging the bureaucracy on the basis of limited contacts and minimal information. Not surprisingly, those one-sided judgments are often harsh and politically self-serving.

One of the most frequently heard critiques is represented by the outstate wilderness view. To many residents of rural outstate communities, the Department of Natural Resources (DNR) is a suspect agency. Many have resented DNR officers who, seeking to ensure proper licensure and practices, have interrupted citizens pursuing fish and game. But the major source of the suspicion has less direct origins. Local opinion leaders, who are often small businesspersons with a stake in natural resource programs, cause much of the discontent because of basic disagreements over program operations. They use the media to portray DNR officers as villainous bureaucrats who cave in to far-off political pressures. This type of criticism, as an agency official noted, "feeds on itself," transforming local suspicions into statewide controversies and often more general challenges to administrative credibility. In one instance, "Damn the DNR" was the well-received title of a lead article by one of Michigan's best-known outdoor writers which appeared in the state's major fishing publication.[2] It was soon posted on many tackle-shop walls in northern Michigan.

The grass-roots political activist's view is another narrowly critical interpretation. Such individuals, usually dedicated to quite specific causes and demanding immediate action, paint pictures of bureaucratic ineptness. They complain about entrenched bureaucrats who use mountains of paperwork, as well as their personal command over programs and legal language, for their own purposes. Veteran lobbyists present another view. They often see administrators as potential interlopers into the lobbyist's stake in policymaking. "Michigan bureaucrats," as one trade association representative stated, "are at once well-schooled, politically naive, and capable of a kind of vindictiveness that will lay you low if you don't protect yourself well when you get in their way."

Such complaints come from seeing but a single part of an agency's work: the careful bureaucratic attention to what the activist wanted done right then or the defense of agency regulations that were objectionable to the lobbyist. A Detroit physician who lobbied public health officials in Lansing spoke more positively but in the same manner about officials who were "incredibly professional, real helping hands in working with the legislature . . . but they fail to warm to offers of friendship."[3]

Indeed, agency officials do not form many friendly, high-contact relationships. The moralistic traditions of the state have provided one important reason, a stringent code of ethics that has been taking shape since 1963.[4] Unlike legislators, agency officials cannot accept lunches with those who lobby them or spend the night at group expense at professional meeting sites where they might make a presentation. Nor are the officials permitted to earn extra income by lecturing or providing information related to their work. With no incentives for cooperation, and wary of suspicions cast on agency personnel who do socialize with clients and lobbyists, Michigan officials act cautiously in their political relationships.

The professional anonymity and sense of distance are rarely breached, but ethics is not the sole reason. Another part of the answer is professional attitude, and a third is the administrator's tenuous political position. In response to the posting of the critical DNR article, one agency officer said, "It does no good to explain official actions in those cases. They just see local results. Just stand there and glare in their face and go about your business." Public relations efforts, in the face of such attitudes, are rare. Beyond that, agency officials understand that they are often expected to take the political heat when elected officials face a controversy. One legislator suggested that "it's much easier to lay blame on bureaucratic ineptness than to explain that a program won't work for everybody or that the legislature – my party – screwed up. They better be willing to take it."

One reason that both reinforces this low visibility and causes the mixed assessments of state administrators has to do with the competing political expectations that surround them. Are they to be judged by how well they represent parts of the state? Or how well they stay out of battles between those parts? Or how well they do the governor's bidding as the state leader? These are not as pronounced at work in all states. As Herbert Kaufman noted, U.S. bureaucracies have been at different times "organized and operated in pursuit of three values" – representativeness, neutral competence, and executive leadership. Kaufman viewed each of these as dominant in different periods of history. "The shift from one to another," he said, "generally appears to have occurred as a consequence of the difficulties encountered in the period preceding the change."[5]

Michigan, however, has broken that sequenced pattern. Beginning at least by the 1970s, state administrators were pressured by changing political conditions to adjust concurrently to each of Kaufman's three values. Despite the competing goals inherent in these values, Michigan's administration attempted to accommodate all three. Today, administering Michigan is best understood in terms of unresolvable tensions reflecting (1) the diverse views of the state's fragmented economy and society, (2) its professional standards of public service as opposed to regional or special-interest service, and (3) the politically charged agenda of its governor in clashes with the legislature.

On one level, Michigan administrators are given a great deal of autonomy by public expectations and a modern constitution that emphasizes both bureaucratic neutrality and political independence. On another level, bureaucrats are so heavily depended on as policy advisers and policy implementers that their actions are repeatedly reviewed and checked. Their critical policy role in recommending and pursuing change makes it unlikely that governors, as McAlvey suggested, can succeed without attempting to exercise administrative leadership. In addition, representativeness becomes important because both clients and legislators, for parochial and individualistic reasons, want officials who reflect more than just the goals of economy and efficiency in their judgments. No wonder, as a relatively new state agency director said, "people just ducked their heads here when I asked them what we do." What he and others found are generally competent employees, with many responsibilities, facing both high and low expectations, who have a hard time defining their political purpose.

SHAPING MICHIGAN'S BUREAUCRACY

What has emerged is not the nation's largest or most independent bureaucracy, but it can seem huge. In 1847 only one wagon was needed to move the state's records from Detroit to the new capitol in Lansing.[6] That wagon could not even have carried the noncomputerized personnel folders of the 27,609 persons state government employed in 1955, nor certainly those of the 70,000 employed in 1979. By 1988 the number had dropped to 60,000 because of hiring freezes and layoffs. Numbers after that surged to over 65,000 in 1990 (see table 10 for a breakdown of state employees by department). By late 1992, numbers fell, through budget cuts and privatization, to just over 59,000 and shrinking. The ratio of state employees to population in the mid-1980s was about 171 per 10,000, a figure less than thirty-five other states, and one that has been steadily declining.[7] In that sense, particularly in the employment of lower-level and service employees, this is one area where modern Michigan has not been driven by its tendencies to excess.

The cost of compensating these employees, however, has not fallen during recent layoffs. In 1985–86, the classified service payroll totaled $2.2 billion, or 80 percent more than the 1979–80 pre-recession payroll.[8] By 1990–91, it was nearly $3 billion. Inflation, of course, accounted for some of this increase. It also reflected a growing commitment to employing a special mix of skilled personnel. Managerial, professional, and technical employees now constitute about 45 percent of the state work force. Salaries account for just under 20 percent of state appropriated general funds.[9] Those employment standards and rewards define the way in which state administration is

Table 10: Number of Employees and Gross Expenditures for Michigan Executive Departments, Fiscal Years 1981–82 and 1991–92

Department	Average Number of Employees		Annual Budget (including federal funds)	
	1981–82	1991–92	1981–82	1991–92
Agriculture	565	525	$31,038,000	$52,930,000
Civil Rights	234	185	9,036,000	12,594,000
Civil Service	458	307	12,147,000	22,698,000
Commerce	1,912	2,475	670,254,000	186,368,000
Corrections	5,673	13,437	218,666,000	893,727,000
Education	2,168	1,949	358,231,000	630,000,000
Labor (MESC)	5,455	3,556	269,921,000	455,137,000
Licensing and Regulation	388	0	14,687,000	———
Management and Budget*	1,377	1,270	135,676,000	1,527,285,000
Mental Health	12,072	7,398	810,791,000	1,308,564,000
Military Affairs	308	829	131,596,000	61,800,000
Natural Resources	3,160	3,616	133,311,000	380,144,000
Public Health	1,823	1,373	189,881,000	421,705,000
Social Services	14,545	13,208	3,277,700,000	5,823,455,000
State Police	2,280	2,219	131,596,000	252,045,000
Transportation	4,250	3,843	670,254	2,309,119
Treasury	4,250	3,708	84,499,000	1,218,591,000
Total	60,918	59,898	6,479,700,254	13,249,352,119

*Includes business services for budgets.

Source: Michigan Department of Management and Budget.

professionalized or skilled, rather than dominated by either political or clerical workers.

A comparison of executive departments over ten fiscal years, 1981–91, provides other insights. While the general trend for departments is fewer employees, there are exceptions. The 1980s saw massive growth, 237 percent, in Department of Corrections staff. The Department of Commerce and the Department of Natural Resources grew by about 500 employees each. These changes reflected the sudden increase in Michigan's prisons and the rise of environmental regulation. The other large increase, for the commerce department, is explained by its merger with the Department of Licensing and Regulation. These increases all reflect major policy shifts. So, too, do the severe cuts in the number of employees in the Department of Mental Health. These trends indicate two things about state agencies. First, they seem relatively immune to protection by important state interests since most cuts are nearly equal. Second, management offices, such as the Departments of Treasury and Civil Service, gain little protection over service departments. The governor's reliance on such departments has not spared them from downsizing. Annual budget data show about the same things.

Professionalism is also evident in the type of programmatic leadership assumed, under political pressure, by agencies over the years. Growth has been greatest among policy specialists rather than administrative generalists. When Governor G. Mennen Williams and United Auto Workers President Walter P. Reuther sought to make the state a "laboratory for social democracy," specialists were needed for such programs as compulsory health insurance, public recreation, and training for the unemployed.[10] Governors Romney and Milliken later supported the building of a higher education system generally ranked second only to California's. Its basis for growth was its specialized employees. The Department of Natural Resources was among the first in the country to shed its conservation emphasis and expand into environmental regulation. More recently, the DNR set precedents by its concern with the entire ecosystem. Both emphases entailed continuing specialization. Governor James Blanchard, facing an ongoing downsizing of the auto industry, emphasized competently administered economic development and employment programs. When cuts were made under Blanchard and Engler, reductions were made among lower-level employees rather than the professional ranks. Some issue specialists with years of tenure found themselves occupying, with pay cuts, college-trainee positions.

Despite this professional emphasis, Michigan's administrative structure is more the result of responses to past problems than the product of a visionary plan. It is, in no small part, the culmination of a series of partially overturned constitutional precedents as well. For example, competitive salaries came early. Indeed, few citizens, however skeptical of executive power, have wanted the state constitution to restrict competent hirings by setting state official salaries, as was true before 1950.[11] Also, in principle at least, many citizens recognized the problems posed by administrative fragmentation. Thus, there was little support for status quo administration when George Romney attacked it in 1962. Little justification could be made for a state bureaucracy consisting of 148 separate units; hence, it became a target for constitutional change.

Professionalism was slow in coming, though, largely because of battles over whether professionalism or amateur government best matched the state's traditions. A slight nod was always given to the former, but only in hiring a cadre of skilled workers. Organization, in contrast, was often left unwieldy. During the early 1920s, for instance, Governor Alex Groesbeck merged or abolished forty-seven authorities. He also created an administrative board with the governor and six elected department heads as members.[12] This plural executive had broad powers to set administrative policy for all agencies. Ungainly as it was, the board worked reasonably well when all members were Republicans, but it deadlocked when several Democrats were elected to statewide office.

In the 1930s, Republican Governor Frank D. Fitzgerald and Democratic Governor Frank Murphy sought to eliminate the administrative board and replace other boards and commissions with gubernatorial control. Many legislators objected because they felt that the governor would have too much power over state administration.[13] In 1948, as a counterbalance to the entrenched board, the legislature reluctantly created a Department of Administration.[14] It had responsibility for preparing and supervising the state budget and establishing systems for uniform accounting, centralized purchasing, and facilities management. The state administrative board, however, still had power to review and approve many of the department's decisions, although it relinquished some functions to the department. The Department of Administration had the capability to serve as the governor's management arm. However, during the 1950s, opposing parties controlled the governorship, legislature, and elected state offices. With this divided leadership, the progressive department and tradition-bound administrative board found themselves at loggerheads.[15]

The sheer number of agencies worsened this conflict in ways not found in many other modern administrative states. Three models of administrative organization developed by the U.S. Advisory Commission on Intergovernmental Relations are helpful in comparing Michigan's brand of professionalism-tinged-with-amateurism to other states.[16] Despite its reforms, Michigan still follows the *traditional* model, which has seventeen or more agencies and a low degree of functional consolidation of agencies. The *cabinet* model creates nine to sixteen agencies and has moderate functional consolidation. The *secretary-coordinator* model has eight or fewer agencies and high consolidation into large, multiple-function or broad single-function agencies. Given Michigan's historical ambivalence toward unchecked gubernatorial powers and direct intervention, it is not surprising that Michigan stayed with the traditional model of administrative reorganization.

The constitutional convention of 1963 restructured state government, but still left Michigan with a traditional administration. It limited the executive branch to no more than twenty departments and reduced the plural executive, establishing only the governor, lieutenant governor, secretary of state, and attorney general as statewide elected officers. For the first time, the constitution declared that "executive power is vested in the governor." It strengthened the governor's office with new powers to make appointments and reorganize the agencies.

But this was a victory for two competing principles, an action that set an example for continuing traditionalism in much of the state's public sector. The new constitution also emphasized what Kaufman called "representativeness" as a core administrative value by keeping numerous powers in the hands of particular agencies as well as the legislature and the public. The previously elected auditor general became a legislative appointee. Formerly elected directors of highways and education became appointees of the Highway Commission and State Board of Education. Several departments gained commissions appointed by the governor, but with staggered terms that limited gubernatorial control.

The provision to limit the executive branch to twenty principal departments is somewhat misleading in overstating the extent of actual consolidation. Several agencies were merely incorporated into their departments for administrative purposes. They retained independent policymaking authority and autonomy, going on their own to the legislature for review. There remained great resistance to change, and the ongoing lack of systematic legislative oversight has been a factor. In fact, over the years, only one state agency has been abolished. The State Board of Mortuary Science, which had little clientele support, accepted its demise with rare grace: "Apparently we are engaged in a hopeless struggle to maintain identity as a separate board. We who are about to die, salute you."[17] Other agencies found proponents who, despite Romney's leadership, rallied the legislature against change.

Concerns about coordination and control in the executive branch today focus largely on goals of more efficient and effective administration. For example, computers were adopted quickly. In addition, both Governors Blanchard and Engler reorganized several departments for improved reporting to the chief executive. Brazen partisan interference in administration and service provision, however, is dealt with quickly and quietly by cooperation between the governor and the legislature, as are various administrative improprieties. Consequently, most state officials and lobbyists take clean and modern government for granted. None of this, however, does much to reduce the legitimate demand for regional and interest-group influence and special treatment. The need to maintain balance within the governor's administration and party and within the legislature makes the goals of servicing regional and group interests incompatible with unrestrained professionalism. So, despite overtures on behalf of efficient state standards, bureaucrats who enforce them either too much or too little pay a price when they deal with issues of representation in service delivery.

Nonetheless, today's executive branch stands in sharp contrast to the dispersed and often personalized agency control that persisted before World War II. Partisan politics and personal agency freedoms often held sway, even in moralistic Michigan with its abhorrence of patronage. In the state's Southern Michigan Prison, for example, the warden sold privileges to prisoners and awarded captains and guards a share. For $25, old-timers claimed, a prisoner could buy a trip to a brothel in downtown Jackson. Business was brisk.[18] Prisons also did more upscale business. The 1945 murder of state senator Warren G. Hooper was allegedly done by prisoners, released for the hours necessary to commit the crime. Since that time, the prisons have been run centrally. The concern for balance today only attempts to give a state prison to every region that wants one. Many communities clamor for corrections department business.

There are, however, forces within the departments that help insulate state officials from some representative pressures. Michigan's civil service system, based on merit employment, is central to the administration's ability to resist regional and interest politics. Civil service sets the value of neutral competence, much like an anchor. Neutrality, in turn, limits direct political manipulation and keeps intact arrangements that assure staffing by those seen to be technically qualified. While Governors Fitzgerald and Murphy were largely unsuccessful in efforts to enhance executive leadership during the 1930s, they still furthered civil service goals by setting the issues in motion. Fitzgerald appointed a study commission; Murphy then capitalized on the findings by ramming a civil service bill through the reluctant legislature in 1937. Three years later, the voters approved a citizen initiative providing for civil service, thus bringing an end to a decade of gridlock over the issue.

The constitutional amendment established a Civil Service Commission with power to appoint, dismiss, and set the salaries for all but a few state employees. Elected officials, court employees, and those in education institutions were exempt. The four-member bipartisan Civil Service Commission now appoints the personnel director. The department is not vulnerable through the appropriations mechanism because the constitution assures appropriations of "not less than one percent of the aggregate payroll of the classified service." Michigan is the only state with such a guaranteed funding provision. But an even more important bulwark is strong citizen support for the civil service concept. A 1987 poll found 80 percent of Michigan citizens in favor of continuing the civil service system.[19] Small wonder, then, that there was little political support for the recommendation of the prestigious Hannah Commission of 1979 to create a department of personnel management separate from the Civil Service Commission and reporting directly to the governor.[20]

Still, even with strong public support, the state's civil service system confronts numerous challenges to its neutral competence. Many of these stem from its own virtues and successes, especially that of equal treatment of employees and prospective state hires. Many critics charge that the system treats employees too equally, especially in protecting senior officials. The most contested issue is performance pay, which is especially hard to sell in a state with strong unions. Insulating promotions from gubernatorial and legislative politics certainly tends to emphasize seniority over accomplishment. Yet proponents of civil service argue that employees are at least given considerable discretion and freedom from interference under present conditions. Nonetheless, at least one reform task force expressed disappointment over the failure to "reward employees with salary increases and possible promotion based upon performance rather than longevity."[21]

Even on this contentious issue, some progress has been made, eroding a degree of neutrality and bureaucratic anonymity. The Classified Executive Service (CES), while not a substitute for systemwide performance pay, does identify positions within civil service where career executives participate directly in the development and implementation of policy. Special attention is paid to those employees who must interact with elected politicians. Each appointment in the CES is made on a one-year probationary basis with careful review. Compensation is then based on predicted and actual performance, with performance standards agreed upon by both the civil servant and the agency's top management. Such discretionary authority over compensation represents a significant departure from past practices. By 1988, approximately 420 career employees had participated in the program, and legislators commented that these individuals came more frequently to the legislature for advice. Attitudes have since remained favorable: "I like the fact that administrators feel free enough from merit constraints to come to the legislature when they have problems. CES has been one of the few things I've seen that break the mold in agency behavior." In January 1994, these rules were modified to encompass a merit-based Senior Executive Service where gubernatorial controls are more possible, even in dismissing executives.

Collective bargaining is another development that detracts from some civil service principles and reinforces others. It also fragments Michigan's bureaucracy. Within eight years after its first authorization in 1980, more than three-fourths of the eligible state employees had both union representation and civil service protection. Approximately 41,000 of these employees are represented by unions that work together in coalition fashion to lobby for protections. To manage this new element, an Office of State Employer was established in the Department of Management and Budget. This office negotiates contracts with bargaining units and recommends wage rates and working conditions to the Civil Service Commission. Despite frequently expressed opinions by both proponents and opponents, no one has assessed the overall impact of collective bargaining on either executive leadership or merit system goals. The only agreement is that it further reduces flexibility in employee reassignments and reductions in force. Employees use both forms of protection in court.

Perhaps, as table 11 suggests, the combined impact is too protective. It is well understood that all actions that advance neutral competence limit a governor's power to appoint and remove administrative subordinates. This further strains official, although not yet public, support for civil service. Each department has but five "exempt" or unclassified positions. The total is 1,700, if members of various boards and commissions are included, but such members are only volunteers whose talents can be flexibly put to work on a part-time basis. Nonetheless, usually departments headed by their own commissions jealously guard their prerogatives both in employment and in seeking and using volunteers. Special interests such as the education community, utilities, hunting and fishing groups, and lawyers also support this balkanization of personnel functions. In doing so, of course, all claim to be standing guard to keep their regulators and policymakers "out of politics," which means out of the mainstream of gubernatorial or civil service control.[22]

The core value of representativeness again comes into play, however. It overcomes some of this rhetoric and also brings these organizations back, at least partially, to the primary flow of state politics. Yet it does so in an oddly unpredictable way, bringing issues of minority rights to all agencies as a central state concern and also playing into racial politics, which are also dispersed regionally. Representativeness has this dual effect because it stresses who will govern. In the nineteenth century, Jacksonians sought to enhance representativeness by electing administrators and commissions. Some proponents advocated patronage for "the common man" in order to assure a bureaucracy that reflected dominant public sentiments and demographic real-

Table 11: Impediments to Effective Management as Perceived by Administrators of Michigan Executive Departments

Impediments	Mean Severity of Impediment	Percentage Reporting Impediment
Civil service procedures for recruiting/selecting personnel	1.7	56
Insufficient appropriations	1.6	52
Legislative expansion of programs but no additional funds	1.4	46
Filling key vacancies/retaining key staff	1.4	45
Inadequately rewarding outstanding employees	1.4	45
Disciplining/dismissing incompetent employees	1.4	39
Process for promulgating rules/regulations	1.3	44
Organizational resistance to change	1.1	24
Paperwork and clearance requirements on decisions	1.1	22
Interest group opposition to agency problems	1.0	23
Assessing organizational performance or program impact	1.0	21
Ineffective organizational planning	0.9	25
Inadequate facilities	0.9	22
Collective bargaining by unit employees	0.9	21
Excessive restrictions on expenditures	0.9	18
Supervisors' lack of management skills	0.9	18
Insufficient time to make decisions	0.9	18

Note: Mean Severity of Impediment, where "not a problem" = 0, "minor problem" = 1, "serious problem" = 2, and "very serious problem" = 3. For entire set of problems, the number of respondents varies between 118 and 125 for each item. Percentage Reporting Impediment is percentage of Michigan administrators reporting a given impediment to be a "serious" or "very serious" problem.

Source: Data collected by Richard C. Elling.

ities. More recently, representativeness has been linked less with amateurism than with social equity. That is, minorities and women want to achieve reasonable parity in public employment.

The number of ranking African-American officials, for example, has increased during the terms of each modern governor through Blanchard. The racial composition of the classified civil service also suggests greater representativeness. In 1992, about 20 percent of the classified service were African Americans compared to 13.9 percent of the state's population. But Afri-

can Americans have been overrepresented in some departments, such as social services, labor, and mental health, where clients are disproportionately
minorities. They are underrepresented in units of the state police, natural resources, and attorney general. Fewer than 10 percent of employees in those
departments are minorities. African Americans hold far fewer top-level positions throughout state administration than do Caucasians.

Various salary grades may also be underrepresented in terms of gender.
Women of all races, except Asian, fell below their male ethnic counterparts
in average salaries. Forty percent of male workers, but only 14 percent of female workers, earned more than $30,000 in 1992. The Civil Service Com-
mission's own task force on comparable worth concluded that even "after
valid and reasonable explanations for pay differentials . . . pay disparities
remain." Findings such as these create coalitions of support between minorities and women. Coalition politics has generated calls for action by groups
that are certainly just in their claims; the action has little to do with neutral competence and often much to do with the state's regional and ethnic
divisions.

The Civil Service Commission, therefore, has been torn between historic
loyalties to the merit system and other values of administration, especially
diversity. The result is that even in hiring, the commission tries to do a little
of everything: gain neutral competence; allow special latitude to those who
can be effective policymakers; and still recruit, train, and promote minority
and female leaders in state administration.

The conflict over the values to be served by the bureaucracy is also reflected in debates about professional standards. This only reinforces the anx-
iety of administrators about whom they should serve and how they should
provide services. For example, Governor Engler found his administration
involved in a prolonged controversy. During the layoffs of the early 1990s,
when twenty-nine African-American administrators lost or were reassigned
from their senior positions, the dismissals were attributed to the governor's
lack of support for minorities. Representative Floyd Clack (D-Flint) kept the
issue alive as chair of the House Civil Service Committee, actively encouraging agency women and minorities to register complaints against the governor. The governor should not have been surprised. There are no easy answers to be found in following the rules of civil service. These rules can
hardly cover each of the competing dictates of Kaufman's three values. The
traditions of state government are too complex. Governor Engler discovered
a simple truth. No matter what gets done with state employees, political controversy accompanies each decision.

PERSPECTIVES ON ADMINISTRATIVE PERFORMANCE

One thing, though, is clear about administrative expectations. The defects in their virtues make state bureaucracies vulnerable to public criticism, especially in light of moralistic traditions of interventionist politics. But the relevance of these complaints is difficult to evaluate. Citizens and elected officials also expect public agencies to exhibit, apart from Kaufman's core values, two other competing standards: stability and adaptability. The exact meaning of these is necessarily unclear. Citizens and policymakers praise bureaucracies for consistency in public service provision but criticize them for resisting change. People also want bureaucrats to emphasize equal treatment for those with whom they deal; yet they complain about such treatment when it shades into treating everyone in an insensitive or abrupt manner.

Nonetheless, performance must be subject to some evaluation. In his pioneering 1976 effort to assess the quality of state administration, Lee Sigelman identified seven standards: efficiency, expertise, information-processing capacity, innovativeness, partisan neutrality, integrity, and representativeness.[23] His work provides some insight for comparing the performance of Michigan's bureaucracy with those of other states. At the time of Sigelman's analysis, Michigan's administrative quality compared favorably to other states. In terms of expertise – that is, professional training and salaries – Michigan ranked nineteenth and fourth, respectively, among the states. It ranked tenth and twentieth in terms of minority employment and minority advancement to higher positions as measures of representativeness. Its ranking for information processing, or the extent to which computers are used, was fifteenth. The Michigan bureaucracy ranked sixth in partisan neutrality as measured by the proportion of state employees covered by civil service.

Modern administrators see these indicators as still useful. All feel that state officials try harder to advance professionalism, diversity, and technology than do policymakers in other states. As one administrator noted, "That's what we see when we compare notes at professional meetings." Administrators feel that the state tries harder at salaries and technology but does less well at training: "Training cuts are always made first during recessions." This, they feel, is one factor that impedes growth in job performance and promotion: "But the bottom line is that our employees are always adequately trained, and those in many states are not." So, despite complaints, we have reasons to think well of Michigan agencies in terms of their capacity to integrate competing values.

Other research confirms that generally positive view. A 1980s study focused on assessing agency problems.[24] Through a mail survey, high-ranking public managers in Michigan and nine other states were asked to assess the severity of fifty-two conditions, circumstances, and practices that might exist in their state or administrative unit that could impede the "efficient and effective administration of the programmatic responsibilities" of their units.

Nearly two-thirds of Michigan administrators believed their units were "very successful" in achieving programmatic goals. The others said their units had been at least "somewhat successful." In Indiana just 45 percent, and 58 percent in South Dakota, reported this highest rate of success. New York, California, and Texas responses were 70 percent or more "very successful." Therefore, Michigan officials fell somewhere in the middle of the states relative to perceptions of doing their jobs well. Of course, few public managers were likely to report "less than successful" operations. Still, the fact that more than one-third of Michigan officials reported only partial success suggests that they believed their performance to be limited by some important factors.

Table 11 shows the relative severity of potential impediments to administrative performance in Michigan. Three basic points stand out. First, fewer than one in four managers saw several potential impediments as serious. A mean of 1.0 indicates a problem is "minor." Only about one-third were identified as being even this serious. No more than one in ten Michigan administrators saw roughly 40 percent of the obstacles as serious. Second, certain problems were severe. Foremost among these were inadequate human and fiscal resources. This reflects, no doubt, the severe cutbacks experienced in the early 1980s.

Third, Michigan administrators, in general, were not concerned with some of the key performance obstacles that public management scholars often see as important, including limited information, program coordination, monitoring and assessing subordinate performance, communications, span of control, complexity of administrative structure, and political intrusion by governors, legislators, or others. It should be noted that administrators from state to state were fairly consistent in their views about the severity of these problems. Often problems that managers across the ten states cited as being severe, nine were among the ten that Michiganians reported as serious.

Michigan managers generally voiced their strongest concerns over personnel matters, including recruiting and selecting personnel in the face of civil service, filling key vacancies and retaining staff, and dealing with incompetent staff. They also complained about collective bargaining impediments. These concerns were seen to be more severe in Michigan than in the other states of the survey. Thus, Michigan's protective personnel arrangements exact what is seen as a comparatively high price in lowering administrative effectiveness.

To judge that, we looked further at this factor. Collective bargaining complaints were strongly correlated with the severity of three related impediments: recruitment, staff control, and discipline. Even in Michigan, however, only one manager in five reported such problems as severe. So problems appear numerous but far from universal, which citizens themselves seem to understand and tolerate. A poll in 1987 reported that Michigan residents, by a margin of two to one, believed that collective bargaining by state employees is "a good thing for the state."[25]

Interestingly, given the state's political uncertainty and highly participative nature, Michigan administrators saw problems stemming from the involvement of outside actors as less severe than did their counterparts in other states. One reason stands out. Michigan public managers were least likely to complain about filling positions on a patronage basis. They did find some political favoritism, though. In particular, administrators suggested that some of their colleagues gain because they develop a close relationship with legislators or other partisan persons.

While more than one-fifth of Michigan's administrators cited inadequate office facilities as a problem, 40 percent saw this to be of no concern. Agencies, the data also show, may confront circumstances that cause one or another potential impediments to administrative performance to be especially severe. Problems relating to federal grant-in-aid programs are a good example. Some agencies cannot get that support, yet others prosper, a result that may reflect the uneven capacity of the Michigan congressional delegation to assist in these efforts.

However, because there are competing standards in judging any performance, some obstacles placed in the way of agency personnel will be especially subject to criticism. There will always be some things that administrators see as irrelevant, particularly political checks and balances. Contrary expectations create that view. Both citizens and elected officials want administrators to act expeditiously and with deference to their own wants, but not in an arbitrary fashion. So procedures to minimize arbitrariness, such as reviews of proposed actions by administrative superiors or legislative hearings, generate the much lamented red tape of bureaucratic lore. This restricts the ability of administrators to get on with their jobs promptly. Not surprisingly, with legislators' district concerns so important in Michigan, the problem of "paperwork and clearance requirements on decisions" emerged as one of the administrators' more serious impediments to what they see as effective management. Department heads and commissioners, so the complaints go, "spend too much time worrying about politics."

Similarly, many Michiganians desire the best of both worlds: lower taxes and increased services.[26] Elected officials respond by wanting to improve services and not raise taxes. Administrators unavoidably feel the pinch. "Insufficient appropriations" and "legislative expansion of program without commensurate increases in appropriations" ranked high as impediments.

Effective administration, as these comments indicate, has not been easy. Yet the agencies manage to cope despite some serious problems. The state's administrative performance appeared in the 1980s to be at least as good as, if not better than, that of the other survey states. Agency administrators in the 1990s believe that there has been little change in the past decade. Both Governors Blanchard and Engler are blamed for injecting somewhat more politics in administration. But that reflects differences in style from Governor Milliken, and it changes the overall picture of inefficiencies very little: "Things have been very constant, even with downsizing and fiscal stress." Legislators and governors intrude more, administrators agree, only because members of the public and their organized interests encourage it. In this case, it seems that Michiganians have competing and always high expectations about state government. These create both hard-to-meet expectations and political impediments to bureaucratic efficiency and effectiveness.

ADMINISTRATION, ACCOUNTABILITY, AND POLICYMAKING

Our earlier analysis of competing expectations confirms what Michigan's career public managers report — "outside meddling" can sometimes be a problem. Moreover, as partisanship has increased, "meddling" may have grown in the past decade. Such views of "meddling" indicate that agency personnel appreciate what we have observed in this and previous chapters, that numerous insiders and outsiders get involved in policy implementation. From the governor and legislators to interest groups and private citizens, political participants consider the conduct of state administration too important to leave solely to administrators. Indeed, nearly everyone in Michigan sometimes seems to be a player. Moreover, increased emphasis in recent years on the core values of executive leadership and representativeness come through in calls for bureaucratic accountability that do impose additional management burdens beyond civil service. In light of these competing

Table 12: Patterns of Influence as Perceived by Administrators of Michigan Executive Departments

	Impact					
	Determining Overall Budget Levels		*Determining Budgets For Specific Programs*		*Determining Major Program Changes*	
Source of Influence	*Mean Impact*	*"Great" Impact(%)*	*Mean Impact*	*"Great" Impact(%)*	*Mean Impact*	*"Great" Impact(%)*
Governor and staff	2.6	63	2.5	58	2.1	37
Legislature	3.2	86	3.1	71	2.7	48
State courts	1.1	11	0.7	6	1.5	21
Agency itself	2.8	66	2.8	74	3.1	80
Federal agencies/ Congress	1.6	26	1.5	23	1.6	27
Federal courts	0.8	7	0.7	6	1.0	13
State Budget Office	2.9	75	2.9	75	2.0	30
State Personnel Office	1.3	18	1.0	12	1.0	8
Other state agencies	1.0	3	0.9	3	1.0	5
Local governments	0.8	3	0.7	6	0.8	5
Professional associations	0.8	4	0.8	4	0.9	4
Agency clientele	1.3	11	1.2	13	1.6	23
State employee unions	1.2	12	1.1	12	1.0	5
Political parties	0.7	6	0.6	5	0.7	6
Media	1.0	9	0.9	9	1.0	7
Interest groups	1.4	11	1.4	17	1.6	18

Table 12 continued on next page.

values, two questions stand out: First, how prominent are state administrators in policymaking? Second, how extensive is the impact of "the meddlers" on policy administration? The research cited above provides interesting answers.

The technical expertise of career administrators, combined with their sustained attention to a narrow range of policy concerns, suggests that agency personnel should dominate service delivery or implementation. Respondents expressed near unanimity that "the agency itself" had a "great" or "very great" impact on day-to-day operations (see table 12). But the legislature, the governor, and the budget office – which is closely aligned with the governor – were seen to be at least periodically influential. So, too, were

Table 12 continued

Source of Influence	Impact					
	Determining Content of Rules		Establishing Daily Procedures		Establishing Daily Operations	
	Mean Impact	"Great" Impact(%)	Mean Impact	"Great" Impact(%)	Mean Impact	"Great" Impact(%)
Governor and staff	1.5	18	1.3	10	1.0	4
State Legislature	2.6	48	1.7	21	1.3	10
State courts	1.5	16	0.9	5	0.8	8
Agency itself	3.3	87	3.5	92	3.7	95
Federal agencies/ Congress	1.4	16	1.1	13	1.1	15
Federal courts	1.1	9	0.7	4	0.6	6
State Budget Office	0.9	8	1.3	19	1.4	23
State Personnel Office	0.7	8	1.5	18	1.4	19
Other state agencies	1.0	5	1.0	4	1.1	7
Local governments	0.8	7	0.7	4	0.9	7
Professional associations	1.1	11	0.7	3	0.9	7
Agency clientele	1.7	25	1.3	12	1.8	30
State employee unions	0.9	7	1.0	9	1.2	12
Political parties	0.5	3	0.5	3	0.4	3
Media	0.9	5	5.5	3	0.9	7
Interest groups	1.7	20	1.1	5	1.3	11

Note: Mean Impact is the average impact of a particular actor on a particular decision or activity area, where the response options were o = "no impact," 1 = "some impact," 2 = "moderate impact," 3 = "great impact," and 4 = "very great impact." The number of respondents ranged between 116 and 124 for each item. "Great" Impact is the percentage of Michigan administrators ascribing "great" or "very great" impact to a particular source of influence.

Source: Data collected by Richard C. Elling.

agency clientele – that is, the customers and beneficiaries. Even in the purest of administrative tasks, then, agencies were seldom seen as sovereign in their operations. In the 1990s, that seems more true, at least in the view of state administrators who reflected on the 1980s survey. As one concluded, "Political forces have been resurrected since the Milliken years, on all levels."

Administrators, by law and design, were also seen as having great influence in determining rules and regulations. Many legislative acts provide only broad statutory goals and objectives, thus leaving the bureaucracy with considerable discretion. The legislature, in effect, delegates to the bureaucracy lead authority to propose rules that give effect to statutes. But administrators did not see themselves as having sole authority in the regulatory process. The legislature was felt to be especially influential. Half the managers reported a great deal of legislative impact on administrative rule making. The warnings given by legislators in routine hearings did seem to be taken seriously. Legislative clout stems from the requirement for house and senate review of any proposed rules prior to final adoption. This gives legislators a final veto. By 1982, forty-one states had some form of legislative oversight of administrative rule making. But only Michigan requires *prior approval* of *all* new rules. Accordingly, no rule may take effect until it has been approved by the legislature's ten-member Joint Committee on Administrative Rules (JCAR).

JCAR approval is far from perfunctory or automatic. The approval vote has been about 75 percent, which demonstrates considerable intervention.[27] Approval rates also vary by department, further indicating that administrators are not all subject to the same level of oversight or controls. Fifty-seven percent of the rules proposed by the Departments of Public Health and Social Services were approved, while the Departments of Agriculture, Labor, and Natural Resources enjoyed approval rates of 80 percent. Moreover, these data do not reveal all there was about legislative intervention. Agencies frequently withdraw proposed rules that even one or two legislators find objectionable. Additional rules are routinely modified to address JCAR's concerns. "That's why we have the damned law," groused one legislator, "to change what they want."

There is a positive side to this intervention, however. Frequent involvement with legislators often places administrators in a better position than they otherwise would be. Contacts allow them to bring problems to the attention of elected officials or to point to deficiencies in policies. This involvement is important in a state where bureaucrats lack a reputation for aggressive pursuit of their most strongly held views. By being required to share their expertise in appropriate executive and legislative circles, agency officials influence developing programs.

Legislators claim that administrators frequently propose solutions that are incorporated into new policies: "This process literally wrings the ideas out of them." In this way, the technical expertise of administrators shapes legislative responses to policy questions even as agency officials hesitate in their public leadership. As our survey data indicated, Michigan public managers felt that they often had great impact in determining the substance of major policy or program changes affecting their units. Thus, while their administrative work was subject to interference, administrators did claim a policymaking position for themselves. Many saw their impact as being more important than that of the legislature or the governor. About one-third of the manager respondents said that they proposed half or more of the legislative actions affecting them. Just 14 percent said half or more of the proposals originated with the legislature. Only five percent saw half or more coming from the governor's office, although, as several administrators noted, the governor's leadership interests meant he usually took credit. This difference in responses indicates that policymaking takes on different forms of political interaction in different parts of state government, with some agencies drawing little attention and others being objects of sharp scrutiny.

Of course, the agencies were not always seen by their managers as getting their own way. Nearly half the administrators saw the legislature's role as very influential. Proposals may originate in administrative agencies, managers noted, but the legislature disposes. Moreover, legislators seek information from numerous other sources, such as lobbyists and legislative experts.[28] Changes in agency recommendations are extensive as a result.

Agency heads saw legislators as having greater influence than the governor. Regular contact appears to be the reason. In another survey of Michigan department heads, only 27 percent ranked the governor as the most influential actor affecting their policies.[29] Indeed, Michigan's governor ranked among the nation's fifteen weakest in total agency impact. One reason is that the governor appoints just 35 percent of the state's major administrative officials, a proportion lower than in all but eight other states. "What's happening here is clear," said one department head; "the governor negotiates an arrangement with us and then it is subject to all sorts of regional and district massaging over in the legislature."

Still the governor matters. The governor's public visibility, as well as the expectation of leadership, gives the governor an advantage in dealing with the legislature – but only when the governor chooses to take it. The pattern of serving several terms also influences the bureaucracy in developing a gubernatorial kinship. Regular cabinet and personal meetings reinforce this only with time, as department heads spread the message that the chief executive is truly watching this or that agency, but not others. If forced to choose between the governor and the legislature, administrators said they would follow the governor's preferences either all the time or most of the time, but not because of political clout alone. "He shares our statewide approach," said one official; "that's the only reason I'd count on the governor." Only 12 percent, in contrast, said they would follow the legislature's wishes if given a choice.

Governors pick their issues and attempt to influence only a portion of legislative or administrative actions. Because their staffs are small and time is limited, chief executives tend to focus on agencies administering programs central to the administration's priorities.[30] Governor Blanchard emphasized economic development; Governor Engler saw international trade as important to the state's economic recovery. Hence, both eventually sought to influence the Department of Commerce. It was no surprise that Blanchard's support for commerce initiatives enhanced the influence of that department, or that Engler's attention began to resurrect that downtrodden department after his earlier dismantling. "Once a governor uses a department," said a legislator, "the more credibility it takes on for us. You treat its people like they know what they are doing."

This attention is important to agency personnel because Michigan governors intervened more actively than those of several other states in our study when crises arose in a program or agency, especially when the potential for political fallout was serious and personal. A crisis has often provided an opportunity for a governor and his appointees in an agency to exert exceptional influence in places where legislators normally dominate. Such was the case with Governor Milliken's involvement with the Department of Agriculture after the PBB accident in the 1970s.[31] "There is some doubt," joked one agriculture committee member of that era, "that he even knew there was such a department before PBB."

Governors who serve more than one term may even make significant inroads into departments where a commission appoints the chief administrator. Yet gubernatorial influence may sometimes be evident in the case of an elected board. Blanchard in 1988, and Engler in 1992, prevailed on the state Board of Education to appoint as superintendent their preferred candidates. Earlier in 1988, the Natural Resources Commission selected the governor's preferred candidate for the directorship. However, Engler was not even able to get that commission to conduct a national search for director, let alone name his choice.

In seeking to understand the relationship between a governor and his top appointees, it would be a mistake to presume that the process typically operates in "top down" fashion. Governors seldom bark orders and find their appointees clicking their heels in obedience. For one thing, energetic and intelligent appointees dislike being puppets. For another, strong governors look for creative appointees who can help them solve problems high on their agendas. The best example from the 1980s was the relationship between Blanchard and Douglas Ross, his first director of the Department of Commerce.

Ross, a founder of the Michigan Citizens Lobby and former Democratic state senator, was no cipher. His involvement in state government as an elected official predated that of the governor. While commerce director, Ross frequently brought proposals for new economic development approaches to Blanchard and convinced him to endorse several that did not seem compatible with Blanchard's pro-business approach to growth. Some of the more surprising initiatives embodied a human investment approach much favored by Ross, a former teacher. A prime example is the Detroit Compact, a cooperative effort involving representatives from business, state and local government, and the Detroit community, which sought to reduce school dropout rates. Programs such as the compact were a sharp departure from those for which the Department of Commerce traditionally had been responsible under previous governors. Their boldness alone elevated Ross to a position where state newspapers discussed his innovativeness and possible gubernatorial future, at least until he quit state government for a Washington position.

Interest groups are another source of influence, but apparently not a strong one involving professional lobbyists. Michigan departmental managers, in the 1980s study, generally reported that interest groups were not exceedingly influential in their administrative activities. In contrast, they believed that clients, who are usually well organized in Michigan, did have considerable impact in determining broad policy. Most of it, though, comes indirectly through the legislature. To some extent, this may reflect our previously quoted public health physician/lobbyist's view that relationships between client and agency are seldom warm even though officials remain helpful. Critics add to this puzzle over grass-roots influence, noting that administrative rule making is sometimes made to order by administrators for friendly interest-group influence.[32] Moreover, a study of state aging interests found the State Office of Aging sympathetic and useful when comparable offices in other states acted contentiously.[33] However, in cooperating with activists on aging, agency officials limited their support to providing information while legislators prodded for administrative cooperation and actively served as group advocates.

Other policymakers also reported that interest-group interaction, if not influence, is comparatively high despite the reticence with which state officials network with others. Michigan agencies tied for third with California agencies in the degree to which administrators and organized interests discussed issues together.[34] Most of this contact, as we would expect given Michigan's code of ethics and the professional demeanor of its agency officials, is initiated by clients and lobbyists. When the agencies seek contacts, they want specific information on how programs are working and what group positions exist on regulation and policy. This interaction tends to be most characteristic of agencies that also work closely with the governor and the legislature, therefore opening doors to broader political contact. Also, interaction appears to be related to the state's political culture. States possessing a moralistic political culture with an emphasis on widespread participation reported the most pronounced involvement between officials and private interests.

The number of interest groups, and disagreements among them, appear to affect their openness with agency officials. Officials from most Michigan agencies reported that they deal with a number of different interests, few of which have been consistently supportive or hostile.[35] The PBB episode, for example, disrupted longstanding cooperation between the Department of Agriculture and the Michigan Farm Bureau Federation. It became apparent to agriculture officials that many farmers disagreed with departmental actions inspired by the Farm Bureau. Contacts broadened dramatically, even including farm protest groups. Similarly, utility companies do not dominate regulators because of the likely intervention of other public agencies, such as the state attorney general's office. Typically, the attorney general intervenes in collaboration with consumer groups in order to counterbalance the narrower private interests involved in rate cases.[36] These examples lead us to agree with the assessments of agency officials. That is, while agency doors are always open to organized interests, access does not ensure active support for them or a closed mind to others. "They listen and listen and listen over in the Mason Building," observed one lobbyist who goes there at least once a week, "and its very problematic that you get anywhere without strong legislative support."

Michigan administrators, according to our 1980s study, had other, often competitive political relationships to which they needed to tend as well. That, today's administrators agree, has not changed at all. Federal agencies and the Congress, for example, influence state agencies largely because of budgetary linkages. The larger the proportion of federal funding of an agency, the greater the federal influence. However, nearly all Michigan agencies complained of federal mandates over service levels and requirements that are too specific.[37] To illustrate, 65 percent of the department managers whose agencies received half or more of their budget from federal sources rated federal agencies as greatly influential. Administrators in other agencies saw federal influence to be much less important.

Intergovernmental tensions involving local governments, which is really another lobbying relationship, were also evident in the rankings. These tensions were no less pronounced than the periodic sparks that fly between state agencies and local governments with their varied regional concerns. One of the oddities of the state is the frequency with which local officials, even career city managers, bemoan those "damned bureaucrats in Lansing." The tension is reflected in both the formal and informal relations between the state's large Department of Natural Resources and, especially, the UP. The state through the DNR, and in contrast to Michigan's history of prodigal wastage, implements policies to protect the ideal of what agency officials regard as the untouched beauty of this natural preserve. Meanwhile, both professional local administrators and lifelong grass-roots "UP-er" activists fume over what they see as suppression of their economic aspirations. Contending views, with economic stakes pitted against preservationist goals, are just too great to support effective cooperation.

Nor is this the only issue separating the agency from UP officials and residents. They seldom see eye-to-eye with DNR professionals on appropriate relations between man and beast. It took twenty-five years before the UP agreed with the DNR to abolish wolf bounties. DNR biologists also advocate a balanced harvesting of antlerless deer and bucks, a plan that UP residents have bitterly fought because many still see doe harvesting as eventually shrinking the deer population and, indirectly, tourism revenues. DNR regulation of local governments in the UP and elsewhere in the state on such issues as sewage treatment, waste disposal, and toxicity also sharpens tensions. However, passage of the Headlee Amendment has at least compelled Michigan to provide the funding necessary to carry out any state mandates placed on local government.

The DNR, though, does score points with local government when it assists in preparing grant applications or floats bonds that place Michigan's "full faith and credit" behind local program initiatives. Where lies the difference between hostility and acceptance? As one retired DNR official explained: "For years we were mistaken. We let UP folks lobby us and we often caved in under legislature pressure. But we did not do one thing, talk to people up there person-to-person. Agency personnel, in my experiences, always walked in as the experts and drew a line in the sand, your way or our way. Even when we lost, we always let them know that their way was just plain wrong, but we never tried to cut a square deal."

Perhaps his comments explain why many agency officials prefer the uncertainties of the courts to dealing with the unrelenting demands of clients and lobbyists. The judiciary is another source of influence that officials saw as having only a modest impact on agencies responsible for environmental management, transportation, and criminal justice. But there is contrary evidence. Courts are much more influential in the policy work of agencies dealing with workers' compensation, taxes, and labor-management relations. This suggests that, to some extent, there are predictable consequences of dealing with litigated issues. However, predictability means only learning to live with the courts as another political force.

The Michigan Supreme Court upholds agency decisions only about half the time, as it eventually did in allowing Governor Engler to reorganize the DNR.[38] "But that is something you learn to live with," said the retired DNR official. "You do not so easily come to understand that, as a trained professional, there are citizens out there who can tell you what to do." Moreover, the supreme court is not particularly activist. Nonetheless, competing tensions go deep into Michigan's public agencies.

ADMINISTRATION AND THE BUDGET PROCESS

The usefulness of the boundaries that public managers set for themselves and the frustrations of negotiating can be seen in state budgeting. Many policy decisions are made as part of the budget process. Tentacles of the budget process extend throughout policymaking and administration because programs and offices cannot operate without dollars. Moreover, budgeting involves virtually all major state policy participants. The process demonstrates the degree to which administrative agencies must involve themselves with many players to secure their budgets. In the intense conflict over whether regional or statewide, legislative or gubernatorial interests will win, a little distance and procedural self-protection are advantageous to agency officials. Quite simply, Michigan is a good place for bureaucrats to avoid political risk. They can do this by stating definitive choices over budgetary allocations and then living with the results. "If you make a request," noted one manager, "then they can't blame you for program failure when you didn't get what you wanted."

Budgetary decision making is more centralized today than in the past. Department directors, the governor, his budget director, and key legislative leaders bargain over policy and program priorities. In this crucial policy arena, however, elected officials, not bureaucrats, call the most consequential shots. The latter wait on tap to advise. Michigan's managers, however, have seen themselves (table 12) as being highly influential in determining funding levels for their unit (66 percent) and program (75 percent) budgets, but only because they know more about program operations than others. Their influence is due in part to the "target-budget" approach that focuses on department programs and priorities for each forthcoming budget year. Knowledge enters in because program managers in the agencies are the key elements in initially articulating budget options and preparing program plans.[39] They can have their greatest impact during retrenchment.

Much budget work is technical, albeit overtly political. The Department of Management and Budget (DMB) acts with the authority of the governor. It seeks to guide the budget process to produce a document consistent with the governor's administrative priorities, which may at times differ considerably from those of the agencies. The Office of the Budget (within the DMB) prepares the annual executive budget, projects revenues, and prepares the governor's annual economic and tax expenditure reports. Public managers are clear about the tasks of the budget office. Three-fourths of them see this office as having great impact on budget levels for their units and programs. The budget office, of course, receives the departmental and unit requests and typically trims them to meet expenditure targets.

The governor is chiefly responsible for the overall integrity of the budget while working with his priorities and purging those things that he finds most objectionable. It also is the governor who vetoes budget bills and those items that he sees as excessive. And it is the governor who issues executive orders to cut budgets midyear if it appears spending will outstrip revenues and produce a deficit budget in violation of the constitution. The director of the DMB, though, is the key staff architect of the fiscal plans which are disseminated through the Budget Message of the Governor and the Executive Budget. That document then becomes the starting point for legislative deliberations.

Action in the legislature revolves around its critical "power of the purse," influence as direct and encompassing as that of any state legislature in the nation. The legislature's professional staff believes members have such great influence because they can obtain competing information as well as devote extensive staff resources to personally directed budget review.

That is, they have great capacity to "meddle," by micromanaging. Michigan public managers, accordingly, saw legislators as exerting more influence on overall agency budgets than any other state officials, closely rivaling the state budget office in setting spending levels for specific programs. Indeed, the rivalry over revenue projections has been so intense that the three finance and budget agencies are now required to collaborate and reach agreement regarding the money estimated to be available to the state for the forthcoming budget. Within the legislature the key players consist of the leadership quadrant from both parties. The four leaders, sometimes discordantly, orchestrate legislative deliberations on the budget to move the process along. Appropriations and, to a lesser extent, taxation committee chairs and members also exert substantial influence on particular issues. But the four leaders matter most because timely movement of the package remains the outstanding failure in Michigan budgeting. Just being the last to be allocated funds sometimes means getting less. This, of course, is largely beyond agency control. Yet the sit-and-wait message that elected officials frequently send to the agencies creates exceptional frustration.

A CLOSING THOUGHT

This process underscores one final point about Michigan's system of public administration. Michigan does not have a runaway, or politically dominant, bureaucracy. Much administrative power is secondhand, exercised at the sufferance of others. As long as agency actions are generally acceptable to major players, as the budget process and other political dynamics ensure, agencies can function with considerable authority and can usually be politically responsive to those whom they serve. If the agency steps outside its customary boundaries, or goes too far as an advocate, these same relationships can be used to bring the errant party to heel. "Getting reminded that policy leadership is not your job," reflected one veteran manager, "is not uncommon. But it's always a terrifying message." The state and its diverse public, nonetheless, depends on the advice of professionally trained, generally secure administrators. Accordingly, public managers do much to improve the quality of public policy debate, even though they seldom assert responsibility for doing so.

CHAPTER SEVEN

The Courts and Their Struggle
to Centralize Control

John Ashby also contributed to this chapter

AN ADMINISTRATIVE COURT

For the last several biennia, chief justices of the Michigan Supreme Court have asked the legislature to change the manner of funding for local courts. Chief justices, from Mary Coleman and G. Mennen Williams to Dorothy Comstock Riley, in their budget requests and in their State of the Judiciary addresses to the legislature, have proposed that the state pay the operating costs of circuit, probate, district, and other lower courts. These courts are now funded by county taxes or other local revenues. Each year the justices promise that local court fees will offset part of the added expense to the state and improve Michigan's system of justice. The legislature's failure to act is a mark of just how fiscally stressed the state has become. Although the legislature shifted the courts in one region to state funding, the action was taken largely to give some fiscal relief to the even more financially strapped city of Detroit and Wayne County.

Legislative inaction also seems to reflect two other conditions. First, it may be that legislators, taking a state rather than district perspective, believe that state government already shares enough of its resources with its local progeny. More likely, the legislature, exhibiting some interbranch rivalry, has little desire to solidify the supreme court's control over the judicial bureaucracy. Committing a further share of the state budget to the courts would set the legislature up to do battle with the court over future budget increases or to a possible court order mandating fund increases. The court has the inherent powers to do so.

For the supreme court, state funding of the entire court system is viewed as nearly the final step in implementing the reforms spawned by the 1963 constitution. That document declares that "there shall be one court of justice in the state" under the "general superintending control" of the supreme court. On the list of judicial reforms in Michigan, as well as in other states, was a unified court system, elimination of nonlawyers from the local courts, professional administration of the court system, and continuing education for judges. Most of these reforms have been attained in Michigan, although not all have achieved their intended goals. Michigan's top court has amassed considerable, but far from absolute, power in bringing about centralized control through its case decisions and court rules. State funding is not essential to greater central control of the system; however, it would give the supreme court considerable leverage in managing lower court judges, staff, and policies.

In 1973, a special commission of judges and legislators reviewed the implications of the judicial article of the constitution. The commission produced numerous recommendations for the future of the judiciary. Since then, supreme court justices have sought more forcefully to bring meaning to the constitutional phrase "superintending control." It is not that the state's top court lacked significant control before, since all judges are professionally committed to abide by the legal decisions of the supreme court and are obligated to conform to court rules promulgated by the supreme court justices. Also, state government has cooperated by implementing other reforms. Since that 1973 special commission, the court has won many victories in the legislature, among them the creation of administrative agencies, such as the State Court Administrative Office, a Judicial Data Center, a Michigan Judicial Institute, and a state Judicial Council. The legislature also eliminated certain courts, established new courts, and provided state funding for the general trial courts in Wayne County.

Still, the supreme court struggles to achieve full superintending control, and state funding for all the courts remains its most elusive goal. This management emphasis, rather than the efforts of a constitutionally interventionist court, remains the primary concern of Michigan's supreme court justices.

MICHIGAN COURT STRUCTURE AND ORGANIZATION

The 1963 constitution established a unified and vertically organized court system, gave the supreme court the power to establish rules of procedure for the lower courts in both civil and criminal matters, and formed the basis for the supreme court's authority to administer the court system through its State Court Administrative Office. A major contribution of the 1963 constitution was that it added to the independence of the court system by putting the supreme court in charge, not only by way of its decisions, but administratively as well.

A second major contribution was the establishment of an intermediate court of appeals between the supreme court and the general trial and special courts. The appeals court is structured to broaden considerably the opportunity for aggrieved parties to appeal from a lower court or other semi-judicial agency, such as the state tax tribunal with its property-tax function. Previously, the supreme court reviewed lower court decisions only as time allowed. Necessarily, the supreme court, operating as a panel of all its justices, had much less capacity to consider actions of the state's major trial courts than the three-judge panels of the appeals court.

A third significant revision mandated in the 1963 constitution was the elimination of the justice of the peace and circuit court commissioners. The justice of the peace, or the J P, system involved the election of persons in each township to serve as the local magistrate over misdemeanors and minor infractions. J Ps were not required to have legal training and usually were not paid a salary. Cynics often said that J P stood for "Judgment for the Plaintiff" because there was no fee for the justice if the person charged was not penalized. The legislature created the district court system, which in 1968 replaced the J P courts and, by 1992, all but five municipal courts as well. These five courts are located in the upscale suburban cities east of Detroit known as the "Pointes." All Michigan courts are now headed by lawyer-judges. The resulting system in a large state such as Michigan directs most of the court's attention to standardizing and managing both a vast caseload and the justices who decide those cases. This leaves less time and room for state politics than many might imagine, especially for nonjudicial issues of the court.

Michigan's court system includes two major sets of courts: trial courts and appeals courts. The first category includes courts of original and limited jurisdiction consisting of the district and circuit courts and probate courts. Also in this category is the Michigan Court of Claims which, in practice, consists of the Ingham County Circuit Court that first hears claims against the state. Included in the appeals category are the Michigan Supreme Court and the Michigan Court of Appeals.

District Courts

Citizens are most likely to encounter the judicial system in the district courts, which have jurisdiction over minor civil and criminal infractions. These courts also administer arraignments, set and accept bail, and hold preliminary examinations in felony cases, even though the trial of such charges falls within the jurisdiction of the circuit court. The district court processes criminal charges for which the maximum penalty is incarceration of one year in the county jail. District courts also issue arrest and search warrants. Civil matters include civil infractions, such as traffic violations under state laws or municipal ordinances, and disputes between persons or businesses. These may involve garnishments, eviction proceedings, and mortgage and land contract foreclosures. Except for the first phase of criminal felonies, criminal cases in these courts deal with misdemeanors.

The district courts do not quite fit the description used to characterize a facility that many Americans see as typical of the courts: "The courtroom is well worn, crowded, and noisy. Row on row of benches are peopled with defendants out on bail, witnesses, friends and relatives of defendants, attorneys, social service personnel, and others. . . . The arraignments, hearings, and conferences which occur at the bench are largely inaudible beyond the second or third row of the spectator gallery. . . . There is a little dignity to the setting. . . . People leaving the courtroom go out a door in the front of the room and off to the judge's left, where outside noise enters the courtroom as the door opens and closes."[1] District court judges work hard to obtain appropriate facilities and staff from county commissions. They also carry out their processes in what court observers often remark to be a dignified manner. This goes on despite a heavy caseload. The annual volume of more than three million cases – one for every three Michiganians and about 11,700 per district judge – also mandates hurried action. Judicially managed haste is particularly evident in the busiest courts, where judges confront as many as 18,000 to 23,000 filings per year.

Not all filings require a judge's time. Magistrates, who are not always lawyers, can process guilty pleas, and many traffic violators do not contest their tickets. Yet, to stay even with the flow, judges and staff must practice hurried justice. Couple this pace with confused defendants and lawyers, or attorneys who often first meet and consult with their clients only moments before they approach the bench, and the scene is hardly pretty.

Traffic cases make up 75 percent of district court work load; civil cases contribute 14 percent, and criminal cases 11 percent. Of the criminal cases, the felony work load amounts to 24 percent, with the remainder comprising misdemeanor offenses. The various cases and issues arising in the district courts often are not insignificant, especially to the parties involved. Nonetheless, the district courts have established procedures to dispose of cases expeditiously. For example, many judges have appointed magistrates to handle many disputed cases under nontrial conditions. In addition, each district court has a small-claims division. Here people or firms may pursue claims against others valued at less than $1,500 without the aid of a lawyer. To work within the framework of the small-claims division, the plaintiff completes a form and files it with the court. This notifies the defendant of the allegations, his or her rights, and a date for a hearing. The plaintiff, and sometimes the defendant, appear, and each tells the judge or the magistrate his or her side of the story in an informal but orderly environment. The judge makes a determination, or signs the judgment proposed by the magistrate, and issues the order. The matter is then ended if the parties agree to comply.

Many small-claims cases involve landlords and tenants or merchants seeking court orders for payment of bills from customers. Nationally, consumer groups were the early sponsors of small-claims court processes because they saw these low-cost procedures as benefiting individuals in legal battles against business and monied interests. However, the "little person" has become the "little defendant" because merchants, landlords, and loan companies who go to court regularly are more knowledgeable about the procedures, and they file and win the largest proportion of these actions.[2] One landlord in a university city periodically goes through apartment dumpsters to find the names of nonrenters who throw their trash there. Then he takes his list of accused and the evidence to court, collecting numerous $100 awards annually. Although default judgments in favor of the plaintiff are common outcomes in such cases, where defendants often do not appear, one major problem is finding the guilty party and collecting on the judgment. But given the courts' management focus, efforts are made to assist with justice.

Some district court cases, of course, involve jury trials. Juries are not large by nationwide standards. District court juries have six members, and in civil cases, five jurors can decide the verdict. In criminal cases, the verdict must be unanimous. A third aspect of district court expeditiousness is Michigan's magistrate process. In many instances, a defendant may never see or talk to the judge. District court judges can appoint magistrates who handle whatever matters are delegated by the judges. A magistrate may set bail, issue arrest and search warrants, negotiate and accept guilty pleas, and impose sentences for certain misdemeanors. In a fourth aspect of hurried justice, litigants are not likely to see a court stenographer punching one of those quiet little "shorthand typewriters." District courts, at the outset, were not courts of record, but that was changed in 1973. However, the proceedings are recorded electronically, and most cases never involve typed verbatim transcripts. Appeals from district court decisions can be made to circuit courts, which sit as appeals courts, but they work with labored difficulty from electronic proceedings.

The district courts are the largest component of Michigan's judicial network. The state has some one hundred such courts covering virtually the entire state, and their caseloads have increased by about 32 percent since 1983. In many respects, the district courts are community courts, linked to community governments – densely populated cities or townships, groups of contiguous townships and cities, or a particular county. Much of this linkage has to do with assisting the court with administrative services, but they also are linked in the sense that these districts constitute the jurisdictional venue of these courts. Matters of district court jurisdiction arising in the district are handled there by the judge of that court. In addition, the 260 judges of this system are nominated and elected from these districts in nonpartisan elections for six-year terms.

Circuit Courts

Circuit courts are the major trial courts of general jurisdiction. They administer those cases that the legislature has determined to be serious. Generally, serious cases involve original jurisdiction in all civil disputes of more than $15,000, all criminal cases where the offense is a major felony or specific misdemeanors with potential punishment exceeding one year in jail, and all domestic relations cases such as divorce and paternity. Circuit courts hear appeals from district courts as well as from probate courts and some state and local administrative agencies. Finally, the circuit courts exercise supervisory control over all other courts within their district, subject to rules of the state supreme court.

Judicial circuits are established along county lines. Usually, each county constitutes a circuit court, but in some places several counties are combined to form a circuit. In these instances, judges hear cases in the several courthouses as needs arise, providing a reminder that Michigan judges once traveled a regular circuit to hear cases. Presently, this component of the judicial system consists of fifty-six circuits staffed with 206 judges. Most of the circuits have 2 or more judges. The highest number is the 64 judges in Wayne County, which includes the judges of the Recorder's Court serving Detroit. The judges of a circuit designate one of their members to serve as chief judge to oversee the administrative affairs of the circuit. While some larger counties have county halls of justice, most circuit judges hold court in the courtrooms of the picturesque county courthouses around the state. For this reason and because circuit courts are linked administratively to the county –

county clerks under the state constitution are clerks of the circuit court – most citizens think of the circuit court as the county court. However, these courts are part of Michigan's single court of justice and have no county status.

Court statistical reports still refer to the Recorder's Court, which was established as a special court in 1857 to hear all felony criminal cases arising in the city of Detroit. In 1986, however, the Third Circuit Court for Wayne County and the Recorder's Court were merged administratively. Circuit judges and Recorder's Court judges also serve six-year terms and are nominated and elected on a nonpartisan ballot. Candidates must be qualified electors, residents of the circuit, lawyers, and older than twenty-one but younger than seventy years of age at the time of election.

The business of these courts, as with the district courts, continues to rise steadily, from some 187,000 cases in 1983 to 232,000 in 1991. Domestic relations cases were the most common component, 41.5 percent, of the work load. These cases included divorce, spouse or child support, and paternity issues. Next in number were cases in the civil area, with 40 percent, followed by criminal cases, with 15 percent. Appeals and court of claims cases constituted a comparatively small 3.5 percent of circuit court filings.

About one-half of the circuit court domestic relations cases, 102,000 in 1991, involved divorce. Fifty-five percent of these were families with children. About one-fourth of the domestic relations cases involved paternity suits under the Uniform Reciprocal Enforcement Support Act, which mandates paternal financial assistance. Other child-support cases constituted the other major category of domestic cases. The state court categorizes civil cases, of which there were 60,000 in 1991, into two major types. The first is tort claims, or wrongs by one person against another or against another's property. The second includes general civil cases such as business disputes, labor relations, contracts, condemnations, housing, and environmental issues. Tort claims accounted for about 45 percent of the 1991 civil cases; of these, 45 percent resulted from automobile accidents.

The third major area of circuit court work load is criminal law. Of the state's 57,000 filings in 1991, about one in twelve was classified as a capital offense. Many of these cases, as happens with many civil cases as well, are not brought to trial. Plea bargaining between the prosecutors and defense counsels settled the overwhelming number of criminal cases. The defendant knows that court dockets are crowded and that a guilty plea to a less severe charge may be a better solution than going to trial and being convicted of a more serious charge. For example, Michigan enacted a well-publicized law in 1977 which adds two years to a sentence if a felony is committed with a firearm. Prosecutors frequently do not charge defendants with the gun offense, or they coax defendants into guilty pleas by dropping the felony gun charge.

The work load of the 206 circuit judges and their staffs remains high. Statewide, in 1991, case filings totaled 1,124 filings per judge. While many of these case filings never reach trial stage, the number of filings per judge in 1983 was 12 percent less. The overload problem could be resolved by adding new judgeships. This, however, involves more financing to pay for judges' salaries and requires legislative approval, which is given in permissive rather than mandatory form so as to avoid conflict with the counties over their responsibility for costs associated with increased staff, courtrooms, and offices.

A major division of the circuit courts is the Friend of the Court, a unit that handles actions related to child custody, visitation, and support issues arising from domestic relations problems. Each circuit court has such an administrative unit that investigates and makes recommendations to the judge. The Friend of the Court offices also receive and disburse child and spousal support payments, some $806 million in 1991. A key issue in family support payments is the extent to which defaults in payment orders contribute to the Aid to Families with Dependent Children (AFDC) caseload. Federal payments aid Friend of the Court offices. So, too, do legislative reforms, such as laws that allow withholding of state and federal income tax refunds and garnishment of payroll checks for those in default. These have lowered the overall default rate. In 1991, about 20 percent of the collected funds were support collections for AFDC families. The annual load of 725,000 cases of the Friends of the Court offices has remained relatively steady since 1987.

Special Courts

The probate court is the principal special court of original and limited jurisdiction. The juvenile divisions of these courts handle cases of neglect, abuse, and delinquency of children under age seventeen. New filings in 1991 totaled 84,100, 60 percent of which were for criminal statute and ordinance violations not related to traffic offenses. Probate courts also handle cases involving institutional commitment, guardianships, and conservatorships for the mentally ill and mentally disabled. Finally, these courts supervise, or probate, the wills and estates of deceased persons. Estate filings totaled some 72,000 in 1991.

Michigan has seventy-nine probate courts staffed by 108 judges, most of whom are full-time. With the exception of eight counties that have combined for purposes of probate court, probate courts are organized along county boundaries and hold hearings in the state's eighty-three courthouses. Probate judges are elected in nonpartisan elections. They, too, serve six-year terms and must meet the same qualifications as Michigan's other judges. These courts have administrative divisions that oversee the placement of youth both for delinquency purposes and for protective custody. Just under 30,000 youth, not including about 17,000 others in the custody of the Department of Social Services, were handled in 1991 by the probate courts.

The Court of Claims hears civil cases involving actions against the state on claims of $1,000 or more.[3] Therefore, it also is a court of special jurisdiction. This court was established to resolve a pronounced work load inequity. Claims against the state had been filed in court at the seat of state government in Ingham County. Consequently, Ingham County incurred a disproportionately high expense in processing state cases. The Court of Claims, as a supplemental court, does not have its own judges; instead, it draws on judges of the Thirtieth Judicial Circuit in Ingham County. For a number of years, about 500 new cases were filed in this court each year. In 1991, however, new filings shot up to 870 as a result of 418 filings against the state Department of Treasury over the single business tax. This worsened an already difficult backlog. Previously, backlogs of two or more years had been resolved in the Court of Claims through mediation with the Office of Attorney General.

Court of Appeals

Appeals courts face problems both different from and similar to those of lower courts. Their function, though, is different. A former Michigan law school dean and U.S. district judge in Detroit said that appellate review has two purposes: "to prevent miscarriages of justice" and to "teach judges, lawyers, and all citizens something about the law."[4] The Michigan Court of Appeals has largely the first function. It provides a broad opportunity for circuit court decisions to be appealed and reviewed. Previously, the supreme court, which, in its public deliberations, always sits as a complete panel of seven, heard appeals. This severely limited the opportunity for appeals to the court. The 1963 constitution, as a corrective, provided for the intermediate court of appeals. Prior to the formation of the court of appeals, litigants had little opportunity to have unfavorable decisions reviewed by the supreme court. If a case was accepted for review, the parties usually had to wait a long

Figure 3: Number of Court of Appeals Filings, 1965–91

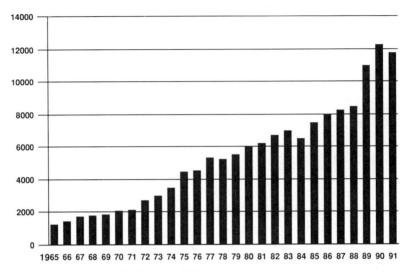

Source: State Court Administrative Office.

time for a decision, which meant – as judges are wont to say in their lobbying – "justice delayed is justice denied."

The court of appeals is designed to speed up the judicial process and to take much of the routine legal burden off the supreme court. The number of appeals has been rising steadily since the formation of the court (see figure 3). Considering that just a little under half of the cases require written decisions, while the rest are disposed of by order, the caseload is substantial. The key to the productivity of the court of appeals is its organization and procedures. The court has twenty-eight judges, a number that has been increased four times since its inception.

Because the court of appeals divides into panels of three judges to hear and rule on each appeal, it can hear at least nine cases at the same time. It can hear even more by borrowing circuit judges when the caseload is high. The court of appeals holds sessions in Lansing, Grand Rapids, Detroit, and Marquette, but assigns the judges to these cities on a rotating basis. This rotation is intended to bring about uniformity of rulings, an important consideration because court decisions have statewide application and are the final adjudication unless the supreme court hears a further appeal. Circuit court decisions are not binding on judges in other circuits. The court of appeals, because of this approach, has brought expanded opportunity for appeal with relatively short waiting periods and has helped restrain the cost of appeals. Judges of Michigan's courts of appeals are elected in nonpartisan elections for terms of six years. They, too, must be lawyers, qualified electors, residents of the district from which chosen, and between twenty-one and seventy years of age at time of election.

The Supreme Court

In addition to the changes already noted, creation of the court of appeals has permitted a subtle change to occur in supreme court deliberations. Michigan's highest court is now more selective in the cases that it accepts for hearing and review. Previously, it had to accept a great many cases that may have involved miscarriages of justice. Now it can focus on cases that provide the best opportunities for teaching, policymaking, and reshaping of law as the court establishes precedents for lower court judges. Thus, the court has gained a reputation as more of a constitutional court than a court for routine review. While the supreme court continues to receive more than two thousand requests for leave to appeal each year, it disposes of the overwhelming proportion of these cases by order rather than by opinion. Indeed, the number of opinion decisions in recent years has declined significantly from the mid-1970s, when the court issued some 175. The 66 opinion dispositions in 1991 were reflective of the court's productivity since 1987.

The smaller number of supreme court opinions occasionally is the subject of editorial criticism. The pattern of the last several years, to be more selective in the cases that the court chooses, seems well established and deliberate. Part of the intent is to avoid being a judicial King Solomon, a wizened body that policymakers look to in times of deadlock. One case it can look forward to receiving each ten years, however, is apportionment of legislative districts. As was discussed in chapter 5, the court in 1982 abolished the state Commission on Legislative Reapportionment established in the 1963 constitution. This eight-person commission, four representing Republicans and four Democrats, was unable in both 1968 and 1972 to generate majority support for one plan. In those instances, the commission presented its plans to the supreme court, which was required to select one of them as usable. This method forced the court to make one of the most blatantly political decisions that any judicial body can make. In 1982 the court abolished the apportionment commission as unconstitutional. It advised the legislature that unless it could devise a plan supported by the two houses and the governor, it would employ a court master to generate a constitutionally proper apportionment plan. With the executive office and the house under Democratic control and the senate controlled by Republicans, it was no contest. The supreme court's plan became the operative one.

Similarly, in 1992, the supreme court created a committee of retired judges to devise legislative districts for the 1990s. This committee hired Bernard J. Apol, the court master from 1982, to prepare a recommended district plan. Neither the committee nor the supreme court was concerned about the plan's partisan effects. Their primary concerns in 1982 were with particular standards, including the maximum allowable deviation in population between the smallest and largest district. While these standards remained matters of concern in 1992, the major issue that year was the effect of any plan on minority representation in the legislature. Such considerations, of course, are not without their political import. For the court, however, the objective was to present a plan that would not be rejected by a federal court for failure to meet civil rights protections. The supreme court dodged in 1982 and again in 1992 the allegations of partisanship that it earned in its earlier reapportionment actions. Both the political balance of the court – with three Democrats, three Republicans, and one independent – and its concern with an enhanced image have been responsible for this shift away from political interference.

This is not to suggest that supreme court justices are of a single mind on the issues that come before them. They are not. Justices follow their personal proclivities on specific types of issues, such as workers' compensation, individuals against corporations, governmental immunity, and criminal matters. As a group, however, they are largely centrist. This moderation and selective involvement in cases makes for a work load that allows, it seems, for careful deliberation. At least, that seems to be the case, since in the last decade other state supreme courts have cited Michigan cases in each of the above areas. On some issues, however, certain justices are likely to be activists due to their ideological beliefs, but such idiosyncracies tend to be rendered ineffectual by majority opinions. As one court observer noted, "The state supreme court of recent years has been about the business of tidying up issues in the law rather than aggressively making new law."

Although that assessment of being tidy rather than aggressive seems accurate, the overall direction of judge-made law can still be somewhat masked by the decisions that justices choose not to review. In Michigan, avoidance of specific types of cases seems not to be a problem. An activist court that annually accepts only some 60 or 70 cases out of the two thousand or more requests that it receives must perceive a great deal of cohesion in the work of the various panels of the court of appeals. It also means the perception of fairness and use of statewide standards. Where once southeastern Michigan courts were known as "labor courts," the general impression among policymakers is that courts now hold to the letter of the quite specific law of the legislature. Some have been surprised that this is the case with recently revised workers' compensation and unemployment laws.

On cases that the supreme court refuses to rehear, it only occasionally issues a remand or reversal order with an opinion. In most instances, the court merely states that leave for appeal is being denied "because we are not persuaded that the question presented should be reviewed by this court." Aside from an occasional dissent, such reports say little about the overall philosophical direction on the court other than that it appears bent toward the practicalities of management. As we suggested, this is much more an administrative court than a political one. In a typology developed by Mary Cornelia Porter and G. Alan Tarr, Michigan has an institutional court rather than one that sets state agendas, complements the legislature, brings federal concerns to the state, or dramatically innovates.[5] But given the court's reputation for some important precedents, plus its unwillingness to restrict state policymaking, justices must get secondary credit for being moderately innovative as a constitutional court as well.

The seven members of the supreme court are elected for eight-year terms. Every other year, the justices select one of their members to be chief justice. This justice presides during oral arguments in court sessions and court conferences and heads the state's judiciary. Each year the chief justice presents a State of the Judiciary address to the legislature which covers judicial issues, such as court financing, court organization, staffing requirements, backlogs, and recommended changes in substantive law. Recent addresses have highlighted victims' rights, juvenile code revisions, the protection and treatment of children in need of care, and community dispute-resolution centers. Most predictably, they request state funding for lower courts.

The Michigan Supreme Court is the final arbiter of the meaning of the Michigan Constitution and Michigan law unless either is challenged by a litigant as violating the U.S. Constitution or other federal law. Appeal from the Michigan Supreme Court, as in all the states, is made directly to the Supreme Court of the United States. Beyond watching for conformity to federal law, the state supreme court has virtually complete control over what it chooses to hear. Under unusual circumstances, the governor may ask it to take newly enacted legislation as original jurisdiction and ask for an advisory opinion on that issue. Requests for advisory opinions do not involve real cases with their own sets of facts. Typically, requests involve recently adopted legislation, often of an emergency nature, that has some questionable legal aspects.

The court accepts few such requests; consequently, governors rarely ask for an advisory opinion. The usual objection is that such cases have no facts or circumstances on which to decide fairness or legality. Moreover, lawyers presenting arguments have no real clients, and lower courts have not heard the case and given their opinions. In addition, any decision is merely advisory; it sets no precedent for judges around the state. As a result, little incentive exists for such use of court time. In general, the court's behavior signals the governors to get an opinion from their own lawyer, the state attorney general. Later, if questions arise, the court may consider an appeal. Again, the effect is to keep the court removed from the politics of other institutions, allowing it to follow its own agenda.

The supreme court prefers cases with specific facts and lawyers with clients who have something to gain or lose. Most often, it agrees to hear cases that involve a major issue of law or where panels of the court of appeals have issued conflicting or contrasting rules. One area ripe for the emergence of the constitutional court is environmental law. Because the Michigan Environmental Protection Act was designed to evolve through judicial precedents, the court has numerous and often unavoidable cause to act. By deciding cases of this sort, the court teaches a point of law to judges throughout Michigan's judicial system, as well as to lawyers, state and community officials, and attentive citizens. Plus, these cases add to the court's national reputation.

The court's procedures for review are fairly simple. If four justices vote to hear a case, the involved parties are notified to provide the court with detailed written briefs, or arguments, several weeks in advance of oral arguments. After oral arguments, the justices discuss the case in conference and hold an initial oral vote on the outcome. The clerk of the court then runs a lottery for the justices in the majority to determine who will write the opinion for the court. Several drafts of an opinion may be required before it gains the approval of at least four justices and is issued as the court opinion. Other justices may write a concurring opinion that explains an additional point or two about the law. Justices who disagree with the majority opinion may write a dissenting opinion. Concurring and dissenting opinions can provide at least some of the basis for later appeals of similar cases. Opinions are released for publication by private companies that bind them in books for sale to law libraries, lawyers, and others.

These books become the court's prime vehicle for communication. The court's procedures, it should be noted, are carried on largely outside of public view. Journalists report on only a small percentage of the decisions, mainly those involving a news celebrity or a reversal of a major public policy. One such case held that the state's single business tax violated the commerce clause of the U.S. Constitution because it treated state-based companies more favorably than those headquartered elsewhere.[6] The ruling had a costly result for the state treasury and gained considerable attention for that reason. Ultimately, it was overturned by the U.S. Supreme Court in *Trinova Corporation* v. *Michigan Department of Treasury*.[7] The level of attention contrasts greatly with that of the legislature, where most differences of opinion and disagreements become visible. Unless there is a leak from a justice, or more likely from a court employee, the public is seldom informed about how these seven elected officials argued points or reached compromises to produce a majority opinion. Justices almost never discuss their decisions with the media. "The opinion," justices say, "must stand on its own." No sunshine laws apply here, where being "above politics" is the standard.

THE POLITICS OF JUDICIAL ADMINISTRATION AND FINANCE

The 1963 constitution implies that the court system will be fully administered by the supreme court. As noted earlier, this interaction derives from the clause that provides a "single court of justice" under the "general superintending authority" of the supreme court. These same phrases also were contained in Michigan's 1908 constitution. During the time that constitution was in effect, though, no efforts were made to act on its intent. The supreme court issued its rules of procedure and lobbied for the judiciary, but, for the most part, it supervised lower courts only through its decisions and the rule that requires judges to apply established precedents to current cases, *stare decisis*.

In recent decades, the supreme court has been more aggressive in carrying out its superintending control. The drive to reform state courts by integrating them into a pyramidal system derives in part from a nationwide reform effort to professionalize courts and remove them from political bargaining.[8] These reforms evidence themselves primarily in three ways in Michigan: internal discipline of judges, central records and resources management, and state financing of costs.

In addition to the oversight provided by the legislature, governor, and local officials, three groups assist the supreme court in disciplining judges and attorneys as officers of the court. Michigan judges, in another unusual bit of isolation, are not subject to recall as are other elected officials. The 1963 constitution empowered the governor to remove a judge for reasonable cause even though the cause may not be sufficient for impeachment. Before the governor may remove a judge, both houses of the legislature must approve, by a two-thirds vote, a resolution detailing the complaints.[9] Supreme court justices are subject to impeachment by the legislature. None of these actions has been used, much less threatened, since 1963.

Such procedures, of course, have strong partisan implications. These processes also permit interference from one of the other branches, with the potential for intimidating those administering justice. Perhaps more important, though, these means of disciplining justices and judges provide but a small measure of discipline. They are used in only the worst of cases, and they involve immense amounts of legislative and executive energy. Time, policymakers indicate, seems better allocated to more rewarding activity in both these branches. For this reason, in 1968, the state constitution was amended to create the Judicial Tenure Commission to administer the disciplining of judges.[10] The governor selects two members of the nine-member commission. The Michigan Bar Association chooses three, and the circuit, district, probate, and appellate court judges as groups name one member each. This system provides a way to discipline judges for causes that may not demand removal, although removal may be ordered. Grievances for behavior involving the commission of a felony, physical or mental disability that renders the judge unable to perform duties, misconduct in office, failure to perform the duties, or habitual intemperance can be filed with this commission. The complaints are then investigated, and if warranted, the commission issues a formal complaint and, without public notice or fanfare, makes a recommendation to the supreme court, which then decides what penalty, if any, to impose.

Judges are subject to additional scrutiny, especially from the U.S. Department of Justice. The number of Detroit-area judges that are either indicted or convicted has not come close to approaching the number in Chicago. In the early 1990s, two Michigan judges were sentenced for accepting bribes, and a third was tried and found innocent of most of the charges. In a separate investigation, an appeals court judge committed suicide following arrest and arraignment on charges of soliciting a bribe. From the courts' perspective, of course, such events undermine efforts to establish a reputation of professionalism. At the same time, citizens recognize that judges are above neither reproach nor investigation.

The Attorney Grievance Commission was established by the Michigan Supreme Court in 1978 to act as a prosecuting agency to assist the court in supervising and disciplining attorneys. This body underwent some restructuring when, in 1991, a newspaper reported that staff had prematurely, and somewhat suspiciously, closed cases and shredded the documents. Justice Dorothy Comstock Riley, embarrassed by the findings, fired the staff and brought the commission under close supervision of the court itself. It still investigates grievances filed against Michigan attorneys and is responsible for filing formal complaints with the Attorney Discipline Board.

Like the Grievance Commission, the Attorney Discipline Board has seven members appointed through the same procedure. The board appoints about three hundred attorneys to serve as volunteers on three-member panels that act as trial bodies. These panels may order dismissal, reprimand, probation, temporary suspension, or disbarment. An attorney may appeal to the full board. Occasionally, they "appeal" cases to the media, as did Assistant U.S. Attorney Michael J. Stern when his colleagues on a panel refused to disbar an attorney for improperly taking $30,000 from a client. Instead, the panel suspended the attorney's license for one year and ordered her to repay the client. Stern argued that the case provided evidence for having non-lawyers, with less of a proprietary interest, on review panels.[11]

Administration and control are no less important to the court than is regulation. Organizing the courts into a single system involves many administrative chores normally associated with managing a large bureaucracy, including training for judges, maintaining records, allocating judicial resources to deal with case backlogs in various circuits, developing policies on such issues as uniform sentencing guidelines, periodic amendment of the court rules, and even publication and legislative relations. According to court records, the supreme court meets in administrative session thirty-five to forty times each year. In some ways, even with greater top-down coordination, administering a judicial bureaucracy may be more difficult than managing other organizations. Part of the problem is with the court system's many independent operations, each dominated on a day-to-day basis by individual judges whom the justices neither select nor, except for gross incompetence or misconduct, fire.

The head of the administrative arm of the supreme court is the administrator. That person directs the State Court Administrative Office, which is responsible for such services as technical assistance, development of manuals and forms, case-flow management, research and planning, and analysis of court rules and legislation. Resource management, also an important role, focuses on judicial assignments, monitoring trial court activity, and case backlogs. The state office also responds to public inquiries and helps to resolve disputes between trial courts and local government boards. Special projects, such as child-support enforcement and procedural rules, need coordination, as does the Judicial Data Center that provides technical assistance to trial courts on data processing, court system design, and development.

The supreme court appoints advisory committees and task forces to recommend action in specific areas of concern. For example, the court has had groups advising it about child-support guidelines, sentencing guidelines, court rules for domestic relations cases, case-flow management, juvenile justice, and gender and racial-ethnic issues. Several of these have gotten the supreme court involved in its teaching role through case selection. More frequently, the justices become personally embroiled in some administrative duties on these issues. In 1988, Chief Justice Riley submitted a letter to Wayne County judges complaining about the abbreviated work schedules of some judges. On another occasion, justices met with seventy judges from the southeastern part of the state to discuss problems that both sides saw in their work. Such involvement produces reactions. Someone leaked Riley's letter. Newspaper accounts of the meeting said that the justices were the ones who "got an earful." One judge suggested that each justice should spend some time each year on a trial court "in the trenches doing some actual work."[12]

All bureaucracies view finances as being of utmost importance. If the framers of the 1963 constitution envisioned and planned for the centralization and independence of the state's courts, however, they left out a key ingredient for those goals. The constitution does not provide an independent funding mechanism for the courts as it does, for example, with the state Civil Service Commission. The courts must compete for appropriations with all other agencies. This explains why forceful lobbying by the court occurs in the legislature. Several chief justices have made various proposals for state funding, ranging from a fixed percentage of state general-fund revenues to gradations in funding by region. In her 1988 State of the Judiciary speech, Chief Justice Riley suggested that the legislature appropriate $30 million to pay the costs of constitutionally guaranteed due process expenses for indigent defendants – jury and witness fees, stipends for court-appointed attorneys, and transcript fees. She envisioned indigent expenses as a series of logical first steps in moving toward state funding. The proposal was not adopted. For the next fiscal year, she requested full state funding of the courts at an increased cost of $200 million or more. If this higher figure was intended to make the previous $30 million request look more attractive, it failed. In recent years, given the condition of the state treasury, chief justices have not renewed requests for state funding, but neither have they set aside this goal.

In 1980 the legislature did reorganize the Wayne County Circuit and Detroit Recorder's Court into the Third Judicial Circuit. The act also spelled out how the state would organize the courts once the consolidation in Wayne County was applied in a statewide plan. The act included full state funding of Wayne courts including the thirty-sixth District Court of Detroit, state retention of all generated fees, and continued provision of physical facilities and a few staff positions by the county and city. Similar state funding was to occur with other courts throughout the state. County commissioners began to pressure the legislature for action, but Attorney General Frank Kelley doused the idea. In a 1983 opinion, Kelley said that each newly assembled legislature has the obligation to determine for itself the purpose for which it appropriates funds, not follow an earlier legislature. In effect, he ruled that the 1980 statutory promise was not really a promise unless a subsequent legislature chooses to appropriate the money.

In 1988, several boards of county commissioners sued the legislature, demanding funding treatment equal to that for Wayne County. The plaintiffs argued unsuccessfully that unequal treatment over the past several years cost the other eighty-two counties as much as $500 million. Without a disruptive decision to uphold such claims, state funding of the entire court system is not imminent. Part of the difficulty that supreme court justices face in securing full state funding, in addition to the strapped budget, is the lack of political gain for legislators in diverting large sums of money to the courts when more influential interests are making financial demands for more publicly visible programs. There was some speculation that the supreme court, one day, would follow the lead of the Pennsylvania Supreme Court and order state funding. The Pennsylvania court held that a constitutional amendment for a uniform state court implied state funding. However, given the Michigan court's lack of aggressive policymaking, the justices have not picked up a case brought by counties for equitable funding.

Why is state funding a centerpiece for court supervision? In addition to reasons noted earlier, a key element is that county governments unevenly provide much of the nonstate funding for courts. Equally important are public controversies over local appropriations between judges and county commissioners. Staff and services not furnished from state funds must be provided by the counties. Fights between judges and county commissions or other local bodies have been embarrassing to the courts. Judges have ordered local commissioners to jail after refusing court orders to appropriate funds. While some disputes have been over such matters as a county's refusal to pay for ink pens bought outside county purchasing procedures, most center around collective bargaining agreements with court employees. But things can get more expensive. For years the courts held that if local court salaries are reasonable and within the financial capacity of the county, then the county must appropriate the money. County boards, however, argue that court salaries are higher than those of other county employees doing similar work. These disputes further explain why the legislature is reluctant to fund the costs of the courts throughout the state. They witness county commissioners mudwrestling with a judge and ask if they, as legislators, want to become embroiled in similar disputes with a chief justice.

Yet the battles go on. In a 1985 decision, the supreme court refined its directives.[13] The procedures in this decision have quieted the intracourthouse and interbranch battles about the comparative costs of decisions. The court, in this case, reaffirmed the authority of the county commission as the legislative body for appropriating funds. Dissatisfied judges may sue the board after specified negotiating and cooling-off periods. Another provision discourages judge-initiated cases, however. It makes the reimbursement of legal fees expended by a judge in a suit against the county a matter to be decided in the trial, rather than an automatic charge.

The courts have been somewhat more successful in making judicial salaries uniform across the state.[14] Salaries of judges had been another point of irritation. The legislature helped equalize the salaries of lower court judges by prescribing formula-based judicial salaries. Circuit judges now receive 92 percent and probate and district judges 88 percent of the salary of a state supreme court justice. The state bears almost all of the cost of judges' salaries, and county commissioners no longer set rates. This decision was not that surprising since legislators frequently retire and run for local judge. "Of course I thought about doing that for a long time," explained one former legislator who was active in raising salaries.

JUDICIAL SELECTION

States select judges in six ways: popular partisan election, nonpartisan election, legislative election, gubernatorial appointment, merit selection, or the combined Missouri Plan, where a panel of judges, attorneys, and laypersons nominates candidates from whom the governor makes appointments. Michigan is one of sixteen states selecting judges through nonpartisan elections. The state supreme court, as a consequence, oversees a single judicial system, but has no direct voice in selecting the persons who staff the various judicial positions. Prior to 1939, Michigan judges were selected by partisan elections. The popularity of President Franklin D. Roosevelt and the Democratic party convinced the still dominant state Republicans to propose an amendment to the constitution which introduced nonpartisan election for all judges. The justices of the supreme court were still nominated by party conventions.[15] The constitution of 1963 continued this process, but allowed the legislature to specify how supreme court justices are to be nominated. The legislature chose to retain partisan nomination at state party conventions and nonpartisan election.[16]

Michigan's process for selecting supreme court justices sometimes produces unexpected results. Candidates must conduct nominating campaigns with those interest groups most frequently aligned with each party. After the nomination, however, their names appear on the nonpartisan ballot in the general election.[17] The state constitutional provision allows any political party to nominate candidates for the supreme court. Major party strength can be broken through this rule. The Michigan Human Rights party was created by former state Democratic party chairman Zolton Ferency and, in 1970, nominated him for the supreme court. Others have had better fortunes by using less radical approaches. In 1972, the Democratic convention nominated Wayne County Circuit Judge Horace Gilmore and Detroit Recorder's Court Judge Robert Evans for the supreme court. One was an old-line Democrat from the "Soapy" Williams era and the other was an African American. This action left no space on the ballot for Appeals Court Judge Charles Levin, who wanted to move to the high court. He formed his own Non-Partisan Judiciary party and, with a well-known political name, ran successfully in the fall election. He has served as supreme court justice ever since.

Others have formed similar parties, and in 1986, the practice generated considerable difficulty for voters, who were faced with twenty-four candidates running for the state's highest court.[18] Only one of the candidates, Justice Dennis Archer, whom Governor James Blanchard had appointed earlier, carried incumbent designation. Being nominated by one of the two major political parties guarantees all straight-ticket votes. Name recognition, or at least name familiarity, also helps. Names such as Williams, Griffin, Levin, Fitzgerald, Kavanaugh or Cavanaugh, Brennan, and Moody have given candidates good head starts. There was speculation that many Democrats must have thought that Appeals Court Justice John Fitzgerald was an Irish-Catholic Democrat when he ran successfully for the court in 1972. In reality, he was a Scotch-Irish Protestant Republican, but also a former state senator and son of late Governor Frank D. Fitzgerald. Candidates for judgeships on the court of appeals have a similar advantage. Still, candidates for either of the appeals courts also need to spend money to get name recognition. In 1984, Justice Patricia Boyle raised nearly $300,000 for her campaign. About $40,000 came from the political action arms of the United Auto Workers (UAW) and over $16,000 from the state AFL-CIO. Former U.S. Senator Robert Griffin obtained more than $30,000 from the Republican party, and Dorothy Comstock Riley got $10,000 from the same ally. Riley's opponent, Justice Thomas Giles Kavanaugh, had $22,000 given him by the UAW and also raised $37,000 from a large legislative-style fund-raiser.

This combination of partisanship, lack of voter knowledge, and campaign expense has brought repeated calls for reform. The late Chief Justice Williams proposed a constitutional amendment to provide for a nonpartisan primary and twelve-year terms.[19] In 1971, the State Bar of Michigan proposed an amendment based on a variation of the Missouri Plan, but voters rejected it. The legislature, of course, has the authority to mandate nonpartisan primaries, but it has yet to find reasons to reject old allies and do so.

Whether justices are nominated by partisan convention and elected on a nonpartisan ballot or appointed, they are still part of Michigan's politics. Attempts by the court to make appointments nonpolitical are only cosmetic and, given the court's greater interest in management than in policymaking, probably not very important. The Missouri Plan would only transfer the politics of judicial selection to the bar and the governor. Governors make choices based on personal and political viewpoints regardless of the selection method used.[20] Nor is there convincing evidence, as some have argued, that the appointment process leads to more qualified judges or to differences in types of decisions made.[21]

Many judges, however, first obtain their positions by appointment. Judges die, retire, change careers, or are removed during their terms. This gives the governor the opportunity to fill vacancies. Some judges deliberately schedule their resignations in order to permit the governor to name their replacements. For example, former Chief Justice Mary Coleman had wanted to retire from the supreme court in 1980. Governor Milliken persuaded her to change her plans. She did so and won another term, but then resigned a year later, enabling Milliken to name James Brickley, who had been Milliken's lieutenant governor and who was heir apparent to the governorship.[22] Similarly, Justice Dennis Archer, who had plans to run for the office of mayor of Detroit in the 1993 election, found himself having to resign from the bench in 1990 when Blanchard lost the executive office to John Engler. Resigning later would have allowed Engler to fill the vacancy. As a result, Blanchard appointed Conrad Mallett Jr., former legal adviser and legislative director, to fill the Archer vacancy. This practice is so common that in states like Michigan, which elect judges to the highest state court, more than half of the judges first gain a seat on the court through gubernatorial appointment.[23] Four of the current Michigan justices first attained the office by gubernatorial appointment. Reelection following an appointment, of course, is not guaranteed, but it is common because sitting judges have the word *incumbent* printed on the ballot alongside their names.

Gubernatorial appointment is a common way to obtain lower court judgeships, too. Milliken served as governor for thirteen years and appointed about 260 judges. Governor Blanchard appointed 99 judges, or almost one-fifth of all Michigan judges, in just his first term. Like governors before him, Blanchard appointed judges from his own political party. He, however, also increased the number of women and minorities on the bench. The procedure used to fill judicial vacancies is straightforward and not very confining to the chief executive. Candidates apply for appointment directly to the governor. When dossiers are complete, all names are sent to the Judicial Qualifications Committee of the Michigan State Bar. The committee interviews each candidate and evaluates the candidate's legal and personal background. Other attorneys familiar with the qualifications of the candidate make both written and oral comments. The committee then rates each candidate as not qualified, qualified, or highly qualified. The governor then selects the person of his or her choice on the list to serve until the next general election. Appointments are not subject to legislative approval.[24]

Not every lawyer who supported the winning gubernatorial candidate, of course, can be appointed to a judgeship. There are not that many vacancies or judgeships, for that matter. For nonappointees, name recognition, rather than experience and credentials in the practice of law, appears to be critical in gaining a seat on the court of appeals. What may be less evident, however, is that political ties, access to campaign contributions, and interest-group support are commonplace and provide reservoirs of support. In 1988, for example, Supreme Court Justice and former U.S. Senator Robert Griffin's son Richard won election to the court of appeals from the third district even though he had practiced law less than five years. Mark Cavanagh, the son of former Detroit Mayor Jerry Cavanagh and nephew of Justice Michael Cavanagh, won an appeals court seat in the same election.

Candidates for circuit, district, or probate court run from much smaller election districts – usually a county or parts of one – and politically attuned voters have a much better opportunity to gain at least some familiarity with candidates, if for no other reason than that many break into the news as prosecutors or attorneys for defendants. Partisan and nonpartisan linkages are essential to win these seats, but it is also essential that candidates have solid reputations. One judge, for example, argues that the turning point in his election was a letter sent by his well-respected physician father to a large number of county residents. This is not to say, of course, that candidates for state judicial positions have inappropriate credentials and reputations. Yet running a statewide race or even running from one of the three appeals court districts requires more than evidence of competence and local trust.

The court system continues to function within the political environment of the state, though not as a routine policy player. While the court system as a whole seeks to enhance its public stature by distancing itself from partisan politics in order to project an image of professional detachment, state politicians and interest groups always look for favorable ears and hearts in the lower courts, the court of appeals, and the supreme court. Few political activists support even the state bar's call for establishing minimum qualifications for judicial candidacy. Judges at all levels have become too important as political decision makers to allow them independence from the forces at play in this politically and economically diverse state.

Yet, despite these tensions between politics and management, the courts are well respected for being above the turmoil of regional and interest battles. As part of its administrative role, the supreme court has made it clear that changes of venue will be considered cautiously. Justices were particularly troubled by tort cases involving African Americans being changed to Wayne County for more favorable hearings. Veteran policymakers are even surprised at such actions: "There was once a rule, be politically responsive." Because the courts now try to stay above interest politics, governors and legislators also worry little about court overrides of state policies, especially when their legislative counsels have anticipated judicial concerns.

The same sense of ease and anticipation of predictability is far less true of federal courts and judges. Shopping for the most winnable federal judge, especially for appeals cases, is common. A Grand Rapids area judge, for example, was targeted by Native American plaintiffs on fishing rights cases: "That may have been the only court in the state where we could have won."

Also, a changing federal regulatory role, where Congress demands more of the states and writes legislation with greater generalization, makes the federal courts, more than the state courts, a party to policymaking. For example, one of the most important factors in keeping school finance reform alive over the years was concern with federal court action. In particular, the governor and legislature worried about Michigan "being in violation of federal equal-opportunity statutes." Thus, while the state courts fail to reflect the current diversity of Michigan politics, the federal courts increasingly fill their political and policy void.

SOME CLOSING THOUGHTS

It is doubtful that the framers of the 1963 constitution clearly saw what they were setting in motion when they wrote the judicial section of the new state charter. To be sure, the section was explicit in wanting to expand the right and opportunity to appeal lower court decisions and in its wishes to abolish the nonprofessional J P courts. The framers could not have known how much more litigious society would become. Nor could they have known how crime rates would increase, expanding the importance of the courts. Hence, it was not likely that the convention foresaw how supreme court justices would seek to bring new meaning to the phrases "one court of justice" and "under superintending control."

The Michigan Supreme Court has struggled to create a cohesive and coherent judicial bureaucracy, one that is willing to follow rules laid out at the highest court levels. In following this approach, the supreme court has modified its own role and, in many ways, has sought to become a manager of this extensive system. It is an uncertain bureaucracy because the supreme court does not select its key subordinates. Those who make it into the bureaucracy often are fiercely independent and quite political persons who do not happily yield to authority. Moreover, it is a bureaucracy that, for quality control and attainment of equal justice, depends on quasi-outsiders – the trial lawyers – to monitor the system through appeals. Such appeals, however, are often a function of client fees. Except for indigent persons who receive publicly paid counsel, nonindigents receive appeal review only if they are willing to pay an attorney.

The supreme court also struggles with its superintending mission because the legislature controls the major decision of how courts are funded. State funding would relieve the lower courts of having to deal with pesky county commissioners. To be sure, having the supreme court bargain in one location with the legislature would probably change the quality, if not the nature, of the bargaining. The supreme court has yet to persuade the legislature of just how the lower courts would benefit by state funding and why permanently assigning a block of revenues to the courts should have a higher priority than other services that use state spending. Nor has it properly convinced the legislature that the supreme court should be, as it is, more about management than judicial appeals. "I wonder," said one legislator, "if we have gone too far in taking the court away from the business of precedent setting and all that it entails." Another added, "We go to the trouble of helping with judicial appointments and elections; we should get judges that reflect more the values of different parts of the state." Such critics miss the teaching side of supreme court justice.

CHAPTER EIGHT

Inescapable Partisanship in a Ticket-Splitting State

Albert F. Palm and Gregg W. Smith are
also authors of this chapter

PARTIES, ISSUES, AND A MORALISTIC STATE CULTURE

Michigan has a strong and enduring attachment to its political parties. Almost all issues take on partisan overtones, even how highway personnel can best fill chuckholes. Because party platforms as well as legislative leaders offer alternative views about government, the state inescapably maintains a tradition of partisanship that encourages direct citizen involvement. Michigan's parties compete to control the offices of governor and lieutenant governor, secretary of state, and attorney general; select members of Congress; and form majorities in the legislature, on the Board of Education, and among the regents of the University of Michigan, trustees of Michigan State University, and governors of Wayne State University. In the counties, the parties vie to control the offices of prosecuting attorney, sheriff, clerk, treasurer, register of deeds, and, in most counties, drain and road commissioners, and to dominate the county commission.

Even nonpartisan judicial and municipal races often take on partisan tones as local cliques rally behind Democratic or Republican favorites. A 1992 race for Isabella County Circuit Court judge, for example, saw the candidates publicly debate judicial temperament and court administration. Another dominant issue in the campaign was the partisan loyalty of the two leading candidates. In this competitive county, the leading candidates wanted to capitalize on both their prior affiliation with one party and the political favors that they had performed for governors of the other. "There is no way," concluded one, "that we can keep this nonpartisan. That word is just rhetoric here."

This intense attachment to a relationship that ties parties, issues, and candidates together remains the most visible legacy of Michigan's moralistic cultural tradition. Connecting these three factors is the state's basic rule of politics. As Daniel Elazar explained in discussing debates over his typology of state cultures, the cultures are not substitutes for ideology and should not be treated as if they are.[1] Thus, a moralistic state is not necessarily liberal, but rather one in which all parts of the political spectrum engage in the difficult task of ascertaining the public welfare. Choices over which direction is correct become viewed in Michigan as property rights of the citizenry.

Democrats and Republicans articulate different views of the public's welfare as a means for providing these choices. This attribute of the state is what matters most in creating partisan intensity and incessant conflict. It also opens doors for escalating the effects of the state's individualistic culture by creating statewide opportunities for the mischiefs of factions. Michigan has not simply attracted partisan and issue-oriented political activists; rather, Michigan traditions have created these individuals and their institutions. As a result, intense regional and interest conflicts are not anomalies. These conflicts are logical extensions of strong partisanship, and they often exist in a party context that varies somewhat from locale to locale.

PARTY DEVELOPMENT AND THE RISE OF
REPUBLICAN DOMINANCE, 1827–1948

Michigan's political parties have formulated issues by emphasizing popular state needs and values, not by relying on cues from the political philosophies of the world or nation. Michigan, due to its New England settlers, already had an established and independent party system when it entered the Union in 1837. The twice-appointed acting territorial governor, Stevens T. Mason, was elected after statehood, serving as a counterpoint to populist President Andrew Jackson, who had removed him from office previously. Yet their differences were not ideological. The territorial conflict with Ohio led to the Toledo War, caused the governor's removal, and split Michigan Democrats from national Democrats.[2] For sixteen of the first eighteen years of statehood, Michigan had a Democratic governor; but the issue of slavery kept driving wedges between Michigan and national Democratic leaders. The slavery controversy isolated the state still further when James G. Birney of Bay City led the anti-slavery Liberty Party as its presidential candidate in both 1840 and, with more impact, in 1844.[3] The vote for Birney in 1844 affected the outcome of the presidential election because votes cast for Birney in Michigan and New York helped elect Democrat James K. Polk president over his Whig opponent.

This peculiar history went on at length. Lewis Cass, a prominent Michigan politician during the period from statehood to the Civil War, was the Democratic party's candidate for president in 1848. His support for the annexation of Texas and other issues that played well in the South labeled him a doughface, a northern Democrat with southern principles. That, along with the emergence of the Free-Soil party, was the major reason for his defeat in a Democratic party that was fighting to hold the states together. Cass finished his political career as a U.S. senator by announcing allegiance to the Republican party and its position in favor of the war and against slavery. Historians laud Cass for his later vote in the Senate in 1868, preventing the conviction of Republican President Andrew Johnson on impeachment charges.

Such decisions led to Michigan's reputation for leadership in the emerging Republican party. Whether the Grand Old Party (GOP) was formed in Jackson, Michigan, or Ripon, Wisconsin, is still a matter of some disagreement among historians. None dispute, however, the importance of the Jackson meeting, "under the oaks," on July 6, 1854.[4] It was there that the Republican party got its name, adopted a platform, and nominated its first candidates. More important, the meeting in Jackson, unlike the one in Ripon, was a mass event, a demonstration of popular support for political change. The Michigan population, swollen by German farmers in midstate and Dutch farmers in the southwest, was vocally expressive about its strong beliefs against slavery. Early Scandinavian residents in the northern part of the state contributed to that support. The Republicans, accordingly, had more success in the state than they did nationally. Republicans dominated Michigan through the Great Depression, during World War II, and until the election of G. Mennen Williams as governor in 1948. By that time, eastern and southern European immigrants along with newly arrived Appalachian whites and southern blacks had developed a strong Democratic base in the Detroit area.

There was more to the state's initial casting as a moralistic state than its Republican, anti-slavery heritage. Michigan previously had been a national leader in the development of the "party in the electorate" – membership by simple, personal identification. Prior to 1827, political parties, as we know them today, did not exist in Michigan. What passed for party politics were unaligned factions, cliques, and groups linked to elite personalities and political patronage.[5] Political parties with identifiable support from specific social and demographic groups and their issues gradually evolved after 1827 and into the Civil War.

Things gradually changed, however, as patronage gave way to different views about government. Michigan's emerging moralistic political culture was receptive to populism and progressivism, and both, especially the latter, had a significant impact on state politics by further encouraging mass participation. Politicians, as a result, were less inclined to rely on support from state elites and their control of local followings, watching instead a shifting and attentive electorate that was prone even then to turn on Republicans. Greenbacks, an early party of the populist movement, along with fusion Democrats nominated Josiah W. Begole for governor in 1882. He went on to win the election by 4,572 votes and then lost narrowly two years later to his Republican opponent. Fusionists still won seven of Michigan's eleven congressional seats, though. Republicans responded to this setback by joining the reform movement, which consequently reduced the influence of the Greenbacker vote in Michigan. The reformist trends also had national repercussions. The Republican gubernatorial candidate in 1896 was a noted reformer who played a key role in keeping Republicanism on a reform path. Detroit Mayor Hazen Pingree helped carry Michigan for William McKinley against William Jennings Bryan, the Democratic candidate and a leading populist.[6]

The Progressive era in Michigan paralleled that movement nationally, but was most intense in the three upper Great Lakes states, which shared a similar moralistic heritage.[7] Results of that reform effort were numerous in Michigan. A state primary election law was adopted in 1905 and modified in 1909. The advent of electoral primaries as a method for selecting party nominees had a lasting impact on the openness of the state's political parties, as they did, to some extent, throughout the United States. Michigan's 1909 law, however, required parties to nominate candidates for governor, U.S. senator, U.S. representative, state legislators, and city officers in Detroit and Grand Rapids through a process of citizen involvement. This allowed the public to put the actual content of political debates in play by linking their issues to choices of candidates.

In 1913, the amendment to the state's constitution that provided for citizen initiatives, referenda, and recalls gave voters still more direct control over issues and politicians. The rules were then set to permit, for example, incidents like the one in 1983 where two state senators were recalled from office for voting in favor of an income-tax increase. This was the catalyst eventually boosting John Engler to the governor's office. Other reforms related to the Progressive movement were also adopted during the period from 1904 to the Great Depression and helped Michigan become a leader in advancing a participative reform agenda that today colors its politics.

After the reform era, partisan politics in Michigan entered a period of relative stability. A Republican electorate, nurtured by its Civil War loyalty to the GOP and its independence from outsiders, was not much affected by the national shift in voter identification that created a new Democratic majority beginning with the election of President Roosevelt in 1932. Even with the Depression of the 1930s and the labor unrest that mobilized the United Automobile Workers, Republicans usually controlled statewide offices as they did the legislature and most county governments. Malapportionment and the state's rural character helped to maintain the Republican grip. But it was also because Michigan's economy weathered the Great Depression relatively well. Hence, Michigan's electoral realignment did not occur until the 1950s and 1960s when, along with the demise of malapportionment, the Democrats with their recent state migrants from the South became a competitive alternative to the Republicans.[8] When the principle of one person–one vote became a reality in Lansing, the state electorate was freed from the vestiges of rural domination. But this did not reverse state politics as many had hoped and others feared. Since then, a surprising number of voters have shopped for parties and candidates much like they do groceries, looking for the best deal rather than just the brand label. These ticket-splitters and their independence from party loyalty determine much about shifts in party competition and politics in Michigan.

DEMOCRATS MAKE THE STATE COMPETITIVE, 1948–66

A new Democratic coalition was born in 1948 and maintained itself through control of the governorship until 1962. This period did much to change the state because it was a time of increasing sophistication among the Michigan electorate. This was true, at least, if electoral sophistication and a tendency to shop for candidates and their issue positions are synonymous. G. Mennen Williams, United Auto Workers President Walter Reuther, August "Gus" Scholle, who headed the Michigan C.I.O. Council, Detroit lawyer Hick Griffiths, and Neil Staebler of Ann Arbor, along with several other prominent liberal politicians, were the catalysts for change. Together, they mapped out a strategy for building a winning coalition in the face of Republican dominance.[9] Faction-plagued Democrats from around the state and representing various ethnic groups had long differed over the ranking of issues used to challenge Republicans and, as a result, had not worked well together.[10] The liberal/labor coalition sought to take advantage of the large number of Democratic labor union members and provide inducements to link them with long disenfranchised liberal intellectuals in the 1948 primary election.[11] The intent, long before court-ordered reapportionment, was to defeat old-guard Democrats who wanted to deny the socially conscious Williams the nomination for governor. The new coalition, guided by Staebler's strategy, sought to appeal to outstate rather than only southeastern Michigan's ethnic voters. It prevailed and became the linchpin of Democratic dominance.

The coalition strategy worked against the old guard and also succeeded in the general election, in part because the Republican party suffered from its own schism. Conservative Republicans viewed incumbent Governor Kim Sigler as too liberal. Accordingly, many Republicans urged the election of the Democrat in 1948, with the hope that they could nominate a conservative candidate two years later and defeat Williams in 1950.[12] The choice-oriented and never captive electorate, bombarded with messages about new directions in state politics, responded. The Republican presidential candidate, Thomas E. Dewey, a native of Owosso, Michigan, carried the state easily. But Williams beat former Governor Harry Kelly in 1950 and later Secretary of State Fred M. Alger Jr. in 1952. Both were close elections, decided only after recounts. In running for an unprecedented fourth term in 1954, however, Williams defeated Donald S. Leonard by a wide margin and, for the second consecutive election, established that the Democratic party was the party of the majority in Michigan. The 1954 election swept Democrats into all state administrative offices, gave them a majority on the supreme court and both U.S. Senate seats, and increased their numbers in the state house of representatives. Malapportionment, though, still kept the Democrats from capturing the legislature.

The 1950s, however, was not a Democratic era. The Republican party carried Michigan in the presidential races of the 1950s. The vote for President Dwight D. Eisenhower on the one hand, and Democrat Williams on the other, provided evidence of increased split-ticket voting. The personal popularity of both Eisenhower and Williams contributed to this voter tendency. More important, the results demonstrated to the electorate that split-ticket voting was useful for controlling politicians and shaping public policy.[13] By the 1960s, ticket-splitters were deciding even more, if not most, Michigan elections.

The Democratic party, nonetheless, continued to develop under Williams, and Lansing policymakers passed considerable liberal legislation.[14] However, to get them to do so, Williams had to appeal to the direct interests of labor voters and use labor activists to promote his agenda. It became obvious that labor had a self-interest that came first. Only when economic times were good did labor support generally progressive social welfare policies. In 1960, with doubts about his continued viability as an avowed liberal in an ideologically mixed state, Williams decided not to run for a seventh term. Nonetheless, he remained in position to pass the party mantle to an heir, even though his years as governor had scarred his reputation from more than just an ideological perspective. As governor, Williams had engaged in many pitched battles with the Republican-dominated legislature. Some of these confrontations, specifically the payless paydays of 1959, gave Michigan and Williams a negative image throughout the country. Lieutenant Governor John B. Swainson and Secretary of State James M. Hare, seeing a likely Democratic victory if Williams was gone, fought a bitter, issue-filled primary for the nomination.

Swainson won both the primary and the general election. But the dispute between Swainson and Hare over the issue of a constitutional convention marked the beginning of the end for the Williams-era coalition. Intellectuals, in particular, felt that demands for change on critical social issues had too long taken a back seat to the immediate political demands of labor issues. Where, they asked, was the promised social laboratory that many saw Reuther and the UAW obstructing? Swainson was unable to handle the unsolved problems left from Williams's administration, many of which were felt to need constitutional attention, or to heal the split created by the 1960 primary battle. In truth, he knew he could afford to eliminate neither liberals nor labor from his personal base of supporters. He also understood that their views were not entirely compatible.

Yet even with this split, Democratic fortunes were on the rise. Although the Republicans controlled the legislature throughout Williams's years, a majority of voters began to vote consistently for the Democratic party. Swainson's demise, therefore, was not bemoaned by all loyal Democrats. The election of 1962 started a new era for the Republicans – and their cooperation with Democrats – when GOP candidate George Romney won the governorship, a post that the party would hold for twenty years. Many voters from both parties saw his victory as a mandate to resolve Michigan's constitutional dilemmas through good-government reforms. In that period, the Democrats kept a plurality among party identifiers, but ticket-splitting became even more widespread. The Democrats, not surprisingly, lost many previously entrenched voters to the reformist Romney.

This milestone in Michigan politics revealed the interests of voters to be more attuned to candidates and issues rather than to partisan and coalition loyalties. In 1964, a year in which the Democrats swept virtually every elective office in Michigan, Republican Romney won by a stunning margin. President Lyndon B. Johnson beat Republican Barry Goldwater by two to one in the presidential race, and the Democrats gained control of both houses of the state legislature. Romney owed his victory to his open opposition to Goldwater and to his strong stand for civil rights as a manifestation of the public interest in what was increasingly an ethnically diverse state. Romney won by skillfully appealing to intellectuals and African-American voters who were felt to be cores of the state Democratic party base. In 1966, Romney easily defeated the even more liberal Democrat, Zolton Ferency, and earned the first four-year term for a Michigan governor. Even with reapportionment, Republicans also won both houses of the legislature.

The 1966 election year also included a bitter primary fight for the U.S. Senate nomination in the Democratic party. Former Governor Williams and Detroit Mayor Jerome Cavanagh both fought hard for the nomination. Meanwhile, the Democratic gubernatorial nomination had gone to Ferency by default. Ferency had been the state party chairman and a self-identified radical who previously had not carried even his party's intellectuals. He was in the race, however, because most prominent Democrats were unwilling to face Romney. Gus Scholle, leader of the state AFL-CIO, was displeased with the prospect of Ferency as the Democratic candidate, but could not persuade any other notable to run. There were good reasons for him to want to dump Ferency, including the fear of potential voter alienation within the party. Although Scholle finally accepted Ferency, he continued to worry about the effect of Ferency's views on an already divisive race for the Senate seat.[15]

Congressman Robert Griffin became the Republican Senate nominee. His coauthorship of the Landrum-Griffin Act, which regulates internal labor-union matters, made him all but despised by state unions. This made it almost mandatory for labor to defeat Griffin or lose face for its inability to control the central electorate of the Democratic party on a bottom-line question of party faith. To complicate matters, the other senator, Democrat Patrick McNammara, died. Romney appointed candidate Griffin to the unexpired term to give Griffin the advantage of incumbency in a heated race. In the election, Romney beat Ferency by 500,000 votes. Griffin won an unexpectedly easy victory with a 220,000-vote margin over Williams. The Republicans also gained significantly in the legislature, while Williams suffered his first defeat at the hands of Michigan's voters. Moreover, Democratic party factions were left especially bitter with one another.

The election results of 1966 summarized well the condition of politics in Michigan. Malapportionment was ended, and the Democratic outstate strategy of appealing to different regional interests had been successful. Despite the state's national reputation as home to "big labor," however, the emergent Democratic party proved that it was not and would not be a captured entity. While unions were Democratic, there were too many internal cleavages for the Democratic party to be union-controlled at the ballot box. Not even union members avoided the appeal of ticket-splitting. What was evident by that time is that Republicans and Democrats alike remained competitive in the state, specifically encouraging controversy and conflict over issues that would shake the very foundations of the "party in the electorate," or the voters' basic partisan identification. The victory was one of the state's moralistic political culture over individualism, where neither union nor any other bosses would determine who it was that voters would favor. There was an insistence that the public be afforded extensive opportunities to consider an array of issues that candidates stood behind. When the Democrats finally made Michigan competitive, they did so by continuing the state's longstanding tradition of keeping parties both important and in check. They did not allow it to be a knee-jerk liberal state or one of partisan gridlock.

THE BIPARTISAN YEARS AND THEIR PASSAGE, 1966–78

George Romney, however, was to be the standard-bearer for setting only the beginnings of a new tone for Michigan politics. He exited quickly. Romney's success as governor, along with his vote-getting ability, made him a potential and, for many, front-running candidate for the Republican presidential nomination in 1968. But a statement made by Romney during a Detroit television interview on September 7, 1967, regarding his October 1965 tour of Vietnam, led to his downfall. In the interview, Romney stated that he had received "the greatest brainwashing that anybody can get" about the Vietnam War at the hands of the U.S. military. This statement made headlines in all the wrong ways for Romney. The national media portrayed him as ill-prepared and too naive to be president. When Richard Nixon was elected president in 1968, he nonetheless appointed Romney as Secretary of Housing and Urban Development and, for all practical purposes, removed him from state politics. This move elevated Lieutenant Governor William Milliken to the executive office and brought in a new political era. Milliken had not even been expected to win in what conventional political wisdom saw to be a Democratic state. But ticket-splitting and public attentiveness to a candidate's issue choices were both still being underestimated. Milliken went on to serve fourteen years, longer than any governor in Michigan history to that point.[16] In doing so, he pioneered the politics of monitoring issues by region and then addressing them to the appropriate crowds.

Milliken first ran for governor in 1970. He faced Democratic state Senator Sander Levin in a typical race, one in which a contested local issue became hot on a statewide basis. The issue was state aid to parochial schools. Early in the race, Levin attacked Milliken for his support of aid to parochial schools, but when Levin seemed to reverse his own early opposition, he lost the support of the important and Democratically inclined Michigan Education Association. Milliken won a close election by a margin of 44,409 votes.

Michigan's two-party politics during the Milliken years was seldom so simple again. With Milliken, and his elaborate polling operations, there was never just one critical issue for the statewide electorate. The governor actually thought regionally, and the strategy of using opinion polls to sample variances in issue preferences from around the state allowed him to do so effectively. The hallmark strategy of these campaigns was to identify issues by region and even community, run ads, and stop frequently in each community to discuss what local citizens considered most important, and then resample opinion to keep the cycle of personal attention current.

Milliken also benefited from several other factors that should not have been unexpected in this state. First, state Democrats were turned by their intellectuals to national issues of civil rights, the war in Vietnam, and other idealistic issues of the late 1960s.[17] Often their energies were consumed more by strife within their own party than with any concern about Republican activities. Second, labor chose to confront rather than accommodate these proponents of "new politics," seeing them as radicals who would cost the party popular support and hurt labor's ability to deliver on its bread-and-butter issues. "These people," said an old labor leader, "were less concerned with protecting old gains in this country than they were with international grievances of every down-trodden group in the world. That scared us, badly." Third, resulting events and disagreements moved the state Democratic party to the left of much of the electorate. Alabama Governor George C. Wallace capitalized on that movement and forcefully attacked the new politics in the state, further damaging Michigan Democrats. As the years of the Milliken administration show, the electorate had moved to a point where it was responding to plain talk about what it knew and liked best. It was shunning what it perceived to be risky, uncertain, and often abstract issues. The public's preference for issue moderation controlled partisan loyalty. Party loyalty, as a consequence, did not move the voters to these new issues, which bitterly disappointed "new issue" advocates who saw Michigan as a liberal base for making national gains.

Student and racial protests during the 1968 National Democratic Convention in Chicago had a procedural as well as issue effect on the Michigan Democratic party in the early 1970s. The Commission on Party Structure and Delegate Selection, better known as the McGovern-Fraser Commission, called for democratized reform of delegate selection to the 1972 national convention. The procedures used in Michigan did not meet the new requirements. As a result, the state party had to change the delegate-selection procedures to meet national party directives. A bitter fight surfaced in the Michigan Democratic party. There was one particularly contentious point. An important clause in the national reforms said: "State parties must overcome the effect of past discrimination by affirmative steps to encourage minority group participation, including representation of minority groups on the National Convention delegation in reasonable relationship to the group's presence in the population of the state."[18] Nationally, and particularly in Michigan, many feared that this was an implied quota system that would change the balance of party power. The state worry was that Detroit would gain in strength while rural influence would erode. To Michiganians, this was a renewal of decades-old regional competition, not an issue of racial justice. Thus, the moralistic judgments of many Democrats determined that such actions within the party were not in the public welfare of the state. Because labor also saw severe disadvantage in these reforms, conflict and distrust escalated.

The new rules also stated that delegate selection was not to begin until the year of a presidential election. However, Michigan law called for the selection of precinct delegates two years before a presidential election. This selection of precinct delegates was the first step in choosing delegates to the national convention. Michigan Democrats were in turmoil. They could not change the procedures without changing the law. Labor Democrats and other party regulars wanted to moderate the reforms by holding new precinct-delegate elections in the spring of even-numbered years. To meet the McGovern-Fraser Commission's guidelines, the proposal called for precinct delegates to be placed on the ballot along with their endorsement of a specific presidential candidate. Those supporting this reform wanted to thwart what they saw as "the radicals" and to keep power in the hands of labor and regular Democrats. In a confusing twist that split the party in three segments, they also wanted to frustrate the possibility of a good showing by Governor George Wallace in any Democratic presidential election. Wallace was running an openly racist campaign for president after a well-publicized tenure as a segregationist governor who attempted to prevent school integration. However, changes in the delegate-selection rules potentially worked to his advantage. But national reform forces cared little about byzantine state problems. A national reform organization, the New Democratic Coalition (NDC), pushed for a presidential primary as a means to meet national party requirements and expand the voters' role in presidential candidate selection. Any reform of the delegate-selection laws needed the governor's help. Luckily for the NDC, Governor Milliken came out in favor of a presidential primary, much to the chagrin of mainstream state Democrats as well as Michigan's conservative Republicans.

Conservative Republicans delighted in the Democrats' possible problems for violating national Democratic rules. They were not pleased at the prospect of letting Democrats off the hook by adopting a presidential primary. Milliken's support of a primary did not sit well with labor because its leaders adamantly opposed the primary and loss of their back-room power in candidate selection. While the proposal to have new precinct-delegate elections did not become law, the fight over the issue of a precinct-delegate election versus a presidential primary created serious disruptions in the Democratic party. Labor did not yield easily. At an open meeting of the Democratic State Central Committee, labor carried the day on the first vote against a presidential primary. However, in a revote, two state party leaders switched their votes, and the central committee endorsed a primary. Labor leaders felt betrayed and again manifested their bitterness at the disruptive results of factionalized party decisions. In the primary, and to the surprise of the "new politics" Democrats, labor's worst fears came true. George Wallace carried the Democratic primary with 51 percent of the vote and, in outstate regions with few African Americans, won eighty out of eighty-three counties.

George McGovern, the eventual Democratic presidential nominee and the "new politics" favorite in the 1972 primary, carried only three counties, all with large university votes. Wallace's strength in Michigan pointed to the serious racial questions facing the Democratic party and the state.

All of Wallace's votes, however, did not come from Democrats. Having an open primary, in a year when Richard Nixon was virtually unopposed in the Republican primary, allowed independents and Republicans to cross over and vote for Wallace in the Democratic primary. Unfortunately for Wallace, labor and Democratic regulars managed to control the selection of the actual delegates to the national convention. Wallace supporters were not familiar with internal party rules and found themselves easily outmaneuvered by the regulars. Many delegates, who by law had to support Wallace, were actually Democratic regulars. They went to the convention as Wallace delegates, but cast their votes only because the law required it. The aftermath was not surprising. In November, Richard Nixon easily carried Michigan while many labor leaders sat on their hands because of their dislike of McGovern and his supporters. As a UAW leader of the era noted, "Ohhh, we hated those leftists, and Nixon was very tolerable. A tough guy who spoke out."

In state elections, little of party consequence went on for the next two years, until Governor Milliken again faced Sander Levin in 1974. Levin tried to tie Milliken to the Republicans' Watergate scandal. Unemployment in the auto industry was also a major issue. While Democrats picked up four congressional seats, Milliken and his campaign of regional issues increased his margin over Levin and the still troubled Democrats. He won by 114,618 votes. This set in motion a period of instate cooperation where Michigan legislative Democrats, if they were to please the electorate, knew they needed to cooperate first with Milliken on state issues and worry later about their national party's woes.

In 1978, Milliken faced State Senator William Fitzgerald, the Democratic nominee and Senate majority leader. Significant to the 1978 race was an issue, mentioned in earlier chapters, arising from a terrible error in a Gratiot County chemical plant. A highly toxic fire retardant, polybrominated biphenyl (PBB), was mixed with a food supplement for dairy cattle. The contaminated feed was distributed to Michigan dairy farmers and, from there, found its way into the consumers' food chain.[19] When the incident came to light in 1974, farmers demanded assistance from the state, but not vocally enough at first to create an electoral issue. Government responses came even more slowly, and by 1976, Democrats were accusing Milliken of covering up the incident to prevent monetary losses for Michigan's dairy industry. In 1978, the governor's response to the crisis became a campaign issue. Yet Milliken survived the crisis with a strong showing in areas of the state thought not to be directly involved in the PBB episode. Indeed, he began his last term as governor with a degree of statewide credibility because of his public disciplining of the Department of Agriculture.

In the same election, Democrat Carl Levin challenged Robert Griffin for the U.S. Senate seat. Griffin had earlier announced that he would not run when his Republican colleagues in the Senate passed him by for the position of minority leader. Griffin said that he had lost interest in being a senator and, for a time, was absent from Senate meetings. Pressured by state Republicans, Griffin changed his mind and attempted to return. Levin beat him in the November election, citing the importance of a senator who truly wants to serve. This gave both U.S. Senate seats to the Democratic party. Showing the voters' sensitivity and ability to continually follow issues, the PBB matter was also an indirect factor in that race.

Many farmers affected by the PBB incident were located in the Tenth District, a crescent-shaped area from Big Rapids to near Cadillac. Normally, Republicans would carry the area. In 1978, however, Milliken, Griffin, and Congressman Elfred Cederberg lost much of the Republican vote of the region. Don Albosta, a Democratic state legislator and farmer, had strongly supported the farmers affected by the PBB incident. Without previous political strength, he became the Democratic candidate and won the election. He did so for one reason, as he explained in 1980, "I put Democrats in tractorcades and on small city streets. While the Republicans talked about farm issues, I wrapped myself in them."[20]

PARTY AND CULTURE: A CUMULATIVE EFFECT

To understand Michigan's shifting two-party competition and its effect on politics in a moralistic yet mixed culture, it helps to recall John H. Fenton's comments in *Midwest Politics*.[21] Although many things have changed since this book was completed, many constants about state government remain. Fenton, like Elazar, emphasized the importance of political culture as a determinant of public policy. He pointed out that, after 1948, Michigan's politics, like those of Wisconsin and Minnesota, were clearly issue-oriented. Illinois, Indiana, and Ohio, in contrast, were focused on political jobs. The Democratic party's *Michigan Declaration* of 1956 is a prime example of this state's emphasis on issues. That document outlined liberal principles of civil liberties, civil rights, economic policy, health, education, automation, and agriculture, all pertaining to highly specific state interests.[22] In contrast, the Republican party adopted a conservative approach toward these issues. As a result, controversial votes in the state legislature were frequently played out along partisan lines that often meshed well with the regional differences between, for example, Detroit and midstate farming regions.

Labor influence became very important during the era about which Fenton wrote, and solidified the state's issue orientation.[23] There existed, after all, a specific interest within the Democratic party that, from both masses and leaders, wanted something tangible for their loyalty. Ideological compatibility with no service was not enough. Today, as it has for four decades, labor plays out much of its political role through the state Democratic party, usually by supporting its candidates.[24] The Committee on Political Education (COPE), created by the labor movement, allowed activists to merge general election politics more directly with the promotion of labor issues in Lansing.[25] COPE remains a legal way for unions to endorse and support partisans with many different resources, especially money and campaign workers. Such support, labor leaders have argued, overcomes the divisive effects of an otherwise factionalized party. In many ways, COPE, as the forerunner of today's political action committees (PACs), made union politics important in Michigan and gained for the state a reputation as the home for organized labor. This was accomplished even though labor leaders, when pressed for concessions, had to acknowledge that their unions were just another set of organized interests in a complex state.

Business, specifically the auto industry, played an important role in the Republican party's response to early labor initiatives.[26] The conflict between auto industry leaders and the labor movement, along with party competitiveness, dominated Michigan politics into the 1970s, declining only with the emergence of bipartisan leadership under Governor Milliken. Organized labor, which now includes teachers unions, is still the single most important element in the Democratic party organization. For example, nearly half the delegates to the 1992 Democratic National Convention were members of organized labor. Auto industry leaders, though, are much less involved in Republican politics. They emphasize issues by taking them to both sides of the political aisle under the guise of state economic development.

The politics of unions and management produced more than just conflict and partisanship in the 1950s and into the Milliken years. Issue contests between these two giants had an impact on the public's attitude toward scandal and corruption, in part because politics was watched carefully with these suspect behemoths so involved. Again, this is an expectation of a moralistic political culture where watching out for the state's ability to deal with the public welfare remains an attribute of the entire political community. Other interests do not want to get into, as one lobbyist said, "a pissing match with a two-ton skunk." Vigilance has remained a watchword that is encouraged by numerous less well financed interests. Wealthy interests could easily outpurchase smaller ones if bribery or even power politics was condoned. The emphasis on issues, or solutions to problems rather than patronage for parties, works with this vigilance to keep Michigan clean. Thus, while numerous other state interests have come into prominence since Fenton wrote, the continued importance of these still vital state interests to the economy means that their issues are always prominent on the state's agenda. "I often argue," said one lobbyist for small business, "that you cannot say no to me if you've just said yes to the big guys. The public won't buy it."

PARTY ORGANIZATION AND PARTY VOTE: WHAT WE NOW SEE

This historical development allows us to consider how parties are organized and how they operate in Michigan. Among the American states, historical precedents create great variability on both counts. Party organizations in the state are based on geographically defined boundaries. These cover all areas of all size throughout the state. They range from the Republican and Democratic state party organizations that cover Michigan from their Lansing headquarters to the party organizations of, for example, the second precinct, first ward, Kent County, of Grand Rapids. While Michigan parties appear from the outside to be hierarchically organized, especially with their strong and vocal central committees, the connection between the upper echelon and lower units is loose. All levels of party organization have a common interest in getting their candidates elected, but the ability of the state organization to dictate policies to local organizations is limited. Often the concerns of the state party differ considerably from those of the local party. These local issues are not cast aside by party operatives; rather, they pick up local issues as their own whenever such issues can be made to fit their purposes.

Political parties can best be seen as quasi-public institutions that are regulated by law and that nominate candidates for election to public office. With the electorate's emphasis on checking extremes of partisanship, regulation in Michigan is taken seriously. Michigan is among nineteen states considered to be heavy regulators of their parties.[27] For example, the selection, composition, and procedures of both state and county party organizations is specified by state law. Compared to other states, however, Michigan laws governing the electoral process are generally supportive of political parties.[28] For example, candidates for all statewide offices except governor are chosen at party conventions; parties are allowed to endorse candidates in primary elections; and voters can cast a "straight party ballot" instead of voting for candidates individually. More than anything, this reflects the historically "clean politics" found in Michigan parties. Bossism and machines that or-

Table 13: Characteristics of Michigan County Democratic and Republican Party Organizations

	Number	%
Have complete set of officers	143	93
Recruit volunteer workers	119	90
Operate under formal rules	110	72
Publish a newsletter	51	39
Have a regular budget	50	33
Have a telephone listing	37	24
Maintain a permanent headquarters	31	20
Employ part-time staff	18	12
Employ full-time staff	12	8

Note: N = 153 respondent organizations. Response rate = 94 percent.

Source: Data are based on a questionnaire mailed to all Michigan county chairs in 1986. See Gregg W. Smith, "The Effect of Party Organizational Strength on Electoral Success" (paper presented at the 1987 annual meeting of the Midwest Political Science Association).

ganize voters through jobs and other payoffs to voters have been relatively rare.

Both Republicans and Democrats have moderately strong state party organizations. In a 1984 study assessing the organizational strength of ninety state parties in forty-nine states, Michigan Democrats were ranked eleventh and Michigan Republicans were twenty-second.[29] Both parties operate a permanent party headquarters, employ a professional staff, recruit candidates for office, and provide assistance to candidates and local party organizations. Republicans, however, do considerably more of all of these things. Democrats, despite their high ranking, often depend on organized union support to get their tasks underway.

County party organizations are also comparatively strong. In a national study ranking the states on the average strength of each party's local organization, Michigan Democrats were ranked twelfth and the Republicans were fourteenth.[30] Because these rankings are based on averages, they conceal the variation that exists between the counties. Some local party organizations are very strong while others are almost nonexistent. A comparative review of county party organizations, their characteristics, and the activities they perform reveals those differences.

Table 13 shows that most county party organizations have officers who operate under a formal set of rules, but few have a permanent headquarters or

Table 14: Campaign Programs Conducted by Michigan County Democratic and Republican Party Organizations

	Number	%
Distribute literature	140	92
Arrange fund-raising events	131	86
Distribute posters or lawn signs	125	82
Contribute money to candidates	124	82
Organize campaign events	109	72
Publicize party with press releases	108	71
Organize telephone campaigns	106	70
Buy newspaper advertising	105	70
Send mailings to voters	98	64
Organize door-to-door canvassing	93	61
Coordinate county-level campaigns	90	59
Conduct registration drives	57	38
Conduct candidate training sessions	46	35
Buy radio or T.V. advertising	45	30
Utilize public opinion surveys	42	28
Arrange other campaign activities	23	18
Coordinate local PAC activity	22	17
Purchase billboard space	9	6

Note: N = 153 respondent organizations. Response rate = 94 percent.

Source: Data are based on a questionnaire mailed to all Michigan county chairs in 1986. See Gregg W. Smith, "The Effect of Party Organizational Strength on Electoral Success" (paper presented at the 1987 annual meeting of the Midwest Political Science Association).

paid staff.[31] The typical county party has the basic elements of organization but lacks the sophistication in campaign technology associated with state and national parties. As seen in table 14, however, this lack of sophistication has not deterred the county parties from conducting numerous programs to get votes for their candidates.[32] In an activist state where nearly everyone can be a player, involvement is not predicated on technical and professional capacity.

But are these active organizations effective at getting votes for their candidates? An analysis of seventy Michigan counties from 1982 to 1986 found that, in general, neither Republican nor Democratic party organizational strength had a significant impact on electoral outcome.[33] County party organizational strength was also unrelated to the percentage of county-registered voters who voted in 1988.[34] These studies cast doubt on the ability of political parties to persuade and mobilize the electorate in Michigan or, perhaps, the need for them to do so. This finding is hardly surprising because Michigan voters tend to weigh issues more heavily than party labels. Another important factor is absence of machines and patronage. Michigan has never had the type of traditional party organizations that can deliver the party vote through an elaborate network of government employees.[35] Unions, ethnic groups, and strong local commitment have apparently not filled that void.

Michiganians are reluctant to support blindly either party, and about 33 percent of the electorate call themselves independents. Hence, most voters do have a party identification. Ultimately, the independents must choose from among party candidates. This means that relative voting strength, as measured by past performance, is important to understanding party influence. An analysis of Michigan voting for both state and federal offices between 1958 and 1990 indicated that the average support for Democratic candidates was about 52 percent and about 48 percent for Republican candidates.[36] Compared to the national vote, Michigan has tended to be somewhat more Republican than the United States as a whole, but is somewhat more Democratic in comparison to other Midwest states. Two factors explain that Democratic vote. First the state's African Americans, 13.9 percent of the population, vote overwhelmingly Democratic. Second, organized labor, which has increasingly been more responsive to African-American issues but which is still beset by ticket-splitting among white members, works hard to mobilize voters. This means that Democrats are heavily dependent on the Detroit, Pontiac, Flint, and Saginaw industrial and minority corridor, where, most of the time, a heavy vote can be mobilized.

Interparty competition appears likely to remain high, in part because state and county political leaders face difficult problems: a declining tax base, less help from Washington, and numerous opportunities to appeal to a shifting set of voters. Accordingly, both parties will continue to be under pressure to formulate policies that produce results. They will also be pressured to foster candidates, especially for governor, who are willing to be held accountable for the condition of the state. Given voting patterns and the great likelihood of voter dissatisfaction carrying over in a troubled economy, electoral stability for one party or the other will continue as an elusive goal.

This instability of the statewide vote shows up in regional electoral patterns over time. Since 1980, a majority of the state's voters have come from only four counties: Wayne, with Detroit as its core; Oakland, just to the north; Macomb, to Oakland's east; and Kent, with Grand Rapids at its center. Wayne is the state's most Democratic county, with consistently more than 65 percent of its residents voting for Democrats. But the other two Detroit metro counties show a partisan division between new suburbs and older places, including the central city. Oakland, with its larger population and up to 60 percent Republican vote, turns out twice as many voters from that party as does Kent. Macomb, which is smaller in size and more blue-collar, tends to be Republican but divides its vote more closely. With such concentrations of voters, other counties matter far less. Democrats usually carry only the western Upper Peninsula and a significantly African-American county, Lake, in the northwest lower peninsula. Republicans, with some exceptions, dominate the lower peninsula's western counties and the central east coast area known as the thumb. Other outstate counties tend to be Republican.

Efforts to maximize electoral gains within this uncertain environment do not, however, concentrate partisan attention on state and federal offices. Quite the contrary. As county governments are forced to become more self-reliant, control of county offices becomes more important as a means of winning voter attention. In 1988, about 66 percent of all county officers and county commissions were Republican. Despite this advantage, the Republican party has not dominated the county vote. Table 15 ranks each county according to its expected percentage of the Democratic vote, with Ottawa being the least Democratic at 32.2 percent and Gogebic being the most Democratic at 69.4 percent. But these figures are somewhat misleading in terms of day-to-day political strategies. The expected vote is only an analytical means of looking at a hypothetical situation, as though issues and candidates were not a factor in an election. In reality, Michigan voters look at much more information than the candidate's party identification.[37] Thus, even county swings for individual candidates are often evident.

So, what really matters in getting voters to the polls? High levels of party competition, a moralistic political culture, a relatively open voter-registration process, and a history of mass involvement all help to explain why voter turnout in Michigan is higher than in most other states. From 1976 to 1988, the average turnout for presidential elections in Michigan was about 58 percent, the thirteenth highest in the nation. In 1992, with President George Bush immensely unpopular but with Republicans making an all-out assault on the state house of representatives, Michiganians ranked somewhat higher. Turnout for nonpresidential elections is much lower. For example, only 38.7 percent of Michigan's voting-age population went to the polls in the 1990 general election. Yet, this, too, reflects higher-than-average turnout and shows the unusual attentiveness of Michigan's electorate and the degree to which local politics matters to its citizenry.

Table 15: Expected Democratic Percentage of the County Vote

Ottawa	32.2	Luce	47.1	Oscoda	54.2
Sanilac	37.3	Oceana	47.8	Muskegon	54.6
Allegan	38.8	Oakland	48.4	Saginaw	54.9
Leelanau	39.2	Lenawee	48.5	Shiawassee	55.0
Grand Traverse	39.5	Ionia	48.6	Houghton	56.0
Missaukee	39.5	Cass	48.9	Alpena	56.0
Hillsdale	40.4	Mason	49.1	Arenac	56.1
Huron	40.7	Isabella	49.1	Presque Isle	56.8
St. Joseph	40.8	Otsego	49.1	Gladwin	56.8
Berrien	42.3	Jackson	49.6	Ogemaw	57.4
Livingston	42.7	Alcona	49.7	Schoolcraft	58.3
Osceola	42.8	Wexford	49.7	Dickinson	58.8
Benzie	42.8	Montmorency	49.8	Lake	58.8
Gratiot	43.7	Crawford	50.7	Memominee	58.8
Newaygo	44.0	Iosco	50.8	Keweenaw	59.2
Eaton	44.4	Lapeer	50.8	Baraga	59.4
Antrim	44.7	Charlevoix	50.9	Monroe	60.1
Clinton	44.9	Roscommon	50.9	Macomb	60.9
Mecosta	45.0	Mackinac	51.1	Ontonagon	61.8
Kalamazoo	45.7	Ingham	51.3	Marquette	62.3
Emmet	45.8	Washentaw	51.8	Genesee	62.7
Branch	46.0	Chippewa	52.0	Delta	63.1
Barry	46.2	Manistee	52.2	Iron	63.5
Kent	46.3	Calhoun	52.3	Bay	63.9
Midland	46.3	Cheboygan	52.4	Alger	66.0
Van Buren	46.3	St. Clare	52.9	Wayne	68.7
Montcalm	46.6	Kalkaska	53.1	Gogebic	69.4
Tuscola	46.8	Clare	53.6		

Note: The expected vote is meant to measure the party identification of the electorate within the county. Its estimation is based on an analysis of votes for the two candidates from each party that run for the State Board of Education every two years.

Source: Gregg W. Smith, "The Effect of Party Organizational Strength on Electoral Success" (paper presented at the 1987 annual meeting of the Midwest Political Science Association).

CONTEMPORARY PARTISAN POLITICS

It has been in the face of this relatively attentive public that Michigan politics has more recently evolved. Governor William Milliken retired from electoral politics in 1982. To a great extent, his way of governing retired with him. While Milliken had conflicts with Democrats in the legislature, he had many confrontations with conservative Republicans as well. Consequently, many, if not most, of his policy proposals needed bipartisan support to get through the legislature. Compromise under Milliken was not especially difficult, however, because he was a moderate in a state party divided between his supporters and conservatives. Moreover, because of his campaign strategy, he reflected the issue preferences of much of the state. In addition, the Democratic party remained fragmented between practitioners of "new politics," labor politics, and, not rarely, reactionary politics.

This stability in the midst of organizational chaos could hardly have lasted. In the 1982 election, Democratic congressman James Blanchard and Republican Richard Headlee competed for the governorship. Headlee was part of the emerging conservative wing of the state Republican party as well as an important figure in grass-roots tax-reform initiatives. Both of these mattered because the conservatives had organized well in local areas in order to seize control of the state party. But, it was from these citizen-run tax protests that Headlee gained his real political standing. He also built on his reputation as a successful insurance executive rather than just another highly taxed complainant. Headlee led a victorious property-tax-limitation initiative in 1978, after having lost in such an effort two years earlier. Another more severe tax-limitation initiative appeared on the ballot alongside the Headlee proposal in 1978. It found a place on the ballot again in 1980 under the leadership of the colorful and self-labeled political amateur Robert Tisch, the Democratic drain commissioner from Shiawassee County. The draconian Tisch amendments were defeated with help from bipartisan and multi-interest opposition by numerous leaders of both political parties and many influential state interests. Even as a conservative Republican, Headlee looked moderate and politically acceptable when facing what was easily portrayed as Tisch's extremism. Moreover, Headlee also appealed to a public made quite suspicious by so many political elites rampaging against one local drain commissioner.

These tax-limitation proposals, while a catalyst for change, were just a part of the picture of Michigan politics in the early 1980s. The national recession at the beginning of the decade had an especially severe impact on Michigan. Auto production was down, and unemployment was high. The result was a serious decline in state revenues and a drastic rise in state unemployment compensation payments and welfare expenses. Handling these problems was the pivotal, and nearly the only substantive, campaign issue of 1982. Headlee insisted that no new taxes were needed to deal with the problem. Instead, he called for a reduction in state services and a "business" approach to the budget. Blanchard did not specifically propose a tax increase to combat the problems, but he promised to continue aiding the unemployed and others of the state's disadvantaged.

The 1982 campaign was both ideological and bitter in contrast to the Milliken era. Ideology finally reared its head in an encompassing way because the prevailing issue became one of more-versus-less state government. Acrimony widened the divide between liberals and conservatives. Headlee, championing his views in a telephone interview with a small campus radio station, charged that Milliken's wife was aligned with lesbians, and then made other charges against her as a radical in the women's movement. The tirade made statewide headlines and dogged him for the remainder of the campaign. Blanchard, perceived as fair, won 53.7 percent of the vote, with strong support from women making the critical difference. A small majority of men voted for Headlee. Democrats, playing on unemployment and bread-and-butter local issues, also won majorities in both houses of the legislature. For the first time in fifty years, they controlled all of state government.

Control was short-lived, although no one thought it would be as short as it was. When Blanchard arrived in office, he faced a deficit of nearly $1 billion and an unemployment rate of 15.7 percent. During his campaign, he had promised that a tax increase would be his last resort. Anticipating four years to recover his popularity, however, he quickly proposed an increase in the state income tax and cuts of $225 million in education and social services. The politics surrounding the income-tax increase/service cut was bitter and partisan. In Blanchard's first 100 days, he obtained the income tax increase and budget cuts. But accompanying these victories were serious political consequences. The final senate vote on the tax increase was twenty to eighteen, with one Democrat voting no and one Republican voting yes. Blanchard, in order to win, was forced to accept limitations on the duration of the increase. Michigan's economic recovery after 1983 was the subject of continuing debate and partisan conflict, one where Democrats and Republicans were split in trying to capture the state's narrowly divided electorate.

As with other tax increases, popular reaction was strong. An attempt was made to recall state senators, a move that triggered overt partisan hostility. Ironically, the two recalls of 1984 took place in white, blue-collar, union counties that in the 1960s and 1970s had been Democratic strongholds, but that were now the state's strongest bastions of conservative politics. As noted earlier, Republicans regained control of the senate.

This affected Blanchard's leadership significantly, even though he was able to win reelection in 1986 with 68 percent of the vote over a comparatively weak candidate, African-American attorney William Lucas. From the bipartisan success of the Milliken years, Michigan politics had moved toward considerable partisan confrontation as both parties and interested groups of citizens struggled to control the state and its tax policy. The reasons behind this change meant that neither Blanchard nor his successor, John Engler, had the opportunity to practice what many saw as Milliken's statesmanship and genteel politics.

Things were rough-and-tumble again, evoking memories of Governor "Soapy" Williams's combative ways. First, Michigan continued to have a well-balanced and especially competitive two-party system, resplendent with ticket-splitters. Second, both parties saw the inescapable issues of rustbelt recovery and economic diversification tied closely to tax policies. Thus, state revenue issues were more controversial than ever before, especially with memories of legislator recalls fresh in politicians' minds. Third, tax issues crowded more easily resolved issues of the 1970s off the short-term political agenda. Tax fright complicated many other issues of recovery that stayed on the agenda, and impeded the mobilization of a solid electoral majority on behalf of any other types of issues. Fourth, the electorate itself continued to break down its party loyalties, pending, it seemed, a clearer idea of what the state economic base would be in the future. Fifth, this breakdown made long-term political volatility more probable than usual. More important, the shifting loyalties were seen as being subject to continuing manipulation as the economic recovery of the mid- to late-1980s moved to the deep recession of the early 1990s. Sixth, party leaders moved actively to affect voter loyalties, both by positioning themselves to win votes during the periods of instability and to convert voters' primary loyalties, if possible, over time. Stronger party organizations were increasingly valued as necessary to accomplish these goals. They, in turn, reinforced the tendency to place a partisan spin on all issues.

Governor Blanchard was unexpectedly defeated for reelection in 1990 by Republican Senator John Engler, who emphasized a 20 percent property-tax cut, less state government, a more favorable business climate, and a pro-life abortion policy. In a close race, he won by 17,595 votes. Given that his was a contentious agenda, the essentially bitter politics of the Blanchard years and the conditions that stimulated them were not to go away. The 1990 election did little to change the balance of power between the parties and the ensuing need to offer choices to the electorate. The Democrats continued through 1992 to control the state house of representatives, sixty-one to forty-nine, the offices of secretary of state and attorney general, eleven of eighteen congressional seats, and both U.S. Senate seats. Republicans retained control of the state senate, twenty to eighteen, and continued to dominate county government. In larger part, however, the public's expectations, and confusion over what was in their general interest, created the conflict. Given the prevailing uncertainty of the 1990s, the public wanted to hear alternative positions. Voicing them meant that divisive and partisan politics would not go away.

SOME CONCLUDING THOUGHTS

The strategies of winning electoral converts in a potentially changing political environment rest on research findings about the popular appeal of candidates that are more disconcerting than merely hostile to Lansing politics. In attempting to learn why the Democratic voters of southeast Michigan recalled their senators over the 1982 tax increase, the national Democratic party concluded that liberal ideals and labor realities may be losing whatever linkages still remained after the Swainson split. The white, blue-collar union members who make up much of Michigan's Democratic base revealed dissatisfaction with social programs, distrust of government, and animosity to African Americans in general and those in Detroit in particular.[38] In contrast to the principles that held old-time Democratic coalition builders together, respondents emphasized that the party supported minority policy goals too strongly and, thus, contributed to the distrust of white voters. Importantly, these opinions were gathered at a time when many blue-collar workers were facing layoffs and enduring Michigan's periodic economic turmoil.

But political activists do not see these as short-term opinions, and there is little evidence in the early to mid-1990s that any degree of statewide harmony is about to break out. If, as leaders of both Michigan parties believe, these blue-collar suburban attitudes mirror those of similar demographic areas of the state, the emerging issues of partisan separation will divide the state further. This will be especially the case in the absence of a strong revival of Michigan's economy.

Regional animosities are likely to sharpen as well. Hence, there will be less willingness to secure outside support or accept nationwide reforms enhancing the status of the state's minorities and disadvantaged. Moreover, regional and special-interest factions, whose cleavages run far deeper than anything seen in the state since the Civil War, may begin to surface. In a place where partisanship is inescapable and tied to popular views of issues, such a partisan future will increase immeasurably the difficulties of state policymaking.

CHAPTER NINE

Influencing Michigan Politics

Delbert J. Ringquist, John Klemanski, and Charles Press are also contributing authors to this chapter

THE CLASH OF COMPETITIVE INTERESTS AND CULTURAL SYMBOLS

Michigan's partisan and interest-group politics, as we saw in chapter 8, are frequently intertwined. Yet much of the necessity for linkage between parties and groups is now gone. No longer do Michigan lumber businesses or automakers feel it necessary to control the Republican party. Nor do intellectuals necessarily forge Democratic alliances. Bipartisan strategies produce bigger payoffs, even when used by interests, such as teacher unions, that remain closely identified with the Democratic party. One reason for this change is the competitiveness that developed in the state's party system and the resulting need to broaden partisan appeal. The other is the rise of independent means of campaign financing. The change to weaker partisan alliances also reflects the growing autonomy of Michigan legislators as they carry out regional and district responsibilities and, in so doing, worry less about their party's leadership. For many legislators, a "partisan issue" is whatever appeals to the largest number of voters in their district. Thus, party issues are often quite localized and personalized rather than the product of state platforms.

What exists today is an extraordinarily competitive interest-group system. It thrives because of regional, district, and economic conflicts and the resulting opportunity to intervene in them.[1] These groups also find their lobbyists and grass-roots activists competing for influence in ways other than among themselves. On the one hand, it is virtually impossible to imagine Michigan government and politics without the involvement of its cadre of well-organized and active interests.[2] Michigan lobbyists, policymakers agree, are prized for their ability to close political deals and resolve issues that are often clouded by regional disputes. Given divisions in the legislature, lobbyists are frequently the state's real deal makers. On the other hand, they are just as likely to become obstacles to policymaking when their own representatives cannot agree.

A comment reflecting despair after house Democrats had failed to support Governor Blanchard's 1988 plan to reform public school finance illustrates the significance and failure of Michigan interest groups in deal making. A handful of legislators walked dejectedly down the capitol corridor, irritated that this issue kept coming back to them. All nodded in agreement as one legislator suggested that tax reform would neither pass nor disappear as an issue until the Michigan Education Association and the State Chamber of Commerce jointly drafted a bill. The two groups, of course, did not – at least, until Governor John Engler almost successfully linked educational equity and a shift in tax policies in 1993. At that point, he insisted that everyone participate or exit the arena. It was not until 1994 that school finance and property tax reform were linked, although the two organizations were not.

In the early 1990s, seemingly unresolvable legislative battles between insurance companies and trial lawyers evoked similar conversations. These interests deadlocked over automobile insurance rates and tied up the legislature for years, even dragging the issue to a failed constitutional ballot question. Modern interest groups, as generally narrow and often unaligned political forces, frequently limit effective decision making. This is where those individualistic, interest-specific elements of the state's predominantly moralistic political culture take on importance to state politics.[3] Groups and regional factions blatantly trumpet their own benefit even though their representatives frequently act as useful policy brokers.

As a result, it seems impossible to imagine a Michigan politics that does not criticize interest groups and lobbyists and treat them as highly suspect, very much in need of regulation. The political climate that provides state regulation leads some interest-group representatives, such as those of Michigan Common Cause, to see themselves more as checks on lobbyists rather than as lobbyists themselves. It also creates opportunities for partisan activists and policymakers to appear statesmanlike by chastening lobbyists. Along with this comes public suspicion and a hostile media. When the legislature refused to adopt a plan to lower automobile insurance rates in 1992, the press gleefully assailed state insurance interests which had agreed to cuts but not to a specific formula for them. This put the blame for policy failure on lobbyists, including the trial lawyers who opposed caps on court judgments. "I just assume," said a reporter, "that I need to suspect and watch the interested groups, not the governor and legislators. I'm not sure why I do that.'' This feature of distrust adds to the competitive environment in which state interests do business.

WHO LOBBIES?

Lobbying of state officials is regulated under the Lobby Registration Act of 1978, an idealistic package aimed at furthering openness in government. The act took effect in 1983, after five years of court challenges by interests opposing disclosure. Opponents argued that the statutes would inhibit communication and restrict needed political contacts. They emphasized, as one opponent explained, ''my vital position in making this government work.'' The act defines lobbying broadly as any direct discussions held with any public officials for the purpose of influencing any public policy. It does not cover interest-group messages aimed at the public or the media. Lobbying, as defined, covers all relevant meetings and contacts with administrators, legislators and staffs, judicial employees, and members of the most potentially controversial commissions and boards. The intent is simple, to establish a public scorecard of all the players for anyone who might wish to inspect it.

The act requires lobbyists to register by client with the secretary of state, file annual expenditure reports, and acknowledge personal compensation for their public affairs work. No other reporting, either of finances or of specific issues addressed, is required of individual lobbyists. Political contributions are covered by the Campaign Finance Act of 1976, legislation that sets the rules for political action committees (PACs). Other than setting limits on contributions and banning corporate giving to candidates, neither that act nor the 1978 act restricts lobbying. Given the history surrounding the passage of the acts, the lack of restrictions in them is somewhat ironic. More than any recent example of reform, this one shows the impact of the clash between individualistic and moralistic cultural expectations.

Michigan was one of the first states to debate political ethics in the nationwide trend of the 1970s, following the Watergate scandals over Republican presidential campaign committee operations in Washington, D.C. With the state's moralistic culture and reform traditions, Michigan policymakers reacted quickly, proposed hastily, and then deliberated for several years over the Omnibus Political Reform Act. The bill was a typical expression of idealism, and its complex provisions had a restrictive tone. The proposal also stepped on too many political toes, and it too harshly challenged the competing Michigan value of open political participation. It could not survive intact. As a result, the bill was broken for further consideration into several sets of rules, two of which eventually passed to cover PACs and then lobbying. Proposed restrictions were dropped, but the acts retained their emphasis on shedding light on lobbying and campaign activities. The media complained vociferously, but to no avail. The courts, in contrast to the press, weakened or eliminated several provisions of each law.[4] The expectation behind sunshine theory is explicit: as long as Michiganians know the array of participants in policymaking, they presumably can count on acceptable behavior in a state such as theirs. The assumption behind sunshine theory is more questionable: that no one in a watchful and moralistic state will do wrong if they have to report on their behavior and actions. Accordingly, reformers still fight to strengthen lobbying and campaign regulations.

Prior to 1983, the law defined lobbyists as only those who sought to influence legislators through direct personal contact. Individuals who appeared before committees or who contacted legislators as constituents were not considered to be lobbyists. Public officials, including administrators advocating their own programs and agencies, did not view themselves as lobbyists and rarely registered. Lobbying was seen as a private-sector job performed by those with specific public affairs responsibilities for their organization.

The number of lobbyists remained relatively constant from 1960, with 367 registrations, until 1983, when 355 individuals registered.[5] Through the 1980s, the number of public affairs specialists who worked in government relations full-time remained at just above 400.[6] However, the number of full-time and part-time lobbyists increased rapidly after 1983, mainly because of the new legal definition and uncertainty over it. Registration increased by over 450 percent from 1983 to 1984 as officials of various types of organizations complied with the new law. During the next two years the number of registered agents rose to more than 2,100. By the beginning of 1988, 2,251 lobbyists and lobbyist agents registered, representing over 550 groups, associations, state agencies, local governments, businesses, and multiclient lobbying firms. In addition, 813 registrants listed but never activated their registrations, indicating that they had not spent or received payment for lobbying in excess of the legal thresholds for reporting. Finally, the registrations of another 1,759 lobbyists had expired. By mid-1993, as familiarity with the process relieved anxieties about penalties for not registering, only 1,250 agents registered. But these individuals represented 300 more organizations than were active in 1988.[7] Thus, registered political organizations were astonishingly prolific – with 850 interest groups, 965 political action committees, 114 ballot-question groups, and 200 state and local political party organizations.

A substantial part of the growth in lobbyist registration came from organizations which, to avoid breaking the law, began registering anyone who they believed might contact a policymaker. For example, Chrysler Corporation maintained only one registered lobbyist for years. But as the definition of lobbying changed, the number of Chrysler registrants rose to forty-three in 1988, even though the company's public affairs efforts expanded very little. Other companies with small public affairs offices, but with frequent political contacts by their executives, also registered several individuals. In 1986, at the peak of the adjustment period, the Michigan Hospitals Association listed 22 lobbyists; E. F. Hutton and Company, 20; Consumers Power, 16; and Perry Drug Stores, 13. The numbers were 16, 20, 16, and 5, respectively, in 1987. These year-to-year changes indicate uncertainty about the state's definition of lobbyist and the perceived lack of importance in disclosure. Many organizations registered only after being challenged for not doing so, or after seeing the principal representative of other organizations challenged for making brief contacts with policymakers.

Still, state lobbying remains largely a private-sector business. Of the 1988 registrants, only 6 percent were state officials, down from 11 percent in 1986. They represented eighteen state agencies. By 1993, with the governor's effort to restrict midlevel administrative contacts with the legislature, that percentage was slightly lower. The explosion of lobbyist registrations, however, came from almost every type of private and nonstate government organization in Michigan. Small-town hospitals, municipal industrial parks, specialized trade associations such as charter boat operators, and sports teams all make contacts with state officials and feel that they must register their officers.

Nonetheless, there has been a bias of representation. Forty-four percent of all lobbyists represented businesses. While this was far more than any other category, the explanation lies in the large number of businesses that have several officials who initiate district contacts with legislators. Also, in a manufacturing state, business represents a diverse range of products and services. Among other interests, 16 percent represented health-care organizations, 7 percent local government, 6 percent citizen and civic reform groups, 2 percent labor, 2 percent farm organizations, and only 1 percent environmental and conservation causes. The latter is the only type that changed noticeably, especially because local environmental groups were among the most frequently challenged for not registering in the mid-1980s.

In one sense, neither these percentages nor the expansion of lobbyist numbers means much to the practitioners' view of their occupation. Most policymakers and Lansing insiders think of lobbyists as only those four hundred or so public affairs specialists who are regularly involved in state politics. These "third house regulars" are the individuals on whom policymakers and other lobbyists depend as deal makers and as the principal experts about state problems.[8] The nonregulars remain less important because they are infrequently involved in the negotiating sessions that resolve policy issues.

State administrators, despite the registration requirements, are rarely seen as "real lobbyists" for yet another reason. As we saw in chapter 6, they occupy a public role for which program advocacy is required. As one trade association lobbyist noted, "How do you call an administrator an administrator if that person won't stand up for what she does. That does not, I repeat, make her a lobbyist though." Moreover, agency officials are often targets of lobbying, although less often than legislators. One legislator summarized it this way, "Lobbyists are like a third house of the first branch of government. The nonregular lobbyists don't belong to the house and the bureaucrats don't belong to the branch." Anomalies in that intriguing dichotomy are the college and university lobbyists who work full-time on state appropriations and capital projects. These individuals have become regulars in the eyes of most policymakers through their association with others: "They get a lot of their credibility because the college crowd also hires a lot of multiclient lobbyists. These professionals have shaped up the other guys."

THE MOST PROMINENT LOBBYING ORGANIZATIONS

An interest group's political influence is never easy to judge. One credible way of doing so, though, is to ask state policymakers and lobbyists to rank the most important organizations and explain the rationale for their selections. With this method, some of Michigan's organized interests stand out from the rest.[9] As policymakers warn, however, influence does not mean that the top-ranked interests can move the same policymakers on all issues. Resources to pursue political interests still vary substantially, as do the opportunities to work with specific policymakers. Not all situations allow skilled regulars to make the difference between organizational success and failure. "For example," reflected one lobbyist who worked on social service issues, "the unionization of state employees precludes many options. It is damned hard to pursue many reforms that impose greater burdens on staff, even when the benefits to clients are obvious."

These variations help explain why no single interest has dominated Michigan politics in the 1980s and 1990s. The state is too economically and regionally diverse. As a consequence, eight quite different interests share reputations for the greatest influence over the past fifteen years: the Big Three American automobile firms of Chrysler, Ford, and General Motors; the United Auto Workers (UAW); the American Federation of Labor–Congress of Industrial Organizations (AFL-CIO); the Michigan United Conservation Clubs (MUCC); the Michigan Education Association (MEA); the Michigan Manufacturers Association (MMA); the city of Detroit; and ad hoc coalitions of anti-tax groups that first organized in the late 1970s. A ninth group, the Michigan State Chamber of Commerce, stands out in the 1990s and has gained major stature for carefully positioning itself during the 1980s. Some, at least for the time being, consider it among the state's most powerful single interests.

The resources and origins of group influence vary considerably. Among the top eight, only the MEA has gained a reputation for its lobbyists' effective and skilled tactics.[10] Even then, policymakers in our survey thought that MEA influence results as much from its large statewide membership of well-educated, locally respected, politically active, and quickly mobilized teachers as from its lobbyists. Members frequently contact lawmakers back home but seldom register as lobbying agents. MEA also benefits from state-directed public affairs work by the National Education Association. The other top-rated interests have their own unique sources of influence. The most unusual of these are the ad hoc anti-tax groups that, with a small core of often changing leaders, routinely coalesce around tax issues. As government outsiders without full-time lobbyists, these groups make superb use of initiatives, referenda, recalls, and, as a result, successful electoral intimidation of policymakers.

MUCC's prominence is based on political factors and its monopoly-like reputation as *the* voice for Michigan's environment and its many outdoor users. A large number of state and regional organizations of environmentalists, preservationists, conservationists, hunters, fishers, trappers, and other recreational users belong to the federation. Many affiliates are local, with primary interest in a single lake or stretch of river. By recruiting the most prominent and esteemed of these groups, and sometimes just the noisiest, MUCC became one of the largest membership organizations in the state. Affiliates have responded to one principal feature of the clubs, the offer of zealous and well-publicized Lansing lobbying. MUCC also gains influence from its mix of individual members who include both professional and blue-collar dues payers scattered throughout Michigan. While its Lansing lobbyists are highly knowledgeable and active in policymaking, particularly Director Thomas Washington, much of MUCC's power comes from its tenacious grass-roots activists who typically concentrate on regional issues. They appear often in Lansing and orchestrate numerous on-site visits from public officials. These activists, in a rare exception to state norms and unlike MEA members, who usually stick to limited contact with home-district legislators, have disdained lobbying registration as unbefitting their citizen status: "When every single union member in Michigan comes out as a lobbyist, I'll register. But only then!"

Detroit's importance is similar to that of MUCC in that it emphasizes local projects and policy rewards for a distinct population within the state. With its own delegation in each house, its solid core of Democratic voters, and its emphasis on the city's position as the leading Michigan group speaking out for African Americans (76 percent of its population), Detroit commands a large and tirelessly negotiated share of state expenditures. Under Mayor Coleman Young, a former state legislator, Detroit represented the nearest thing to a cohesive patronage machine in modern state politics, bringing with it periodic examples of political corruption and payoff. Young's lack of enthusiasm for Governor Blanchard in the 1990 election led to an uncharacteristicly low voter turnout and aided John Engler's victory. Young's successor, Dennis Archer, moved into the mayor's office without the machine, but still kept alive the perception that Detroit is a prominent state interest.

The UAW benefits, in a defensive way, from prominence in the Democratic party, the ability to raise campaign funds through well-organized union locals, and the backlog of state laws that protect workers employed in a cyclic industry. It also has gained from rejoining the AFL-CIO. As a result, UAW representatives provide well-funded electoral support for candidates who, in turn, largely defend existing law. When its members want new state – or federal – programs, which has been seldom in recent years, the union is much less able to deliver unless it argues loud and hard that its members are neglected by emerging state policies. Then they may get a share, but often a small one. The strength of the AFL-CIO is not much different than the UAW, except that its members do not hold many prominent positions within the automobile industry (plant transportation is an exception) or do not have the same ability to affect directly that segment of the state economy through collective bargaining and strikes. For that reason, most Michigan policymakers continue to view the UAW as a separate political entity. The AFL-CIO benefits primarily from its broad base of members: Detroit teachers, state and local government workers, skilled trades, and another recent affiliate, the

Teamsters. It also uses the influence that comes from being able to manipulate existing laws in ways that would not be possible in a weak union state.

The automobile companies and MMA – an association of large and small businesses – have yet another source of power, the economic hopes of the state.[11] Policymakers have frequently criticized both interests for poor judgments in their decades of neglect of manufacturing quality. But, especially with new quality commitments, policymakers find it difficult to vote against industry proposals when their defeat could add to the state's loss of jobs and revenue as well as enhance the state's anti-business reputation. Both the auto and manufacturing interests work as closely with the governor as with the legislature. The importance of the economy as a statewide issue, the need to work through a comprehensive development strategy, and the governor's high profile and personal decision to identify with the state's "big issues" all account for this emphasis.

This common strategy sometimes obscures the fact that the Big Three and MMA have different agendas. The auto industry focuses on more easily defined policies favorable to production costs, while MMA deals with the more nebulous goal of economic diversification. MMA, which allied itself with Governor Blanchard, lost considerable access and reputation when John Engler was elected. Still, its agenda reflects what are generally accepted by most policymakers to be state economic needs. Thus, MMA remains a respected, though isolated, participant even though Governor Engler's economic views have been more compatible with those of the State Chamber of Commerce. That compatibility caused many veteran legislators to look anew at the State Chamber of Commerce after 1990, seeing it as likely to replace MMA in state influence, especially if manufacturing continued to lose jobs while small business gained. As one explained: "A group like the Chamber, it gains power from being at the right place at the right time."

The list of second-ranked interests includes fifteen very diverse associations and seven sets of loosely allied though still autonomous organizations. Individual associations ranked as having great influence with policymakers include Blue Cross/Blue Shield of Michigan, the Michigan Association of School Boards, Michigan Automobile Dealers Association, Michigan Bell Telephone, Michigan Wine and Beer Wholesalers Association, Michigan Farm Bureau, Michigan Merchants Council, Michigan Milk Producers Association, Michigan Hospitals Association, Michigan Insurance Federation, Michigan Retailers Association, Michigan State Medical Society, Michigan Trial Lawyers Association, Right to Life of Michigan anti-abortion activists, and the United Transportation Union.

The semi-permanent coalitions of loosely allied but still independent and often competitive organizations include groups representing the aged, banking, local governments, oil industries, public utilities, state higher education, and tourist associations. These interests are familiar to Lansing politicians even though their demands do not continuously confront the large numbers of policymakers who must contend with the top eight interest groups and the State Chamber of Commerce. Unlike the major state interests, these groups in the second tier lack a constant presence on nearly all of the largest and most recurring state issues. Policymakers often note that these interests are different for only one reason: they cannot define a winnable position for themselves on as many issues as can the big eight. These more narrow interests either have restricted credibility on such issues or have limited resources to use in influencing them. Thus, they are heard on far fewer occasions.

Organizations from this second tier are noted both for their more restricted interests and a more restrained effect on state policy. "You know, for example," said one legislator, "that the education lobby will not wreck a budget deal or get in a debate over the state's economic future. They only want a share and then they shut up." The second-ranked groups are, as a result, especially individualistic. "Most just will not get into the great debates about the public interest of the state," concluded one frustrated legislator. Many policymakers also note that these groups could be added to the list of the most influential state interests if that list were redefined to include all organizations that usually win on the issues that they choose to contest. At least, representatives of these organizations can almost always force some compromise on issues of intense importance to their members, as long as they do not stray too far from their core concerns.

Three reasons stand out for the perceived influence of these twenty-two second-ranked state interests. Some, such as the Michigan Beer and Wine Wholesalers Association, once had skilled lobbyists who were close to specific policymakers. Others, including oil and tourist interests, are believed to be integral and unique to localized, but important, parts of the state economy. As such, the organizations that represent their interests are quite active in ongoing state programs that relate to the use of natural resources. Others, such as Right to Life of Michigan and the handful of senior-citizen organizations that cooperate with the Association of Area Agencies on Aging, benefit from numerous and active members who are somewhat less organized than those of, for example, MUCC or the UAW. Right to Life, in particular, capitalizes on the Republican party's inability to dodge the abortion issue and avoid a public alliance with the group's core supporters. As a Republican legislator noted, "I'm really pro-choice but these people hang on me like barbed thistle seeds. They make it impossible to vote or even articulate my beliefs." In essence, private influence is dispersed among numerous players who follow a variety of strategies for a wide range of reasons.

INFLUENCE AND CAMPAIGN FINANCING

Despite this diversity of interests, critics claim that only money moves interest-group politics. "I see it like the old movie title," said one reporter, "*For a Few Dollars More.*" Given the state's history of politically dominant big business and big labor, that assertion has some merit. Certainly the titans of those two manufacturing-centered camps control much of the flow of campaign contributions. However, their involvement is not the major factor in PAC operations.[12] The major characteristics of campaign finance, which do generate media and public suspicions, are twofold. First, despite the expansion of influence explained above, a relatively small number of PACs dominate contributions. But that number includes far more interests than just unions and auto industries. Second, the largest PACs contribute a great majority of funds to one type of legislator – incumbents.

For all state candidate races in 1986, PACs gave nearly $7.5 million. This exceeded the combined amounts that PACs contributed in either 1982 or 1984, demonstrating both the escalating involvement and increased reporting by interest groups during the decade. By 1986 some 850 PACs, or about 90 percent of those active in 1982, were contributors. PAC growth, through 1993, saw about twenty new committees added per year. Their candidate expenditures were up to $11.4 million in 1990 and $11.7 million in 1992. In addition, PACs spent about $14.5 million on 1992 ballot proposals, an indicator of how much these initiatives matter to state politics.

The aggregate giving and total number of organizations has been misleading, though. The state's largest fifteen PACs (see table 16 for the top fifteen in 1984 and 1992) contributed nearly $4.5 million of the total PAC contribution of $7.5 million to all candidates in 1986. For the largest fifteen PACs, this was more than a 40 percent increase from 1984, a year with no state senate elections. However, with total PAC contribution so much higher in 1986, the top fifteen PACs were obviously still reporting increasing expenditures. They contributed about 60 percent of the amount given by all cam-

Table 16: Michigan's Top Fifteen PAC Contributors, All Candidate Elections, 1984 and 1992

1984

Rank	Amount
1. Michigan United Auto Workers PAC (MI UAW PAC)	$389,028
2. Michigan State AFL-CIO COPE	336,221
3. Civic Involvement Program (General Motors)	308,905
4. Michigan Education Association PAC	290,790
5. Democratic National Committee (non-federal)	223,500
6. UAW SEM PAC	202,614
7. Michigan Democratic Party Policy Committee	183,228
8. House Democratic Victory Fund	152,627
9. Realtors PAC of Michigan	115,225
10. Allstate Insurance Company PAC	113,465
11. Region 1-D UAW PAC	112,711
12. Republican Majority Committee	111,338
13. House Republican Campaign Committee	110,020
14. Michigan Beer and Wine Wholesalers	92,924
15. UAW Greater Flint CAP Council	88,840

1992

Rank	Amount
1. Michigan Education Association PAC	$333,742
2. Trying to Help Underdogs with Money	273,739
3. Michigan UAW PAC	261,277
4. Young PAC	257,595
5. Detroit Auto Dealers	232,330
6. UAW SEM PAC	215,793
7. Michigan Realtors	213,845
8. Michigan Trial Laywers PAC	198,850
9. Michigan Beer and Wine Wholesalers	197,544
10. AFL-CIO COPE	195,840
11. Committee for the Future of Michigan (Republican Cacus)	163,655
12. House Democratic Campaign Committee	156,149
13. Hospital Association	149,255
14. Michigan Bell	149,099
15. Region 1-D UAW PAC	147,103

Note: Figures do not include ballot issues or inter-PAC contributions.

Source: Summaries by Campaign Finance Reporting, Bureau of Elections, Michigan Department of State, 1985 and 1993.

paign organizations to candidates.[13] By 1990 and 1992, the fifteen largest PACs were contributing 29 and 28 percent of all PAC spending. Amounts per major PAC were noticeably smaller than in previous years.

As also can be seen in table 16, interest groups are not the only ones that operate PACs. However, the state's largest PACs tend to be managed by representatives of interest groups that are ranked by policymakers as most influential. In fact, only groups that were ranked as influential were on the 1980s lists of big contributors, even though they ranked higher in years when major legislation affecting them was before the legislature. In 1986, for example, medical malpractice liability brought nearly a threefold increase over 1984 in contributions by the Michigan Doctors PAC. While corporations cannot contribute to candidates, their employees can raise PAC dollars voluntarily through the public affairs office of each firm. Thus, the General Motors Civic Involvement Program is a large and recognizable contributor. The UAW's level of contributions, in contrast, is understated in the list because each local can operate its own committee, as long as the different committees do not openly collaborate with one another.

By 1990 and 1992, with PAC contributions smaller for the biggest givers, more second-ranked interests were among the top fifteen. The Michigan Trial Lawyers, with insurance reform before them, were notable players. Michigan Bell, in the midst of regulatory battles, was a 1992 addition. For the first time, Detroit was represented through its mayor's Young PAC. Michigan Beer and Wine Wholesalers kept their ranking. However, by the 1990s, MEA continued to top the PAC lists by a wide dollar margin.

Among the state's eight major interests, only the anti-tax groups and MUCC have not been major PAC players. Anti-tax forces, however, have raised large sums of money to direct against legislative and gubernatorial candidates not of their liking. Environmental groups encourage individual, rather than PAC, contributions from their members. Detroit's operatives have for years helped legislators from the city delegation, often by intervening with the UAW. Quite clearly, money, and the ability to raise it for officeholders, is strongly associated with group success. For that reason, lobbyists from state universities have fought hard on their own campuses to create PACs: "If we don't, we're not players, I fear."

As the example of the environmental groups shows, the ability to see who contributes remains somewhat clouded despite disclosure laws. Just under half of all legislative contributions were from individuals during the 1980s.[14] The same remains true in the 1990s. Much of this giving is orchestrated by the PACs of political parties (see table 16) and by legislators themselves.

Some of that money, but no one knows how much, results from lobbyists who encourage individual contributions by people whom legislators and other recipients will clearly identify with the firm, group, or interest.[15]

Multiclient lobbyists are particularly adept at this strategy, often arriving with small packages of checks from all of their clients at the annual fund-raisers held by legislators. This brings into the money game the raft of small organizations that use multiclient firms. It also distributes access to policy-makers quite broadly among Michigan's organized interests: "We all play and we all lean on other employees to buy tickets from us so we can contribute together as a block." It also, as Michigan Common Cause points out, leaves those who are unorganized at some disadvantage. But that hardly seems to be the only problem. Actual donations are hard to estimate because, in defiance of the sunshine theory, many lobbyists refuse to report their organized client contributions. "Those are costs of doing business, not lobbying expenditures," explained one active solicitor. "It would be like reporting the rent on the building. Many of the folks, in fact, are only on retainer, not actively lobbying an issue through our office."

The economics of gubernatorial elections are somewhat different from legislative contests because Michigan, with its reformist tradition, provides public funds to candidates.[16] For candidates who agree to limit campaign expenditures and to seek qualifying contributions only from individuals, the state provides two public dollars for every one raised by the candidate. These funds are available only after the candidate raises five percent of the $1 million expenditure limit. While this has taken PACs out of gubernatorial races, it leaves many lobbyists heavily involved with each campaign: "Of course it does. I want to be able to show the governor's staff how much my people added to that war-chest that they were working so hard to fill."

The degree to which interest-group representatives emphasize their work with active policymakers points to the advantages of incumbency in raising PAC contributions. In the 1984 elections, for example, incumbent candidates averaged 59 percent of their total campaign contributions from PACs. Challengers who won averaged only 38 percent in PAC contributions. Losing candidates fared far worse, receiving only 24 percent of their funds from PACs.[17] Losing candidates, meanwhile, spent less than $8,000 each on that election. Winners spent an average of $37,869.[18] The 1986 election was no different; winners again raised nearly 60 percent of their funds from PACs.[19]

PAC giving to incumbents also increases with the incumbent's tenure in office. This reflects the closer working relationships that exist with senior legislators, who are more likely to be chairs of important committees. It also results from the difficulty of turning down the requests of senior members. "You cannot say 'no' to a winner," observed one PAC manager, "and it's really hard to say 'yes' to a loser."

To some extent, lobbyist cooperation with partisan leaders is a vestige of the state's previous pattern of groups and parties attempting to capture one another. Another remnant is the inability of some state interests to break partisan strings. The largest labor PACs gave at least 99 percent of their contributions in 1986 to Democratic candidates and party organizations, with a considerable emphasis on the latter.[20] The MEA, as can be seen in table 17, gave 91 percent to Democrats, but mostly to candidates for office. Michigan Bankers PAC and the State Chamber of Commerce gave 82 and 88 percent of their funds to Republicans. For most of the state's most influential groups, however, less partisan strategies are followed in organizing PAC contributions, allowing their lobbyists to claim that they do their electoral interloping across party lines. "We want to do this," explained another lobbyist of his bipartisan contribution. "We want all of our friends to know that we can help out in the truly grueling ordeal of raising campaign funds. In fact, that's how we convince many that we are their friends, regardless of whether or not we want anything from them. For these legislators, the fund-raising process is a nightmare that you cannot comprehend until you've tried to do it."

A BREAK FROM THE PAST

The close relationship between incumbent policymakers and a comparatively wide circle of important state interest groups is a sharp departure from the way Michigan's politics was once perceived. The Big Three and a few smaller automobile companies and subcontractors once ruled as the prevailing economic powers because they overwhelmed other industries in stature. In the 1950s and 1960s, the Big Three and UAW were the major interests in a state where organized interests, in general, had little political influence compared to state political parties.[21] The UAW worked on behalf of a comparatively well paid and regionally dominant blue-collar work force centered in southeast Michigan. But it had scattered statewide members. Increasingly high wages and union rules, especially the closed shop where only dues-paying union workers could work in a unionized plant, brought considerable money to Democratic party politics. Other organized interests found it difficult to compete for attention. Competitors' tasks were made all the more difficult because both the Big Three and the UAW had political influence that was usually exercised through the state's actively competing but transform-

Table 17: Top Contributions to Michigan Party Candidates, Party Caucuses, and Party Committees, 1986

Rank	Percent by Party
1. Michigan UAW PAC	99–D
2. Michigan State AFL-CIO COPE	99–D
3. Michigan Education Association	91–D
4. Michigan Realtors Association PAC	74–R
5. Region 1-D UAW PAC	100–D
6. Michigan Beer and Wine Wholesalers	56–D
7. Medical Society of Michigan	67–R
8. UAW SEM PAC	100–D
9. Detroit Auto Dealers PAC	65–D
10. Michigan Trial Lawyers Association	86–D
11. State Chamber of Commerce	88–R
12. Michigan Bankers PAC	82–R
13. Law PAC	63–D
14. Hospital Association PAC	54–R
15. Consumers Power PAC	64–R
16. Civic Involvement Program (General Motors)	77–R
17. Michigan Auto Dealers PAC	52–R
18. Physicians for Fairness	67–R
19. Region 1-C UAW PAC	100–D

Source: William S. Ballenger, "PACs Increase Power in State Politics," Inside Michigan Politics 1 (September 4, 1987): 3–4.

ing political parties. Conventional lobbying techniques of gaining access to policymakers and winning them over with policy-relevant information was only a second line of attack in that environment to soliciting partisan favors. Michigan's parties, however, could not maintain that control over time.

The professionalization of state government and the legislature was a significant catalyst in dispersing influence. With numerous large and competent agencies and, especially, many informed and well-staffed elected officials, other interests commanded attention. Established but less dominant interests representing agriculture, the timber industry, tourism, the furniture industry, and oil businesses were long organized but without much influence in Lansing. In effect, they were squeezed out by lack of attention and, to a lesser extent, by the laissez-faire attitudes of a malapportioned legislature. The new problem-solving, bipartisan approach to government introduced by Governor William Milliken in the late 1960s encouraged neglected interests to argue for economic diversification, relief from the boom-and-bust cycles of automobile production, and development assistance for other industries.

Milliken appeared to care little about party discipline and more about policy change. His administration completed the task of professionalizing the bureaucracy. At the same time, committees gained power in the full-time legislature.[22] Moreover, both administrators and legislators were given considerable latitude in gathering information and formulating policy ideas. As a result, neglected issues – previously held in check by partisan and electoral conflict that generated attention to big business and big labor – found spokespersons in a state capitol where party leaders could increasingly be bypassed. Environmental problems, minority rights, and small business all developed specific champions in state policymaking.[23]

Thus, a wide variety of organized and well-financed interests now influence policymakers because these officials feel it essential to work on various development projects and to protect the state's natural resources.[24] Successful problem solving, policymakers believe, requires private sector and citizen cooperation, especially in securing the information needed to address problems effectively. This also ensures that agency clientele will cooperate in implementing programs. What can be called "bidirectional lobbying" is frequent as well; state officials make policy requests of private interests that further their lobbyists' influence over prized state programs.[25] This exists, in part, because government has become more important to the life of the state and an activist force in its own right. By raising the stakes of decision making by adding programs, government attracts and even leads to the organization of more interests. State financial specialists estimate that 50 percent of the state's voters are direct beneficiaries of state funding – as program recipients, employers, or grant beneficiaries.

To these ends, lobbyists and other representatives of established interests have become policymaking partners as well as sources of campaign funds. Their advice and recommendations are now seen as routine elements in policymaking.[26] Certainly the form that professionalization has taken in the legislature, with its emphasis on political intelligence and the avoidance of electoral risks, makes lobbyists generally closer partners with legislators and staff. However, state agencies also have become highly valued, if more aloof, allies in this partnership. As a result, securing the cooperation, though perhaps not the active support, of agency officials remains a goal of most state interests. "One of our critical difficulties as agents of influence is our lack of opportunity to show bureaucrats that we understand their problems and that we can relate to them as people. Elections [and our campaign contributions] don't grease the skids [for these people] as they do in the house and senate."

LOBBYISTS AS POLICYMAKING PARTNERS

The growing interdependence of policymakers and interest-group representatives helps explain why participants distinguish between regular and part-time or amateur lobbyists, and why, in contrast, registration requirements emphasize a broad definition of lobbyist. The focus of negotiated policy settlements takes place in Lansing as lobbyists manage their issues in what participants perceive to be a highly professional setting. But the real source of influence often rests on the political and economic resources of specific organizations. These resources, depending on the interests, enable regular lobbyists to be heard in the first place. Skill is rarely seen as the major determinant of an organization's influence. Yet because of the state emphasis on lobbying professionals, skill and technique are important.

Because of this concentration of political and economic power, rumors of an occasional scandal are sometimes heard. In 1987, a multiclient lobbyist was indicted but later acquitted by a jury on charges of bribing a state representative.[27] Many respondents to two 1986 and 1987 surveys of policymakers and lobbyists said that some lobbyists, commanding large budgets, will offer illegal gratuities to a few policymakers.[28] However, the respondents also agreed that resourcefulness, not corruption, controls the tempo of state lobbying.

Thus, all players follow similar rules and beliefs about strategy. However, variation exists in the ways in which lobbyists employ their resources. Lobbyists differ from one another in personality and behavior but follow a conventional pattern of lobbying that interest-group scholars have labeled "professional."[29] The actions of professional lobbyists in Michigan are easily outlined.

First, target the appropriate policymaker. Second, establish contact. Third, have well-researched and substantiated information. Fourth, determine a way to use the information to create a response from the targeted contact. Fifth, recognize that the district approach will get the best response: "What does this mean back home?" Sixth, show the strength of the group or firm's position. Seventh, negotiate an agreement with that individual. Eighth, follow that settlement through to closure within the policy process, deviating as little as possible unless the initial target agrees. In summary, professional lobbyists see themselves as brokers or, as they like to explain, "issue managers." In the words of another lobbyist, "Professionalism in the third house means employment of basic public relations skills in bringing numerous unaligned players together. The better you do it, the more professional you are."

The policymaking environment also facilitates this issue-management style. In a 1986 survey of legislators and lobbyists, Michigan lobbyists were found to have easy access to and considerable respect from policymakers. Ninety percent of legislative respondents said that they were readily accessible to lobbyists. Seventy-five percent of legislative respondents agreed that they and their colleagues "will talk to anyone who will bring them fresh information." Ninety-four percent of them regarded information as "a strong source of power to lobbyists." In addition, 68 percent of legislators believed that the "legislature could not function as well as it does today without lobbyists." In agreeing with the importance of lobbyists, 87 percent of legislators called them "competent professionals," and 96 percent felt they knew "their business well." Lobbyists, in similar proportions, agreed with those statements. These findings still apply, policymakers believe, in the 1990s.

The key to this generally comfortable interaction with lobbyists was the information that they gave others. Lobbyist respondents noted that the provided information depended on the specific identity of the targeted contact, a strategy that promotes flexibility and makes lobbyists uniformly important across all of state government. "Everyone out there has a need to know something that remains elusive," said one lobbyist. "My job is to fill the void." Administrators, according to lobbyists, primarily want positive or value-free information on how their programs or assignments can meet expected goals. They want it quickly, and then they want lobbyists out of their offices. The governor's staff and close gubernatorial allies want the same type of information. They also like to get information about legislative actions to which only a few lobbyists can be privy: "We milk them, but you wouldn't believe the voluntary calls that come to the office." Lobbyists believe that legislators want to know about only what specifically concerns them. Legislators claim to be mostly concerned about furthering favored policy concerns within their committees and learning how their districts and regions will be affected by bills. Complete details of programs are of less concern. For example, a Detroit legislator will want to know about specific gains for the city from an economic development program rather than its statewide effect or its chance for recruiting jobs for all of Michigan.

As the above suggests, political information, or district intelligence work, is as important as policy information. Lobbyists must have command of both. Legislators want value-laden but factually specific information as to which of their constituents will be affected by an issue, how these people will react, how their reaction can be dealt with, and what that reaction will likely mean to public opinion in the district. "That explains why I cannot lobby on too great a range of issues," noted one lobbyist. "My links to the district level are generally specific to only one type of business."

Two rules of thumb suggest the importance of regular lobbyists in sustaining partnerships with policymakers. First, the lobbyists' job demands that they provide both program and political information to likely participants as early as possible in deliberations on any issue of consequence to their client. Second, the appropriate information, selected on the basis of what concerns the various targets, must be disseminated to each participant likely to be of help in resolving the issue. "Don't ever play the game of secret-information-man," observed one former legislator. "As a lobbyist I give all my [relevant] information to all those who need it. I don't get burned for playing favorites then." The regular lobbyist, as a result, not only promotes the issue by gathering and communicating information; he or she often plays a pivotal role in resolving the issue by using knowledge to link together the political needs of the governor, legislators, staff members, and administrators. "By running back and forth with that information," explained the lobbyist quoted above, "I can keep the issue defined my way in front of all affected parties." Of course, this seldom is necessary if a lobbyist's job is only to stop legislation, as with the Michigan Trial Lawyers PAC and insurance reform.

The need to manage issues from the inception of policy ideas to their resolution explains why lobbyists are highly regarded by most of those who control organized interests as well as by state policymakers. Grass-roots representatives who more rarely are called on to lobby themselves – from business executives and university presidents to social activists and politically astute hunters – express the fear that an interest cannot succeed unless it has a regular lobbyist, namely, a Lansing political insider, a professional.[30] This belief has done much to increase both the number and reputation of multiclient lobbying firms that serve a diverse clientele for, usually, a smaller fee than the amount required to add another lobbyist or two. Operating either on annual retainer or for a specific assignment, multiclient lobbyists have gained great prominence.

Of the more than 2,000 interest representatives registered and studied in 1988, 256 worked for a total of thirty-seven multiclient firms. As total registrations dropped by a third over the next five years, multiclient lobbyists grew to an estimated high of 270 and firms ranged in number from thirty-five to forty. Reorganizations and mergers accounted for the variation. Most all of the firms have been located in Lansing. Some of the twenty to forty organizations represented in Lansing by Washington, D.C.–based lobbyists employed multiclient firms from the nation's capital. One firm, Honigman and

Table 18: Ten Most Effective Multiclient Lobbying Firms, 1986–87 and 1993

1986–87	1993
Capitol Services Corporation	Public Affairs Associates, Inc.
Dykema, Gossett	Governmental Consultant Services, Inc.
Fitzgerald, Hodgman, Cox	James H. Karoub Associates
Governmental Consultant Services, Inc.	Muchmore Harrington Associates
Huffman and Associates	Michigan Legislative Consultants
James H. Karoub Associates	Cawthorne, McCollough
Kheder and Associates	Noordhoek and Associates
Michigan Legislative Consultants	Capitol Services Corporation
Public Affairs Associates, Inc.	Dykema Gossett
Public Sector Consultants, Inc.*	Husband, Cusmano and Associates

*This firm registered no clients and, technically, is a research organization that exercises considerable influence through its analysis.

Sources: William S. Ballenger, "Lobbyists in IMP Survey," Inside Michigan Politics 1 (November 2, 1987): 2–3; and Ballenger, "Multi-Client Firms (and Muchmore) Top Lobbyist Survey," Inside Michigan Politics 7 (May 10, 1993): 1–3. The results were found by William P. Browne and Delbert J. Ringquist during the 1986 session of the Legislature and follow-up work in 1992.

Associates of Detroit, employed nearly half (121) of the multiclient lobbyists in 1988. Lobbyists owning these firms, or employed by them, have developed reputations for influence that are disproportionate to their numbers. Of the individual lobbyists ranked as most influential in the 1987 Ballenger survey of Lansing activists and political observers, fourteen of the top-ranked twenty-one most effective representatives were members of multiclient firms. Moreover, according to the same survey, four of the most effective lobbying organizations were multiclient firms. The other six were public affairs staffs or trade and professional associations. None was employed by individual business firms or by grass-roots organizations. The 1993 Ballenger study found ten of the state's ranking lobbies to be multiclient firms, which employed nineteen of the twenty top-rated lobbyists. As can be seen in table 18, only six of the ten top-ranked 1986–87 firms retained their ranking in 1993.

Multiclient firms reported, that they had clients from 431 organizations in 1987, but this did not include those on retainer who were not actively lobbying an issue that year.[31] The ten firms ranked as the most effective registered on behalf of from zero to seventy clients. According to executives of the firms, the largest served between fifty and one hundred clients that year. The number, respondents noted, grew steadily throughout the decade, but with few firms going over one hundred clients.

Active clients divide between those who use lobbyists-for-hire as their only representatives and those organizations already employing their own in-house lobbyists. The latter organizations want multiclient firms to mount comprehensive lobbying strategies by covering more contacts, generating greater information, or undertaking more public relations and polling assignments. The firms differ significantly from one another though. Law firms do mostly technical legal work and execute only limited follow-through, either legislatively or by litigating. The most prominent multiclient firms also divide between those whose lobbyists are most noted for their ability to gain favors from an old-boy network and those whose representatives specialize in planning strategy, putting an appropriate lobbying team together, preparing materials, and adhering to a schedule. This second type makes extensive use of computers and quantitative information, as opposed to personal friendships and insider knowledge. Other differences among firms include their varying emphases: appropriations, certain types of policy, partisan connections, and many other specific political needs.

The emphasis on working closely with key contacts and managing policy deliberations is misleading in that these activities glamorize the lobbyist's job. This mystique of the professional lobbyist as political insider overlooks a frequent admission by lobbyists: "I don't do anything that clients can't do for themselves." Lobbyists simply work with greater knowledge about the dynamics of policymaking. So a difficult job for a Muskegon businessperson or a Birmingham environmental activist becomes an easy one for a Lansing lobbyist who knows the policy participants, understands the legislative process, and is close enough to stay informed about various procedural actions.[32]

Both multiclient lobbyists and those employed by organized interests emphasize that they cannot succeed unless their cause attracts the attention of policymakers. They suggest that a winnable issue must be backed by public opinion, have an actively mobilized constituency, or have a financially committed membership. The latter was particularly emphasized: "It's real, real hard for a legislator to say 'no' to constituents who are economic stakeholders in an issue. They'll scream and haunt the member forever." To this end, nearly all legislators arrange meetings between policymakers and constituents who belong to or otherwise support the organized interest. "The exception," a typical respondent acknowledged, "is the lobbyist who has a powerful legislator as a close personal friend."

In Michigan, despite the search for balance, some issues clearly get more backing than others because of strong public opinion and forceful displays of constituent concern. Issues affecting the environment and conservation, labor, and industry all find responsive politicians in Lansing. The 1967 riots in Detroit brought the problems of African Americans to the state's policy agenda, even if the events apparently escalated racial tensions among many Michiganians. The taxpayer revolt – with grass-roots–mandated statewide tax-limitation referenda in 1976, 1978, and 1980 – gave that issue lasting agenda status. Representatives of aged, fishing, motorcyclist, anti-abortion, farm, private school, or medical interests all staged disruptive protests on the state capitol grounds at various times in the 1980s and early 1990s. Legislators, in most cases, were convinced that protesters had legitimate – and neglected – positions, and policy momentum resulted: "It scares you when voters ring the Capitol. You don't know how many of them are yours or what they say to their friends back home."

But many other issues are not able to gain such enthusiastic grass-roots support and, therefore, legislative attention. Their appeal is either too narrow or, ironically, too complex and technical. For these groups, financial contributions and in-kind campaign assistance become particularly important in drawing policymaker support. The high cost of campaigning and the strong financial incentives (relatively high salary, retirement benefits) for incumbents to stay in office make such assistance valued commodities for legislators. Those factors encourage a wide range of state interests to raise whatever they can to assist legislators. This cooperation explains why money – in tandem with numerous meetings with executives and constituents to remind recipients as to why organizations provide it – is a central feature of interest politics. But the large number of PACs is only one example. Fund-raisers for individual legislators, for which few lobbyists can afford not to buy tickets, are a nightly event in Lansing during much of the year. Other donations flow into campaign committees controlled by legislative and party leaders. Honoraria for legislators to speak at and attend meetings of association members and firm executives are commonplace, frequently suggested by those who receive the fee. Influential interests with highly organized members, such as the UAW and MEA, find this feature of Michigan politics useful on issues that do not generate a cohesive statewide position, such as workers' compensation and state funding of education.[33] Groups with small but financially strong members, such as Michigan Beer and Wine Wholesalers, also gain advantage by being able to raise large sums of money quickly.

Such actions bring the most frequent criticisms of interest groups from state officials, lobbyists, and political critics. The implication is that while

organized interests cannot control policymaking, they often play too dominant a role. Efforts at insurance reform in 1992 provide an excellent example. The media and numerous policy participants reacted vociferously when
the legislature deadlocked after months of negotiation. With trial lawyers
allied with Democrats, and insurance companies allied with Republicans,
neither the legislative leaders nor key lobbyists could broker a deal. Turning
the issue over to an electoral initiative, as happened, was distasteful for everyone. However, the one bill that did make it to the executive office was
vetoed. The anticipation of large campaign contributions from each set of interests made it hard for legislators to push their group allies to settle: "The
flow of campaign money was tremendous." A daily bipartisan observer of
the Lansing scene commented: "Auto insurance is the best example I can
think of that shows the legislature is owned lock, stock and barrel by competing special interest groups."[34] Transfer of the battle to voters did little good.
They, too, rejected the insurance reform proposal, even though they found
lower rates appealing. When the legislature finally passed a similar bill with
an evenly split Michigan house, opposing interests once again filed petition
for a ballot question to overturn the law in the 1994 elections.

THE WATCHDOGS

As the above quote indicates, criticism of Michigan interest groups and their
policy partners is extensive and directly tied to money. Because this criticism has great symbolic importance in a state that emphasizes ethical standards, it carries influence. Thus, the watchdogs for impropriety, who themselves are stakeholders, also must be considered here.

A few good-government groups, such as Michigan Common Cause and
the Michigan Citizens Lobby, can be found in the state. Despite the self-image of these groups, policymakers see them as but another set of organized
interests with narrow agendas. Accordingly, their mostly amateur-style efforts are not given special recognition. "I don't see where they differ," explained one legislator. "In a sense all lobbyists are out trying to expose one
another." His comments ring true because the reform groups' alternate role –
broadening public awareness – produces few analyses of state policy and
politics. The most widely recognized is the informational guide of the Michigan League of Women Voters, which profiles candidates in a noncontrover-
sial fashion. Traditionally, these groups have been neutral with respect to
ballot questions as well. However, in 1992, the League was outspoken in opposition to property-tax reform, and the Citizens Lobby opposed the insur-

ance reform proposal. These actions brought the two groups closer to the mainstream of influence politics.

Watchdogging, or monitoring state politics for questionable actions, is left then to the media.[35] Despite the media's near monopoly on the watchdog's job, state government is seldom the target of investigative reporting. Although a small legion of reporters may converge on a hot story for a few days, there have been few sustained news events. The PBB disaster involving contaminated cow feed was a rare exception, rather than a recurring example of reporters focusing on state government. It is a surprising, even shocking, story when individual legislators are held out for public scrutiny.

A more typical example was a week-long preoccupation of several reporters with 1992 purchases of state capitol office furniture. The story was considered hot because of its symbolism: several hundred thousand dollars were to be spent amidst looming budget cuts in government programs. Also somewhat typical, although unusually persistent, is *Detroit News* columnist Pete Waldmeir's continued hammering of Governor John Engler for his handling of the Michigan Education Trust (MET). Such stories remind politicians that the media can create a degree of public visibility and potential outrage, even when no great breech of public trust is obvious.

Thus, Michigan reportage generally is neither intense nor controversial. It may be somewhat biased – reflecting the subtle differences between the conservative *Detroit News* and the more liberal *Detroit Free Press* or the boosterism that local reporters give to their district legislators – but mostly state reporting is low-key and short on detail.

The reason is quite simple. Relatively few media resources are directed to Lansing. Editors feel that their readers find stories on state issues and procedures to be difficult to comprehend and, hence, boring.[36] This produces interdependent relationships between reporters who need cooperative politicians for good stories and political officials who need coverage from the media.[37] Consequently, the more familiar American theme of independence in journalism often becomes secondary to producing formatted, general information news. The lack of big stories, at least partially because of the relative efficiency and honesty of state politics, encourages cooperation and routines. As a reporter noted, "They set up photo opportunities; we cover them. They screw up and we show up; the staff arranges a production with all the explanations. Then we out-of-town guys are done."

Watchdogging is done by a small cadre of regular reporters who have far more limited opportunities and incentives to dig deeply into controversies than most observers realize. About thirty-five reporters have full-time Lansing assignments. Few media outlets have their own correspondents in the capitol. Most state newspapers, television stations, and radio stations depend on wire-service messages and reports that local legislators provide with partisan staff assistance. Two newspaper chains, Booth and Gannett, have small local offices to serve their Michigan papers, which number among the state's largest. Only the two Detroit daily papers, a single TV channel, and the Lansing media (which see all this as local news) provide full-time staff to the state capital. These reporters cover state leaders first, local legislators second, and everything else as incidental. Little issue expertise or institutional memory develops among the reporters. As one noted, "When someone in Lansing suggested I cover the need for lobbying reform, I thought I discovered the story. Later I found it comes up in the papers every three or four years when someone suggests it to a reporter."

When special events are scheduled in advance, several more papers and stations send reporters and news teams. To draw broad coverage, these events usually focus on the governor, the legislative leaders, or a well-orchestrated and vocal interest-group protest. The result is that big picture items get considerable coverage and commentary, but usually only as managed media events.

Also, local and regional issues, which dominate the legislature's attention, get ignored by the regular press corps, which is focused on events of statewide interest. This neglect leaves local legislators to deal directly with their district media. Frequent trips back home enable most media outlets to cover their legislators on local turf. These trips also allow highly personal contacts with the media that let legislators put their own spin on nearly every story.

For example, Senator John Pridnia (R-Harrisville), in a very unusual story, was singled out by the *Detroit Free Press* for moving "through Lansing like a vacuum cleaner sucking up the money of political action committees." He sought his defense in local district papers.[38] Accusing the *Free Press* of "tabloid reporting," Pridnia made several headlines and scored numerous points with northern Michigan constituents with his follow-up rhetoric. Local papers played especially on his "cool head," the lack of believability in "Detroit papers," earlier *Free Press* endorsements of Mayor Coleman Young, labor leader involvement in the attacks, and the legality of the senator's actions.

Interdependence prevails because public relations staff are easily accessible in the governor's office, in the legislature, and for most state interests. The reluctance of state administrators, other than departmental executives, to volunteer information means that reporters gravitate to gubernatorial and legislative staff for insights on agency matters. The same reticence is often true for the judiciary. So, investigative reporters usually cover only scheduled events, and they get most of their information from those who do the scheduling. The unusual story of Senator Pridnia was made possible because both opponents and allies cooperated with information or startling quotes. The State Chamber of Commerce called Pridnia's behavior "shameful," and noted the need to be "sensitive to the perception that special interests control the agenda."[39] Many saw this as a good way to shift the critical spotlight from lobbyists to a deserving legislator.

While reporters work with a skeptical eye on state officials, their own schedule and space limitations make the use of public relations assistance normally quite sufficient to their needs. Television favors visual events and seldom allows more than sixty seconds to show them. Radio likes even shorter sound bites – often just a ten-second quote. Newspaper stories are often three to six column inches long, with a twelve- to fifteen-inch story being a major feature. Hence, the need to produce a great deal of information for most stories is rare. One reporter explained, "If things don't smell fishy after I cover the bases with all the press officials, than I just let it go and put their stuff together as I need it. I could actually get by with never doing anything more."

The capacity of the media to influence politics under those circumstances is quite limited. Reporters lack the resources and, with a few exceptions, the professional experience of lobbyists and public officials. Most quickly rotate off the state government beat. The media, however, do matter because state officials want to place their names, their faces, and their identification with popular issues before the electorate. Accordingly, access is open, and the opportunities, if not the time, to probe are almost unlimited. Moreover, state officials, as sources of leaks, are useful in providing information. The interdependence that characterizes relationships between elected officials and media representatives keeps most activities subject to public scrutiny, especially because many young reporters would like nothing better than to report a hot story to advance their careers.

Help is available in generating leads for hot stories. A second set of specialized media provides even closer scrutiny and leads for stories. Columnists from the two Detroit dailies; the operators of the *Gongwer Newsletter,* the *Hannah Report,* and *Michigan Information and Research Service* (MIRS), which provide daily status reports and special information on state government; the entrepreneur behind the newsletter *Inside Michigan Poli-*

tics; and the host of the public broadcasting network's weekly *Off the Record* television program are all recognized personalities who seek capital stories every day. Moreover, most of them report with great detail and considerable innuendo. This puts state officials and lobbyists in the spotlight and on the defensive, even as these same people clamor to gain more coverage. While these specialized products appeal primarily to political junkies, the audience of insiders helps keep state politics open and controversial. Long gone, as a result, are the days when an auto lobbyist could sit at a legislative leader's desk and help direct floor activity without someone calling public attention to its inappropriateness.

SOME CLOSING THOUGHTS

The convergence of media watchdogs, grass-roots activists, and regular lobbyists produces an usual mix of influence agents in Michigan politics. It remains far too simple to follow the money trail and draw conclusions about what interests matter most. Michigan politics is too complex. The attentiveness that legislators give to district reporters and activists counterbalances the resource advantages of major statewide interests. At the same time, high finance is truly a way of life in interest-group politics, though it remains difficult to judge what that money buys in terms of public policies. However, all the major players and many of the truly minor ones get a significant share of what often seems excessiveness in state programs. It appears truly trying for Michigan officials to say "no."

CHAPTER TEN

Economic Problems:
Issues and Policy

David Murphy, Noelle Schiffer, William Sederburg, and
David Verway contributed to this chapter

ECONOMICS AND POLITICS: INSEPARABLE LINKAGE

A large part of the linkage of politics and economics in Michigan can be attributed to the state's boom-and-bust economy. When the economy has prospered, state revenues have been available to expand programs (see figure 4). With about 25 percent of state revenue in the early 1990s coming from the personal income tax, another 17 percent from sales and use taxes, and about 11 percent from business taxes, the state has been vulnerable to revenue surges and declines. The 1994 replacement of 75 percent of local school-district property taxes on homesteads with an increased state sales tax, and other tax shifts, increased the likelihood of such ups and downs. Each of these taxes contributes more to state coffers when times are good, less when the economy dips. Shifts can create great volatility in program allocations. Even when the state depended mostly on sales and use taxes, things were little different; when income rose, leveled, or fell, personal expenditures, and therefore tax revenues, were affected.[1] Of course, with most incomes affected marginally and some stability built into other revenue sources, revenues and expenditures have not fluctuated as wildly as average personal incomes. There always remained sources on which to draw and even against which to borrow for a base budget. For example, the state had budget shortfalls in 1979 and had to withdraw from its budget stabilization fund. Over the next four years, revenue surpluses were put into the reserve fund. The years 1987–92 again saw withdrawals. By 1992, the state also remained $781 million in debt to the federal government for its share of federal unemployment costs, a debt that every other major industrial state had paid off.

Figure 4: Michigan State Expenditures and Revenues, in Billions of Dollars, 1976–91

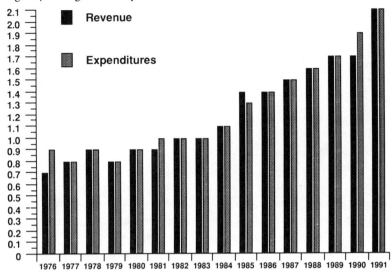

Note: Figures not adjusted for inflation.

Source: Comprehensive Annual Financial Report, Michigan Department of Management and Budget.

In general, revenues and expenditures have shown growth beyond inflation. Both modestly increased from 1976 and 1984. Then there was a decided upswing through 1991, even as imbalances occurred. In fact, expenditures increased about 20 percent in that latter period, with personal income taxes supporting one-third of that growth. Adjusting for inflation, this growth pushed state expenditures up 39.5 percent between 1971 and 1991. Such growth creates two budgetary stresses for the state. First, there is the constant demand for more funds. Second, when revenues increase, newer costs get built into the state budget, which then become burdensome when the economy declines. This problem is even more severe than it first appears. Because increasing revenues can be generated under marginal economic conditions, growth may not reflect the health of the state economy. This same principle applied when cash reserves from unexpectedly high 1993–94 revenues were deducted from the proposed sales tax increase before voters in March 1994 could get to the polls to resolve the school finance issue. Funds were diverted away from rainy-day reserves.

This shows how the state has played out its moralistic inclinations. These expenditures satisfied a wide variety of claims in a very individualistic fashion. But they leveraged the state into financial difficulties and, in most cases, led to investment in capital assets that have to be maintained when the economy falls into recession. The best example can be seen in the 79 percent increase in expenditures for public safety and corrections between 1986 and 1991. With more prisons, operational costs soared. In 1994, it led to a concern about whether a boom-and-bust state could sustain school finance levels.

All budget problems, however, are not of the state's making. Federal assistance counts for about 26 percent of state revenues. These funds do not come without their own costs. Federal regulations and requirements for matching assistance accompany federal funding and have pushed up state expenditures more than is commonly understood. For example, the state general-fund share of Medicaid grew 33 percent in 1981–91, requiring a 50 percent match for every federal dollar spent in Michigan. During the period of rapid growth, 1986–91, policy areas of federal interest or expenditure increased most. Social services, general government, and health care were significantly affected by federal mandates, ranging from childhood welfare assistance to safety regulations. State expenditures in those three areas rose a combined 28 percent, 8 percent above the state average. Only corrections grew faster among state programs, and only school aid came close – with a 26 percent increase prompted by Governor Engler's attention to education. In addition, these three areas of federal interest grew at a combined 29 percent rate in the previous five years, a period of otherwise modest growth.

In this chapter we do three things: explain in more detail the economic conditions that have made this cyclic economy even less manageable, examine political responses and economic programs that result from structural changes in the economy, and draw some implications about the state's policy future in a period of downsized personal and state budgets. Our point throughout explains Michigan's most critical dilemma: how do political leaders try to balance, in some acceptable fashion, losses in public program benefits while still dealing effectively with statewide economic problems?

THE MICHIGAN ECONOMY

Even when Michigan was a growing industrial giant, the state was beset by exceptional problems of governance, especially given the many reasons to spend whenever it was made possible by the state's increasing revenues. From 1914 to 1953, through four national business cycles of recession and surge, Michigan was first among the thirty-three largest states in economic volatility.[2] It was the state most variable in average depth of cyclical decline and average height of subsequent expansion in manufacturing employment. Michigan also was fourth in average rate of cyclical decline and first in average rate of cyclical expansion. From 1909 to 1953, Michigan was fifth in average growth rate in manufacturing employment. In short, Michigan moved into the manufacturing era with an unstable economy; it remained so even though it was also one of the fastest growing state economies in the first half of this century. Although Michigan politics was dominated by rural laissez-faire interests, the demand for state infrastructure supports to sustain this emerging manufacturing economy was intense. Under this strain, policymakers pushed for some of the nation's earliest federal grants, just before the turn of the twentieth century.

Modern Volatility

Michigan's manufacturing dependence was producing great difficulties for the state as early as 1956, first as military demand shifted away from land-based transportation vehicles and then as demands for civilian durable goods after World War II were met. This coincided, quite by chance, with Michigan's new identity as a progressive labor state, one in which human service expenditures were escalating sharply. As a result, Michigan entered a high expenditure/high expectations era just as its revenue base faced great instability. State leaders soon observed the beginnings of a fundamental shift that would haunt Michigan into the present: U.S. manufacturing was growing less rapidly, automobile manufacturing was falling behind rates of other manufactured goods, and Michigan's share of auto production was declining.[3] State unemployment in 1961 was 10.1 percent compared to a U.S. average of 6.7 percent. Moreover, the national economy was becoming more dependent on information-based industries. More people were selling, distributing, acquiring, and analyzing information than were actually manufacturing durable goods.[4] The sunbelt states gained the most from these new industries that were not dependent on being close to old centers of wealth and manufacturing.[5] Michigan benefited little from this new industry. Nor did Michiganians try to capture these industries and the federal government contracts on which they grew. One of the major difficulties was high industrial wages – 26 percent above the national average – which led to high state worker expectations and discouraged emerging firms from locating here.

This shift toward less consistent growth exaggerated the volatility that

Figure 5: Michigan Unemployment Rate, in Percent, 1960–93

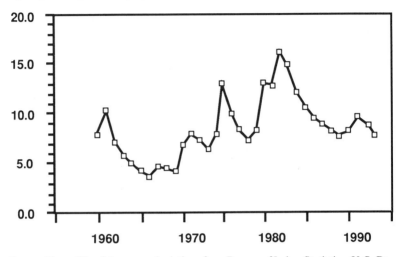

Source: House Fiscal Agency calculations from Bureau of Labor Statistics, U.S. Department of Labor.

Michiganians had come to expect in their economy. Booms and busts, as reflected in figure 5, came more quickly and predictably than before: unemployment lows followed the recessions of 1957, 1960, 1969, 1973, 1979, 1981, and 1990. Durable goods manufacturing, particularly of autos, only made gains when external events pushed up consumer purchases. The end of the Korean War, suburbanization, interstate highways, and increased federal government spending all boosted sales. Negative trends remained, however, with overall income in the manufacturing sector off by 10 percent from 1960 to 1981. Moreover, Michigan's unemployment rate began a long-term upward trend from 1966 to 1982.

The situation grew worse for employment after the 1981 recession. While the unemployment rate dropped after 1982, structural adjustments in the auto industry changed the state's job mix by forcing many auto workers off the line. The automobile industry finally began adjusting to the information age, switching when possible to more capital-intensive and more high-technology assembly methods from its previous labor dependency.[6] Just thirty years after the information age arrived, Michigan's share of national total per capita personal income had declined from 5.2 percent to 3.7 percent. Its problems were severe even for the rustbelt. Michigan's share among the economies of the five Great Lakes states fell from 23.6 to 21.9 percent over this period. Its poverty rate was the highest. Moreover, high percentages of the state's work force were being lost as industry automated. Low-skill jobs, for reasons of cheap labor, moved overseas and to Mexico. By 1992, Mexico employed one General Motors employee for every three left in Michigan, many at less than two dollars per hour. Changes in industry structure no longer matched the job skills of many employees, creating many general welfare recipients when unemployment benefits ran out. These employees were not counted in the unemployment rate after their benefits expired. At the height of the recession in 1982, 12.9 percent of Michigan residents were on welfare and 13.2 percent in poverty. Even by 1988, a period of economic recovery, 10.6 percent of the population was still on these assistance rolls. This does not count auto workers whose jobs were bought out through early retirement and those who left the state in frustration.

Unlike the recessions of earlier decades, Michigan personal incomes of the 1980s were no longer recovering their national share of wealth. In 1973, Michigan's growth in income had still not approached its 1969 pre-recession share. By 1981, national economic recovery no longer guaranteed that the income of Michigan residents would rise above pre-recession levels. In fact, income continued to fall below levels of 1976 throughout the 1980s. The result was that Michigan's historically high state expenditures leveled off to only modest growth. While the state for decades had been about 10 percent above the national average in expenditures, it dropped to seven percent below by 1982.

None of these changes of the 1980s, especially those that tightened budgets, were lost on political leaders. During each of the recessions of the last thirty-five years, the governor and legislators rededicated efforts to what was always called "diversifying the Michigan economy." Predictably, this first response was never sustained. As market demand for cars would rise and the economy expand, diversification would recede from the headlines. For example, during recovery, even lakeshore communities would look beyond tourism and service-job gains as they cast envious eyes at the rapidly developing suburbs of southeastern Michigan. Attention would then turn to recruiting an auto parts supply firm, or citizens groups in the most unlikely places would clamor for their officials to bid for something like General Motor's new Saturn Corporation. Hence, meaningful long-term budget and fiscal policy reform was never forthcoming.

The hope for recovery, especially a recovery tied to the automobile industry, is understandable. The costs of doing something else with Michigan's economy are extraordinarily high: people and firms simply do not voluntarily phase out procedures and facilities in which they have invested capital that cannot easily be shifted to some other productive use. So politics, in a state like Michigan that is responsive to its residents' demands, protects assets that are sunk into existing ways of doing business. With so many organized and regional interests, with intense party competition, with independent and active voters, and with a legislature built on its members' political careers, no one wants to assume the risks of proclaiming the state's need to sacrifice and adjust its standard of living. Most often, policymakers engage in rhetoric and posturing about making cuts to improve the state's quality of life. This can be seen in the taxation bills introduced by legislators in the 1980s and early 1990s. From 1981 through 1992, approximately 10 percent of all bills were tax proposals. Tax-reduction bills led tax-increase proposals by about four to one, with both Democrats and Republicans leaning to cuts. Almost none of the bills passed.[7] Things only intensified under Governor Engler in 1993 and 1994 as he led the effort to break finally the property-tax impasse.

The state also cannot afford to see further unemployment in the sizable percentage of its work force employed in the auto industry. As the vestiges of an updated version of prodigal wastage from automobile manufacturing now show, little can be done with an abandoned plant or an uneducated assembly-line worker who has no transferable job skills. The best strategy is to keep future auto manufacturing losses as low as possible and look for marginal gains in other economic sectors.

Michigan, clinging to its industrial character, goes on quite rationally, though somewhat unrealistically given structural changes. Two things about the state's economy clearly explain why: durable goods manufacturing still dominates despite its losses, and automobile manufacturing still remains king in that sector. As from its frontier inception, the state remained, even through most of the 1980s, a place where brawn and raw resources, rather than financial wizardry or high technology, marked progress. Even today, manual laborers are more abundant than technicians and designers.

Automobile Dominance

Government statisticians first recognized automobile manufacturing as a distinct industry in the U.S. Census of Manufacturing of 1905; 9,023 of the 20,161 motor vehicles made in the United States that year rolled out of Michigan factories. The state's industrial leadership grew. In 1914, as automobiles accounted for over 36 percent of Michigan's manufacturing value, its factories produced 443,072 cars, trucks, and buses out of a national total of 569,054. Production in Michigan and nationally continued to grow until 1929. By 1935, Michigan was leading not only its own economy but that of the nation out of the Great Depression with vehicle production records. The post–World War II boom was also led by automobiles, as Michigan factories worked to satisfy pent-up national demand for new cars and trucks.

The importance of the automobile to the state economy can be seen by looking briefly at Michigan's postwar employment patterns. The state reached its auto employment apogee in 1956 with 411,700 workers. That figure fell, though, to 288,500 only two years later as Michigan plunged into a deep recession. Numbers never again reached that level, but generally grew until 1978. Auto was still king. By 1978, however, 30.2 percent of the labor force was in durable goods manufacturing; 9.7 percent, or 409,600, made automobiles.[8] After 1978, the number of employees declined rapidly, even with periodic economic growth. By 1985, 25.6 percent of Michigan workers were in durable goods manufacturing, a 15.2 percent reduction from 1978. Auto employment dropped even more, 18.5 percent. By 1990, only 21.5 percent of the Michigan work force made durable goods, which was another 23.7 percent decline from 1981. Auto jobs again dropped a bit more. Even with heavy manufacturing still so important, and with the auto industry in its second round of technological adoption and hiring of more skilled employees, it was no wonder that the logic of diversification and the realization that Michigan's economy had fundamentally changed finally hit home. The instincts of state policymakers during this period were severely tested: tending to gravitate to the old automotive stalwart, yet anxious for relief from its negative effects.

What manufacturing did for income was extremely important in resisting change, however. As we noted in chapter 1, service jobs (which are defined in table 19) pay considerably less. That differential, as seen by referring to figure 1 in the first chapter, kept state income averages well above national averages, but only as long as Michigan kept manufacturing jobs as its labor core. In the boom years of the 1970s, apart from Alaska with its unusually high cost of living, Michigan's auto cities led the nation in average workers' salaries. When manufacturing jobs declined in the 1980s as the auto industry furloughed and replaced workers with technology, Michigan lost its standing as a high average income and expenditure state. An increase in service jobs through the 1980s offset some manufacturing job losses, and service jobs proved somewhat more "recession-proof" in the downturn of 1990–91. Nevertheless, a service economy does not provide the standard of living that

Table 19: Michigan's Private-Sector Manufacturing and Service Jobs as a Percentage of Employment in Each Sector, July 1991

Manufacturing Jobs (23% of state total)	*Service Jobs* (25% of state total)
Durable goods (74%)	Business services (18.2%)
Motor vehicles (28.6%)	Engineering, accounting, and
Industrial machinery/computers	management (8.6%)
(13.1%)	Social services (6.5%)
Fabricated metals (12.6%)	Hotels and lodging (3.9%)
Primary metals (4.3%)	Automotive services (3.4%)
Furniture and fixtures (3.8%)	Health services (3.4%)
Other electrical equipment (3.5%)	Private education (3.2%)
Stone, clay, and glass products	Other (23.2%)
(1.8%)	
Other transportation (1.7%)	
Lumber and wood products (1.6%)	
Other (2.7%)	
Nondurable goods (26%)	
Rubber and plastics (5.7%)	
Chemicals and petroleum (5.4%)	
Food and kindred products (5.3%)	
Printing and publishing (4.9%)	
Paper and allied products (2.4%)	
Apparel (2.1%)	
Other (0.4%)	

Source: Bureau of Labor Statistics, U.S. Department of Labor.

a large percentage of Michigan residents had come to expect in their industrial heyday.

Michigan residents in the 1990s thus were forced to grapple with questions of what state government should and could still do. However, any assessment of future policy actions was difficult because, for all practical purposes, there was no place to start over. The reasons for this inflexibility were simple. Michigan's political economy – as a merger of public policy decisions and economic conditions – severely limited the options, both by characteristics that the state lacked and by political forces that were created in the manufacturing era. This lack of flexibility produced political complexities that did not make it easy for the state to restore manufacturing to its optimal level. The diversity of the state meant there were several important groups that were not enamored with a return to such an economy: outstate residents who were never part of that labor mix, service industries that could not compete for prize employees against high-paying manufacturing jobs, agriculture and tourist industries that saw mixed benefits in manufacturing, and various anti-development interests and people who had moved outstate to retire, play, or seek a less competitive economy.

Despite this diversity, Michigan's economy has created conditions that give the state its own particular character. Although they are not always appreciated by state residents, these conditions produce issues and historical problems that define much of the state's politics.

High Touch, Late Development

Years of manufacturing growth have brought about a state political economy that is every bit as specific and as deterministic to Michigan as its mixed political culture. There are three relevant parts to that political economy, the first of which is its historical development. The political economy and the issues that it continues to generate were structured by what was manufactured in the state and how it was done. Unlike the West Coast of the United States, which cultivated industries that both matured and suffered reversals later, Michigan's capital-intensive, resource conversion manufacturing was high touch as opposed to high tech: large numbers of laborers spent long hours repeating tasks that were less mentally demanding than they were emotionally tedious. This was true of auto workers and, to a varying extent, those employed by steel, furniture, appliance, boat, food-processing, and chemical firms around the state. Industrial leaders concentrated on plants with massive production capacities, workers trained in narrowly specialized jobs, and scientific management techniques to promote efficiency. Workers were monitored carefully with, by the 1960s in General Motors, as many as fourteen layers of highly bureaucratized management. This was costly and, as it later proved in competition with Japanese companies, inefficient.

Nor was research and development much more than high touch. While each major automotive manufacturer began developing high-technology cars produced under increasingly exhaustive scientific standards after World War II, these produced limited changes in the industry. Concentrations of new technology in auto electronics and robotics that focused on improved manufacturing techniques and automobile quality did not appear until the early 1980s. Prior to that, the industry emphasized performance and appearance, but not quality. Large-scale use of computers awaited a second wave of technology in the late 1980s that carried into the 1990s. The state, like its region, was noted as a place not "much interested in the man with the Ph.D. and what he can contribute to the opening of new frontiers. It has failed singly to exploit . . . educational resources. . . . [It] has not developed much enthusiasm for staffing high concentrations of people who have the highly technical background required to do creative work."[9] Instead, the auto industry prized its trade-schooled machinists and toolmakers, while, for example, California's aerospace industries depended on metallurgists with doctorates. Mechanical engineers stayed in Michigan to retool the industry, while the state's best electronic engineering graduates moved to the West.

Even growth industries that were coming to depend on high technology exited a state that they found to be little receptive to their needs. Willow Run, one of the nation's premier aircraft production facilities during World War II, was converted to producing automobiles for an ill-fated joint Kaiser-Frazier assembly plant. Eventually, until its closing was announced for 1993, the site was to become a General Motors assembly plant, while aircraft manufacturing flourished in states that were to benefit immensely from aerospace developments.

These conditions produced two problems that the state and its industries still face, both in diversifying the economy and in strengthening the automotive industry. First, the conditions led to a poorly educated work force. Michigan's school dropout rates have been excessively high for Americans, nearly six percent in 1985–86. Literacy rates are low, with 14 percent being below eighth-grade reading abilities. Only 77 percent of adults over age twenty-five have graduated from high school, and only 17.3 percent of adults have graduated from a four-year college program. Quality of the work force has become a major issue, with firms like General Motors getting reports from its plants that unskilled Mexican laborers prove more reliable. The quality of education, not surprisingly, has become a contentious issue, especially among businesses that now need more capable employees. Detroit's public schools, once among the finest in the nation, began a long and steady decline in 1929 as divisiveness split the district.[10]

Second, independent and largely blue-collar industries have not fostered strong relationships with higher education, other than hiring their graduates. Historically, except for unique programs such as those in mining in the Upper Peninsula, with its links to Michigan Tech University, demands for educational services and research have been weak. For years, the General Motors Institute served as that corporation's largely private college; its students could learn precisely what they needed to know, with no frills, from inside the industry. Technology transfer from academia has been low. As a result, new state educational investments with specific economic returns have been called for. But while universities want the financial support that comes from programs such as state Research Excellence grants, they often lack knowledge of how to use the funds to meet business needs.

While Michigan has all of the educational institutions, opportunities, and diversity of programs expected in a moralistic state, critics question education's relevancy and its dedication to help the state solve its problems. They charge that colleges and universities continue to produce surpluses of teacher candidates and fail to give graduates the necessary work skills for cutting-edge technologies. Business leaders cite out-of-state industries and their educational ties as sources of innovation for their needs. Education asks how its institutions can suddenly become involved with industries that never needed them before. Educators also note extensive investments made elsewhere, such as at Stanford University and in research centers in Colorado, by General Motors, Ford, Dow Chemical, and other Michigan corporations. If these expenditures had been made in Michigan, chagrined and budget-strapped administrators note, they could have boosted the state economy and, in the long term, Michigan competitiveness.

Economic Concentration

A second part of the Michigan political economy and its issues results from the economic structure and concentration of its major industries. Auto manufacturing is the best example, but not the only one. In the early 1920s, more than one hundred American companies produced automobiles. Most were small firms. By the late 1920s, less than half were still in business.

General Motors moved from a holding company with seven divisions to an integrated corporation that continued to make a profit throughout the Great Depression.[11] Chrysler gained strength from reorganization, acquisition, and the development of several product lines. By 1930, the Big Three, with Ford thriving because of its innovations in assembly-line manufacture, dominated the industry, much of Michigan politics, and, especially, its Detroit home base.[12] The depression did even more for state manufacturers, leading to the collapse of most non-Michigan auto firms and concentrating 90 percent of U.S. production in the state.

Although other types of manufacturing never rivaled the size or political power of the auto industry's Big Three, large firms have been a common feature of Michigan's economy and its political landscape. Some firms, such as mining companies in the UP and steel foundries in southern Michigan, were giants long before concentration existed in the auto industry. Detroit and Bay City housed the nation's largest ship builders in the 1890s. Others grew alongside auto manufacturing: Whirlpool appliances in southeast Michigan, Chris-Craft pleasure boats on Lake Michigan's central shoreline, Huron Portland Cement in Alpena, and Kellogg breakfast cereals in Battle Creek. Still more dominant firms emerged later, most notably Amway's household products firm and Steelcase and Herman Miller office furniture manufacturers. These and other large firms helped transform Grand Rapids and west-central Michigan into the state's most rapidly growing area of the late twentieth century.

The rise of Grand Rapids to a premier urban center in the 1980s is illustrative of much of Michigan's past. Big business, as a key to the state's political economy, had a threefold impact on Michigan and its politics. First, regardless of their diversity of product and location, large manufacturers created community dependency wherever they located. Lumber firms, for example, controlled whole cities throughout northern Michigan at the turn of the century.

Second, dependency produced a state politics and a business climate that addressed industrial problems of labor and resource availability far more than it addressed the concerns of the downtown merchant, the investment banker, or, later, the high-risk entrepreneur.[13] In that sense, local politics as a special set of business problems and demands came to state government. This intensified already strong regional sentiments about government. When big business was represented in Lansing, it was through company presidents and corporate officials rather than chamber of commerce members, as in much of the rest of the Midwest. Tax deals, as they were negotiated in 1959 under Governor G. Mennen Williams, for example, were completed with auto lobbyists sitting in the offices of legislative leaders and providing coordination. "The damned Chrysler lobbyist sat there with his feet on the Speaker's desk," remembered one former legislator. In the 1930s, as labor unions fought for protection, Henry Ford and other auto executives intervened with governors and legislators. Despite such efforts, however, big business never really dominated state politics. In part, this was because the auto industry never sought an activist state government – other than for its own favors. Also, there was always competition in the legislature, first from nonindustrial rural interests and then from organized labor.

Third, big business eventually brought the rise of organized labor to Michigan.[14] Without the concentration of unskilled workers in large manufacturing industries, there was no basis for a successful labor union movement in any state. Michigan was ideal. When union leaders rebelled against unfair production practices and low wages, a sufficient mass of workers existed to support the sit-down strikes and plant closings of 1936 and 1937. There also was enough of a worker base to elect, on Franklin D. Roosevelt's coattails, Democratic governor Frank Murphy. Murphy, who refused to bow to judicial and business demands to use the National Guard to clear the strikers from plants, was not responsive to a business-driven politics that often corrupted local leaders. He had other powerful constituents to worry about, especially at the ballot box, where a new form of interest-group influence was being joined to state politics.

As a consequence, big labor followed big business, and the two set in motion their own politics of balance, a balance that by the 1950s became more prominent in state politics than urban-rural contests. While business continued to advance a conservative tone for the state, its leaders usually were more interested in profits than policy. They periodically checked labor union demands that might lead to higher taxes or other costs of doing business. But through the 1960s, business seldom defeated labor's liberal agenda of employee protection for its members and social welfare for the rest of Michigan's citizenry.[15] Their executives, untroubled by competition, simply passed on the costs of these programs to auto buyers, accepting such public policies for their usefulness in keeping a stable work force available for the expected booms and busts in Michigan hiring. Business reserved its clout for other issues, while labor benefited in social policy from its electoral majorities. This balance tipped the scales toward increased state expenditures and programs, and furthered the state's image as a moralistic culture where powerful organized interests oftentimes watched out for the statewide concerns of others. In reality, it was no less the uneasy truce of individualistic interests.

Manufacturing Dependence Continues

There remains a third and final important feature of Michigan's manufacturing-centered political economy, beyond that of assembly and production processes and business concentration. The degree to which manufacturing's economic contribution dominates the state's other two major industries remains overwhelming. This makes diversification difficult for Michigan.

Measured in terms of economic importance to the state, tourism and agriculture rank second and third. International competition and the farm-debt crisis of the 1980s hit Michigan and its relatively small-scale farmers hard, dropping the entire industry behind tourism – or travel and vacations – for the first time. But both industries are an odd mix of strengths and problems, leaving them vulnerable to numerous forces outside the state as well as to their own weaknesses.

Agriculture, with its $37.5 billion impact on the state economy, is highly touted in Michigan, especially for its diversity. With more than fifty crops grown commercially, Michigan is one of the top three states in range of production. Agriculture is also regional within the state, making it a leading industry in several regions. Wine production and fruit on the west coast of the lower peninsula, dry beans and sugar beets in the eastern "Thumb" region, and the herbs of central Michigan are well-known Michigan crops. Consequently, while legislators generally favor agriculture because it has a place in so many districts, the sector's fragmentation produces no clearcut policy guidance for improving its viability. The economic importance of this diverse production is as limited to the state as it is fragmented, which creates further problems. Six of the seven top state agricultural commodities are grown nationally, and in states with more of a competitive edge: dairy, cattle, hogs, corn, soybeans, and wheat. Moreover, except for livestock, all of these crops are in chronic surplus. In 1989, these six accounted for 52 percent of all state commodity cash receipts, a decline from a 65 percent share in 1985 that resulted mainly from taking Michigan land from production. Only when all vegetable farm receipts are combined do the more visibly prominent but specialty products break into Michigan's top seven commodities. Thus, most state farms are vulnerable to domestic price and international marketing fluctuations. Their plight is made more difficult because food-processing industries in Michigan are not adequate to handle an expansion of nonsurplus crops for which identifiable markets exist.[16]

Nor is agriculture as big an industry as either the size of the state's rural areas or the industry's economic rank indicates. Agriculture's share of the economy pales before auto manufacturing and retail trade stores (see figure 6). In any case, it is tiny unless food processing and agricultural manufacturing are added. Agriculture's ranking shows how varied the combination of other sectors really is. In perspective, Michigan agriculture – despite the state's size and open spaces – ranks only twenty-first among the fifty states and accounts for only 1.8 percent of United States food and fiber commodity cash receipts. Moreover, in the 1980s, only one rural Michigan county was considered by the U.S. Department of Agriculture to be agriculture dependent, a county where 20 percent of total income and personal cash receipts came from farming.[17]

Figure 6: Michigan Industries as a Percentage of Gross State Product, 1990–91

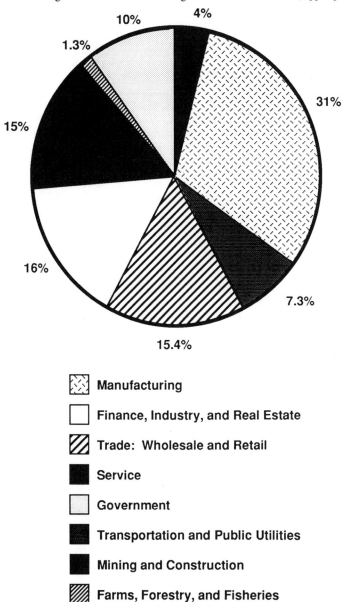

Manufacturing

Finance, Industry, and Real Estate

Trade: Wholesale and Retail

Service

Government

Transportation and Public Utilities

Mining and Construction

Farms, Forestry, and Fisheries

Source: Michigan House of Representatives Fiscal Agency.

In looking at the problems that Michigan would have in competing on major crops with more productive states, many policymakers and business leaders see tourism as a better investment. "The best economic shot in the arm for most Michigan farmers," observed one policy expert, "would be part-time jobs in tourism and recreation." Tourism has been more of a growth industry. Michigan is a major tourist state. Northern Michigan long ago became a playground for state residents who formed the principal economic base in the south, creating both rural employment and development hopes. Areas such as Traverse City, Mackinac Island, and Houghton Lake grew for years on the basis of the summer resort and tourism business. Casino gambling has contributed in Traverse City and less traditional tourist towns, such as Mt. Pleasant, as Native Americans claimed operational rights through federal courts. Even the UP saw a 5 percent decline in unemployment in the late 1980s, due largely to tourist growth. Beginning in the 1880s, although often interrupted by recession, this growth has been a constant for outstate Michigan, so the trend appears sustainable. Indeed, the rural population has generally held its own since 1950, staying at just less than a quarter of the state's population. Traverse City is now an urban growth center, having become the commercial and financial capital of northern Michigan as well as a job relocation choice for professionals who leave southern Michigan and other U.S. cities. These trends facilitate tourism by stabilizing the population of vacation areas, creating a mass of people to support attractive local businesses.

Yet, as with agriculture, there are problems, not the least of which is the low pay of service jobs, especially those that require the less skilled work often associated with tourism. Even on average, service jobs pay only 70 percent of state manufacturing wages; in the North, service jobs outnumber manufacturing jobs by more than four to one. Communities content with a tourist economy resign themselves to economic circumstances well below the expectations of many other parts of Michigan.

Moreover, tourism is cyclical. In northwestern Michigan, tourist businesses do 60 percent of their trade in the three summer months. Employees are often hired as temporaries or are laid off for much of the year, making them eligible for costly state assistance programs. Given these problems, capable employees are hard to find.

Tourism also is as recession prone as automobile sales, a factor that does little to stabilize the state's economy. During the years of economic upswing, from 1982 to 1989, tourism's economic contribution to the state increased at an annual rate of nearly 10 percent, while the number of out-of-state visitors increased by about 6 percent per year. But 1990 through 1993 saw growth fall flat and then suffer a harsh decline, leaving many tourist businesses financially plagued by recent expansion and newly incurred debt.[18]

Addressing either agricultural or tourism development is fraught with political and economic risks, especially because there may be little payoff for rural areas. In fact, most tourist jobs are not even outstate or in rural places. Nearly half of all tourist dollars are spent in the three-county metropolitan Detroit area. Seven of the top ten counties in tourism spending are urban rather than rural or nonmetropolitan. In all, 57 percent of the state's tourist industry jobs are in these seven counties. Unlike outstate areas rich in scenic beauty and natural resources but with few jobs, these counties support other full-time, nonseasonal employment. The allure of tourism continues to motivate Detroit developers and local political leaders to deflect more growth their way. This inspires local coalitions to formulate central-city redevelopment plans dependent on mixing new sports stadia, new casinos, and existing theaters. However, it also further regionalizes and fragments state tourist interests.

Hence, the job gains and long-term political benefits for tourism in rural communities are quite limited; estimates place the total number of full- and part-time positions there at between 65,000 and 145,000.[19] But in conjunction with agriculture, even part-time work is meaningful. Most of those who operate Michigan's 55,000 farms derive about 60 percent of their family income from off-farm sources, including second jobs. In fact, only 51 percent of Michigan's farmers regard agriculture as their primary occupation. Hence, Michigan's two most recognized rural industries bring few full-time employment prospects.

For rural residents, other options for development and employment seem unlikely. While retirees have been moving into the northern part of the lower peninsula, government employment and income transfers are threatened by the state's declining economic base and its more limited budget. Expansion of manufacturing to these regions is questionable as urban centers compete harder. The investments of major industrial employers are nearly always near their headquarters or plants, while rural communities are left, at best, with subcontractors – such as a steering wheel producer. This means that Michigan's political economy is bifurcated beyond its more obvious regional splintering. On one side is a declining but dominant urban-centered durable goods manufacturing sector; on the other is the vastness of rural regions for which there are even fewer answers as to how to create jobs. That split, not just the transformation of the auto industry, set the stage for economic redevelopment policies as they became important in the 1980s under Governor James Blanchard. The continuing expectations of residents and policymakers that everyone will get a share in what the state does makes anything else impossible. Governor John Engler recognized it again in making school finance reform, especially for outstate areas with low property-tax bases, a key issue approaching the 1994 elections. Unfortunately, the politics of balance made economic redevelopment policies both hit-and-miss in their political success. Engler was rebuffed badly by metro Detroit voters on a school and tax ballot proposal that carried the rest of the state in 1993. In 1994, these voters were only slightly more receptive to his proposal.

JOB CREATION AND ECONOMIC REDEVELOPMENT

Until the 1980s, even with earlier expressed concerns about industrial diversification, the state had few economic development objectives. What it did have, when business was moved to fight, were battles between state interests over business policy, specifically whether programs supported by organized labor had made Michigan uncompetitive and overly expensive as a place to locate. Also, under Governor William Milliken, it had a few experiments in assisting business. The period since the 1960s has been characterized by an endless ebb and flow of pro-business and pro-labor proposals. Most failed, though some gave minor cost relief to business in return for other gains for labor. The action was much like a checker match, and just as exciting to follow. Aggressive action was left to local governments, allowed by the state to offer tax and service inducements to relocating industries.

By 1982, as Milliken was leaving office and Governor Blanchard was moving from Congress to replace him, perceptions of the state economy and its needs were noticeably worse than they had been in previous recessions. Downsizing in the auto industry was permanent. Cities were getting little by competing for business relocations. More often, governors and mayors from Indiana, Ohio, and Tennessee were visiting state sites and inducing Michigan firms to leave. This was especially true of smaller industries and manufacturing subcontractors who, lacking the flexibility of big business, were financially disadvantaged by public policy concessions that allowed their larger counterparts and big labor to coexist.

What Blanchard faced early in his administration was a startling realization that even the bitter gubernatorial campaign, with his slogan of "Jobs, jobs, jobs," had not made clear. This was no simple situation. Seven formidable forces were converging: the effects of back-to-back recessions were still not over; revenues did not grow as projected, and the state faced a budget deficit; state personal income was once again falling; demand for state assistance and social services was high; government costs were going up; technological changes in the automobile industry meant that thousands of workers would never be called back; and the tax revolt led by Robert Tisch and Richard Headlee was very much alive.

Economic development policy made sense, and not just because other states were doing it. It was incumbent on Blanchard to do something decisive. The necessity of either ordering severe budget cuts or raising state taxes, but probably doing both, mandated an especially popular and appealing alternative. Few of these were available. As cuts were agreed on and a tumultuous tax battle ensued, choices were made about how to start carrying out economic development.

There were three options.[20] The first was to focus on the apparent problem of state competitiveness and mount a recruitment campaign that Michigan, with its high cost of doing business, was not then equipped to win. It also was a strategy whose costs, both in the politics of changing laws and in the level of expenditures needed for recruitment incentives, were too high for the state to undertake. This was of limited use.

A second choice was to enable Michigan firms to thrive, or at least to survive. This became the state's guiding principle in the 1980s for both state and local economic development. Even the last vestige of the UP mining community, the Copper Range Company, received state loans to help it stay afloat. So, too, did a venerable Detroit chocolate company, Sanders. "Work to keep what you have before you go after other businesses" became the administration's motto. While the state could and did adopt some policies to lower the costs of doing business, many firms still failed. Fewer regulations, lower worker compensation costs, and less costly unemployment benefits were helpful for already competitive industries or for those that regained their competitive edge. Nonetheless, anticipating recovery and renewed competitiveness, Blanchard and the legislature worked with bipartisan and multi-interest support to develop, even with labor support, a consensus for change. That strategy wiped out whole neighborhoods in order to provide sites for such new manufacturing plants as GM's Poletown plant in Detroit. It also secured the engineering and design centers for General Motors' new Saturn Corporation, even though the company's first manufacturing facility went to nonunion Tennessee, with its lower labor costs and a better offer. What the strategy did more than anything, however, was to stem much of the pessimism that gripped the state, giving industry leaders some faith in investing in Michigan. This allowed reinvestment a chance to work during economic recovery.

That strategic option also provided a link to the third choice of strategies, one that was more dependent on concentrated redevelopment than diversified development. The last major option was to build on the state's strengths and previous investments. Translated, it meant that the state – as the automobile industry was already doing – would reverse directions and seek to develop a high-technology automated manufacturing capability. There would be no abandonment of the automobile industry nor even a turning away. Robot users and robot manufacturers were already very much present in Michigan. Although it would take over a decade to make full use of the capabilities of such acquisitions as Electronic Data Systems and Hughes Aircraft, the Big Three were buying these and other firms because of their experience in industries that were felt to eventually be useful to auto manufacturing.[21] Computers, robotics, and related electronic products were especially encouraged by a state government that was again following a changing industrial leader, as it had in the 1920s and earlier in the lumber era. State leaders envisioned a technological transformation of the state's manufacturing facilities into "factories of the future." Under this strategy, auto products would also change. High-tech vehicles, while produced with fewer workers, would have more components and be more costly. Thus, over the long term, the industry would still grow and contribute at least as much as it had to the state economy.

Surprisingly, Michigan policymakers recruited a new joint-venture plant between Ford and the Japanese corporation Mazda and machine-tooling operations from Toyota and Nissan. These were exemplary prizes because most Japanese plants were being built outside the Midwest states, where labor union influence was less and wages were lower. Using a recruiting package involving partial property-tax waivers, state loans, and subsidies for training workers, Michigan was able to win significantly in the recruitment game with Mazda. Later, as it became apparent that Japanese industries could operate successfully in Michigan, other corporations from Japan found sites that allowed them quick entry into the mainstream of Detroit's still internationally acclaimed auto world. By 1991, 274 Japanese firms had set up operations in Michigan, many as subcontractors to Mazda and out-of-state assembly plants. The eventual downside, however, was that Japanese firms purchased little from Michigan companies, creating some conflicts that extended all the way to Lansing by the elections of 1992. "We should be forcing open contracting on these plants," said one legislator whose district businesses were not getting Japanese business. Another problem was that many Japanese firms suffered financial reversals just as the Big Three and its suppliers grew in 1993 and 1994.

Michigan's economic development, or perhaps we should say its manu-facturing redevelopment, plan merged the three strategies with three basic programmatic components.[22] One part involved assisting fledgling but promising companies to gain financial resources – companies to which banks ordinarily are unwilling to extend loans. Investments were expected to be made in industries that could service the state's major corporations, free-ing up their capital to modernize plants without the expense of creating a support infrastructure for electronics and robotics. This was important be-cause even the state's newest factories were obsolete when they opened in the early 1980s. Assistance also was intended to draw entrepreneurs and in-vestment capital to the state. Loans were possible because Michigan, despite its economic weaknesses, possessed strong financial resources.[23] The first such project, begun in 1982 before Blanchard's election, allowed high-tech-nology equity investments to be made with state retirement funds. Blanchard later consolidated two Milliken programs into the Michigan Strategic Fund to create venture capital for direct loans to some companies, while encourag-ing banks to make riskier loans to others. The Strategic Fund was to be a cat-alyst, bringing in private money over state-funded support. Financed outside the normal legislative process, funding decisions could be handled as admin-istrative decisions without legislative concurrence.[24]

A second leg of the overall strategy involved transforming the state's uni-versities, especially those doing major research. This was a correction needed quickly. Some work went on through the governor's High Technol-ogy Taskforce, another pre-Blanchard policy that was refined by his staff. Two research institutes were created with ties to the University of Michigan and Michigan State University. Through the Industrial Technology Institute in Ann Arbor and the Michigan Biotechnology Institute at East Lansing, the state showed a commitment to growth strategies that was unique in Michi-gan's history. Key objectives for these institutes were, first, to avoid past patterns of neglect, as with aerospace, and, second, to generate new technol-ogies and convert them into useful applications and products. State indus-tries could then use technology to create new jobs. The institutes were funded from oil and gas extraction revenues directed through the Strategic Fund. Universities were also tapped through the Research Excellence Fund. Unfortunately, that program quickly became tainted by charges of pork-barrel politics. The legislature changed the governor's initial proposal to fund major research efforts in only four state universities to one of guaranteeing funds to all of the state's fifteen public universities, regardless of previous research performance.

A third redevelopment component was direct, hands-on assistance. Its first target was industry. The Metropolitan Center for High Technology (MCHT) became the most publicized example. MCHT, with state appropriations, took over the former S. S. Kresge headquarters in one of Detroit's depressed neighborhoods in order to establish a business incubator for high-tech enterprises. This center started slowly but eventually gained momentum. It benefited from the support and involvement of major Detroit-area corporations and recruited several appropriate tenants. MCHT, as a matter of balance, was also an expression of support for Detroit. Small ventures included a firm that designed a device to help engineers analyze the performance of engines, one that developed pharmaceuticals from micro-organisms, a company that designed voice-activated computers, and a firm that made solutions to control bacteria in water. By the end of 1988, seventeen incubator companies occupied the facility.

Industry was not the only target; changes were affecting workers as well. As part of state efforts to create jobs, labor received job retraining funds. In addition, at the urging of policymakers, the United Auto Workers bargained into its contracts with the Big Three a set-aside fund for retraining union members for any other field of employment, including newly available high-tech jobs as well as questionable ventures, such as charter boat operation. State universities were encouraged to undertake innovative retraining programs, even offering new academic programs onsite. Yet, along with addressing the long-term institutional problem of inspiring change in educational delivery systems, the state allowed transfer payments to operators of training programs who had never before thought of themselves as running schools for job placement. These programs often failed to create employment skills.

But structural unemployment left other scars that retraining could not correct, largely because many former auto workers had no educational background that facilitated learning new skills.[25] This was one reason why so many alternative educational programs were funded. There were also demands to do things for cities that had lost outdated plants and gained few replacements. Through the 1980s, Detroit, for example, had more than 20 percent unemployment and a welfare population of nearly 18 percent. Beyond targeting sites such as MCHT for the city, there were few state responses; nor were there even many suggestions as to what could be done. The most notable effort was an inner-city youth Jobs Corps. Projects were created around the state for the summer months in the hope that participants would gain basic work habits.

Assistance to the state's diverse business firms and to segments of organized labor was insufficient for dealing with the entire array of prominent regions. The Department of Commerce created a Michigan Rural Development Strategy with a leadership team to advise community and business officials locally.[26] Agriculture and tourism also gained their share in economic policy, mostly through direct assistance programs. In 1985, Michigan State University's extension and research activities were supplemented with a gubernatorial initiative, the Agricultural Assistance Network. Workshops on farm survival, loan programs, funding for management analysis, and a statewide farm financial survey were its key features. Beyond that network of supports, the state tried to facilitate the creation of new and more varied food processors and encourage export assistance for prepared and packaged, or value-added, food products.

Farm assistance paled in comparison to tourism efforts, though. Governor Blanchard became personally identified with the "Say Yes to Michigan" program, which advertised Michigan travel and vacation activities throughout the nation. As part of that campaign, the Michigan Travel Bureau established ties with nearly every component of the industry, from charter boats to motels, as well as regional groups across the state. Both funding of materials and technical advice were offered to clients.

By the end of the 1980s, Michigan's economic redevelopment package was well developed and subject to national praise.[27] Its balanced approach to many problems was central to its success. So was the fact that most new jobs, in a departure for the Michigan economy, were being created by small businesses.

Yet the package was criticized by Blanchard's foes for its flaws. While most agreed that the state was richer for the confidence restored by the new policies, many questioned the price of the effort. High rates of business failure were found among state investments. By 1989, one-third or more of the loans made by the Strategic Fund were in or near delinquency. Auditors found other loans at great risk. The recession in 1990 only worsened those problems. A lack of significant returns from programs assigned to educational institutions, a continuing trend by business to go out of state for research support, an inability to slow the rate of farm failures, a lagging entrepreneurial investment, and a lack of relevance in many state assistance projects also were cited as problems.[28] In addition, programs were faulted for their lack of coordination, especially as bureaucratic turf wars fragmented initiatives. Legislators struggled in vain to determine exactly what was funded as economic development policy and what it cost. Programs were also were criticized as being used by Blanchard to enhance his personal image rather than the welfare of the state.

When John Engler defeated Blanchard, economic policy was relegated to secondary status. The Department of Commerce, which had seen a 44 percent increase in operating revenues under Blanchard, was cut by approximately half in its employees and budget. It was then given licensing and regulation responsibilities. Many administratively created programs were dropped. Funding became much tighter for those remaining, such as the university institutes and the revamped "Yes, M!ch!gan!" program. In part, this downgraded status reflected the program's disfavor in a new administration and a desire to create markets rather than to supply products for unspecified and uncertain sales opportunities. Downgrading also reflected the new governor's absorption in other matters at the onset of another recession, mainly in downsizing Michigan's government as a different way to balance the state's economy with its levels of expenditure. Engler's decisions also reflected a belief that many programs had served their initial purpose – that is, getting businesses sufficiently competitive where possible, so that they could continue to redevelop on their own.[29]

That decision proved to have its own problems, which reaffirmed the importance of Blanchard's strategy. The first difficulty was that it made the state appear inattentive to business relocations and financial problems. Some business people saw a return to laissez-faire economics in a competitive national and international marketplace: "I just decided to leave for Indiana at that point." Beyond the appearance of inattention, state and local development officials found themselves without the tools needed to compete for businesses. They, in turn, complained vociferously to the governor. This, not unexpectedly, led to a systematic search for restoring the best elements of the Blanchard package – without, of course, lending the former administration credit. Economic development, on the whole, is perhaps the best example of the state's excesses, under two governors, as well as a case in point about how balance works in Michigan.

CHANGING THE FOCUS

Regardless of who was governor, and which party had control, the 1990s were to be a time of changing economic policy. Periodic economic downturns left the state each time with less personal income and, consequently, less state revenue. Because Michigan's state/local tax burden took 17.5 percent of average per capita personal income from its citizens, ranking it fourteenth of the fifty states, tax hikes were effectively embargoed. Michigan ranked fourth in corporate taxes among the American states, tenth in property taxes, and twentieth in personal income taxes in 1992. This high-tax status garnered severe reactions. Anti-tax groups and fears of further business losses are powerful deterrents to new taxes, unless they are disguised as carefully selected user fees and combined with the prospect of a property-tax cut.

Moreover, Michigan lacks other fiscal policy tools to compensate and get more from state revenue. As state officials found in 1992, the Budget Stabilization Fund, established for financially rainy days, is inadequate. There were insufficient dollars in the fund to meet the state's legal obligation to balance its accounts annually. By 1993, despite careful use, the fund was nearly exhausted. Neither have the state's experiments with periodic reviews of programs been successful. The Program Budgeting Evaluation System (PBES) to justify total programs was abandoned because of bureaucratic resistance, legislative distrust, and a reluctance to evaluate government outputs and subject them to controversy. In addition, "sunset" clauses, which set ending dates for programs, have proven ineffective because the legislature has nearly always renewed programs before their expiration date. Clientele get built in and work legislative committees. In short, state policymakers have been reluctant to allow general oversight or to loosen legislative committee controls over program operations. Indeed, authorizing committees often lock funds in restricted accounts, independent of budget appropriations, so that the governor and appropriations committees lack flexibility and discretion. Sometimes governors do the same to make future change unlikely. In 1988–89, nearly 60 percent of total state revenues were either in restricted accounts or otherwise earmarked by federal funding controls.

Another limit on budgetary accountability and responsibility is what policymakers call "budget gimmicks." Both in the early 1980s and the early 1990s, the state did three things: overestimated revenues, understated likely spending, and switched accounting procedures to recover costs from one fiscal year to the next. All three simply delayed budgetary accountability. For example, revenue projections were nearly $1 billion off for both 1991 and 1992. Executive cuts and appropriation callbacks were about half that total each year. Another strategy, with more long-term problems, has been to avoid necessary capital improvements and repairs: "We shift monies from facility care to salaries and then pay the price later when roofs leak and foundations crack.''

Budget adjustment and fiscal reform are not easy. Oftentimes policy initiatives, made even as policymakers are grasping for a more adjustable budget, proceed in the direction of further tightening up expenditures. When Governor Blanchard faced charges of being ''soft on crime'' for continuing early prison releases, he began the largest prison construction project in state history, a ten-year plan to quadruple capacity. Because such capital-intensive facilities need continuous operational dollars, Blanchard only added to the state's inability to adjust in future recessions.

Satisfying everyone, or engaging in the recurring excess of Michigan's politics of balance, produces the same uneven results. The lessons of economic development, even with its intended focus on bringing technology to state manufacturers, demonstrated that point forcefully. Manufacturing redevelopment quickly took on a shotgun approach in which policymakers tried to conjure up something for everyone. This meant that state economic policy had to shift in the early years of the Engler administration. But the degree to which it shifted was surprising in both cause and effect. The change was not inspired simply by structural transformations in the economy that promised less for Michigan. Nor was the shift caused by a realization that state industry was well on its way to recovery. The reverse expectation was feared. Policy changes were made in a year when the newly competitive Big Three auto manufacturers lost a record $7.6 billion, at a time when auto company analysts estimated that plant production capacity worldwide was 40 percent above future requirements.

Engler's economic policies took on many characteristics of fiscal policy: cut budgets whenever possible, regard education as a funding priority to correct past problems and to produce a more competent work force, keep taxes low to stimulate investment and industry interest in the state, and rely on existing resources to compete with other states. The emphasis turned, as economic conditions dictated, to downsizing government and limiting intervention by the state as a means for achieving a balanced politics. Unlike his predecessors, however, Engler did not plan to give something to everyone, or even to all of his allies, in the search for balance. Downsizing (or, as some officials claim, ''right-sizing'') was also a strategy for avoiding many of the pitfalls of Michigan politics that make governing the state so difficult – that is, meeting multiple demands, letting everyone add his or her own piece to the puzzle, and allocating benefits with regional equity. Downsizing government was a reversal of course that attacked not just its bigness but, more fundamentally, the idea of Michigan as a proactive state.

Under such conditions, and with expectations that more jobs could be gained through less government, both Michigan and the Engler administration proved vulnerable to states still chasing smokestacks. Faced with competition from Texas, where inducements were given to General Motors, Michigan lost its huge Willow Run assembly plant in 1992, while a similar plant stayed open in the Lone Star State. Michigan, through the governor's office and Department of Commerce, had also offered inducements. However, without a well-articulated economic development strategy and with the costs of business not yet lowered as Governor Engler wanted, criticisms of the chief executive – and of the United Auto Workers – ran rampant after the announcement. Altogether, in GM's 16,000-person downsizing of 1992, Michigan lost over 9,000 jobs, and the manufacturing future of this recession-prone state looked even more threatened. Yet, as ever, the state rebounded in the next two years with increased auto sales, worker overtime, and promises of new hires by Ford and Chrysler.

SOME CLOSING THOUGHTS

The state economic development policies of the 1980s were fascinating experiments that generated high marks from outside observers. Yet, for every old wrong seemingly corrected by those policies, obvious mistakes were made as well. The economic development initiatives proved two things about state government and politics: first, the state could innovate by playing on its strong resources; second, it could also make bad investments by responding to everyone rather than just appropriate targets.

Michigan is indeed held captive by its past. While technology and factories of the future are beginning to deliver on their promises, they cannot reverse economic trends beyond the state's control. Michigan's auto industry is desperately trying to stay competitive. It shows signs not only of improved quality but also of better sales and price competitiveness. But Michigan public policy did little to facilitate that change. Nor did the improvement remove Michigan's accumulated problems of time and history.

For that reason, a state government that previously showed little fiscal restraint is now facing fundamental changes, ones that may cost the state its innovative and humanistic edges. Downsizing the government and lessening direct intervention and support in its citizens' lives will be as difficult for state residents to cope with as automation has been for the Big Three and organized labor. Although past levels of public policy performance probably will not be repeated, expectations still remain high. Thus, frustration over the heavy loss of General Motors jobs was particularly intense. Even when Michigan's early 1993 unemployment fell to a national low for all industrial states, and Engler claimed credit because of an improved business climate, the state worried. Future economic and fiscal policymaking promises to be a tough job for Michigan.

CHAPTER ELEVEN

Michigan Environmental Politics: Battleground of the Political Titans

James P. Hill and Robert W. Kaufman are also authors of this chapter

FROM IMBALANCE TO BALANCE

If the battle for private-sector employment is the yin of Michigan politics, is-sues of the environment are its yang. As we emphasized earlier, Michigan has been plagued for two centuries with an economy driven by what Bruce Catton called prodigal wastage. For that reason, the politics of economic growth and that of a sound natural ecology hit one another head-on. Analysis of auto industry costs by the University of Michigan blames high environ-mental regulation costs as well as high taxes and electrical rates for the state's competitive disadvantage. So obviously this is not a consensual arena in which Michiganians know that they must pull together. Most interests want someone else to pay the costs of environmental responsiveness.

A vivid example of the yin and yang and shifting interests occurred in the 1980s when the U.S. Navy sought to install in the U P a communications grid for its submarine fleet. The first response was from enthusiastic local resi-dents who would benefit from construction jobs. This was followed by an environmental howl that induced the navy to modify the project severely rather than face its loss. Pro-jobs forces helped the navy at every step, creat-ing often bitter relationships among once close but quickly divided neighbors.

But nowhere in state politics was such an unavoidable reaction between jobs and their environmental consequences more evident than when the gov-ernor proposed to reorganize the Department of Natural Resources (DNR). Governor John Engler's attempt in 1992 to reorganize the DNR through exec-utive order set off a reaction that can best be characterized as a clash of Mich-igan titans in the state's environmental politics. These influential interests, divided into two relatively stable coalitions, are key actors in state environmental policy. The resulting events, often with bitter contests, remind many of Michigan's politics of the 1960s, when business and labor competed for control of the state. In one coalition are the titans of business and industry. The groups that represent them are such familiar ones as the State Chamber of Commerce, the Michigan Farm Bureau, the Michigan Manufacturers Association, and the Michigan Chemical Council. The Big Three auto companies and state members of the Business Roundtable are also primary players in this camp. The other coalition, dominated by Michigan's environmental titan – the Michigan United Conservation Clubs (MUCC) – is composed of a loosely knit alliance of state hunting, trapping, and fishing interests. Boating and recreation interests, as well as state affiliates of such national environmental protection groups as the Nature Conservancy and the Sierra Club, coalesce with MUCC.

Environmentalists have been especially eager to protect their longstanding interests in and relationships with the DNR. Accordingly, they have been suspicious of the motives of Governor Engler and the support for his reorganization plan by the Michigan Chamber of Commerce. The environmental alliance united their varied interests and filed a circuit court suit that, on the eve of final action, enjoined Engler from implementing his reorganization plan. The resulting fury highlighted the power of MUCC and those it can mobilize when fundamental concerns of the out-of-doors and the environment are at stake. Industrial and business interests had clearly wanted reorganization.

Certainly the history of environmental politics in Michigan has not been balanced in the way that state policies so routinely are. Until recent decades, the balance emphasized resource use and environmental neglect. But that neglect, inspired by general ignorance of environmental costs, extended far beyond Michigan. Conservation during the first century of Michigan statehood was largely dominated by the lumbering, farming, trapping, and fishing interests that settled the state, as well as the commercial sectors that serviced them. Environmental protection groups – or more accurately, conservationists – existed only when wealthy landowners from cities wanted to protect their own recreational developments from exploitation by others. Indeed, the near elimination of the beaver because of overtrapping, the killing of more than one million now-extinct passenger pigeons in one hunt in Petoskey in 1878, and the leveling of Michigan's forests in a mere sixty years, when they were projected to last five hundred, are prime examples of the imbalance that existed in Michigan politics.

The environment was so neglected that as late as the 1950s, Walter Reuther of the UAW took leadership on many conservation issues because no other prominent person would do so. However, after a century of prodigal wastage, a new sense of environmental awareness and the emergence of well over a hundred environmental groups throughout Michigan brought a symbiotic balance to the state's politics. Progress has been notable.

The current balance sways with the attempts of leaders of industry and commerce to move the state into the national economic mainstream. Heavy emphasis is placed on removing regulatory hurdles that taint the business climate. On other issues, where conservation imposes few costs but pays obvious quality-of-life benefits, these leaders make few objections and often cooperate actively. The general public has wistfully mixed views. While all emphasize a healthy environment, some citizens complain that the state is overly pristine while others see it as hopelessly degraded. Usually, these divided views can be traced to the complainants' other interests – as homeowners, developers, job seekers, or business owners.

But even efforts to reduce economically burdensome regulations are countered by a relatively new and entirely different set of policy players, many at the grass roots in local groups, and many who are idealistically motivated by Michigan's rich natural resources and scenic beauty. They, as a small but influential cadre, have become the core of the state's environmental protection movement. With the slogan "Think globally, act locally," environmentalists work hard to fit well with even such seemingly odd allies as hunting groups. This, of course, expands the core of environmental players. The Michigan Hunting Dog Federation, with its slogan "Dedicated to preserving the right to free cast our hunting dogs afield," is a prominent M UCC member. Environmentalists, with their grass-roots focus, also fit well into state politics, which often behaves as if all the state's issues are to be determined by local wants. Environmentalists, accordingly, are given respect by campaigning politicians and legislators negotiating in Lansing.

Environmental activists are also somewhat different from the members of other organized state interests in that, despite their localism, they have a decidedly world view of their issues.[1] This is a disadvantage in that some of their policy ideas are hard to integrate into state politics because they threaten economic growth and freedom of enterprise in uncompromising ways. Environmental protection issues often go to the heart of rejecting a capitalist economy, which certainly describes Michigan. However, two complementary forces in state politics keep some intemperate environmental demands credible and moving along, even though similarly uncompromising stands would be rejected if raised by other organized interests.

The first grouping consists of the environmental protectionists who want more for Michigan than the federal government will provide through national policy initiatives. The protectionists want a state free of degradation, a persuasive sales pitch that appeals to much of the public. Yet the idealistic nature of the goal makes it necessary for policymakers to adopt the general dimensions of environmental demands but to rely on others to mold proposals into workable programs. This works because of the second grouping of activists, environmental pragmatists who are willing to do that necessary molding. For example, multiclient environmental attorney lobbyists do big business. MUCC's executives are no less involved as brokers. Because environmental solutions are so critical to the state and its development, even regulatory opponents acknowledge that Michigan needs an environmental protection lobby to raise issues that business would otherwise neglect. These two forces, activists and arbitrators, have taken Michigan from nowhere to being a frontrunner among the American states as a steward of its natural resources.

A NEW ENVIRONMENTAL ORDER

Michigan's 1963 constitution marked an important point of policy departure because, in one of those efforts to avoid neglect, it provided a clear environmental mandate to the legislature.

> The conservation and development of the natural resources of the state are hereby declared to be of paramount public concern in the interest of the health, safety, and general welfare of the people. The legislature shall provide for the protection of the air, water, and other natural resources of the state from pollution, impairment, and destruction.[2]

It was not the constitution, however, that directly brought new life to the state's environmental politics. This provision was only a catalyst. Moreover, like other constitutional provisions of 1963, it was inserted to please specific interests represented at the convention. For them, including some labor leaders, it was a point of balance against "big business." In 1970, in a far more significant move, the legislature followed the constitutional mandate by adopting the Michigan Environmental Protection Act (MEPA). The heart of this brief, yet revolutionary, act is contained in the following paragraph:

> The attorney general, any political subdivision of the state, any . . . agency of the state or of a political subdivision thereof, any person, partnership, corpora-

tion, association, organization or other legal entity may maintain an action
. . . for the protection of the air, water, and other natural resources and the
public trust therein from pollution, impairment or destruction.[3]

With this act, the general adversarial relationship between advocates of
economic development and those of environmental protection became institutionalized in Michigan. It became easy to challenge any perceived degradation. Many activists argue, both pro and con, that it created insurgency
against environmental pillage and provided common citizens with usable legal tools. This statute certainly reordered the political power of those with
competing interests in natural resources. It gave citizens, both grass-roots
environmental activists and just aggrieved neighbors, a legal standing to in-
voke the public trust doctrine and to seek a court injunction for relief in cases
of threatened damage to any natural resource. Previously, individuals wanting to protect the environment had no legal right unless they could point to
some direct personal or economic interest that gave them standing in court.
In addition, MEPA standards were set forth to be used to review or challenge
all other state statutes in protecting Michigan's natural resources. This was a
precedent, both within the state and nationally. Several other states and the
federal government followed in adapting this approach to their own circumstances, but usually not in such open-ended fashion.

MEPA created a legal procedure for settling environmental disputes because activists who supported the law were suspicious of the state's tradition
of depending on negotiated policy settlements. The idea for the legislation
came from Joseph L. Sax, professor of law at the University of Michigan.[4]
The key to Sax's strategy is the integration of four elements provided in the
statute: (1) the citizen's legal standing to sue; (2) the role of courts as the instrument of decision; (3) the application of the public trust doctrine to natural
resources; and (4) the framework within which a common law on environmental questions can develop.

This legislation views the citizenry as the ultimate owner of the natural
environment – which is defined in the law as a public, as opposed to a private,
property right. Historically, individuals have had limited standing to sue in
U.S. courts. During Michigan's past, individuals have also had difficulty influencing state agencies that oversee natural resources; administrators were
more attuned to their organized statewide clients than to individuals and regions. In fact, until MEPA, many of these agencies excluded citizens from
even their planning process. Also, agencies behaved as closed organizations

because they tended to translate public goals into their own preferences, usually the defense of ongoing programs. This tendency not only grated on Michiganians, with their sensitivity to the out-of-doors, but, in the case of passing MEPA, it also led legislators to look for ways to strengthen their constituents' hands in dealing with administrators.

The legislation also institutes court procedures to settle disputes. These procedures are designed to identify the critical issues behind a complaint and to resolve them without sentiment or prejudice to either side. Because the adversaries in environmental disputes were seen to be unusually determined foes, with full intentions of carrying out extensive campaigns, the legislature chose the courts as arbiters. Advocates of MEPA feared the consequences of either the normal routine of negotiated compromises or of gridlock in the legislature or the administration.

Moreover, in a key – and now highly contentious – point that creates obstacles to development, the potential for judicial injunction provides a way to halt environmentally dangerous projects before irreparable damage is done. The procedure requires a judicial hearing at which the plaintiff must persuasively argue the merit and importance of a complaint before gaining even a temporary injunction. Using the courts, of course, does not restrict environmental activists from either encouraging public debate or simultaneously going to other policymakers to resolve disputes.

In addition, MEPA is based on the doctrine of public trust as found in Roman law, where perpetual use of common property was dedicated to the public. The full scale of judicial pronouncements outlining private rights, however, has overshadowed the development of public rights. From the outset, public rights to clean water and air, for example, were vague and subject to broad interpretation in court. Ensuing court actions, as a consequence, set precedents in law from the very beginning.

As such, MEPA represented a fundamental change in political decision making, one that redefined both the various environmental battlegrounds and the balance of forces on them. On most issues, elected policymakers and administrators are the usual allocators of common public resources. They allocate public resources in pursuit of public goals as they see fit, sometimes with overriding private benefits that go to a private interest. Yet, under MEPA, the process to resolve environmental issues was seen as being different. Even going to state officials, it was argued in MEPA debates, may have negative environmental consequences because of bargaining inherent in the normal policy process. Public agencies may be too willing to work with interests seeking private benefits, and, jointly, the two may capture the legislature's attention. The public trust doctrine provided a procedural and substantive limitation on such relationships, one that would eventually be well detailed in law. With numerous court decisions being rendered over time, the doctrine was also seen as having the potential to gain the same status in law as private property rights.

How? It was here that MEPA was the most innovative, due to the inclusion of Sax's fourth strategic point – the framework for common law. Common law is judge-made law, as contrasted to statutory law enacted by legislative bodies. English judges, and later those in the United States, decided disputes based on prevailing custom and, once these decisions were made, applied them to similar situations. This use of precedent gradually became common to the entire nation. Although legislatures have passed a number of laws regulating environmental matters, the public trust doctrine remains without specific statutory definition. Also, society lacks a widespread consensus on what additional statutes should require. As a corrective, MEPA set up a framework in which a series of cases over time would contribute to continued evolution of a public trust doctrine in the fashion of other common law. In Michigan, that common law for the environment continues to develop, altering the battlegrounds of interest politics at each step.[5]

The emergence of an environmental common law under the Michigan Environmental Protection Act has been proceeding at a timely pace. The act has been used extensively. Because of such regular use, it has been a frequent tool for environmental protection groups to use to confront even the state's most influential business and industry titans on the most otherwise unwinnable issues. Examples are numerous: Development has been blocked from wetlands. Polluting industries have been ordered closed. Dozens of environmental cleanups, with fines, have been ordered, even one against the city of Detroit. In all instances, MEPA's public trust doctrine has been the linchpin for cases brought forward.

Obviously, MEPA itself was not without challenge. In 1975, the Michigan Supreme Court confirmed the constitutionality of the act by holding that it was appropriate for the courts to develop such a common law of environmental quality. A key paragraph from that case reads:

MEPA signals a dramatic change from the practice where the important task of environmental law enforcement was left to administrative agencies without the opportunity for participation by individuals or groups of citizens. Not every public agency proved to be diligent and dedicated defenders of the environment . . . MEPA imposes a duty on individuals and organizations both in the public and private sectors to prevent or minimize degradation of the environment which is caused or is likely to be caused by their activities.[6]

In its success, M E P A has gained important and very public political support. Governor William Milliken defended the statute as giving "our citizens the right to defend themselves from all forms of environmental pollution." He called it a "precious gift" to all succeeding generations.[7] Milliken assumed a leadership stance behind the bill – even though it was brought to the legislature only four months into his tenure. However, Milliken's enthusiasm explains much about why Michigan has been able to be a proactive environmental policy state when so many of its other policy efforts have proven futile and filled with delay. He "won" because of extremely fortunate circumstances: (1) M E P A benefited from the intervention of the West Michigan Environmental Action Council (W M E A C), whose leadership asked Joseph Sax to draft the bill and then mobilized the rest of the emerging environmental coalition; (2) W M E A C was advantaged by the existing base of conservation groups that filled legislative hearings with M E P A supporters; (3) because of Walter Ruether's longstanding conservation interest, the U A W was equally supportive and active; (4) supporters highlighted numerous environmental hazards in the state as reasons for new legislation; and (5) these supporters pointed, very effectively, to a lack of assistance from the federal government. This convergence of factors allowed the legislation to pass with only minor amendments, despite business opposition and Attorney General Frank Kelley's contention that the act was redundant.

Governor Blanchard also gave support to M E P A and, in 1987, identified the environment as one of six elements in planning for Michigan to become the "best state . . . [in which] to live and work and raise a family."[8] One of M E P A's strengths was in its recognition by the U.S. Environmental Protection Agency (E P A) as a formidable set of standards. This meant, on most issues, that Michigan laws were recognized by E P A and that decisions made in the state took precedence. Federal conflicts, thus, were minimized. Yet for those who encounter the threat of M E P A in business and private practices, it remains a contentious and unpopular tool that heightens the prospect of political conflict and losses over numerous issues of the economy. In that sense, while muting bargaining, it has had the ironic effect of still leading to the large-scale employment of those specialized attorney lobbyists who attempt to reconcile conflicts before M E P A is applied.

MICHIGAN'S ENVIRONMENTAL BATTLEGROUNDS

The conditions are ripe for vigorous disagreement. Almost any entrepreneurial effort generates some threat to natural resources. Reviewing the most common environmental battlegrounds demonstrates both the nature of the issues contested in Michigan and the points of agreement and disagreement between the titans that are most active in the two contesting interest-group coalitions. This is important because as natural resources are distributed differently among the states, issues and conflicts vary accordingly. For example, reclamation has not been a concern for Michigan, with its plentiful land and space. Even attempts by the state to buy more public lands are of limited interest. In the main, the most contested issues are those of toxic substances, hazardous waste, water quality, and a clean and usable rural landscape.

Toxic Substances

Toxic chemicals significantly stimulated the evolution of environmental policies in the state. Under MEPA, the courts have been major actors in developing toxic substance policies. MEPA's influence is easily judged. The Michigan Court of Appeals ruled in 1968 against the Environmental Defense Fund in a case involving the spraying of the pesticide dieldrin on farm areas. It found that prior to MEPA the Michigan Department of Agriculture (MDA) acted within its discretionary authority in its effort to eradicate the Japanese beetle.[9] By contrast, in a 1978 case, the Organic Growers of Michigan filed a court challenge against the MDA on a similar mission. In this case, the courts applied MEPA as a new decisional rule and restrained the department from spraying dimlin to control the gypsy moth.[10]

The most far-reaching incident relative to toxic substances was the PBB accident of 1973 discussed briefly in earlier chapters. It became what many consider the single worst food contamination disaster in U.S. history. The event not only changed the course of state elections but also demonstrated that state agencies were then unable to respond quickly and effectively to a toxic threat to public health.[11] Statewide losses included 24,000 cattle, 1.5 million chickens, 34,000 pounds of dried milk, and 865 tons of feed. As many as eight of every nine Michigan residents were contaminated with PBB.[12]

The PBB tragedy was widely perceived as a case of bureaucratic incompetence as state agencies failed to identify the problem initially and then minimized its seriousness once the cause became known. Governor Milliken, apparently satisfied with the MDA's initial decisions, took no immediate action to order a thorough investigation.[13] However, in a later effort to preclude a similar episode, the legislature established a watchdog agency, the Toxic Substances Control Commission (TSCC), whose fundamental goal was to protect the public health.[14] Its purpose was to monitor and investigate toxic substance problems dealt with by all state agencies. The TSCC was also charged with making recommendations to the governor and legislature on toxic substance control and was empowered to declare toxic emergencies with the concurrence of the governor. In such emergencies, the TSCC directs and coordinates all state responses, thus superseding all other state agencies. In addition, the law authorizes scientific research and data collection.

Creation of the TSCC touched off a lengthy administrative turf battle. Specifically, it was the target of criticism from those agencies that it had been created to oversee – primarily the Departments of Agriculture, Natural Resources, and Public Health. The contest was intense because the TSCC's authority originally was to expire at the end of 1982. Affected agencies wanted to see the TSCC expire on schedule. These politically entrenched departments objected to TSCC operations, terming its management style "disruptive" and "unaccountable" even though it required the governor's approval to declare a toxic emergency. While opponents created a controversy, they did not prevail, and the TSCC was extended.

The TSCC controversy reflects an organizational problem and political issue in Michigan's government that is of recurring significance: the extent of gubernatorial control over departments. Governor Engler's 1991 executive order to reorganize the DNR, and abolish the TSCC, was not so much a battle over the need to reorganize the DNR as it was a battle over the extent of his power to do so unilaterally. Legislative autonomy, for both legislators and groups with access, was a consideration.

In the PBB incident, the MDA reported not to the governor but to the Michigan Agriculture Commission. The governor appoints agriculture commissioners but has limited power to remove them from office. The governor appoints and may remove the director of agriculture, but control over policy implementation rests with the commission. Further, the commission traditionally is made up of active members of the Michigan Farm Bureau (MFB), one of the state's two major farmer organizations.

Ironically, MFB Services, a business arm of the Farm Bureau, was the agent that mixed PBB with cattle feed. The mixed loyalties and conflicting interests contributed significantly to the uncertainty of how to deal with the problem. For example, as charged on many other issues as well, MFB control of the Agriculture Commission led to its protecting MFB Services rather than promoting government assistance for dairy farmers. Interest-group penetration of centers of government policymaking in this case proved a national embarrassment to the state.

The PBB accident was the nation's first such incident to have extensive economic and social consequences. The charge was leveled that the nation's advanced chemical industry outpaced the sensitivity of public officials to establish appropriate public health safeguards. Systemic toxics were widely manufactured, sold freely, and often dispersed into the environment with abandon. The Michigan incident, with its international publicity, was portrayed as a larger disaster waiting to happen. Michigan consumer activists registered their alarm at toxic substances entering the food chain and, for the first time, argued more generally against unrestrained technological innovations entering the marketplace. The incident and the ensuing reaction produced one major effect: state policymakers disagreed with the routines of government negotiation and called for better controls for the manufacture, transportation, use, and disposal of toxic chemicals. As a result, programs were developed by the state and federal governments to address related problems.

Hazardous Waste Cleanup and Disposal

Hazardous waste policy is a major concern that produced a reaction following the PBB incident. In the late 1970s, chemical contamination from hazardous wastes became a national issue. Congress enacted the Comprehensive Environmental Response, Compensation, and Liability Act of 1980 (CERCLA), which has consequences for Michigan. This act established a $1.6 billion Superfund to clean up sites where hazardous wastes have been released into the environment. Congress extended the act for five years in 1986 and re-funded cleanup at $8.5 billion, with the money being raised largely from taxes on the petroleum, chemical, and waste-disposal industries. Superfund pays 90 percent of the cost of cleaning up privately owned sites and 50 percent of those governmentally owned.

The act also ordered the U.S. Environmental Protection Agency to prepare a national priority list of contaminated sites. The 1982 list contained forty-two Michigan sites; by 1992, there were seventy-nine sites on the list, ranking Michigan as one of the most contaminated states in the Midwest. Michigan's waste problem, because of its long industrial past, also ranks well above the national average. Superfund programs require response legislation from the states in order to qualify for federal monies. To finance the state share of cleaning up, Michigan voters passed a $300 million bond issue in 1988.[15]

But Michigan refuses to be federally dependent. In 1993, for example, there was serious consideration given to dropping out of Superfund, thus letting the federal government clean up sites on the national list and using Michigan resources on state-designated problems. (Figure 7 shows the

Figure 7: Number of State-Funded Environmental Surface Cleanup Projects Initiated, Fiscal Years 1984–91

NUMBER OF SITES

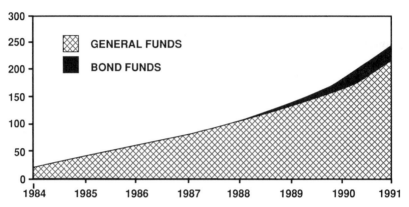

Source: Michigan Department of Natural Resources, April 1992.

number of environmental cleanup projects initiated during fiscal years 1984–91.) Part of the reason was the inexact federal standards that allowed some cleanup contractors to pad billings, do unnecessary work, and add costs to the state. The state also has its own statutes regulating waste disposal and hazardous substances in ways that go beyond federal standards. These add complexity to Superfund cleanups. Three of the more important laws that keep federal officials less involved in Michigan environmental issues than with those of other states are the Solid Waste Management Act, which regulates municipal-industrial sludge, commercial-industrial wastes, and community government disposal standards; the Pesticide Control Act, which regulates the sale, use, and commercial application of poisons for insects, rodents, herbs, and fungi; and a hazardous waste act that governs solid, liquid, and gaseous wastes that could endanger health or the environment.[16] These acts add to the financial burdens of polluters and have raised the stakes in state environmental politics. One example of the magnitude of the problems in this area is the need to inspect almost 70,000 underground tanks in the state for leakage under the federal L U S T program (Leaking Underground Storage Tanks).

The hazardous waste act excludes nuclear materials, municipal sewage flows, and point discharges, which the government regulates by permits. Waste handlers must record movements of toxic substances from "cradle to grave." The "graves" must be constructed and operated under D N R guidelines. Laws to control poison chemicals and toxic wastes were followed by another act giving workers the "right to know" of dangers inherent in chemicals used in the workplace. Similar considerations come into play as the state ponders, while landfills fill to the brim, the "bury, burn, recycle" trilemma of disposal alternatives.

Michigan continues to seek a policy governing waste disposal, but the debate is clouded by interests that are advantaged by different alternatives. Should waste be buried? burned and then buried as residue? recycled? Should the volume of waste be reduced? How does government take any of these actions? Who gets the contracts? Landfills create the greatest disputes, however. With their accompanying truck traffic, blowing debris, and potential for spoiling groundwater, an "anywhere but here" syndrome spawns controversy in numerous locales and precludes large modern refuse facilities in populated areas. Yet trash haulers are well organized and politically connected. At times, they have turned these issues into demands for state support of recycling centers and then sought to get recycling contracts under locally run state projects that work in conjunction with landfills.

Landfills, however, lead to land contamination, which, in turn, causes some groundwater contamination. While the former may be controlled or contained, the latter cannot. Groundwater moves, over the long term, in unpredictable directions at unpredictable velocities. Because water is so essential to life and because many rural areas depend on groundwater for drinking, the demand for its protection is strong. Episodes of groundwater contamination in various places throughout the state have convinced officials and citizens that groundwater, once contaminated, is next to impossible to reclaim.

Rejection of waste burial is not easy, however, even on the basis of the best possible alternative. Objections to burning include the concern that airborne residues may be hazardous and that pyrolysis facilities will always cry for fuel, thus encouraging the production of more waste. Environmentalists argue that whatever policies are adopted, they should encourage less, not more, waste. The ambivalence of state policy, when no clearly superior alternative exists, was seen in former Governor Blanchard's endorsement of a pyrolysis system for the Detroit area. Environmentalists cited the incident as a political decision made in haste to reward Detroit, by which many Michiganians will be "parboiled for years." A court case under MEPA is expected to be brought by one or more citizens because the problem will not go away and because politicians, not unexpectedly, have learned to shy away from Detroit's incinerators.

The episode illustrates how public officials are themselves burned in touching many environmental issues. Detroit is a powerful force in Lansing. Not only is the Detroit delegation in the legislature large and influential, but the city's severe economic depression has instigated numerous calls on the state treasury for bringing money and jobs to Detroit. Most have been made on the basis of racial equity and balance. In the view of environmentalists, however, Blanchard's decision was an example of how the concern for jobs – not fairness – overrides environmental protection.

In the face of such controversy, the recent environmental emphasis on waste disposal policy since MEPA has caused concern but not outright rancor in the business community. Unlike Detroit, industry has articulated a typical Michigan "split the difference" attitude. That stance softens this particular battleground. Closely identified with the Republican party, but able to work well with Governor Blanchard on economic issues because of bipartisan lobbying strategies, the business community resisted any kind of government regulation in the 1980s. But the arguments about public health have become salient, and business generally has modified its response to cooperate, while still arguing against unnecessary or too stringent regulation. This transition was accomplished with some ease during the 1970s under the leadership of Governor Milliken, an avowed environmentalist. With the onset of the environmental era, business modified and expanded its legislative offices to deal with those new policy issues. Groups such as the Michigan Oil and Gas Association recognized the need to publish additional technical information for their members and a rationale for cooperating. Some placed environmental specialists in corporate structures. Organizations such as the Michigan Chemical Council (MCC) developed and then lobbied for common positions on the proposed policies to regulate industrial practices and products.

MCC includes several Michigan-based multinational corporations, such as Dow Chemical, Union Carbide, Monsanto Chemical, Upjohn, and Parke-Davis. These are principal producers in the state and in the world of chemicals and medicines, some of which become hazardous waste. MCC has been active in legislative politics to advance its views, including ease and cost of disposal.

MCC argues that member companies have "a responsibility to provide information on hazardous chemicals to the public." As legislators consider more legislation, MCC points out that the requirements for such information are already found in federal and state laws. MCC opposes indiscriminate use of landfills, but acknowledges that manufacturing processes, as well as incineration, produce wastes and residues for which appropriately designed landfills must be available. It urges a reconciliation of federal and state requirements to reduce the industry's burden of compliance. MCC also maintains that "society as a whole" benefits "from industry's production of goods and services and that industry, government and society alike must necessarily have a responsibility for the proper management" and must share in the costs associated with wastes.[17]

One reason for the chemical industry's political responsiveness to the environment is self-interest. In seeking relief from escalating insurance and tort costs, MCC supported legislation to reform product liability so as to limit contingency fees, reduce the statutory limitation of repose, and modify "joint and several" liability claims. In 1988, MCC supported proposals for environmental cleanup at $300 million, solid waste projects at $125 million, and $75 million for wastewater treatment. It opposed bond funds for economic development or for recreation facilities while attempting to be environmentally supportive. Other industrial and commercial interests, however, were skeptical of such precedents.

In this set of environmental issues, a wide variety of policy positions typifies responses from the larger business community and illustrates how environmental protection is pitted against economic development. Familiar arguments note that new environmental policies should evolve slowly; business should endorse reasonable environmental protection, especially when threats to public health are evident; and business should avoid supporting extraneous projects and should keep the costs of environmental compensation low. Also, government involvement should be designed for an acceptable burden of risks, not for a completely risk-free environment. With such positions, where compromises are possible, business gets recognition as an active participant in waste-disposal reform rather than as an obstruction.

Low-Level Radioactive Waste

Michigan's environmental politics, even with MEPA, are not always progressive and compromising. Nor is the federal government always happy with the state's environmental stands. The politics of NIMBY ("not in my back yard") are most evident when it comes to disposing of low-level radioactive waste.

The genesis of the issue in Michigan can be traced to a congressional decision to undertake responsibility for disposal of high-level radioactive waste and leave low-level waste disposal to the states. Michigan joined an interstate compact with other midwestern states to develop a regional disposal site for these low-level radioactive wastes. When Michigan was eventually designated as the site for disposal of the waste of all of the states in the compact, the Blanchard and Engler administrations balked at the prospect. Lawsuits ensued.

The outcome of this fiasco has been the booting of Michigan from the compact; the refusal of South Carolina, Nevada, and Washington, the existing disposal sites, to continue to receive Michigan's low-level radioactive waste; and the resulting storage of this material in fifty-three temporary state sites, which have a combined capacity of only three years.[18] Although Michigan politicians continued for years to avoid construction of a waste site by pursuing federal litigation to require out-of-state acceptance of Michigan's low-level radioactive waste, the prospects of doing so encountered formidable barriers. Still unresolved, despite Michigan's expenditure of $7 million on the issue, this conflict appears to be a problem that the usual state interest-group politics will not settle alone. It may ultimately require resolution by the federal government, perhaps in court. Such results will underscore the state's not infrequent tendency to let gridlock overtake public officials.

Water and Air Policy

The story of zealous environmentalism is similar for programs designed to protect Michigan's lakes and streams, but without the gridlock. In addition to Michigan's more than 3,000 miles of Great Lakes shoreline, the state has more than 11,000 lakes, is drained by fourteen river systems, and has a high water table. All are fresh water and sources of potable water for the state's communities. Most of the northern waters, even in the lower peninsula, are relatively clean, compared to those of other states and nations.

Michigan signaled its intent to protect this unique natural resource in 1929 by creating the Water Resources Commission (WRC).[19] The act granted the commission "control of the pollution of surface or underground waters of the state and the Great Lakes." The key responsibilities, proclaimed in the state's best moralistic fashion, were to "protect and conserve" water resources, "prevent any pollution," and "promote the public interest" in any lake, river, stream, or other waters of the state. Initially, the WRC exercised independent and exclusive authority with respect to water resources.

The Natural Resources Commission (NRC), after customary turf battles between the DNR and WRC, is now responsible for many original WRC functions. Governor Engler's reorganization plan transferred WRC authority to the NRC. In 1994, after dealings through litigation, the WRC lost its quasi-judicial functions, rule-making authority, and control over permits and orders regarding point-source pollution where a specific point can be identified as a discharging source. The DNR and the attorney general were responsible only for enforcing the WRC rulings. The WRC also exercised responsibility to control soil erosion and sedimentation that involved nonpoint-source pollution. It licensed persons at excavation sites or other pollution-generating sites to supervise treatment control facilities. Only enforcement duties were assigned to the DNR.

In addition, the WRC was the state agent for implementing the federal water pollution control amendments. The responsibilities in executing the National Pollution Discharge Elimination System (NPDES) reinforced and expanded the commission's authority. All point-source discharges had to obtain permits and agree to comply with federal and state effluent standards, including Michigan's groundwater quality rules. These rules, linking with hazardous waste policy, were designed to protect groundwater as well as surface water users. Discharge into groundwater was permitted only under a strict variance policy of MEPA's affirmative defense. Few exceptions were made under these stringent policies.[20] Reorganization serves the purpose of integrating prior WRC tasks more fully into the DNR, but some question that these policies will be as rigorously followed as under the WRC.

Strict policy enforcement still remains likely because of the strong emotional attachment of Michiganians to the Great Lakes. To arouse Michiganians, an outside force need only suggest that the states of the parched western sunbelt be permitted to draw fresh water from the lakes. Former astronaut and 1984 U.S. Senate candidate Jack Lousma gained his greatest public recognition when he proclaimed, "The only water that will leave the Great Lakes will be in a can of Vernors."

Both environmentalists and developers oppose the use of Great Lakes basin water by others. It was from this consensus that the Council of Great Lakes Governors, with ties to the Midwest Council of Governors, was established in 1982 as a private, nonprofit corporation. As noted in chapter 2, its Great Lakes Charter became the instrument to protect and manage Great Lakes waters on an intergovernmental basis. The critical policy in the document is the strategy of "prior notice and consultation" on any proposed diversion or consumptive use of Great Lakes waters. Provision is made for convening a meeting on any proposal and for annual consultation among the participants on the cumulative impacts of diversions and consumptive uses. Congress codified the power of the council by providing each Great Lakes governor with a veto power over any new out-of-basin diversion.

The Council of Great Lakes Governors is organized to identify whatever policies are seen as being in the mutual interest of the participants. More recently, the council has become an active environmental arbiter. In contrast, the Great Lakes Commission, ratified by Congress as an interstate compact commission, has been primarily a technical agency accumulating and analyzing economic and environmental data on the Great Lakes. With the immediate threat of diversions, the council has injected a new significance into the commission.

For Michigan, as for the Great Lakes waters, toxic pollution is the foremost environmental water issue, even though diversion gets the greatest public attention. As a result, a second agreement of the council dealt with toxic substance control using a similar proactive strategy.[21] The Great Lakes Water Quality Initiative is another ongoing effort to improve the water quality of the lakes by establishing consistent standards for the whole of the Great Lakes. It, too, has raised considerable controversy, as more stringent water quality levels mean increased costs for business and other polluters.

Nonetheless, the Blanchard and Engler administrations have given considerable emphasis to the Great Lakes and to water resources. Such leadership on a popular topic helps to keep public opinion favorable to the governors, and they use it for numerous photo opportunities. One example of gubernatorial support was the appointment in 1985 of a Great Lakes and Water Resources Planning Commission for the state, which issued a draft action plan in 1987. A second effort was the creation of the Office of Great Lakes, also in 1985. Its first annual report unveiled a bouquet of water protection reforms and goals to be achieved by the turn of the century.[22] But even without these initiatives, Michigan displayed a notable array of water protection policies during the 1950s, 1960s, and 1970s, including legislation on submerged lands, shoreline protection, wetlands conservation, lake levels, natural rivers, and flood-plain rules.

These, too, are not issues without conflict. Air pollution control, regulated by the Air Quality and Air Pollution Control Commission, raises problems as well. The tighter the air emission standards, the less room for economic growth in severely air-degraded regions of the state, especially in southeastern Michigan. In addition, it is estimated by the Air Quality Division of the DNR that approximately $2.8 billion has been spent in the state on air pollution control equipment.

The federal Clean Air Act Amendments of 1990 required a new approach to air regulatory programs, imposing a permit and fee structure that will create a new economic dimension of conflict among polluters in Michigan. This

market approach, when implemented, will likely stimulate new efforts di
rected toward a more consensual approach to air pollution reduction. The
impact on the relations among Michigan's titans of environmental politics –
business interests versus M U C C – remains to be seen.

From Hunting Conservation to Environmental Protection

While several state agencies attend to the well-being of the state's natural environment, these agencies have not always been alert to present threats. Nor
are they judged by environmental activists to be consistent in anticipating
potential dangers. Both the state's industrial character and the rural emphasis
on wildlife conservation and recreation are blamed. For example, E P A officials have long felt that Michigan's Department of Natural Resources, despite its strong traditions, was soft on one specific issue, loss of wetlands.
Consequently, organized interest groups have been more important than the
state's agencies in shifting state policy from simple conservation to environmental protection.

Organized interests have been influential in many instances because they
have been able, through M U C C, to represent many specific interests under a
common banner. Some of these groups are old-line conservation organizations – the fur, fish, and game interests that want to preserve natural habitat
for hunting. These interests put the environment on the policy agenda initially, but primarily from a user perspective. More recently, other interests
have cast themselves as environmental activists employing scientific concepts of natural cycles and ecology in their advocacy briefs.

Despite these differences, most Michigan conservation and environmental groups generally cluster under the federated Michigan United Conservation Clubs, formerly Michigan Sportsmen Associated and the oldest and
largest outdoor group in the state. They rarely undermine one another, giving the groups impressive solidarity. M U C C's members traditionally have
come primarily from local hunting and fishing clubs that still determine most
of its legislative agenda. The strong pro-hunting emphasis of the federation
can be seen in the slogan of the Michigan Bear Hunter's Association: ''Militant Defenders of Our Wildlife Heritage.''

However, M U C C's lobbying has evolved and extended to many other policy areas, such as air and land pollution and ''right to know'' legislation, as
well as to policies regulating solid, toxic, and hazardous wastes. M U C C also
initiated Great Lakes United, a citizen's lobby based in Buffalo, New York,
and devoted to protecting all five of the Great Lakes. M U C C prides itself on

taking specific complaints from affiliated organizations and casting them as attainable policy goals. This dual focus, with issues of conservation and environmental protection reinforcing one another, adds up to potent political influence, which is further reinforced by the uncertainties of political numbers. Because no one knows just how many people belong to one or another local or state environmental group, public officials sometimes suspect that it is nearly everyone.

MUCC, for example, mobilized – almost single-handedly – sufficient support from its affiliated clubs and other environmental activists to place an initiative on the ballot in 1976 and then pass Michigan's disposable-bottle bill. The law requires a deposit on all cans and bottles containing soft drinks, beer, or wine. Other less noted groups have had similar success by bringing together even extremely radical environmental activists and by developing moderate policies. The West Michigan Environmental Action Council (WMEAC) initiated a contract with the School of Law at the University of Michigan seeking more direct involvement of citizens in decisions on natural resources. MEPA ultimately resulted from that relationship. WMEAC also was instrumental in creating the Michigan Environmental Council (MEC) in 1980. MEC is another coalition of sixteen local groups lobbying to protect public health and natural resources. Solid and hazardous wastes, especially low-level radioactive materials, are high on MEC's agenda.

Other environmental groups give more specialized attention to specific bills and resulting programs than does MUCC or MEC. For example, the East Michigan Environmental Action Council contributed a major effort on a stronger wetlands bill and to evaluating Michigan's environmental system. The Sierra Club worked successfully for many years to establish additional wilderness areas in Michigan. The Michigan Lung Association vigorously attacks air pollution. Tobacco smoke and "whatever else contaminates the air" are on its agenda.

SOME CLOSING THOUGHTS

Because of these groups, and the general though mixed identification of Michigan residents with natural resources, the environment will be a continuing battleground. Environmentalists have tasted victory in many political contests that just a few years ago would have been seen as lost causes. Accordingly, they want to build on those successes to prevent a return to the state's prodigal wastage. Scholars, scientists, professionals, union leaders, and a host of other supporters of the environment are extremely wary of disasters ahead. The invasions of exotic species into the Great Lakes through the St. Lawrence Seaway, from the sea lamprey in the 1940s to the zebra mussel in the 1990s, are symptoms of the problems that environmentalists see lying ahead. "Ecosystem" has become a buzzword in Michigan politics, as has "jobs," and the two compete for attention.

State government persists in its efforts to provide jobs, even if ecological problems are sometimes created by their proposals. This often results because the state's emphasis remains on resource use rather than restoration. Some public officials even ignore environmentalists who warn against development and interfere with job creation. They are a distinct minority, however. Many politicians try to capitalize on what they see as the public's widespread environmental fears. To reduce this problem, Governor Engler appointed an Environmental Science Board of twenty-four scientists to systematically prioritize environmental problems. The intent is to avoid, in Engler's words, "the environmental crisis of the month." The governor, with MUCC already angry about DNR reorganization, had little choice but to look for such an alternative agenda setter if he wanted to avoid future political scars. In addition, the environmental policies put in place the 1970s and 1980s are now institutions of law that make unrestrained development impossible. If negotiations do not yield appropriate results, MEPA can be used to throw up at least temporary roadblocks. Consequently, there can be no complete victory for either environmental or business interests if one or the other chooses to be uncooperative with state efforts to find the desired balance. The task that confronts Michigan policymakers is largely about continuing the effort to generate employment within a healthful and enjoyable natural environment. It has been and will be a bumpy road.

CHAPTER TWELVE

State-Local Relations: The Uneasy Sharing of Resources

A STATE WITH MANY GOVERNMENTS

A discussion of Michigan politics would be incomplete without considering the array of local governments where many policy decisions are made and carried out – in the communities around the state. Much of the state's success in dealing with the issues of race, jobs, and the environment depends on local involvement and cooperation. Community responses to state initiatives and regulations are diverse. Their variability owes to the many different conditions that state officials seek to influence and to the numerous ways of organizing local government authority and responsibility.

Nationally, there are 84,955 local governments organized as cities, villages, townships, school districts, and special districts – an average of 1,699 per state. Michigan, with 2,726 local units, ranks thirteenth among the states in total numbers.[1] There are at least three reasons why Michigan has a large number of local governments. First, Michigan was established out of the Northwest Territory. The states of the territory were surveyed into thirty-six-square-mile areas, most of which were later organized as townships. Thus, before the state itself was organized, it was destined to have many local governments. Today, the state has 1,242 townships.

Second, until 1970, as few as 750 people were required to incorporate a new city, 150 to form a village government. In 1970, through the state boundary commission, Michigan began supervising more closely the formation of such governments, thereby slowing the rate of increase in new city and village formations. Proliferating municipalities were thought to be delivering services with little efficiency and with significant service duplication.

There was a third reason for the large number of local governments. Local taxing powers and government boundaries were incongruous with residential and commercial regions. When municipal boundaries did not correspond to economic developments or to service needs, but were legally fixed, people looked for compensating institutions. Local officials, accordingly, formed single-purpose governments – mostly special districts – to overcome certain tax limitations and coordination problems. These districts help rearrange local government by letting another independent unit deliver specific services. Special districts in Michigan have been forming at a rate of more than ten per year, offsetting by several times reductions in school districts through consolidations.

State government has the legal authority to control and manage local governments, but Michigan's conglomerate of local governments is far from planned. Rather, it is the result of political bargaining – negotiations between the state and local governments as well as negotiations among local governments themselves.

STRUCTURAL FRAMEWORK

Michigan's local governments can be classified as general purpose and special purpose. Counties, townships, cities, and villages are the general-purpose units because they provide a broad range of public services and may exercise a variety of regulatory powers. Special or limited-purpose governments usually carry out one or two highly restricted functions. School districts, community college districts, and intermediate school districts are the most common form of special local units in Michigan.[2] Other special districts operate airports, parks, water and sewer systems, parking garages, and other facilities. To the extent that Michigan's local governments bear any mark of having been planned, it appears among the general-purpose governments by historical tradition. Counties and townships, early on, were intended to govern rural areas as well as to carry out state government functions throughout Michigan. City and village governments, on the other hand, were organized to address the needs of people in local settlements.

Counties

Michigan, like all but two states, has border-to-border county governments. The county has its roots in old English government, a system brought to America by early settlers. James Bryce, a professor of civil law at Oxford University, came to the United States in 1788 to see how the country was organizing itself.[3] He observed that New England colonists depended mostly on town and township forms of local organization and not on counties. The southern colonies, however, depended entirely on counties for local government. The middle colonies of New York, Pennsylvania, and New Jersey combined the two patterns. It was this mixture and resulting complexity that the settlers of Michigan brought with them from the East.

Counties were an essential component of state government in a time when travel was difficult and long-distance communications were slow. As late as 1900, state government had few employees to administer its laws. The legislature depended primarily on local governments to implement state law. Counties were the principal substate regional governments carrying out state responsibilities. The state uses the same strategy today, but does not depend on local units as much as it did in the past. For instance, Michigan requires a person to have a gun permit before buying a pistol. This document is obtained from the county sheriff, not the state police. Many state officers and state departments have counterparts in each of the counties. The county clerk, for example, is locally accountable for many functions – keeping official records and administering elections – for which the secretary of state is also responsible in Lansing. County prosecutors are the local counterpart of the state attorney general. Of course, both the state and the counties have their own treasurers, and both have police forces.

A similar pattern exists with respect to some departments. The state mental and public health departments depend heavily on county or multicounty mental and public health departments to administer their programs. The state Department of Transportation has counterparts in county road commissions that maintain much of the state road and highway system. By far, the largest part of the state's judicial system is operated through county and subcounty court systems. Although less so now than in the past, the counterpart state and county officers depend a great deal on each other to carry out their duties. State offices would be considerably different were there no county officials to extend their authority throughout Michigan. State government might organize its relationships to local governments differently if the state were being settled today. With modern computer technologies, rapid communications, and shortened travel times, the state could have made many public functions state, rather than local, responsibilities. The DNR with its regional offices would be a likely model.

A county is also a local general-purpose government with officials who are elected by its residents. As such, counties conduct many programs to address local needs, just as they follow state mandates. Local county tasks are often unconnected to state functions. Examples of local empowerment are land-use planning and zoning. County airports are another. Some counties operate extensive park systems and senior-citizen programs. Counties conduct programs of this sort, not because the state requires them to do so, but because officials and citizens determined that such programs are desirable.

County government is largely organized along the principles of Jacksonian democracy. In general, Jacksonians believed that anyone could do government work and that everyone should have the opportunity to do so. To achieve these goals, they made many government positions elective and kept the terms short, in some cases one year. Michigan counties today, with several elected administrators, reflect this philosophy and embody amateurism in local government management. Jacksonianism, however, also opened the gateway to partisanship. With so many offices, voters needed party identifications to keep candidates straight. Among the elected line administrators are the clerk, treasurer, sheriff, prosecutor, register of deeds, and drain commissioner. The 1963 Michigan constitution changed the term for each office from two to four years, at least lengthening the time to gain expertise. Some counties also elect road commissioners as well as a land surveyor, and some UP counties elect a mine inspector. Members of the legislative body, the board of county commissioners, are elected to two-year terms from single-member districts. Heading the board is a chairperson chosen by the commissioners. Although the chairperson is recognized as the head of county government for many purposes, this official has few formal powers. The position bears the mark of the Jacksonian weak-mayor style of executive leadership.[4]

The state constitution imbeds many Jacksonian characteristics into county government. Yet it also permits counties to reorganize under a locally drawn charter.[5] While charter counties must continue the elected officers, the charter may strengthen the executive role by establishing an office of elected county executive or appointed county manager. Also, a separate statute permits counties to reorganize under "optional forms," either elected executive or appointed manager. However, counties have been slow to adopt these new forms of organization. Bay and Oakland Counties have elected executives under the optional forms approach, and Wayne County has reorganized by adopting a county charter. No county has adopted the county manager model, although several have administrators who work at the behest of the commission.

Other than Michigan's affection for amateurs in government, why have counties been slow to reorganize? No county, other than Wayne, has seriously considered becoming a charter county. One reason is that the charter statute permits little real change in operation. The legislature made special provisions for Wayne County. Second, there has been no groundswell of pressure to have the charter county act liberalized and county government modernized. Neither elected county commissioners nor elected line officers have pushed for reorganization. Experience from the three reorganized counties indicates that an elected executive will infringe on the powers of other county officials. Hence, leadership for reform, if it comes, will probably have to originate from outside county government.

Townships

Townships came with the territory and statehood. Like counties, townships remain bastions of amateur, rather than professional, government. Alexis de Tocqueville, in 1835, said of New England towns, "The township is the only association so well rooted in nature that wherever men assemble it forms itself."[6] This was almost the case in Michigan. Thomas Jefferson, as a member of the Continental Congress, was enamored with the direct democracy being practiced in the New England states in the late 1700s, so he lobbied the Congress to write a provision in the Northwest Ordinance of 1785 to have the territory surveyed into six-by-six-mile areas. He envisioned that when the territory was settled, these township areas would become "pure and elementary republics." Townships today bear some marks of the New England town governments, but most elements associated with participatory democracy have faded. Although many Michigan townships still conduct an annual meeting each spring, many of the powers that once belonged to that citizens' forum have been delegated to the township board. Township residents, though, exercise considerable control over local boards and their decisions by limiting taxing powers.[7]

Originally, townships received limited service, regulatory, and taxing powers because they were intended to serve rural areas having little need for a wide range of municipal services. Mostly, they were subdivisions of counties and the final state agency in administering activities, such as property taxation, rudimentary justice through the justice of the peace, and state and federal elections. They also administered some basic services, including fire protection, road maintenance, cemeteries, and welfare.[8]

In much of the Midwest, townships waned and counties assumed most of their functions. In Michigan, however, townships gained influence. After World War II, residential, commercial, and industrial developments exploded beyond city boundaries. Township residents, often with an anti-city bias, began to count politically in state legislative races. Township officials, developing a new self-awareness and organizing a new state association, began pressing for change in their service and regulatory powers. In the language of today, these newly developed urban/suburban areas might be referred to as "edge cities."[9] The language of the past saw them differently, as rural and Republican strongholds in an urbanizing and Democratic world.

Responding to townships' growing political muscle, the legislature gradually expanded their powers. As a result, while they often lack the operational flexibility of cities, townships can exercise important service and regulatory powers over public water and sewer utilities, police and fire protection, zoning and building codes, and other services usually accorded to cities. This presents problems. Townships traditionally lacked even the limited boundary integrity of cities in Michigan, a fact that led to many battles between cities and townships over annexation of territory. As we note later, because of boundary differences, both types of units raid each other's geographical domains. Townships were also denied the financial flexibility of cities with respect to authority to tax property and personal income. Neither did Michigan townships gain the organizational flexibility of cities. Jacksonian values dominate the township form, restraining them in developing professional and business practices. Each township elects three key administrators: the supervisor, clerk, and treasurer. Each office has its own statutory duties. These three officers, along with two or four – depending on the size and type of the township – elected trustees, constitute the township board. All board members now serve four-year terms.

Township reform has been limited. In 1947, the legislature passed the Charter Township Act, which provides some centralized administrative control and expanded taxing power and boundary protection. Most of the approximately one hundred charter townships in 1993 reorganized to gain boundary protection, although other criteria also come into play before a township becomes immune to annexation. Perhaps the most significant long-term reform of township government has been the change in their function – a shedding of state services and an expansion of local services for residents.

Municipalities

Cities and villages are distinct from the other two forms of local government because they exist as an overlay on the grid of counties and townships. Cities and villages are organized only in populated settlements. Both have authority to deal with the governmental needs of people in urban and rural communities. Initially, the legislature approved charters in the form of local acts for each city and village. The legislature spelled out the form of organization and the powers that could be exercised by each unit. These local acts made the units vulnerable to the whims of legislators. Political mischief might have involved a legislator proposing a change in a city charter as a way of getting even with political enemies back home or perhaps exchanging favors with a mayor who gave the legislator's brother a city job. Luther Gulick noted that "when the states stepped in to clean up the local messes, especially in the 'wicked cities' – which were generally of the opposite political faith – there was always the tendency to go too far and pass over into raw political manipulation of local affairs."[10]

Reformers insisted that most laws be general and that local acts be especially difficult to pass. Targeting just one community with legislation was made more difficult. The major reform, though, was the inclusion of municipal home rule in the 1908 constitution.[11] It was one of the chief planks of the Progressive movement, along with initiative, referendum, recall, the direct primary, and women's suffrage. Home rule meant that city residents could organize their government on their own and determine its taxing powers, services, and regulations. An elected committee of citizens would write a proposed charter and submit it to local voters for approval or rejection. Except for a few general restrictions and limits, the legislature was invited to stay out of these local affairs. For the most part, home rule has limited state legislative interference. However, an occasional issue arises that moves locally concerned legislators into action: for example, an economic development initiative that rewards some local interests over others.

Home rule was conceived about the same time that reformers were searching for a different management model for cities. City government had depended largely on an elected mayor and council, along with political appointees to run local services. The Progressives thought that city governments should be run more efficiently and professionally.[12] Business, with its board of directors and appointed chief executive officer, provided the model. The council-manager form has since become the dominant one among Michigan's small and middle-sized cities. In Michigan's larger and, especially, older cities, residents are more socially and economically diverse and less amenable to the manager model. The city of Flint changed to a strong mayor form after having experimented with the council-manager approach; Grand Rapids kept its city manager but also installed a full-time mayor. Residents in these communities appear to have concluded that elected leadership and responsiveness are as important as administrative efficiency.

The village is an intermediate form between city and township. It typically has authority to deal with the needs of small population centers that require more service than an ordinary township provides. Unlike cities, which separate from the township upon incorporation, villages remain part of the township even while having their own corporate identities. This permits villages to organize without being responsible for all local functions, such as state and federal elections and local courts. For the most part, the structural and functional differences between city and village governments are indistinguishable to most village residents today.

Single-Purpose Governments

Special districts are the fastest growing form of local government in Michigan, in part because they compensate for the extent to which settlement patterns overlap political boundaries. The prevailing types of single-purpose districts provide education services. Indeed, school districts were the original model. Public school, community college, and intermediate school districts have their own elected officials, levy property taxes, hire their own employees, and establish their own policies. In addition, their activities take place within the context of their own local politics. These districts finance their services by a combination of state aid and property taxes, and, in the case of community colleges, tuition. Other user fees, such as tuition, are becoming common in Michigan. One special characteristic of Michigan special districts is their economic vulnerability. They may not raise millage rates without voter approval. Furthermore, they are dependent for most of their revenues on property assessments.

Michigan law permits a variety of single-purpose governments. Cities, townships, and counties – and sometimes state government itself – create these units for three reasons. First, lobbyists urge them on the legislature as solutions to specific problems. Because a special district with taxing power cannot be organized without voter approval, such proposals pick up little opposition in the legislature. Second, special districts provide a specific service that an existing government cannot provide either because it does not have the resources or because the service area extends beyond the unit's boundaries (e.g., airports and public bus systems). Governor Engler proposed "charter schools" as single districts to compete with local public schools as a challenge to increase the quality of education. Other special districts carry out functions such as water and sewage treatment, parks and recreation, and library services. Third, a special district or authority, once approved, can issue its own bonds or order its own property-tax levy without drawing upon the limited taxing or bonding powers of the sponsoring units. Special districts also generate funds from the fees they charge system users (e.g., water and sewer customers and bus riders).

Special districts have their own governing boards. Members are usually appointed by the sponsoring governments. Nonetheless, district boards operate rather independently of their sponsoring units. These boards typically exercise their functions through a hired executive manager. Except for their employees and for interest groups with a stake in their function, board members are usually unknown to and unwatched by the general public. Unless they run into financial problems, employee strikes, or scandal, the media rarely report their activities. Michigan school districts tend to be an exception to this anonymity, both because they are seen widely as the cause of high property taxes and because the perceived failure of public education is seen as hurting economic growth. Nevertheless, special districts are extremely important to state politics because they expand the service points for numerous state programs, ranging from vocational education to air transportation.

STATE-LOCAL RELATIONS

Michigan's constitution, which is otherwise a detailed contract, provides only for the basic existence of local governments, leaving it to the legislature to round out the bulk of local powers, home rule notwithstanding. Hence, the legislature decides what powers local governments may exercise and how various programs are to be carried out. It is around these issues that state-local relations revolve.

The basic ground rule is that local units may do only what state law permits. This rule was expressed in an Iowa case in the 1870s. Judge John F. Dillon wrote, "It is the general and undisputed proposition of law that a municipal corporation possesses and may exercise the following powers: first, those granted in expressed words; second, those necessary or fairly implied in or incident to the powers expressly granted; [and] third, those essential to the declared objects and purposes of the corporation – not simply convenient, but indispensable. Any fair, reasonable, substantial doubt concerning the existence of power is resolved by the courts against the corporation, and the power is denied."[13]

To offset some of the severity of this language, the Michigan Constitution directs judges to construe local government powers "liberally, in their favor."[14] The constitution also provides home rule for cities, villages, and counties but directs the legislature to spell out what home rule means in practice. Home rule provides greater latitude for cities and villages than it does for counties, but in no case does it permit absolute escape from Dillon's Rule that local governments exist at the state's pleasure. Nor does it entirely prevent the legislature from occasionally imposing its will on community governments.[15]

The legislature has several strategies for limiting local autonomy. Passing general statutes is one method. The legislature, for example, passed the Uniform Accounting and Budgeting Act in 1968, which outlines specific standards that each unit must follow in maintaining financial records. In addition, the statute establishes procedures for state intervention when a local government borders on bankruptcy. Other statutes impose rules for how local boards and commissions must conduct their meetings and the conditions under which they may deny citizens access to public documents. The legislature also set up a Mobile Home Commission and effectively removed much of the cities' and townships' discretion over these developments. Generally, local units have not challenged these laws as infringements on local autonomy, even though they limit local flexibility.

A second stratagem is to enact permissive general legislation allowing local units to exercise a function such as zoning. Once a local unit is granted zoning powers, state law spells out the procedures to follow in exercising such powers.

In a third approach, the legislature can declare a particular function as falling under state jurisdiction and can remove it from local control. This happened gradually with the administration of social welfare, which was a county responsibility until it was changed entirely to a state function in 1979. However, the transition began in 1965 when legislators first took aim at nonuniformity in benefits. In another example, Detroit had a rent-control initiative on the ballot in 1988. The legislature intervened with an act removing rent control as a matter of local authority. Also, in 1989, Senator John Kelly (D-Detroit) introduced a bill to require Detroit Common Council members to be elected from districts rather than at large as provided by the city charter. Kelly objected to the strong commitment of the mayor and council to downtown redevelopment rather than to neighborhood problems. Although the bill died in committee, it served its purpose by warning city councilors that they were not beyond the reach of the state capitol.

The legislature also reassigns functions periodically. Perhaps the major reassignment involved removing local streets and roads from township responsibility and assigning them to the county in 1931. More recently, state officials have discussed – some would say threatened – transferring elections administration and property-tax assessment to the county. A related tactic is to pit localities against each other and against the state. For instance, when solid waste disposal approached crisis conditions, the state mandated local area planning for disposal. Counties have the first option to develop the plans. If a county declines, units within the county can band together to make plans. If local units fail to undertake the project, the law orders the director of the Department of Natural Resources to do so. This approach usually works because local officials and their citizens tend not to look favorably on having state bureaucrats plan a program for their home communities.

What motivates the legislature to alter local authority? That question and the answers it evokes point to how local government problems become intertwined with state politics. Often, changes in local authority occur because one interest group or another wants the ground rules changed. In the case of welfare administration, the federal government pays a share of the cost and insists on uniform standards throughout the state. The state assumed responsibility rather than trying to get Michigan's many county-directed welfare offices to operate in a sufficiently uniform manner in order to meet federal requirements. The state's assumption of welfare administration also reflected the power of the state's social welfare bureaucracy and the state bias in favor of professional administration. Having commissioners in each county determine who qualifies for benefits, and for how much, did not sit well with modern social welfare administrators. State administrators in public and mental health expressed similar concerns about their programs, which are operated under extensive county controls.

In the case of mobile-home legislation, mobile-home manufacturers and dealers argued that they could not build housing or provide mobile-home parks to meet widely diverse local standards. The construction industry made similar arguments when they suspected local governments of using their building ordinances to give area contractors an advantage over outsiders. Mobile-home and construction groups, with statewide interests, would much prefer to lobby for regulations at one location – Lansing – rather than in eighty-three counties or 1,500 cities and townships.

State bureaucrats lobby for some of these changes. The Department of Natural Resources did so very effectively on the issue of landfill siting. In another case, state election officials proposed reducing the township and city role in elections administration. Indeed, legislators often cooperate with agency requests for greater state administrative discretion because they see such changes as remedies for bothersome issues.

For the most part, for legislators at least, changes that give greater authority to the state develop as responses to personally troublesome problems rather than from philosophical convictions. That is, legislators do not deliberately review government functions and decide rationally which should be administered by the state and which by local governments. Still, the main tendency has been to move services and regulations from local to state administration. But even as the state has asserted service delivery responsibilities, most state agencies experience considerable pressure to take local needs and differences into account. State police reallocation of post assignments to meet local problems better is a good example. Some legislators argue that if government functions were originally decentralized to the counties because communications were slow and travel difficult, they no longer need to be so dispersed and so costly in times of modern technology. This, of course, would also give legislators more opportunities to oversee state service delivery.

Local officials and their associations often resist such changes and delay them for years. When certain changes seem inevitable, local officials negotiate the best deal possible or extract the highest price that they can in return for conformity. Local government groups have various resources with which to wage political battles. One is the access of local officials to legislators both at the state capitol and in the home district. Many local officials know their legislators personally and have worked with them on other issues. Moreover, the local official and the legislator may be of the same political party and may have helped each other in election campaigns. Thus, local officials often have a reservoir of good will built on personal acquaintance and political cooperation that bodes them well in challenging the state.

Perhaps a more important resource is the law itself. As noted, the state constitution affords local units and their officials at least some protections. First, the 1978 Headlee Amendment to the constitution gives local governments even more protection against an imposing state legislature because it requires the state to pay the costs of newly mandated programs.[16] Local officials have not been reluctant to claim their rights under this provision. For example, the Delta County Board of Commissioners in the Upper Peninsula successfully fought off the solid waste disposal act over this point. In 1988, several counties began a lawsuit claiming more than $500 million in delayed state funding for the courts. State officials, operating under increasingly stringent budget conditions, are reluctant to compensate local units for mandated programs. In part, they believe that the state should conduct the program itself if it pays the costs. At the same time, legislators realize that the state, with its accustomed reliance on local units, would have political and administrative difficulty in reaching out to all regions with a broad range of mandated programs.

A second protection for local units of government is that the Headlee Amendment requires the state to disburse 41.6 percent of its tax revenues to local units.[17] Agency officials and many legislators think that sum is plenty, and they resent being bothered with reimbursing local units for relatively small amounts. A good deal of the politicking between state and local officials is over who will impose a tax and who will spend the proceeds. This provision, too, has been the subject of lawsuits filed by local officials against the state. The most recent suit was settled by agreement just after Governor John Engler took office. Pending before the state supreme court was an action by Oakland County asserting that state aid for mental health programs should not be counted against the 41.6 percent allotment because the mental health programs are joint state-county programs, not state assistance to a local program. With a potential judgment ordering payment to counties of more than $600 million at a time when the state budget was already in deficit, the governor and county executive reached an agreement. The county did not insist on reimbursement of foregone aid, and the state no longer counts mental health funding against the Headlee allotment.

Local governments have used other constitutional provisions for leverage with state officials. An amendment passed in 1946, for example, guaranteed cities, villages, and townships one-half cent from every dollar of retail sales.[18] Two cents of each state sales tax levy was dedicated by the constitution to the state's school-aid fund. In 1976, though, voters approved a referendum to exempt food and drugs from the sales tax so as to make that tax less regressive.[19] Local officials did not oppose this referendum because it contained provisions to shield them from losses from reduced tax revenues. (Beginning in 1994, four cents of the six-cent levy goes to schools.)

City, county, and township associations and employee groups have been especially important in determining the various tasks of government and how such tasks are undertaken. Often the effect of the tasks negates sensible changes because they are so organized around narrow interests. Local officials are represented by many organizations in Lansing. The Michigan Municipal League, for example, looks after the interests of cities and villages. Detroit interests, though, have seen themselves as different enough from those of other cities that they send their own lobbyists to Lansing rather than depend on the league. Similarly, Wayne County usually has its own representative rather than rely entirely on the Michigan Association of Counties. Outstate interests often differ from those of the state's largest city and county. Outstaters usually look at proposals from Detroit and Wayne County with suspicion and often bargain with opponents of such propositions until they, too, get part of the assistance requested from the state.

The Michigan Township Association looks after the interests of township governments, and the Michigan Association of Counties, whose members are county commissioners, attends to the affairs of county government. Similarly, because local officials in the UP and northern lower peninsula often see their interests being overlooked by the statewide organizations, they have their own subgroups, if not lobbyists, to articulate northern Michigan interests. Each group of county officers – clerks, registers, sheriffs – has its own association to follow its affairs in Lansing as well as in individual counties. Together, these officials also have an umbrella organization to look after their common interests by watchdogging the legislature and state agencies.

There also are several groups that attend to public education. The Michigan Education Association, representing teachers, is among the most powerful of the education groups. Yet the MEA often disagrees with the Michigan Association of School Boards, which represents the management side of education. Other smaller school associations, such as the "middle cities" group and the "out-of-formula" districts, make sure their interests and appropriation needs are stated and at least considered by state officials.

State legislators and state administrators must also deal with many other local government organizations. These add to the diversity rather than coordination of political demands on the state. City, township, and county clerks, for example, have a direct stake in election laws because they administer such laws. Accordingly, the state Bureau of Elections must deal with three organizations representing clerks. The state highway department must deal with the road commission association and the city public works officials and also with their allied private-sector associates in road building and contracting. The Association of Mental Health Boards bargains with the state mental health department, while the powerful Michigan Sheriffs Association must be reckoned with on county jail rules, road patrol, and criminal procedures.[20] Complicating decision making even more is the fact that many of these multi-interest deliberations also include representatives of employee groups that seek to influence policy formation and appropriations.

On another level, divisiveness goes on because local units and state agencies compete for state resources. Allocations of funds for police and for road maintenance and construction are cases in point. The struggle over police funds perhaps should have been handled as a policy question, with funding decisions following. A policy resolution would have clearly defined the specific functions of the state police throughout Michigan. That is, should state police provide exclusive patrol service to the state expressway system and fulfill highly specialized and technical needs, while leaving to county sheriffs and other local police the responsibility for routine road patrol and public safety? No one can say with certainty. The battle since 1982, however, has been waged over state assistance to county sheriffs for secondary road patrol. The Michigan Sheriffs Association argued that the counties could not afford to fund police patrol in their rural areas and that the state should assist with small grants to counties meeting maintenance-of-effort conditions. During the intervening ten years, the amount of the state grants has grown to tens of millions of dollars. State police officials see these dollars as coming at their expense, especially in light of state budget reductions and the layoffs that they have experienced in recent years.

Competition for funds derived from vehicle and gasoline taxes is one of longer duration. These revenues, which are earmarked for transportation, are divided among three major interests – the state Department of Transportation, county road commissions, and city and village street departments. While the overall formula is complicated, the basic numbers over which these groups fight is their percentage share of the pie. The allocation among the three parties was in dispute for much of the 1980s. Temporary allocations were authorized several times pending future studies. The state agency that previously received just under half the funds was unable to hold off the local forces, who contended that the state share should be reduced because state obligations for expressway construction were declining. It was time, the locals asserted, for Michigan to bring local roads up to standard. The arguments and pressures were successful. At the end of the decade, the state share of transportation revenues had dropped to 39 percent, the same as the new county share. The city and village proportion had risen to 22 percent. That settlement, however, did not end state-local controversies. By 1992, local transportation officials were appearing regularly around the state on regional evening TV news broadcasts to explain the need for enhanced state revenues for county use.

It should be noted that in doing battle with local interests in the legislature, state officials are somewhat disadvantaged. Agency bureaucrats are less able than local government associations to lubricate the wheels of legislative decision making. Making campaign contributions, offering open electoral endorsements, and delivering blocks of votes are not the tools of civil servants. Unless their friends in the private sector come to their aid, or unless a legislator's personal interest is affected, state agencies are vulnerable in fights over resources.

Losses by state agencies are not unexpected then, despite the general move of service functions from local to state government. Because of their well-organized associations and active involvement in politics, local government interests exercise considerable clout over issues that concern them. State agencies fare best when local interests cannot agree among themselves, which is frequently the case. Often, several associations or units of local government collaborate to battle against other groups and forms of local governments. A case in point is the running dispute between teachers and school boards over collective bargaining by public employees. MEA has been pressing for the right of teachers to strike, something current statutes do not permit any public employees to do. The school board association opposes teacher strikes and wants stronger laws allowing back-to-work injunctions, which courts are reluctant to give. The controversy reached one of its periodic peaks when Bobby Crim was Speaker of the house of representatives. Unable to resolve the differences in the dispute, he assigned MEA and school board lobbyists to a Lansing motel where they were ordered to hammer out a compromise. After several days of meetings, agreement still evaded them. Only in the aftermath of the 1994 school finance reform was the legislature able to specify penalties for teacher strikes and lockouts.

Usually, differences between local interest groups are first negotiated. The groups develop a compromise and then present it to the legislature for enactment into law. The situation is similar when differences exist between a state agency and the contesting interest groups. Legislators rarely and reluctantly take issues aggressively in hand to resolve unless a more powerful third party presses for resolution. More commonly, the legislature waits until the competing groups hammer out a compromise. This characteristic of state government, as much as anything else, gives influence and discretion to Michigan's local governments because they usually favor either the status quo or a plan to send more state resources their way. Disagreements, however, leave many local policy problems unresolved, as many interests often favor. Thus, changes on behalf of effective and efficient state and local governance are often incomplete.

BUDGETS, REVENUES, AND INTERGOVERNMENTAL RELATIONS

Financial difficulties also lie at the heart of these local policy controversies, owing both to resource scarcity within the state and to growing levels of competing expenditures in some policy areas. Other difficulties are created by rules governing taxation and spending. Still more are created by increased state and federal regulations that require local government compliance.

Despite the lack of definitive data, pieces of the budget and revenue puzzle can be tentatively linked. Federal revenue assistance to Michigan cities, counties, and townships fell more than 46 percent from 1983 through 1990, a drop of nearly $282 million. This was partially offset, for the state as a whole, by a more than $142 million increase in aid to special districts and a $28 million increase for school districts. Financial stress, in the wake of such losses, clearly accrued to Michigan's multipurpose governments, from Detroit to outstate units.

This, however, was not a time of decreased state revenue sharing. From 1981 to 1990, state assistance to multipurpose districts went up nearly 46 percent, or almost $440 million, which more than offset federal revenue losses. School districts also saw their total state aid go up significantly, by over 50 percent to more than $3.1 billion. Thus, Michigan assistance to local governments offset federal cutbacks. As a city manager observed, "We were not unduly affected. In fact, we received every state grant we really targeted." Few local administrators disagreed. However, the flow of intergovernmental dollars has not been the same for all local governments. In fact, there exists a general relationship between ability to raise revenue locally and intergovernmental assistance – that is, more capable governments get more grants.

The offsetting impact of state and federal spending is also challenged by local administrators who point to regulatory requirements. In particular, city and county inspection costs have risen dramatically as environmental, health, safety, and product codes have been adopted to meet regulatory requirements. Estimates range from a low of 100 percent in once well-staffed local governments to 600 and 700 percent increases in previously understaffed communities. School districts faced some of the same facility requirements as cities and counties, but also saw regulatory mandates having a greater effect on their instruction programs. Major expenditure increases for education included special-education facilities for the disabled and cultural diversity. State estimates indicate that regulatory requirements, and the side effects that they produced for transportation and facility operation, offset most of the increased state and federal aid of the 1980s. For example, as state school aid increased by about 47 percent in the 1980s, the state share of school operating revenues remained at 29.5 percent. About 80 percent of state aid was for operational assistance. Schools were rapidly consuming available dollars.

These data point to a major stress point in local government that was removed only when school finance changes were finally made in 1994. As the local share of school operating revenues increased by 43 percent from 1971 to 1980 and another 40 percent from 1981 to 1990, all local governments were affected. Three factors were responsible. First, local governments primarily raised their own funds through property taxes, which accounted for 62 percent of all locally generated revenues and 40 percent of total revenues. Charges of various sorts, from water fees to traffic fines, accounted for another 32 percent of locally generated funds.

Second, Michigan ranked twelfth among the states in property taxes in 1990 and 30 percent above the national average. This added high costs to businesses, which often left the state – and, of course, the community – for that reason. It also rankled citizens, inspiring vocal taxpayer complaints. Increased property taxes, as a result, have been reluctantly implemented. Third, property taxes above fifteen mills for all units combined, to a maximum of fifty mills in any single location, had to be voted on by local residents. This opportunity for citizens to resist extra costs gave local officials even greater pause in recommending millage increases.

The increasing local share of school operating revenues had several other effects as well. The growth in school revenues, because of tax limits, directly squeezed services of cities and counties. It also produced great disparity in the capacity to fund comparable services statewide. For example, spending per student in 1992 varied in Michigan school districts from $2,814 to $9,040. This variation was widely seen as unfair. Units of government were advantaged by growth in commercial and industrial tax base, disadvantaged by federal and state tax-exempt facilities, and severely harmed when property values fell. Detroit and its older suburbs suffered the most.[21] But other problems, such as falling farmland values in the 1980s, had the same effect. Some heavily agricultural counties took as many as six years to recoup taxroll losses.

Adjustments to new problems and circumstances are far from easy for multipurpose governments experiencing fiscal stress. Commonly, when new tasks are required, new employee assignments are gained by layoffs elsewhere. Facing the upper-level fifty mills, even prosperous cities and counties were affected. Thus, to build a new jail prior to tax reform, for example, a county would have to reduce its operational budget for each department over a multi-year planning period. The limitations imposed by the Headlee Amendments further limited responsiveness and slow the addition of new facilities.

The convergence of competing forces, imposed by variably distributed resources and public values, makes local government budgeting a source of contention throughout the state and in intergovernmental relations even with reform. Under pressure, local officials turn whenever they can to Lansing, well convinced that federal assistance will be limited. As a local government official accurately speculated, "The politics of the 1990s will be about the state relieving local pressure by reallocating state dollars and responsibilities to the grass roots. We always have real confidence that we can win in Lansing while we feel shut entirely off from Washington."

INTERLOCAL DISPUTES AND COOPERATION

Local governments compete locally as well. Individual cities and townships, for example, have had classic battles over boundary adjustment or annexation. The fights were most pronounced during the 1950s and 1960s, when urban growth was spilling over city limits and into the townships at unprecedented rates. City officials or township residents could initiate annexation proceedings that would take land and population from townships and attach them to cities. County boards of supervisors had ministerial responsibilities to set the date for the voter referendum on the proposed annexation. The rules then said that county boards had to handle the petitions in the sequence in which they were received.

Those rules often sparked races to the county courthouse. Township supervisors, on getting wind of an annexation petition being circulated in the city, would hurry to the courthouse with their own petitions to form a city or incorporate the township as a city. If the supervisors won the race, the incorporation issue would be placed on the ballot first. As a consequence, many suburban cities adjacent to older central cities were formed through political battles rather than by planned incorporation.[22]

Such contests are now history because of state action and, in this case, interest-group cooperation. At an evening meeting in a Lansing restaurant, Municipal League and Township Association representatives hammered out a compromise that resulted in the creation of a state boundary commission to supervise annexation and incorporation. This change, along with other lesser changes in annexation laws, has tempered the annexation problem. No longer can a city council target an industrial plant for takeover by connecting the plant to the city by a railroad track to meet the contiguity requirement for annexation. The battle over boundaries has come to an end for the state's largest cities, such as Detroit, Grand Rapids, Flint, Kalamazoo, and a few suburban cities that used such ploys. That is not the case with respect to middle-sized and smaller cities, such as Midland, Holland, Mt. Pleasant, and Big Rapids. Councils of such cities and developers in those areas regularly ask the state boundary commission to approve annexations. Townships battle back vigorously. They fight proposed annexations at boundary commission hearings and often in court, sometimes for years. Their other tactics include "defensive" or "blocking" petitions presented to the boundary commission in order to buy time and some freedom from further annexation actions. More recently, township forces have successfully interrupted the contiguity of boundaries necessary for annexation by initiating detachment procedures – a kind of reverse annexation – to counteract annexation moves.

Other disputes and cooperative experiences surface over competition for commercial and industrial development. Central-city downtowns have suffered physical and economic devastation because of shopping centers constructed in suburban communities. Many industrial plants have been built in the suburbs as well. Central cities have fought back. Often as the sole producers of public water and sanitary sewer services, they seek to preserve their own tax bases and to head off suburban developments by withholding service hookups. Not uncommonly, cities insist on annexation as a condition of service extensions.

Eventually, older central cities agreed to sell these services to the suburbs – usually at a higher price than was charged consumers in the city. Detroit, for example, provides water services to most of the suburbs in southeast Michigan. In other instances, central cities and suburbs have developed agreements to share federal grant monies for the construction of new offices or industrial facilities. Central cities gain from suburban commitments to repay the grant funds and share resulting property-tax revenues or from commitments to provide a number of jobs to city residents. Other agreements work in reverse. Townships agree to release territory to the city for a specified period or even permanently. In return, they receive a share of the property taxes and personal income taxes generated from new industrial or commercial facilities.

Local officials cooperate in many other ways. They agree to share police and fire personnel in emergencies. They also cooperate because conditions in federal grants require the sharing of water and sewer services beyond city boundaries. Units cooperate in establishing public transit systems and 911 services. Conflicts, of course, draw more publicity than cooperation arrangements. Cooperative efforts, however, are more common than conflict in the interlocal area.

At the center of both conflict and cooperation are tax revenue and development. Officials in most units compete fiercely for development. Local governments search for industrial and commercial projects that provide tax revenue and jobs because townships and counties, as well as many suburban cities, rely heavily on property taxes to finance their municipal operations. The older central cities, and a few suburban cities, also levy a personal income tax on residents and suburbanites who work in the city. In all but Detroit, rates are one percent on residents and one-half of one percent on nonresidents. While most units do not tax property at their maximum authorizations, officials generally are loath to increase tax rates. Property assessments, of course, typically increase annually, but these tend to track or follow inflation. The result is that local governments gain additional purchasing power and expand only when they obtain new developments. Since the late 1970s, when federal assistance first began to decline, many municipalities have been unable to keep pace with growing service demands. Hence, as federal cuts intensified, many cities cut back on police, fire, and other services and increased their efforts to gain new businesses and industries.

Public schools, in this discussion, are a special case. School officials are generally not involved in promoting new development, even though they received the major portion of local property taxes before reforms took effect in 1994 – 60 percent of the state total for operating revenue and another 11 percent to service bonded debts in 1991. School funding came from state aid as well as local taxes, and gains in local revenues often meant an offsetting reduction in state aid. The tax benefits of economic development thus were smaller for schools. In addition, though, taxpayers in southern Michigan generally honored school boards' requests for higher property-tax authorizations when the burden of financing schools shifted in the 1980s from the state to local taxes. Northern schools have had greater problems with voters and, as a result, were more concerned about improving their local economies. This shifting revenue base and regional differences produced a difficult problem for the state as it struggled with a four-to-one gap in per student expenditures between the highest and the lowest school districts. High spending districts – usually those outside the state aid formula, anyway – had been reluctant to support a general tax increase without a gain of state aid. Their voters, meanwhile, sought relief from one of the nation's highest property taxes.

As wealthy districts registered their commitment to education with higher property-tax rates and as other districts lagged, the spending gap grew. Equalizing per pupil spending was an intractable problem. A so-called Robin Hood plan, adopted in 1991, divided the state into three regions; in each district, the increased property-tax receipts from the new industrial and commercial tax base would be shared in reverse proportion to the per capita tax base. This plan held the promise of at least slowing the expansion of the spending gap between rich and poor districts within the same region. However, the plan was halted by a lawsuit before it could take effect.

Actions to close the gap had to deal with the issue of the level at which the state should fund schools – the median? the seventy-fifth percentile? Actions also addressed whether or not the state should cap spending by the wealthiest districts in order to hasten the closing of the gap. Then there remained the questions of need and of South versus North. Equalization of spending assumed equality of need, an assumption barely tenable when one considers the widely varying social and economic characteristics of the state's regions. State legislators, lobbyists for the teachers and the school boards, various groups of school districts, and others struggled annually to devise a school-aid plan that would make education less dependent on local property taxes and that would reduce spending disparities. Yet even a rare combination of gubernatorial leadership, bipartisan cooperation, multi-interest bargains, and a property-tax/sales-tax shift was defeated in a special election to correct many of these inequities in June 1993. Those favorable factors could still not unite all state interests or overcome voter differences between metro Detroit and outstate. In frustration, the legislature, with the governor's support, simply abolished school property taxes in July of 1993. Legislators then had one year to work on reform, freed from the protectiveness that previously characterized educational reform efforts. In that crisis environment, both greater equity and increased state aid were finally forthcoming. Still, however, the state's wealthiest school districts will lose resources under that plan unless they enact a special millage available only to previously high-spending places.

Southeast Michigan has also become a special case with respect to shared wealth and responsibility. At the heart of the seven-county megalopolis that spreads into Ohio lies the city of Detroit and Wayne County. Sharing that space are other major metro governments, especially the rapidly growing counties of Oakland and Macomb. The U.S. Bureau of the Census now designates this region as the Detroit–Ann Arbor metropolitan area, a definition that belies its lack of interlocal unity. This is the nation's sixth largest metropolitan area and home for more than half the state's population. Massive residential, commercial, and industrial complexes like Michigan's metro represent a special problem for the governments of any state. The problem is one of bringing a degree of coordination and cost sharing to the governmental functions of hundreds of local and county agencies. Michigan's metro is no exception and, in some ways, is a worst-case example.

This region's efforts to coordinate itself date back to the mid-1950s, when the boards of county supervisors, as county commissioners were then called, from Wayne, Oakland, and Macomb Counties formed a committee to discuss common problems and, where appropriate, to plan together. This was a precursor to what came to be known nationally as councils of government, or COGs. In the Detroit area, the council came to be known as SEMCOG – Southeast Michigan Council of Governments – and included, in addition to the original three, Livingston, Washtenaw, Monroe, and St. Clair Counties.[23]

SEMCOG began and remained a voluntary planning and development arm of those area governments that chose to participate and fund it. It was not intended to become a super-government or to deliver municipal services. It was, though, something of a model for the state. Following a report by a special commission in 1972, Governor William Milliken designated fourteen such regions to cover all of Michigan.[24] Later, the legislature began making modest annual appropriations to fund these regional agencies. During the 1970s and early 1980s, COGs thrived on federal grants to conduct studies and administer the A-95 review process for federal grant proposals. The goal of this federal process was to assure that grants in the region supported projects consistent with regional plans. As federal grant programs diminished, however, and as they were converted to block grants under state coordination, the role of the regional agencies diminished. Today they have little influence. SEMCOG was the exception and continues to coordinate the more closely connected local governments of its region.

Coordinating any governmental functions in a region as complex as southeast Michigan is difficult at best. Areawide projects must be negotiated with all the affected governments, and no two governments are affected in exactly the same way. Of concern, of course, are questions of who pays and who benefits. Disputes arise from self-interest as well as from questions of inefficiency and inequity. There are also issues of timing, scheduling, location, service points, rates, and the like. Then there are issues of how to handle existing facilities. For example, the city of Detroit led the area in bus services. When the suburbs formed the Southeast Michigan Transportation Authority (SEMTA), Detroit decided to continue operating its own mass transit, independent of the regional system. The debate over developing a comprehensive transportation system within the region, the form it should take, and deciding how to pay for it continues. Former Mayor Coleman Young's administration advocated a subway system. SEMCOG officials think that a light rail system would be more cost effective. The debate goes on, becoming an issue for the new Dennis Archer administration.

Similarly, the Michigan Department of Transportation (MDOT) bargained with communities for nearly a decade over locating a freeway across southern Oakland and Macomb Counties. The many small cities along the path were concerned that the roadway not divide their communities or destroy neighborhoods and their small commercial centers. Despite SEMCOG's survival, coordinating governmental functions in southeast Michigan hardly provides a textbook example of how things should be done. A mobile "People Mover" public transit system was built in downtown Detroit in the 1980s, but only to serve key commercial interests. The effort failed to generate sufficient operational revenues. Thus, public services in the region remain like a patchwork quilt, widely perceived by public officials not to be examples of governmental efficiency, though usually functional.

The region, however, continues to experience difficult problems. Even in economic recession, the metro expands into undeveloped areas of northern Oakland and Macomb Counties, leaving in its wake a further weakened central city as well as declining inner suburban cities, such as Warren and Inkster. Most serious is the city of Detroit. Crime is high. Much of Detroit's private and public housing stock has become outdated and, in numerous instances, abandoned. While there are some signs of localized rebirth – the downtown area, the renewing theater district, and a few new manufacturing plants – the property-tax and personal income-tax bases have been in sharp decline. To offset the decline, the city and school districts have increased tax rates, an action that adds to the flight of residents and businesses from the city and further weakens local governments. At the close of the 1990 federal census, Detroit's population reached only one million so Mayor Young demanded "a recount." Census Bureau officials reestimated the population to include those missed by the official count. Both white and African-American middle-class residents have fled from the city. This trend, it appears from declines through 1992, will continue as long as crime, poor public education, and a deteriorating bureaucracy and infrastructure remain uncontrolled and poorly managed.

The erosion of the city's tax base and the dependence of its population on public services also affects Wayne County since Detroit constitutes such a large part of the county. In some respects, the impact is even more pronounced on county government because the county bears large portions of the costs of indigent health care and costs for the prosecution and incarceration of criminals and drug addicts. In 1987, the county bordered on bankruptcy largely because of uncontrolled health care costs. Under the direction of County Executive Edward McNamara and with changes in state law, the county regained a degree of financial stability but only through exhaustive budget cuts.

State government has granted some assistance and relief. In 1988, the legislature passed a series of bills to relieve somewhat the county's financial pressures. The state, as a first step in restructuring the state court system, assumed financial responsibility for local courts in Wayne County. The city and county no longer bear the costs of social welfare because the state administers the system. The state also has been appropriating funds to help support the city's cultural facilities, such as the Detroit Institute of Arts and the Detroit Zoo. However, the Engler administration, with its own deficit problems, eliminated or reduced these grants. During the Milliken and Blanchard eras, the state encouraged economic development in the city. Most notably, the state coordinated the Poletown land clearing project for a new General Motors plant. The city and state have collaborated on other projects, as well. Detroiters, though, insist that the state has not done enough. The claim has been louder during the Engler years, although the governor lowered expectations by asking all of Michigan to sacrifice and by reducing the size of state government. Mayor Coleman Young worked closely with Republican Governor Milliken, but relations with Governor James Blanchard were less friendly than might be expected from a fellow Democrat. Given the mayor's criticism of Blanchard, Young remained surprisingly quiet about Engler. Young's first real volley against the governor was in attacking the 1993 ballot proposal on school and tax reform, a plan that Young felt did not bring enough dollars to Detroit schools or other favors to the city.

Some of the initial quiet toward Engler came from Young's and now Dennis Archer's need for state and business cooperation. The policy cornerstone of the Young administration was apartment buildings and office complexes in the downtown core and riverfront. These have been linked by the federally assisted People Mover transit system. In addition, rebuilding efforts have expanded the exhibition center and constructed the hockey arena in the same vicinity. During the early 1990s, hot discussions about building a new facility for the city's American League baseball team were interrupted by the owner's decision to sell the franchise. The main proposal from the city and county was to build a new ballpark near the central commerce area. As a indication of the weakened city and an aging mayor, it was the county executive who took the lead in advocating public backing for the facility. During his first months as owner, Mike Ilitch, a Michigan pizza king and new owner of the Detroit Tigers, was silent about new stadium plans other than to say that the club needs an improved ballpark in downtown Detroit. While the old stadium was refurbished and a new stadium will be built somewhere, Ilitch's tentativeness reflected widespread local suspicions about Detroit's future even among its biggest boosters. When Ilitch later offered to pay for a new downtown stadium, concerns over state and local infrastructure costs still created uneasiness in Detroit.

Like numerous other cities, Detroit has also considered gaming halls as an additional boost for economic revival. Though Mayor Young vigorously supported the proposal, four times voters rebuffed his efforts to bring casinos to the city. The politically important African-American churches and their ministers successfully warded off casino gambling until 1994, when voters finally relented even with the opposition of their new mayor, Dennis Archer. The lights of the Canadian casinos shining across the Detroit River at Windsor were evidence that, one way or another, casinos would be a fact of life in the Detroit area.

Critics argue that renewing the city's core has done little for the city's neighborhoods. They can make a good case. In a survey of one neighborhood, residents complained that 67 percent of the houses were abandoned. In 1992, the U.S. Department of Housing and Urban Development (HUD) seemed to concur. In awarding a $21 million grant to the city, HUD required the city to contract out administration of the grant rather than leave it to the city bureaucracy. A year earlier, HUD publicly criticized the city housing authority for leaving housing grant funds lie idle while nearly half the city's public housing units were vacant and in disrepair. It was not the only instance of the city's inability to respond to community service problems. In 1992, Detroit lost a $475,000 federal grant to provide services to persons with AIDS because the city could not muster program plans to use the money.[25] One city official even suggested that some whole neighborhoods be demolished and then fenced off to prevent vandalism and crime.

Young's strategy, despite these strong negatives, was focused on the long view by addressing the city's essential raison d'être. The mayor, who chose not to run for reelection in 1993, often stated that the metro needs Detroit.

Others express doubts. Both sides have a point. The city began as a trading and shipping center because of its location on the Detroit River. That past fostered the auto industry. Detroit may still be seen as the international automobile capital, but not in the way it once was. Car design, production, and marketing may be guided and directed from Detroit, but manufacturing is scattered around the country and, indeed, the world. The strategy for rebuilding the city, therefore, seems to acknowledge the decline of auto manufacturing by seeking to attract business and commerce of all types, including convention and tourist activity. Given Detroit's reputation, these things are hard to cultivate. At the least, it remains to be seen whether new businesses can generate the jobs and income to stimulate a housing demand sufficient to rebuild Detroit's many crumbled neighborhoods.

Questions often arose, therefore, about Mayor Young's legitimacy in the eyes of his public. For example, after voters rejected casino gambling the third time, Young and his developer allies attempted to turn gambling over to Native Americans so as to avoid the issue of local citizen support. Avoidance, however, was at first rebuffed when Young was forced to place a nonbinding gambling initiative before the city's voters in 1993. It failed, even when sold as a means of promoting minority gains. Young, nonetheless, worked with Governer Engler and business leaders to incorporate the possibility of casinos in a later agreement reached between the state and the tribes to finalize state support of Native American gaming. Hence, polarization grows as numerous interests and regional representatives express disagreement about both the spirit and the achievements of Detroit's costly redevelopment policies. Dennis Archer's campaign for mayor in 1993 played successfully on that theme, allowing him to defeat his Young-endorsed opponent.

Many of the most difficult aspects of both interlocal and state-local relations in Michigan stem from efforts to solve financial problems in Detroit and Wayne County. In the past, the legislature usually made exceptions in what were otherwise statewide policies relating to local governments. For the most part, exceptions provided alternative structural arrangements and local tax policies. More recent patterns, though, have involved state taxing powers as well as state expenditure programs. These have not fared well. Other regions of the state generally have been willing to let Detroit and Wayne County have their way on the organizational and local tax questions. However, in an austere and transforming period, most other state residents draw the line on more central-city aid and insist on sharing in programs that distribute state resources to the city and county. Those dynamics forestalled a more effective role for the Michigan Commission on Intergovernmental Relations (MCIR), appointed in 1988 to study and improve state-local relations. Both partisan and regional differences plagued the commission, and in 1993, it lost its state funding. MCIR was but one example of why Michigan has a potential social and economic disaster in its midst in Detroit, one that the public has no apparent resolve to either tolerate or mitigate.

SOME CLOSING THOUGHTS

Relationships between the state and its local governments, as well as among local governments, are both competitive and cooperative. The relationships are often stressful as governments compete for power and financial resources. Local officials see themselves as being on the front line of providing government services. They assert that their units are closest to the people and more in touch with common needs and how to fulfill such needs. The state, local officials maintain, should either facilitate delivery of these services or desist from interfering with local operations.

State officials, meanwhile, seem to follow Dillon's Rule that local units exist at the pleasure of the state, which, in a strictly theoretical sense, is valid. The state, though, plays a redistributive and equalizing role, taking from resource-rich areas and delivering to the resource poor. In addition, the state exercises an oversight and superintending responsibility. Both sets of tasks are bound to contribute irritants to state-local relationships. Add to that the competition for resources for the state's own use, and state-local relationships are inevitably stressed to their limits.

Relationships among local units, while also competitive and cooperative, are marked more by limited cooperation than by conflict in most areas of concern. Resource problems and budget difficulties have driven them there. School-financing reform and Detroit are the exceptions. In a moralistic state, we seem likely to see demands for greater cooperation and efficiency grow between local governments. Budget problems and revenue declines will mandate change in a state where anti-tax sentiments remain strong. Service sharing will become greater, perhaps more equitable. However, poverty and decay remain sticking points that could undo gains from interlocal cooperation.

CHAPTER THIRTEEN

Problems and Prospects in State Government

THE PROSPECTS FOR CHANGE

We began this book by citing Floyd C. Fischer's exultation of Michigan as the "isolated empire" of rich and abundant resources.[1] While his prose reflected the heady times of the 1950s and 1960s, when American manufacturing drove the world economy and Michigan literally provided the engines, things have changed. One 1992 economic forecast used a mix of resident characteristics, industry characteristics, and business costs to conclude that over the next five years, Michigan would rank forty-ninth among the American states in job growth.[2] Another forecast by Michigan's leading public issues firm predicted a decade of sluggish economic growth and shrinking state revenues.[3]

As the world economy has shifted toward international dependency, the seraphim and cherubim no longer stand guard over the state's industrial corridor. If they did, General Motors would have recaptured its lost shares of the auto market rather than announcing intended layoffs of 74,000 employees by 1995, including the closure of three plants and the dismissal of up to 10,000 management personnel in Michigan. The heavenly chorus that residents now hear – and mostly join – is one that raises its voice for change. Chrysler Motors' recovery to an automobile leader was not enough. Factors that make for that low projection in job growth, many have argued, must be reversed by state government. They simply do not agree on the degree to which change needs to occur, or the mix of variables that bring desired change. The state is in an economic transformation from its industrial dependence on union-organized, highly paid, low-skilled jobs. Even new automotive line jobs require technical skills. That transformation, during the 1980s and early

1990s, has been marked by decline, not just the bust of a boom-and-bust cycle. Moreover, what will happen with Michigan's government and its intertwined economy remains unclear. The only certainty is that political isolationism and pretending that state government can control the world economy will be futile. Otherwise, there are many mixed signals about whether this decline can be reversed and, if so, what governmental changes are needed to facilitate the reversal.

POLITICAL CONSTRAINTS

Politics is an activity in fostering change. Despite the state's long tradition of grass-roots political momentum, no clear opinions exist as to exactly what the public wants in the 1990s. Fragmented interests and regions, as enduring features of Michigan government, give rise to competing ideas of what should be emphasized in political and economic changes. Some regions and interests within them, as a first priority, want controlled and environmentally friendly growth. Others are far more committed to jobs, and they want those jobs to be connected with their own region's distinct manufacturing past. Some losses in the quality of government services and in the environment, to many of these citizens, are worth accepting if they mean more jobs or higher income.

Polls indicate that most of the public is stuck in the middle of those two positions.[4] Jobs and economic growth remain the highest-ranked issues in the state. However, the public also realizes that Michigan's rich natural resources and well-established government services add to the state's attractiveness to employers. Citizens worry about needing a healthy environment, better education, better transportation, and better law enforcement – among other things. The only other issue that holds the citizenry together, and gives clearer policy guidance than the economy, is the disdain for increased taxes. Yet, as individuals, Michiganians often deviate even on taxes, when perhaps a small adjustment upward might help one's favored service. Education has been the best example. But little agreement exists on which services carry statewide value, so the electorate rallies around a generalized no-increase position. Policymakers, in response, are uncertain what to do and whom to follow. Despite Governor John Engler's championing of unemployment insurance and product liability reforms as key parts in his economic agenda, the Republican-controlled senate allowed these reforms to flounder throughout 1992. Yet the presumed experts are most often stuck in the middle over what to do. Analytically, the relationship between jobs, an improved economy, a decent environment, and lower taxes is hard to sort through in a comprehensive plan.

The dilemmas of property tax relief and school finance reform, despite the 1994 success, remain excellent examples of disagreement over the appropriate policy response. The 1992 ballot proposal, championed by Governor Engler, offered a 30 percent reduction in school property taxes and a restricted ceiling on annual increases. In that sense, it lowered the costs of business production and directly addressed Michigan's competitive disadvantage. While all stakeholders agreed on the significance of addressing competitiveness, other factors created opposition. Projections of state revenue losses by critics varied from a half to three-quarters of a billion dollars.[5] For many, such large projected deficits implied service cuts or other compensating tax increases, both of which were feared as driving businesses and citizens away. These critics pointed to Michigan's existing patterns of economic growth as a warning. Firms were not merely seeking inexpensive sites, which could have included downtown Detroit, for their operations. Business executives, such as those who planned the move of Chrysler Motors headquarters to the far northern suburbs of the metro, also sought quality-of-life amenities in job sites.

All of the dominant characteristics of Michigan's politics come into play when a policy question like school tax reform illuminates competing views about economic growth. Not only are a bewildering array of professional opinions and reports brought out for display, but the uncertainties in any plan for economic recovery also give rise to vigorous and opportunistic political contests involving both the state's active parties and many of its well-organized interests. On the "cut and cap" proposal, Republicans rallied to the importance of lowering taxes. Democrats warned of other tax hikes and of chaos in the state economy and its services. Yet there was considerable reluctance and much foot-dragging among partisans who held public office.

Engler had to speak publicly against the opinion of his state treasurer, who was one of his most trusted political insiders, and also against his state director of education, a recently hired, showcase appointee with whom the governor identified quite closely on issues of education policy. Democrats, however, found no greater solidarity on their side. Numerous Democratic legislators and candidates found it impossible to speak against such a cut in rural and suburban districts where anti-tax sentiment was especially strong. Even the Speaker of the house, Lewis Dodak (D-Birch Run), found constituent support for "cut and cap" impeding his ability to attack the proposal with great enthusiasm.

Those partisan cleavages and often regionally inspired splits only intensified interest-group politics. The State Chamber of Commerce, seeking to solidify further its growing importance in state politics, emerged as the proposal's chief advocate. The Michigan Education Association led a multi-interest coalition, Advance Michigan, in opposition. MEA, fearing a loss in school revenues and, thus, the loss of increased teacher salaries at bargaining tables, was also motivated by gains to be made in its state reputation. But these would be won only if its actions could strengthen faltering Democratic resolve against "cut and cap." With such mixed messages in front of them, Michiganians followed their normal inclination to vote against ballot proposals.

The dynamics of school tax reform were important less for their specifics than for what these responses revealed about the complexities of Michigan politics. Unlike in many of the American states, no partisan machine or "good ol' boy" network exists to rally behind a relatively popular governor to propel a proposal of statewide importance.[6] Governor Engler found increased opposition and disagreement on "cut and cap" and other issues even as his popularity in the polls was increasing. His approval rating, which never went up much above 50 percent, increased fifteen percentage points from November 1991 to July 1992. Despite growing public perceptions of his good job in office, he was still vulnerable to several likely electoral challengers.[7] By 1994, four Democratic challengers with considerable political experience were running against him. This surprised many. As a transplanted out-of-state lobbyist acknowledged, "In this state, you cannot get away with telling people to support your boss because he's both popular and the guy in charge. That was an astonishing lesson to me."

That observation summarizes our biggest worry about Michigan's ability to deal effectively with its economic future. Citizens and legislators depend on Michigan governors to take the lead in resolving statewide problems. On questions of the economy, though, governors face severe limitations and an often fleeting set of followers. The economy, in the first place, is not seen as only a statewide matter. Regional demands enter in. As Governor James Blanchard discovered, a coherent and well-focused package of economic development goals can be suddenly stretched into an extensive array of pork-barrel items. The politics of Michigan's modern era, post-1950, has been one of balance and a tendency to be exceedingly generous in its policies and programs, given its resources.

The political conditions that create that balanced and generous pattern of distribution are influential parties, influential interests, strong legislators, and localized regions with different needs. All are out to win, and they will continue to press for their goals in the future. Saying "no" to any of them is a challenge. Unless the public offers better and more unified cues to what they want than they did in the 1980s, or unless economic analysts can agree on a policy approach that is generally accepted as correct, things appear bleak. It appears, under those conditions, that no modern governor can offer overly assertive leadership on issues of the economy. No one will want to be forced to repeat "Soapy" Williams's sad lament, that he moved too far ahead of his constituents and found himself gone.

Fortunate Resource Conditions

Individualistic features of Michigan's political landscape suggest that state government may not work well on issues of economic recovery. Particularly troubling was the contentious laugh of one 1992 candidate for the state house from northern Michigan as he reflected on General Motors' just announced white-collar labor reductions: "Now those high-rollers in Birmingham and Bloomfield Hills can share the pain." At the same time, however, the state's past traditions of decline and resurgence provide us with competing expectations. We also see, historically, a larger set of macrolevel dynamics. In a macropolitical sense, as judged by the overall adjustment of the state's political economy to changing conditions, Michigan has shown a remarkable ability to succeed after each collapse. While Bruce Catton wrote principally of the carnage of prodigal wastage, as the state exhausted one resource after another, he also revealed Michigan's recurring capacity to adjust.[8]

The state has repeatedly used a new resource base to prosper after an old one was depleted. Michigan has reversed economic decline before – as furs, wildlife, lumber, and mining each gave out. There are also three sets of indicators that suggest a degree of foolishness in betting against Michigan. All start, as did Fischer's euphoric litany, with an emphasis on state resources and the circumstances surrounding them.

First, plentiful resources are available. Not only is the state bounded by one-fifth of the world's fresh water supply; lumber and assorted extractive and tourist industries still contribute significantly to the state's economic base. In an international economy faced with resource problems, Michigan could convert at least some of these resources to its competitive advantage. Moreover, despite the permanent demise of low-skill employment, the central strength of the economy is its manufacturing sector and associated new technologies. Building on that sector, with both its large corporations and new array of smaller firms and its related service industries, remains more than possible. The state, after all, produces more manufactured goods than at least two-thirds of the world's two dozen largest industrial nations. The state's modernization of that sector, moreover, outpaces all but just a few of those national economies – most notably Germany and Japan. Even firms from those countries have established offices and cooperative ventures in southern Michigan to gain from the technological capital of the region. Results showed in economic gains for the state by mid-1993.

Second, manufacturing's use of resources need not be seen as narrowly regional and divisive. Manufacturing-dependent counties, where 30 percent of generated revenue is industrial, are found not only in southeastern Michigan and the Grand Rapids area but also in counties located throughout both the east and west coasts of the northern lower peninsula and in the Upper Peninsula as well.[9] Moreover, manufacturing aspirations remain high in parts of all three regions. While relatively different industries dominate in each location, those patterns provide the strategic base for thinking about manufacturing as Michigan's leading industry on a statewide basis.

Political leadership, by emphasizing statewide manufacturing dependency, could go far in muting regional disagreements about development strategies. A skilled leader could rely on familiar regional vote trading. Cooperation would entail considerable legislative and local community involvement in formulating policies to promote and supplement a manufacturing strategy for integrating the state. Local investments would certainly be demanded, and needed, for developing the infrastructure, transportation systems, and jobs training. Nonetheless, these would be more efficient investments than those seen in the ever-expanding Blanchard packages, where nearly every tourist provider and crop producer became eligible for some state-supported subsidy. This leadership could be advantaged by pointing to recent growth in all the adjacent rustbelt states of the Midwest.

Third, resource use generally lacks the militant opposition in Michigan that exists elsewhere. Despite a uniquely strong state Environmental Protection Act and a history of progressive environmental policy, environmentally conscious manufacturing firms and their cleaner technologies would find the state a more compatible home than many other places. If the state could ensure freedom from excessive costs and nuisance suits under MEPA, firms could gravitate to Michigan with greater assuredness.

One of the two reasons for Michigan's lack of militancy lies in the organization of the state's environmental lobby and the unique statewide constituency from which it evolved.[10] Even without a statewide economic development vision to challenge their cooperation and their brokerage skills, that lobby has been moderate in its demands. As one legislator noted, "There are few of the real crazies here. Our environmental activists are inclined to be thoughtful and politically skilled people." The federated governing structure of the Michigan United Conservation Clubs is one important reason. M UCC's structure certainly creates numerous environmentally active groups in this state, such as bear hunters and dog owners, by mobilizing them on behalf of the state's ecosystem.

That interest-group structure also restrains extremist positions of both the "go-slow" and "go-fast" persuasion. Presently, M UCC members almost always refrain from attacking other members, and they also are relatively careful not to offend many of the economic views of the diverse range of members who populate affiliate clubs. In addition, the political prominence and visibility of M UCC squeezes more extreme environmental groups out of both Lansing politics and from media coverage. For example, the activities of Greenpeace have long been ignored in Michigan as those of the extremist fringe. The more moderate Sierra Club, whose state organizations dominate the environmental agenda of many states with no-growth proposals, plays a role in supporting M UCC.

The other reason for relatively moderate state politics concerning resource use lies in the orientation of most state environmental programs. Despite the long list of regional complaints, the Department of Natural Resources has worked as well as possible to foster state development. Environmental use dominates its programs, with the emphasis on use. Both state officials and interest-group leaders appear responsible for the tone; yet there has never been any systematic debate on philosophies of resource stewardship in Michigan. The state's handling of its Great Lakes fishery provides an excellent illustration. Michigan pioneered most of the recovery of the lakes as an economically viable industry. In restoring the fishery, Michigan broke ranks from the onset with the efforts of federal and other state rehabilitation efforts.

That split was astonishingly pronounced.[11] Where the federal government had sought to restore natural reproduction of lake trout, Michigan perpetuated its fishery through as extensive a hatchery-release program as the forage base would allow. The difference is not subtle. When resource managers meet, the main debate has been between Michigan and everyone else.[12] Michigan's fish managers, like their other resource colleagues in the state, are interventionists, committed to creating desirable changes through science. In effect, Michigan's environmental managers generally respond to the development and use goals of those who pay their salaries. Accordingly, with the Great Lakes fishery, they emphasize several species of fish. They also promote put-and-take techniques, which get as many fishers as possible on the water and vacationing in Michigan. The prevailing philosophy elsewhere is to restore a native species, the lake trout. Restorationists portray intervention as dangerous ecological tinkering and want to rehabilitate old habitats and original occupants. They are not focused on development and use – or on political responsiveness.

This fisheries approach is revealing for what it demonstrates about Michigan politics. In the public policy sector, as a whole, the prevailing emphasis has been on how the state and its people can best use their natural resources while also sustaining them for future generations. Government has long been interventionist, from the point in the nineteenth century where it encouraged lumbering and the construction of ports. The same attitude applies to influential state conservation supporters. When Walter Ruether spoke of his fondness for northern Michigan, he emphasized its usefulness to UAW members for rest and recreation.

Even with the state's surge of environmental awareness and its increasingly strong regulations, it seems that Michigan would only most reluctantly leave its interventionist ways behind. There is likely to be no serious debate over this, even though some continued expectation of future environmental degradation must be taken as a given.

Some environmentalists find that position objectionable and no doubt will make themselves heard in future policy decisions. The chances of their prevailing over policymakers who seek to balance jobs and the environment are minimal, especially when economic hardship confronts the state. Governor Engler's science advisory board only facilitates this moderation, as does his mostly completed reorganization of the DNR. The board allows careful consideration of long-term options, with the corresponding opportunity to look comparatively at the most desirable state responses. The ability of policymakers to frame environmental policy solutions in different ways, from regulatory standards to abatement subsidies, will help the state adjust to and accommodate much of the environmental agenda.[13] Michigan's interventionist and user-oriented approach will still encourage environmental policy gains, but those gains are unlikely to be as incompatible with manufacturing as the gains in states where restorationists achieve political control or where a highly prominent disaster looms.

The moralistic political culture, as the factor that sets the state's macropolitical mood, seems the direct reason. That culture appears to be what

Michiganians fall back on when it comes time to reorder micropolitical conflicts into more favorable macropolitics. While no panacea, Michigan's political culture brings the state several favorable attributes that are useful in wrestling with its uncertain future.

THE EFFECTS OF A MIXED POLITICAL CULTURE

The cumulative effects of political culture are nearly impossible to measure. Nonetheless, they are observable, especially in generalizing about the overall responsiveness of the state and going beyond the minute details of its politics. Two points seem especially clear about the state's cultural legacy.

As noted in chapter 1, Michigan has followed a consistent if imperfect goal of moralistic inclusion. State officials have generally searched for encompassing policies and rules that eventually favored everyone. This reflects a strong public commitment to the well-being of the state. However, this does not mean the state is a liberal place, or one that provides only collective goods to be used equally by all citizens. Rather, the moralistic culture is concerned, first, with a balanced view of the public welfare and, then, a relatively balanced distribution of government benefits. Those balances play out in some share of most policies for everyone, yet allowing regions and interests to pursue different wants. Of course, under such circumstances, the threads of a more individualistic culture were impossible to stop from spreading in the state.

Michigan's predominantly moralistic but mixed culture, in consequence, provides no guarantees of equitable treatment and satisfaction of all needs. This is why its attributes have not been such an obvious part of daily politics. The distribution of who gets what is and has been decided only after intense conflict linking ideologies, parties, interests, issues, and candidates. This process, as it airs information, means a distinct moderation of state politics – but not because all contenders accept each other's wants and seek to help one another. They simply take it as a political given that benefits for all will be forthcoming from whatever total budgetary appropriation the state can afford.

This means, by necessity, that state politics will be intense, rancorous, and deeply divided over what seems fair. It also means that all available funds will be spent, and perhaps overspent, and that tax cuts will be hard to make. That political process will also appear ponderously slow to those desiring immediate change. The question of revenue availability for the budget must be – as it long has been – the central point of contention in all periods of even minor economic change. Many state activists, intervening on behalf of the disadvantaged, have long argued for higher taxes and redistribution of wealth. During periods of economic growth, they won. They did so – and narrowly – only by linking support for the disadvantaged with the provision of more government programs beneficial to other economic classes.

When the comparatively high taxes that sustained high levels of services for all became widely viewed as a drag on the economy, the expectations that underlay the state culture did not change. From the late 1970s and through the present, Michigan politics often seemed meanspirited as budget pressures intensified. It has been impractical to argue for some greater protection of programs benefiting the core of the state's disadvantaged than for others. Services for all types of citizens are institutionalized in modern state government, just as austere measures were once the governing rule of thumb for Michigan under malapportioned rural domination. Consequently, the budget cuts of the 1980s and 1990s did not entail much redistribution because there were few self-sacrificers. All users of government services, including the poor, faced losses. Most residents supported the process, even if they disliked the results.

That balancing process, despite its general acceptance, has nonetheless furthered hostility and sometimes intense animosity as the state, in its own way, has followed moralistic determinants. Detroit is only the best example, not the only one. However, these animosities were not new. They were apparent even in the entry of new forces to state politics during Michigan's manufacturing heydays. For example, it took years for the state to provide political representation to its exploding southeastern industrial corridor and its blue-collar work force. In the 1950s it did, though, and the United Auto Workers then used its emergent power to reshape much of state politics.

The politics of race has been similar. Too many intervening years went by before the state recognized that African Americans were a significant part of its population. While racism and its effects have been little mitigated, and while poverty and unemployment persist by race, African Americans now compete ably if not always equally for a share of the state government pie. They have since the early 1970s. In the eyes of most of those who set the political pace for Michigan, the empowerment of the UAW and the recognition of an African-American share were acceptable. Some were ecstatic. To those who lost influence and control over public programs, and especially to many of those who were taxed by these "intruders," acceptability was grudging at best and always perceived as too extreme. Regional tensions became more resolute.

These and other newcomers to state politics have been no less aggrieved. Their progress has been tedious, blocked repeatedly, and, for labor and African Americans, marred by riots and violence. Laws had to be changed to ensure equality, and securing change was harder than defending the status quo. Events surrounding the passage of new laws often had little to do with the need for union or African-American justice, but everything to do with obstructionism.[14] Moreover, when their representatives did gain legitimacy, the same political culture that eventually forced the opponents of unions and African Americans to acquiesce also created reversals. Hopes for a liberal laboratory for social democracy, whether they were UAW led in a Williams era or African-American led in a Milliken era, made only limited progress. The self-perceived needs of the activists and those they represented, as a result, were largely unrealized. "In both cases," reflected a labor leader of the 1950s and 1960s, "we won recognition but we lost the battles. The state never gave us, except very briefly, any more real assistance than anyone else. And our people, workers and blacks, seemed to have real problems that other state residents did not." Thus, following changes, the winners and losers found increasing antagonism within the state's moderately balanced politics. Compromise between haves and have-nots was never easy but grew even harder. There likely will never be an enthusiasm for redistributive public policy in the state, as demonstrated by the neglect of Michigan's Native Americans and their retreat to federal courts.

If a moralistic culture fails to hasten change, lessen the antagonisms of individualism, and remove feelings of inequality, where does it contribute? That question is the vital one for Michigan if, as we suggest, such a culture is the state's key for setting the mood in regenerating its economy. What we are suggesting is that, despite Michigan's fortunate history, the next recovery is always culturally dependent, at least in part. The explanation is simple.

Economic policy success, as it involves state politics, is dependent on avoiding a future that further sharpens distinctions between Michiganians. Acute distinctions lead to an emphasis on micropolitical conflicts, which bar collective commitment to capitalizing on commonly held resources. Should the state's fostering of manufacturing and technology become embroiled in intense battles between regions and among state interests, progress toward increased jobs will bog down. A no-growth philosophy of resource use would encourage further gridlock. Unlike the UAW and African Americans, manufacturing interests will not linger angrily in Michigan. Their mobility in light of competition from other states and nations precludes their being held in place. They will locate elsewhere, continuing the trend of the past several decades.

So we have an answer to our question of where the state's moralistic culture contributes and why. It does so by emphasizing constructive resource use on behalf of all claimants in the state. It possibly mutes the destructive urges of the state's competing and now intense individualistic co-culture. The moralistic culture of Yankee forefathers, it must be remembered, emerged under conditions of prodigal wastage. Yet what political culture contributes, it can also take away. Political culture will have a decidedly hard time being of use in the future unless all claimants get on with the business of agreeing to what each needs from state politics, or unless a strong leader finds a way to encourage that cooperation. Given the depth of disappointments in state politics, neither task will be easy.

THE STRUCTURE OF MICHIGAN GOVERNMENT

Michigan's handling of its economic future is quite different from that of other states where undeveloped and antiquated institutions prevail. Oklahoma is an excellent example, with its balkanized and independent county governments on one hand and its more than two hundred state agencies on the other.[15] Governors there found the idea of leadership, as expected in Michigan, well nigh impossible on even executive branch issues. Michigan's modern governor, in contrast, is supported by a strong but professional legislature, a relatively streamlined and very policy-attuned bureaucracy, and a universe of state interests that has largely escaped "good ol' boy" politics. Government is also clean and honest. Moreover, its competing political parties provide alternative visions of where the state should go on most issues, yielding citizens both a choice and plentiful information with which to decide.

Indeed, if the prevailing pattern of United States government, with its democratic separation of powers and its checks and balances, will work anywhere, then this pattern should work in Michigan. It remains quite popular, in fact, to describe Michigan's governmental structure and patterns of open political participation as a near mirror of the U.S. government. Washington lobbyists who also work Michigan often make such remarks. Some see "a microcosm of Capitol Hill, with the same degree of professional government found in the best federal agencies and the [lobbying] offices of K Street." Others remark that Michigan is better: "The state's level of professionalism is uniformly high, but the difference is that all segments of Michigan state government get nearly equal treatment. In Washington, there are more obviously second-ranked agencies and third-rate committee seats."

Room for structural improvement exists, of course. Greater agency consolidation and improved accountability from legislative committees are at the top of the list. It would be hard to conclude, though, that such reforms in an already quite modern government would significantly improve the performance of state government. In particular, those reforms would not address the crucial problem of what James Madison called the "mischiefs of faction."[16] The lack of strong gubernatorial control found in the separation of powers, as Madison predicted for the United States, means that factions wreak havoc with the state's moralistic commitment to the common good.

Factionalization, by region and by organization, meets the strong suit of the legislature as well as the spirit of the state's partisanship. Both are perfectly attuned to partially satisfying and at least actively representing every claimant. As a consequence, rewarding each faction with an education facility, a recreation program, or some piece of an economic development package has become a way of life in Michigan politics. In short, the ongoing search for balance leads to excess. This pork-barreling goes on regardless of what issue comes to the state's agenda. In that sense, the great diversity of the state – by place, by economic sector, and by ethnic origin – puts factionalized mischiefs in a higher-stakes game than they are in states with either greater homogeneity or less of an openly activist and competitive tradition. Quite simply, there are many opportunities for diverse interests to win in Michigan.

What this translates to in a highly professionalized state is the increasing utilization of greater resources on behalf of specific constituencies: "We seem to want a university in every city, a prison in every region, and economic development money for every city and county." Staff keep their legislators better attuned to the district. Policy experts in the agencies are torn between following the governor, emphasizing neutrality, or being broadly representative in their service. Lobbyists, in judging their own professionalism, rank themselves according to their ability to broker among the most individualistic forces in state government.

What exists in state politics, therefore, is largely a paradox. While the efforts to professionalize and modernize government have been carried on in the best moralistic traditions, the effects have been to lessen commitment to statewide policies and agendas. If anything, furthering moralistic attachments to the good of the entire state by selectively rewarding each of its components has expanded that segment of the state political culture that practices individualism.

The independence of the Michigan voter was as pronounced as ever in 1992, with a high turnout of more than two-thirds of registered voters and considerable ticket-splitting. Voters showed sophisticated issue concerns that reflected the broad interests of Michigan. President George Bush lost by a wide margin, 7 percent, to Arkansas Governor Bill Clinton. At the same time, Bush's state spokesperson, Governor Engler, showed increased popularity in polls and in support for his endorsements in state house races. Bush was blamed for ignoring domestic job losses while, to most Michigan voters, Engler was addressing those issues as well as lowering the costs of government. His administration proudly noted Michigan's spending cuts in 1991, a year when thirty other states raised taxes. Voter criticism of Democrat Clinton, nonetheless, was extensive for his support of higher automobile emissions standards and, ironically, along with Bush and Engler, support of the North American Free Trade Agreement. Both proposals were feared as likely to cost more Michigan jobs. Within the Democratic party, former Commerce Director Doug Ross was winning converts as he traveled the state speaking about his own economic strategies. The popularity of his message grew as he proposed capitalizing on the state's strengths. The fact that he denied political aspirations helped his appeal. Meanwhile, House Speaker Lewis Dodak, who was Engler's most visible statewide opponent, lost a close election in his home district.

That mixed assessment of old chief executives and potential new ones was accompanied by no further postprimary turnover in Michigan's congressional delegation, with a final tally of ten Democrats and six Republicans in the House of Representatives. Democrats won each district in which they were competitive. Turnover in the Michigan house was high, but of the twenty-seven new members, only six defeated incumbents. In a stunning shift, five Republican candidates each won by less than four hundred votes. Their party gained five seats and a 55–55 split in the house. One Democrat won by seven votes after a closely watched recount. Gains were strong for Republicans outstate, even where Clinton did well. Republican gains were attributed, by officials of both parties, to the governor's popularity on the jobs issue and to his appeals for legislative majorities to break the partisan impasse. Increased Democratic votes in many districts showed that enthusiasm to be regional and far from uniform, however. In particular, many aging

Democratic voters in blue-collar areas, such as Macomb County, returned to their own party after years of voting for President Reagan, Governor Engler, and conservative legislators. But Republicans still carried that old labor enclave and others like it in the suburbs. Archconservative David Jaye was comfortably reelected from Macomb County to the state legislature. In short, electoral signals were as mixed as they can get in this ticket-splitting state.

Ballot proposals, or referenda votes, had promised to be of great interest to the state's political future, even though they did not help prioritize the service preferences of the public or show what the public wanted in the battle over jobs and the environment. In the end, voters proved little, other than that Detroit, metro, downstate, and outstate voters were divided by the politics of place. The "cut and cap" property-tax proposal, linked closely to the governor, failed by 18 percent. So, too, did a Democratic proposal to limit annual rates of increase in property taxes. An insurance reform proposal also failed because of a suspicious electorate. Largely because the proposal was sponsored by the insurance industry, Michiganians voted not to cut their automobile insurance rates in return for reduced awards in court settlements. One important proposal passed – the amendment limiting the terms of members of Congress, the state legislature, and the four elected statewide offices. That result was widely seen as a blow against big government, for continued change, and for a reduced role for professional politicians. Or was it a blow for the state's always important political amateurs and a reassertion of the constitution's "We, the people" principle? Many newly elected Republican legislators endorsed term limits during the election, but it was also a proposal with national appeal. During the 1992 election, thirteen other states passed similar referenda.

Overall, the 1992 election was reminiscent of the citizenry's no-tax-hike theme as it had been articulated by one anti-tax activist: "Be against it if you can't feel good about anything else." In this case, with "cut and cap," Michiganians failed to support even a property-tax cut, with most opposing voters not believing that lost funds for schools would be replaced as promised from general revenues.[17] In fact, several local anti-tax groups campaigned against both proposals, holding out for a better deal later.

Issues of manufacturing jobs and high taxes were at the forefront in an indirect way. Unlike other states, however, the referenda allowed Michiganians to seize some degree of personal control even in the absence of a specific prescription. They failed to do so. What the referenda indicated was that, statewide, voters favored change and distrusted the status quo. Outstate and in the suburbs they were willing to give Engler an opportunity to succeed on tax reform, state school aid, and insurance-rate legislation. In other words, they provided an electoral message that, despite some regional splits, provided Michigan government with a rare chance to see if it could work better without divided government. With a Republican governor, a Republican senate, and a divided house numbering at least six conservative Democrats, Engler's agenda seemed within range. Even though Republicans and Democrats agreed to share the house Speaker's job and all committee chairs, there was little that Democrats could do to tie up the governor's proposals permanently. Thus, Republicans were on notice to produce economic improvement quickly. Engler, in the face of that challenge, remained optimistic: "It's easier to break legislators of their regional habits when there is no budget fat. And we certainly face lean conditions in solving our problems."[18]

That optimism was soon broken by events that at first seemed positive for the governor. First, his leadership was advantaged by a postelection analysis that found the budget $370 million in deficit. This made Engler's demands for reform and spending cuts easier to accept. The March 24, 1993, closing of northern Michigan's Kalkaska public schools, and warnings of serious financial problems in several other districts, contributed to a sense of urgency. Meanwhile, in the transition to a new house leadership, bipartisan investigations found improper use of House Fiscal Agency funds under the old Democratic guard. While former Speaker Lewis Dodak received some criticism, Representative Dominic Jacobetti took most of the blame because the agency was under his direct control and because payoffs were made over several years to some of his closest associates. House Democrats quickly removed Jacobetti from his powerful Appropriations Committee chairmanship. Even though the chair was now shared with Republicans, Jacobetti's ouster removed a major obstacle, along with many of his friends, blocking Engler's agenda. The scandal episode closed with confessions and prison time for several participants.

These circumstances led to an emergence of bipartisan cooperation greater than any seen in Lansing since the Milliken years. Insurance reform passed, even though negotiations on its immediate effect were bitterly divided and opponents filed petitions for a second vote on the issue. With Republican house pressure on the governor, several contentious items were wrapped together for solution. Property-tax cuts, a cap on their future growth, a 2 percent sales-tax increase, a statewide minimum per pupil expenditure of $4,800, a reduction in school-tax millage, and guaranteed school district retiree payments were combined. This combination squarely linked quality education to job creation through property-tax reduction. Because of the sales-tax inclusion, the package was required to be presented to state voters in a constitutional referendum.

Engler's leadership and bipartisan legislative support brought those old enemies, the Michigan Education Association and the State Chamber of Commerce, together with a coalition of businesses and school districts. At the outset, the governor indicated a strong possibility, "60 percent," of passage. The former Milliken and Blanchard state education director, Phillip Runkle, was recruited to direct what he proclaimed to be "the mother of all millages." However, the public proved a hard sell, which seriously undermined the spirit of future state cooperation.

The United Auto Workers, Detroit Mayor Coleman Young, and an assortment of Macomb and Oakland County taxpayer groups were the only forceful opponents. While they were outspent approximately thirty to one for campaign ads, their opposition proved formidable. In particular, they argued that the agreement could not be trusted to prevail in legislative implementation, that business was the primary beneficiary, and that metro-Detroit schools would lose in the bargain. Despite polls that showed the proposal leading until the week of the election, those arguments won. Voters, according to those same polls, did not believe the promised revenues would go to education: "Remember the lottery." Proposal A, as it was called, was defeated 54–46 percent, with the "yes" vote winning only 5 percent more than won by supporters of "cut and cap."

Proposal A lost by nearly three to one in the three metro-Detroit counties while handily winning in most outstate counties. Other eastern, industrial-corridor counties narrowly voted against the proposal, which indicated continued UAW influence and a hardening of cynicism among labor voters: "Our members are believing less about government's performance daily." The defeat also meant an impediment to both coalition building and bipartisanship. As a legislator explained, "There was a high price to pay for that cooperation, and we got nothing for it. It's back to Robin Hood plans, tax fights, and an escalation of this particular regional battle that Proposal A began." For Governor Engler, and what only months earlier seemed like his secure policy agenda, it meant a very uncertain political future.

This uncertainty led to a most unusual solution. Democratic Senator and gubernatorial candidate Debbie Stabenow proposed, and Engler accepted, the idea of eliminating school-operating property taxes by the 1994 school year – with no prospect of restoring the old plan. This provided the benefit of minimizing regional battles in any piecemeal reform of educational policy.

With the old rules gone, and a funding deadline in view, the political costs of transacting change were lowered. In July 1993, the house agreed, 69–35, and the senate provided an even larger endorsement, 34–5. With that, the legislature and governor finally passed a reform package for more equitable funding and some changes in school operations.

With lawmakers operating under a self-imposed Christmas 1993 deadline, the solution almost proved to be a worst-case scenario of Michigan politics. Once again, a tax plan required an all-night session of the legislature. Any sense of bipartisan cooperation was lost, though, and the political process failed to present Michiganians with even a vague sense of steady policy direction. Worse yet, in a March 1994 special election, the public was forced to choose between two tax plans to make up for lost school revenues, and polls indicated that voters understood neither.

A plan endorsed by Engler and most Republican lawmakers went to the electorate to raise the sales tax to 6 percent by constitutional amendment. It also restored part of the school property tax for homesteads and all of it for businesses. But, a statutory fall-back plan was to go into effect if this new Proposal A failed. Most Democrats, with the fall elections in sight, favored this alternate raise in the income tax, from 4.6 to 6 percent. It restored twice as much of the property tax on homesteads as did Proposal A. The battle was not only partisan. Interest-group cooperation fell apart, particularly because their leaders worked legislators and the governor to include numerous other tax increases and exemptions in each plan. For example, farm property gained the homestead rate.

The Michigan Education Association and organized labor led opposition to Proposal A. But they were backed by a quirky partner – up to $4 million in advertising came from national tobacco interests trying to avoid Proposal A's stiff cigarette tax increase. Once again, anti-tax groups opposed the plan. Most state business interests favored A, as did Detroit's new mayor Dennis Archer. Because the sales tax increase favored business competitiveness, most state papers endorsed it. But an intense three-week-long media blitz was hailed by Michigan political observers as the most misleading campaign they had seen. The more heavily funded anti-A forces were critized the most for implying that the electorate could avoid change by voting "no."

There were two results. First, public cynicism intensified, even though the sales tax won by a huge margin. Second, this new Proposal A passed, 70–30. Once again, outstate voted overwhelmingly "yes" and, by a two to one margin, Detroit said "no." Other metro areas were split. Nonetheless, Governor Engler had his long-promised property tax cut and a huge personal victory, more than double the amount that he promised. But he also faced declining support in the polls in the months prior to the referendum and after the property tax cut. In the wake of electoral confusion, he also lost much of the public's faith that Michigan would follow his promised policy direction. It really was more of the same old squabbles.

A FINAL CLOSING THOUGHT

We are only cautiously optimistic about Michigan's political and policy future and, therefore, its economic future. The 1992 elections seemed to create a mandate repudiating politics as usual. Numerous interests and partisans responded, in ways that many state political observers felt impossible. After all, the public still wants, and the state still needs, decisive action to enhance Michigan's economy.

Yet the ballot questions of 1993 and 1994 clouded that positive outlook. The 1993 proposal brought numerous major players together but bifurcated the state in a way not recently seen in Michigan history. School-financing reform, while resolved, did not heal that split. It was more like the 1950s than the 1980s. Only on one dimension was it worse: the public was openly cynical about government. Voters also demonstrated their reluctance to follow the majority opinions and leadership of the state capitol. Few state interests and policymakers sought or hoped for defeat in 1993. Institutions that were both numerous and flexible enough to enable policymakers to work together to formulate a planned approach did not produce their desired ends.

The results made cooperation difficult in 1994 and onward. Who wanted to ask constituents for sacrifice? As "Soapy" Williams found, even in the heyday of the state's moralistic culture, policymakers cannot afford to get too far ahead of those who decide their fate. In what is now a more individualistic state, can policymakers lead at all? They can, but only if they cast their coalition nets wide and with a common purpose. Perhaps Senator Joanne Emmons phrased it best one day after the 1993 proposal's defeat. In opening the senate with its daily prayer, she added, "Now we come to You as always, somewhere there is a solution." She was right. Too often, though, as in the following months, Michigan fails to find one that gives any semblance of unity. Meanwhile, the state prepares for the next contest as former Congressman Howard E. Wolpe seeks the governorship.

Resources for the Study of Michigan Politics

Theodore M. Rusesky and Leo F. Kennedy are the
principal authors of this chapter

LIBRARIES AND ARCHIVES

Those wishing to study Michigan government and politics can tap the holdings of several libraries and organizations. The Library of Michigan, an agency of the Michigan legislature, is a complete source of information. Its books, pamphlets, newspapers, government documents, and journals constitute a thorough collection on Michigan's history and government. The Library of Michigan also prepares a number of publications designed to help a researcher find materials and makes available many other materials through its designated depository libraries located throughout the state and the country. The Library of Michigan, now housed in the spacious new Michigan Library and Historical Center in Lansing, has been the official distribution center and clearinghouse for Michigan documents since 1843. Documents published by Michigan state departments are distributed to sixty other designated depository libraries, including forty-eight libraries within the state. Exchanges are also maintained with state libraries in California, Illinois, Indiana, New York, Ohio, Pennsylvania, and Wisconsin.

The Michigan Documents Collection of the Library of Michigan includes all available state government publications issued since 1805. This collection, now containing over 100,000 items, is an excellent resource for both historical and current information. An ongoing project is to catalog all of the Michigan documents held by the library. When completed, the 33,000 periodical publications, 12,000 books, and 500 maps in the library's Michigan Documents Collection will be accessible by subject, title, agency, department, and series name through a computerized online catalog, which is available to remote researchers through microcomputer modem dialing. In addition, all documents processed since 1966 are listed in *Michigan Documents*. Now distributed in paper format, the publication is arranged by issuing agency, call number, and title. The *Michigan Magazine Index,* published from 1967 to 1991, provides selective subject and author indexing for articles about Michigan that appeared in more than 170 state and regional periodicals.

While the academic libraries of Michigan's colleges and universities are excellent sources for information, the public libraries of Michigan's major cities are also useful. Many city libraries have strong local collections that include official documents and records of local governments, pamphlets or books on local history, and indexes to local newspapers. Libraries in Battle Creek, Bay City, Lansing, Flint, Grand Rapids, Detroit, and Saginaw are excellent sources for such information as the records of city council, school board, or county commission meetings. County and city budget documents, local history and genealogy materials, and photo collections are among the other types of resources available at these facilities. Some of these libraries are also Michigan State Document Depository Libraries.

Some researchers may wish to use primary resources – letters, memoranda, unpublished reports, or private manuscripts. The official repository for records of enduring value that are created or received by state and local government agencies is the State Archives of Michigan, a section of the Bureau of History, Michigan Department of State. It is located in the Michigan Library and Historical Center. There are also regional archival depositories located at Western Michigan University's East Hall, Oakland University's Kresge Library, the Burton Historical Collection at the Detroit Public Library, Central Michigan University's Clarke Library, and Michigan Technological University's Van Pelt Library. In addition, the State Archives itself serves as a regional center. These regional depositories have collections of county government records and private manuscripts.

Included among the 80 million documents in the State Archives are evidentiary materials – documents dealing with policy development – and informational records – documents of a more general nature, such as a listing of Michigan veterans of World War I. The State Archives also has one of the best photo and historical map collections in the state. None of these materials can be circulated or accessed through interlibrary loan. Staff archivists will attempt to respond to inquiries by telephone or letter, but, in most cases, the researcher must visit the archives to review documents. Published in 1977 by the Department of State, *A Guide to State Archives of Michigan: State Records* lists the holdings of the State Archives.

All three branches of state government are represented in the State Archives. Executive branch records include those of the governor's office and the various departments and agencies. However, only governors prior to G. Mennen Williams placed their public (but not all their private) papers in the State Archives. Legislative branch holdings consist of records from both the house and senate, including committee records. The State Archives has a strong collection of house standing committee records beginning with 1970. Senate standing committee records begin in 1980. In addition, audiotapes of the house sessions are available (the senate does not record sessions). Records and other materials relating to the work of special legislative committees or task forces are also available, though these are often difficult to trace. An increasing amount of material from the judicial branch is also being deposited in the State Archives.

The private manuscripts of individuals and organizations constitute another smaller part of the holdings of the State Archives. The largest nongovernmental collection concerns the Cleveland-Cliffs Iron Company, a prominent mining firm that has long been active in the Upper Peninsula. The State Archives also houses a collection of nearly 500,000 maps and over 300,000 photographs reflecting such activities as lumbering and mining, Great Lakes shipping, and Michigan community scenes.

Other sections of the Bureau of History can also be helpful. The Publications Section oversees the distribution of *Michigan History Magazine* and a variety of other materials, such as *Traveling through Time: A Guide to Michigan's Historical Markers*. Those interested in historical preservation may wish to review the files of Michigan sites listed in the National Register of Historic Places and the State Register of Historic Sites. Research in the collections of the Michigan Historical Museum located in the Michigan Library and Historical Center may also be undertaken, but only with the written permission of the director of the museum.

Michigan boasts other outstanding archival centers as well. Established in 1935, the Bentley Historical Library at the University of Michigan in Ann Arbor is a nationally renowned archival center. A wealth of materials on Michigan politics and public policy is available in the library's Michigan Historical Collections. In contrast to the State Archives, the Bentley Library is devoted to collecting private materials. Included among its holdings are the records of the state Democratic and Republican parties and the private papers of twenty-eight Michigan governors, the most prominent U.S. senators and U.S. representatives from Michigan, leading Michigan legislators, and other individuals and groups that have influenced the course of Michigan political history. The library's collection on the temperance movement and prohibition is particularly strong, as is the collection of materials relating to minor political parties.

Two other archival centers on the University of Michigan campus, one dealing with pre-twentieth-century materials and the other with more recent times, may also be useful. The William L. Clements Library contains a comprehensive collection of primary materials dealing with early American history, from the voyages of Columbus to the mid-nineteenth century. Its collection includes books, manuscripts, maps, prints, broadsides, and newspapers written or published at the time of the events with which they deal. The greatest strength of the Clements Library is in the general areas of American military, political, religious, and exploratory history before the middle of the nineteenth century. A superb source for a variety of materials relating to Americana, it has an extensive collection of drawings and sketches depicting life in that era.

A presidential library administered by the National Archives and Records Administration, the Gerald R. Ford Library, was opened in 1981. This library's holdings include former President Ford's congressional, vice-presidential, and presidential papers. It also has the files of more than one hundred White House advisers and staff assistants. The material on Republican party activity is particularly strong. About 60 percent of the presidential files are open to the public, and additional material is opened for research (sometimes following declassification) as it is arranged, reviewed, and described by library archivists. The audiovisual holdings include 283,000 photographs, 750 hours of videotapes, 700,000 feet of film, and 2,100 hours of audiotape. In recent years, the breadth of the collection has grown to include additional information on political affairs and domestic and international economic policy. The Gerald R. Ford Museum, also part of the library, is located in downtown Grand Rapids.

There are two premier archival resources located in the city of Detroit. On the campus of Wayne State University is the Walter P. Reuther Library of Labor and Urban Affairs, the official depository for nine major international unions. Because of organized labor's involvement in political, social, and economic causes, the archives also include the private papers and records of politicians, civil rights and community leaders, and other organizations. In addition, the Reuther Library has an extensive audiovisual collection consisting of hundreds of thousands of photos, motion pictures, slides, posters, memorabilia, and nearly 5,000 audiotapes. More recently, the Reuther Library has begun to collect information on urban affairs, and the facility also serves as the official archives for Wayne State University. Oral histories are used extensively to supplement the archival collections, which total more than 50,000 linear feet.

The Burton Historical Collection, a special department of the Detroit Public Library, provides research material for the study of the history of Detroit, the state of Michigan, and the Old Northwest Territory. It also has a genealogy section for all of the United States and parts of Canada. The facility serves as the official repository for the archives of the city of Detroit as well. The Burton collection includes the Local History Index, Great Lakes Index, Genealogical Index, and Biography Index. This collection includes extensive vertical files, a picture and map collection, and a number of private manuscripts of individuals, including former Detroit mayors and other local politicians. The Biography Index, for example, is a catalog file that includes cards indexing biographical information on prominent Detroiters and Michiganians from newspapers, books, periodicals, and the other vertical files.

Another good archival resource is the Michigan State University Archives and Historical Collections in East Lansing. Encompassing a broad range of interests, the holdings include more than 950 collections of various organizations and individuals and contain materials that can be useful in studying such topics as the history of lumbering and agriculture in Michigan and the early growth of the automobile industry. There is a fine collection of materials from and following the Constitutional Convention of 1961–62. This facility also serves as the official archives for the university.

The Clarke Historical Library, located on the campus of Central Michigan University in Mt. Pleasant, maintains a collection that has grown to include more than 70,000 volumes, thousands of maps, photographs, other graphic materials, and a large manuscript collection. The major focus is on the history of Michigan and the surrounding states of the Old Northwest Territory. There are extensive materials on the history of slavery, the lumbering era, and presidential candidate biographies. This library also has a sizable collection of materials from Michigan counties, townships, and cities.

A researcher should also keep in mind that other cities, as well as other colleges and universities, may have useful collections, most of which will deal with regional development and individuals. The *Directory of Historical Societies, Agencies and Historic District Commissions in Michigan,* published by the Historical Society of Michigan, provides a list of other such archival sources.

REFERENCE MATERIALS

As a book that claims to be "of ready reference to every student in the political history of the mother State of the lake region of the country," the *Michigan Manual* is an indispensable tool containing information on state government, public officials, colleges and universities, and election results. This publication – sometimes referred to as the "Red Book" or "Legislative Manual" – has been published every two years since Michigan's admission to the Union. Serving primarily as a resource handbook for the legislature from 1836 through 1957, the book's earlier editions include material relative to the conduct of legislative business. Beginning with the 1959 volume, the manual's focus shifted to that of being an official state manual. Recently, responsibility for this publication has been returned to the legislature and, beginning with the 1989 edition, the manual is published by the Legislative Service Bureau under the supervision of the Legislative Council.

By consulting the current volume of the *Michigan Manual,* the researcher can find the text of the state constitution as well as a table reflecting the vote on ballot proposals to amend the constitution. There are brief biographies of the state's public officials, descriptions of components of the executive branch, including various boards and commissions, and such other information as the "Report of the State Treasurer's Common Cash Fund." Older volumes can be equally valuable. Information on state finances, Michigan's railroads, and various agricultural, manufacturing, and mining statistics appear in these earlier editions. The biographical sketches are not only helpful in garnering personal information on public officials throughout the state's history, but they can also be entertaining in that they reflect the rich prose of a bygone era. A helpful aid in locating biographical information in the *Michigan Manual* is the *Biography Index to the Michigan Manuals, 1923–1973.*

The legislature and its agencies generate a great deal of material. While not verbatim transcripts of session activity, the journals of the house and senate contain the record of official action taken on measures. A typical journal includes the record of daily attendance, reports of standing committees, messages from the opposite house, proposed amendments, action taken on Second Reading or General Orders or Third Reading, roll call votes on the final passage of bills, votes on procedural motions made during debate, motions and resolutions, executive orders and messages from the governor and other state officers and agencies, "no vote" explanations, statements made under personal privilege, notices, and information on the introduction, printing, and enrollment of bills.

Analyses of pending legislation are prepared by the Senate Fiscal Agency Legislative Analysis Unit, the House Legislative Analysis Section, and, on numerous occasions, by state departments and agencies that may be affected by legislation. Some libraries have compilations of bill analyses from past sessions, which generally begin with the 1975–76 biennium (though some analyses from the late 1960s are available).

The Legislative Service Bureau, a nonpartisan agency that provides bill drafting, research, and other services to both houses of the legislature, produces a number of useful materials. In addition to publishing the *Public and Local Acts of the Legislature of the State of Michigan, Michigan Compiled Laws,* and the *Michigan Administrative Code,* the LSB publishes the *Michigan Legislative Telephone Directory* and annual summaries of public acts in cooperation with the house and senate analysis agencies. Published monthly since 1984, the *Michigan Register* is designed to fulfill the same function for the state that the *Federal Register* does for the federal government.

Among the other excellent legislative publications that a researcher may wish to use is the *Michigan Legislative Handbook,* containing information on legislators, committee assignments, the rules of the house of representatives, the senate, the joint rules, and the state constitution. This pocket-sized publication is issued biennially by the secretary of the senate and the clerk of the house. *A Citizen's Guide to State Government* and the *Michigan Taxpayer's Guide* are abbreviated volumes distributed at state expense by individual legislators. Another directory that merits attention is the *Michigan Government Directory* prepared by Public Sector Consultants. An advantage of this directory is that it contains information on voting records as well as biographical information. Old issues of the discontinued *Capitol Profiles* are useful for similar purposes.

A considerable amount of economic, statistical, program, and comparative budget and revenue information is compiled, primarily by the house and senate fiscal agencies, in support of appropriations decision making. This information is in addition to that provided by individual departments and agencies or the Department of Management and Budget. The fiscal agencies offer a variety of reports, including comparative summaries of departmental appropriations and analyses of the governor's budget recommendations. The Senate Fiscal Agency offers subscriptions to its *Notes on the Budget and Economy, Michigan Economic Indicators,* and *Budget Status Report* publications. This agency's annual *Statistical Report* contains a variety of tables and graphs that present current and historical data relative to the state budget. The agency also issues annual reports dealing with the governor's budget recommendations, state spending by county, and enacted appropriations measures.

Once an elective officeholder of the executive branch, the auditor general became part of the legislative branch with the adoption of the constitution of

1963. The auditor general, assisted by a staff of professionals, is now responsible for postaudits and performance postaudits of all branches, departments, offices, agencies, authorities, and institutions of the state established by the constitution or by law. The auditor general also conducts a number of specific audits and reviews as required by other laws. The resulting audit reports provide a continuing flow of information to assist the legislature in its oversight of state agencies. It is a key source for detailed information on specific programs and agencies.

The departments and subunits of Michigan's executive branch generate a wide variety of publications. Some of these are issued on an annual or semiannual basis and can generally be accessed through the depository libraries designated by the Library of Michigan. Because of the nature of their distinct administrative responsibilities, some departments are more prolific in producing such publications. This material, which can be identified by using *Michigan Documents,* is so voluminous that it would be impossible to comment on all of it. There are, however, some very useful categories of information that demand attention.

Most departments and a number of subunits issue annual reports, which can provide more detailed information on a particular department or agency, its programs, and its expenditures. However, some annual reports are issued sporadically and not always on schedule.

Many departments prepare and distribute periodic newsletters or similar publications designed to keep their own employees, as well the public, informed about a number of developments. Departmental newsletters include the *DSS Digest* (Department of Social Services), *Civil Service Focus,* and the *Michigan Civil Rights Commission Newsletter.* Other publications include *A.I.M.,* published by the Office of Services to the Aging and *The MESC Employment Report,* prepared by the Department of Labor.

The Department of State is an especially important source of information, particularly its Bureau of Elections. As the most centrally located source of voting statistics, the elections bureau issues the official canvass for general, primary, and special elections. Depending upon the election, the official canvass may contain voting statistics on federal offices; state executive, legislative, and judicial offices; and state ballot proposals. The data are available on registration and on voting precinct bases. In addition, statistics are available on registration and on voter turnout. More general information on voting statistics is in the *Michigan Manual,* which contains voting data similar to those published by the Secretary of State. The Department of State also has responsibility for regulating the state campaign finance law. It is possible to obtain information concerning funds acquired and expended by political action committees, candidates, and committees from the Bureau of Elections. A third area of election law responsibility is the registration and compilation of lobbyists and the collection of information on how much money they spend. The Bureau of Elections also issues *The Polling Place,* a publication designed to keep local officials abreast of the latest developments in election law.

Statistical information also abounds. *The Michigan Labor Market Review* is published by the Michigan Employment Security Commission (MESC). Similar statistical analyses for labor in various regions of the state are also issued by MESC. The Agricultural Statistics Service prepares various statistical materials. The Office of Highway Safety Planning issues *Michigan Traffic Accident Facts,* which is compiled annually by the Department of State Police.

Decisions of the Michigan Supreme Court and Michigan Court of Appeals are published in *Michigan Reports* and *Michigan Appeals Report,* respectively. However, these publications do not include all decisions handed down by these courts. Circuit and district court opinions have little or no binding effect outside of their respective circuit or district, although the Ingham County Circuit Court is sometimes an exception because it decides cases involving state agencies. At any rate, copies of circuit and district opinions can be obtained only through the clerk of the court or court reporter and can be relatively expensive. The *Michigan State Courts Annual Report,* published by the Office of the Court Administrator, provides a comprehensive look at the state's court system. In addition to a description of the various courts and support agencies and a listing of judges, the book contains a host of figures and tables that present comparative and analytical data on court filings and information on the activities of the Attorney Discipline Board, Attorney Grievance Commission, Judicial Tenure Commission, and State Appellate Defenders Office. The Office of the Court Administrator also publishes *The Statistical Supplement,* which provides detailed statistical figures on each court's caseloau.

Some departments produce material that can serve as general reference tools. For example, the Department of Education issues several annual bulletins, such as *Analysis of Michigan Public Schools Revenues and Expenditures, Five Year Summary of Expenditure Data for Michigan Public Schools,* and *Michigan K-12 School Districts Ranked by Selected Financial Data.* In regard to the state budget, the Department of Management and Budget (DMB) publishes the *Budget Message of the Governor* and *Comprehen-*

sive Annual Financial Report of the State of Michigan. The DMB also prepares the *State of Michigan Telephone Directory,* which contains number
listings and addresses for all universities, employee organizations, and
Michigan's congressional delegation. The phone directory also reveals the
organizational structure of executive departments. Prepared every two
years, *Elective and Appointive State Officers, State of Michigan* lists the
members of boards and commissions, judges of the state, and various county
officials. DMB's Office of Health and Human Services prepares the *Michigan State Health Plan* and has issued reports on such topics as use of hospitals, health-care costs, and the supply of physicians in the state.

The Department of Treasury's Taxation and Economic Policy Office has
prepared comprehensive analyses of Michigan's property taxes, sales tax,
single business tax, income tax, and tax increment financing. These analyses present basic tax data, including some comparative figures from other
states, and discuss the current issues concerning each tax. This office also issues the *Tax Expenditure Appendix* to the *Executive Budget,* which provides
information on the tax revenue foregone because of exemptions, exclusions,
or deductions from the tax base, and credits or preferential tax rates.

Several publications produced by state agencies deal with women's issues. Members of the legislature have prepared booklets such as *Women on
Michigan Boards and Commissions, A Historical View of Michigan Women
in the Legislative Process,* and *Laws and Programs to Assist Minority,
Women, and Handicapped Entrepreneurs. Women on Michigan Boards and
Commissions* provides data on the gains that women have made in membership on state boards and commissions over specific time periods. Published
by the Michigan Women's Commission, *Michigan Women* is an annual publication that contains short articles and status reports on state and federal legislation affecting women, as well as such other things as gubernatorial appointments of women.

Secondary Sources

Some of the best resources for information on Michigan politics can be
found in the newspapers of the state. A listing of newspapers in the *Michigan
Manual* displays each paper's place of publication, its publisher, and the frequency of its distribution. Generally, newspaper coverage in Michigan is local in nature. While there is no central place where all current newspapers
are available, the *Detroit Free Press* and the *Detroit News* are available at
college or university libraries and at most local libraries. The Library of
Michigan receives more than forty current newspapers from other cities, in-

cluding Lansing, Flint, Jackson, Grand Rapids, Marquette, Muskegon, Battle Creek, and Alpena. Older issues of these and hundreds of other papers are available on microfilm.

Newspapers on microfilm are identified in the ongoing electronic catalog prepared by the Library of Michigan and are available for use at the library or via interlibrary loan within the state. The Library of Michigan also has an extensive newspaper clipping file that dates back to 1955. Subject file clippings of the *Detroit News* and *Detroit Free Press* are available from the library on compact disc (CD-ROM). Full texts of newspapers are available other ways as well. The *Detroit Free Press* is available on CD-ROM from Dialog (a fee-based online service) retrospective to 1988. The CD-ROM of the *Detroit News* is available from Newsbank beginning in 1992. The full text of the *Detroit Free Press* since 1988 is available on Dialog.

Access to newspaper articles is available through indexing services. The *Detroit News Index* (title varies) offers coverage retrospective to 1976. Dialog provides indexing and abstracting of the *Detroit News* and *Michigan Chronicle*. The data from 1984 to 1988 are in the database file *Newspaper Abstracts,* and data from 1989 to present are in the file *Courier Plus.* There are additional indexes in paper form from some other Michigan newspapers. Only three are currently published: *Kalamazoo Gazette, Lansing State Journal,* and *Grand Rapids Press.* These and other newspaper indexes are described in *Michigan Newspaper Index* at the Library of Michigan. Of particular interest is the state's major African-American paper, *The Michigan Chronicle.*

Many university and local libraries can provide access to the *Michigan Compiled Laws* and annotated compilations prepared by two private publishers, West's *Michigan Compiled Laws Annotated* and *Callaghan's Michigan Statutes Annotated.* Several law reviews also may prove useful. The University of Michigan publishes the *Michigan Law Review* and the *University of Michigan Journal of Law Reform.* Other law reviews are the *Detroit College of Law Review,* the *University of Detroit Mercy Law Review, The Wayne Law Review,* the *Thomas M. Cooley Law Review,* and the *Michigan Bar Journal.* These law journals are indexed in the *Index to Legal Periodicals* and in the *Legal Resource Index,* a microform service which is also available on Dialog. CD-ROM versions are Wilsondisc and Legaltrac.

Although issued only intermittently, reports produced by university research bureaus cover a wide scope of topics. Wayne State University, through its Center for Urban Studies and the Bureau of Business Research, issues topical and statistical reports on Michigan. As part of the U.S. Census

Bureau's State Data Center Program, the Michigan Metropolitan Information Center in the w s u Center for Urban Studies is the official Michigan processing center for machine-readable census data. The center has issued reports containing 1980 census profiles on Michigan senate and house districts. In 1987, it issued a statistical profile on how the Detroit area has changed since 1967. Another current processing center is the Michigan Information Center (mic) in the Michigan Department of Management and Budget. mic produces custom research products using census data in paper and diskette formats and on maps. Although it focused more on economic issues, the former Bureau of Business Research issued reports on topics ranging from county income patterns to the Detroit economy. The bureau also published the *Michigan Statistical Abstract*.

Although the series was discontinued, papers and pamphlets issued by the Institute of Public Administration at the University of Michigan have become classics in the study of Michigan state and local government. The Institute of Public Administration was reorganized in 1968 into the Institute of Public Policy Studies. Most of the work by the Institute of Public Policy Studies is national in scope, but a number of the working papers prepared by the staff deal with subjects that focus on Michigan politics and government.

A national and international focus is present in much of the data available through the Institute for Social Research's Inter-University Consortium for Political and Social Research at the University of Michigan. However, the information available in the Detroit Area Study collection can be useful for data on attitudes and actions of residents in the Detroit area. This annual survey has been conducted by the University of Michigan since 1951. A variety of topics have been examined, including metropolitan and neighborhood problems; social problems and social change in Detroit; activities and attitudes of party leaders at the county, district, and precinct levels; and racial attitudes, community issues, and political participation. There is also some survey data of outstate rural residents.

A number of institutes at Michigan State University also have prepared reports focusing on Michigan governments. The Cooperative Extension Service and the Agricultural Experiment Station publish short pamphlets on such subjects as community development, the law, local government, and leadership development. Although somewhat dated, reports prepared by the Social Science Research Bureau or its predecessor in the 1950s and the 1960s, including *The Michigan One-Man Grand Jury, Guide to Michigan Politics,* and *Politics and the Press,* merit attention. The office of Community Development Programs, now assigned to the Department of Resource

Development, has issued a number of guides to local government in Michigan, including the *Guide to Michigan County Government, Managing the Modern Michigan Township,* and the *Michigan Local Property Tax Primer.* The Institute for Public Policy and Social Science Research also has been working on Michigan-specific projects.

Many private organizations prepare reports, pamphlets, and newsletters and offer a great deal of insight into political developments. Public Sector Consultants annually publishes *Michigan in Brief: An Issues Handbook,* which presents a discussion on the major issues facing the state at a given period. For over seventy years, the Citizens Research Council of Michigan has prepared some informative reports on public policy issues. The League of Women Voters of Michigan has also issued various brochures and pamphlets. Somewhat new to the scene is a newsletter entitled *Inside Michigan Politics,* edited by William S. Ballenger, which presents a "newsy" approach to national, state, and local political developments of importance to Michigan. In the same vein, Gongwer News Service's *Michigan Report,* issued five days a week, contains an excellent summary of legislative, judicial, and executive actions in Michigan's capital. The *Hannah Report* and *MIRS Legislative Report* provide similar but often different coverage of issues and events.

Some interest groups prepare useful newsletters, including the Michigan Hospital Association, the Michigan AFL-CIO, the Michigan Municipal League, the Michigan Education Association, and the Michigan State Chamber of Commerce. Michigan is also fortunate to have two excellent history journals. *Michigan History,* a popular glossy publication, is published by the Department of State. *The Michigan Historical Review* is issued by Clarke Historical Library, Central Michigan University. The Historical Society of Michigan, which cooperates with these journals, also publishes a bimonthly magazine entitled *Chronicle.* From time to time articles on Michigan politics appear in the *Michigan Academician.* These articles are refereed by the Michigan Academy of Science, Arts, and Letters.

A good deal of statistical information on Michigan government and politics is available from several sources. An excellent collection of basic statistics on Michigan is found in the *Michigan Statistical Abstract,* which was last published in 1987 by the Bureau of Business Research at Wayne State University. This publication contains information on a wide scope of subjects, ranging from election results to government finances and employment to demographic statistics. The abstract cites the sources being used and may lead a researcher to additional information. For comparative purposes,

States in Profile by State Policy Research, Inc., presents state-by-state rankings and national averages in the areas of demographics, economics, taxation and finances, and other selected topics.

Universities have begun to collect large sets of electronically accessible data on Michigan's economy, government, and people. Michigan State University's Institute for Public Policy and Social Science Research (formerly the Center for the Redevelopment of Industrialized States) has collected a wide array of materials, with one data set containing information on Michigan counties; another consisting of entries for all fifty states, the District of Columbia, and a national total; and a third consisting of data on Michigan cities and townships.

The University of Michigan's Research Seminar in Quantitative Economics (RSQE) engages in forecasting and creating computer models from which predictions about the Michigan economy can be formulated. The RSQE model has been used to generate projections on state employment, personal income, and state tax revenues. Also at the University of Michigan, the Institute of Labor and Industrial Relations has developed two models that may be helpful in studying Michigan's economy. The institute has developed a short-term (two to three years) econometrics substate model that can be used to examine specific industries by SMSAs. It also has a long-term model that can be used to conduct an economic impact analysis of a structural change in Michigan's economy. The latter model has often analyzed the effect of a major industrial plant moving into the state or the effect of a major federal project on the state's economy.

Eastern Michigan University's Institute for Community and Regional Development produces semi-annual economic forecasts for various regions in the state. Researchers may also be able to draw on databases from the University of Michigan's Institute for Social Research. Although most of the data are again national and international in scope, data sets in any number of areas, from legislative roll calls to mass political behavior and attitudes to community and urban studies, are available. Users must work through a university that is a member of the Inter-University Consortium for Political and Social Research.

Although a nonprofit agency, the W. E. Upjohn Institute for Employment Research in Kalamazoo conducts research on the causes and effects of unemployment and measures to alleviate unemployment. Much of its work is national in scope, but this agency has conducted research on unemployment insurance and workers' compensation in Michigan. The institute also uses a regional model which utilizes a combination of input-output and time-series analysis to assess the factors contributing to the growth or decline of five southwestern Michigan regions.

In recent years, there has been a quantum leap in the use of public opinion polls by candidates for federal, state, and local offices. Public opinion firms located both within and outside of Michigan do polling work for candidates and party organizations. Candidates and party organizations may be somewhat reluctant at certain times to share polling data, but one should not be shy in asking for such compilations. Persistence may unveil a gold mine of information. The *Detroit News* and *Detroit Free Press* contract with polling firms to conduct polls before primary and general elections reflecting voter preferences on both candidates and ballot proposals. These excellent sources may provide the only polling data available on many subjects.

The primary sources for information on how Michigan legislators have voted are the journals of the senate and the house of representatives. Through the journals, specific votes or a set of votes on a number of issues can be identified. In addition, the Department of Political Science Polimetrics Lab of Michigan State University has coded breakdowns on tape for all senate and house of representatives roll calls between 1945 and 1965 and will supply this information at cost. From time to time, an article may be published which examines roll call voting in the Michigan legislature. The only major effort in this regard, however, was that conducted by the late Vincent Hauge along with Spencer A. Hill of Michigan Technological University. For a number of years during the mid-1980s, Hauge and Hill prepared a series of reports entitled *Major Issues in Michigan Politics*.

SOME CONCLUDING THOUGHTS

Michigan is fortunate in having exceptional public and private facilities that provide useful information for researchers. In addition, the variety of materials and publications that may be useful continues to grow as both governmental and private-sector agencies introduce new publications. However, those interested in research should not overlook the value of actually talking to the policymakers and public officials who must deal with important issues every day. Not only can individual interviews supplement other information, but on occasion they can be crucial to determining what happened on a particular issue or in an election. At any rate, the people, places, and things that are the keys to analyzing the political developments and issues of this state are plentiful.

SELECTED DOCUMENTS AND SOURCES

Capitol Profiles. Lansing: Capitol Publications (biennial, but no longer published).

Chronicle. Ann Arbor: Historical Society of Michigan (bimonthly).

A Citizen's Guide to State Government. Lansing: Michigan Legislative Council (biennial).

Thomas M. Cooley Law Review. Lansing: Thomas M. Cooley Law School (three times yearly).

Detroit College of Law Review. Detroit: Detroit College of Law (quarterly).

Directory of Archives and Manuscript Repositories in the United States. Washington DC: National Historical Publications and Records Commission, 1988.

Directory of Historical Societies, Agencies and Historic District Commissions in Michigan. Ann Arbor: Historical Society of Michigan, 1988.

A Guide to the Archives of Labor History and Urban Affairs by Warner W. Pflug. Detroit: Wayne State University Press, 1974.

A Guide to the Michigan State University Archives and Historical Collections by Frederick L. Honhart, Suzanna M. Pyzik, and Saralee R. Howard. East Lansing: University Archives and Historical Collections, Michigan State University, 1976.

A Guide to the State Archives of Michigan: State Records by Valerie G. Browne and David J. Johnson. Lansing: Michigan History Division, Michigan Department of State, 1977.

The Hannah Report by Joe Goedert. Lansing: Hannah Information Systems (five times weekly).

Index to Legal Periodicals. Bronx NY: H. W. Wilson Company (monthly).

Inside Michigan Politics by William S. Ballenger. Lansing: Inside Michigan Politics (biweekly).

Major Issues in Michigan Politics by Vincent Hauge and Spencer A. Hill. Houghton MI: Politics Press of Michigan, 1984 and 1986.

Michigan Academician. Ann Arbor: The Michigan Academy of Science, Arts, and Letters (quarterly).

Michigan Administrative Code. Lansing: Michigan Legislative Service Bureau (revised periodically).

Michigan Appeals Reports. Rochester NY: Lawyers Cooperative Publishing Company (from 1965 on).

Michigan Bar Journal. Lansing: State Bar of Michigan (monthly).

Michigan Compiled Laws. Lansing: Michigan Legislative Council (revised periodically).

Michigan Compiled Laws Annotated. St. Paul MN: West Publishing Company (from 1948 on).

Michigan Documents. Lansing: Library of Michigan (quarterly).

Michigan Government Directory. Lansing: Public Sector Consultants (biennial).

Michigan Historical Review. Mt. Pleasant MI: Clarke Historical Library, Central Michigan University (quarterly).

Michigan History Magazine. Lansing: Bureau of History, Michigan Department of State (bimonthly).

Michigan in Brief: An Issues Handbook. Lansing: Public Sector Consultants (biennial).

Michigan Law Review. Ann Arbor: The University of Michigan Law School (eight times annually).

Michigan Legislative Handbook. Lansing: Michigan Secretary of the Senate and Michigan Clerk of the House (biennial).

Michigan Magazine Index. Lansing: Library of Michigan (quarterly).

Michigan Register. Lansing: Michigan Legislative Service Bureau (monthly).

Michigan Report. Lansing: Gongwer News Service (five times weekly).

Michigan Reports. Rochester NY: Lawyers Cooperative Publishing (from 1843 on).

Michigan Statistical Abstract. Detroit: Bureau of Business Research, Wayne State University (biennial, but no longer published).

Michigan State Courts Annual Report. Lansing: Office of the Court Administrator (annual).

Michigan Statutes Annotated. New York: Clark, Boardman and Callaghan (from 1936 on).

MIRS Legislative Report. Lansing: Michigan Information and Research Service (five times weekly).

Public and Local Acts of the Legislature of the State of Michigan. Lansing: Michigan Legislative Service Bureau (annual).

State Policy Data Book. McConnellsburg PA: Brizius and Foster (annual, but no longer published).

States in Profile. Birmingham AL: State Policy Research, Inc. (twice yearly).

The State We're In. Lansing: League of Women Voters of Michigan (revised periodically).

University of Detroit Mercy Law Review. Detroit: University of Detroit Mercy School of Law (quarterly).

University of Michigan Journal of Law Reform. Ann Arbor: University of Michigan Law School (quarterly).

The Wayne Law Review. Detroit: Wayne State University Law School (quarterly).

Notes

CHAPTER ONE

1 Floyd C. Fischer, *The Government of Michigan* (Boston: Allyn and Bacon, 1966), p.9.
2 Many of these data are taken from F. Clever Bald, *Michigan in Four Centuries* (New York: Harper and Row, 1961), pp.475–76.
3 The Hudson Institute, *Michigan beyond 2000* (Indianapolis: The Hudson Institute, 1985).
4 Bruce Catton, *Michigan: A Bicentennial History* (New York: W. W. Norton, 1985).
5 See also *Roger and Me,* a movie about the closing of auto plants in Flint. Michael Moore produced the film in 1989.
6 Daniel J. Elazar, *American Federalism: A View from the States,* 3d ed. (New York: Harper and Row, 1984), pp.135–36. Also see John Kincaid, ed., *Political Culture, Public Policy and the American States* (Philadelphia: ISHI Press, 1982).
7 Wilbur Rich chronicles the network of black political leaders in Detroit in *Coleman Young and Detroit Politics: From Social Activist to Power Broker* (Detroit: Wayne State University Press, 1988).
8 William Kornhauser, Harold L. Sheppard, and Albert J. Mayer, *When Labor Votes: A Study of Auto Workers* (New York: University Books, 1956).
9 Charles Press, "The Reagan Block Grants: Implementation in Michigan," in Marilyn Gittell, ed., *State Politics and the New Federalism* (New York: Longman, 1986), pp.215–30.
10 U.S. Advisory Commission on Intergovernmental Relations, *Significant Features of Fiscal Federalism,* vol.2 (Washington DC: ACIR, 1992), p.268.

11 Comparison by Lynn Harvey, Department of Agricultural Economics, Michigan State University.

12 *Detroit News,* November 4, 1990, p.14A.

13 Walter DeVries and V. Lance Tarrance, *The Ticket-Splitters: A New Force in American Politics* (Grand Rapids MI: William B. Eerdmans, 1972).

14 Thomas E. Cronin, *Direct Democracy: The Politics of Initiative, Referendum, and Recall* (Cambridge MA: Harvard University Press, 1989).

15 William P. Browne and Delbert J. Ringquist, "Michigan Interests: Diversity and Professionalism in a Partisan Environment," in Ronald J. Hrebenar and Clive S. Thomas, eds., *Interest Group Politics in the Midwestern States* (Ames: Iowa State University Press, 1993), pp.117–44.

CHAPTER TWO

1 Two studies that are useful in looking at state politics from a geographical perspective are Daniel J. Elazar, *Cities of the Prairie: The Closing of the Metropolitan Frontier* (Lincoln: University of Nebraska Press, 1986); and Janet E. Kodras and John Paul Jones III, ed., *Geographical Dimensions of United States Social Policy* (London: Edward Arnold, 1990).

2 Jon Gjerde, *From Peasants to Farmers: The Migration from Balestrand, Norway to the Upper Middle West* (New York: Cambridge University Press, 1985).

3 Jeremy W. Kilwar, *Michigan's Lumbertowns: Lumbermen and Laborers in Saginaw, Bay City, and Muskegon, 1870–1905* (Detroit: Wayne State University Press, 1990).

4 Oliver P. Williams and Charles R. Adrian, *Four Cities: A Study in Comparative Policy Making* (Philadelphia: University of Pennsylvania Press, 1963).

5 Daniel J. Elazar, *American Federalism: A View from the States,* 3d ed. (New York: Harper and Row, 1984).

6 Information provided by state demographer Ching-li Wang, 1991.

7 William P. Browne, "Political Values in a Changing Rural Community," *Policy Studies Review* 1 (August 1982): 55–64.

8 Charles Press, "The Reagan Block Grants: Implementation in Michigan," in Marilyn Gittell, ed., *State Politics and the New Federalism* (New York: Longman, 1986), p.218.

9 Lynn M. Daft, "The Rural Poor," *Policy Studies Review* 1 (August 1982): 65–71.

10 John Kincaid, "From Cooperation to Coercion in American Federalism: Housing, Fragmentation, and Preemption, 1780–1992," *Journal of Law and Politics* 9 (Winter 1993): 333–430.

11 For example, Northern Michigan University in the UP received $5,627 per stu-

dent in state aid while the three regional schools of the lower peninsula averaged $3,636 per student in aid. Wayne State University in Detroit got $7,918 per student (1990 figures). Senate Fiscal Agency, "Higher Education Appropriations Report," 1991.

12 Elazar, *American Federalism,* pp.135–36.

13 Ibid.

14 Peter V. McAvoy, "The Great Lakes Charter: Toward a Basin-Wide Strategy for Managing the Great Lakes" (draft of paper for presentation at the Great Lakes Legal Seminar: Diversion and Consumptive Use, Cleveland, 1985).

15 Nancy Webb Hatton, "The Plot to Steal the Great Lakes," *Detroit News,* special edition, November 28, 1982, p.15.

16 Richard Oakland, "Sister Relationships Build Trust – International Trade, Too!" *Michigan Municipal Review* 66 (July 1988): 202–3.

17 Ivo D. Duchacek, ed., "Federated States and International Relations," *Publius: The Journal of Federalism* 14 (Fall 1984 – entire issue); John Kincaid, "State Offices in Europe," *Comparative State Politics Newsletter* 6 (August 1985): 22–28.

18 Interview with state senate leadership by William P. Browne as research for chapter 9.

19 Kenneth N. Bickers and Robert M. Stein, *Federal Domestic Outlays, 1983–1990: A Data Book* (Armonk N Y: M. E. Sharp, 1991).

20 Richard E. Cohen, *Washington at Work: Back Rooms and Clean Air* (New York: Macmillan, 1992).

21 Quotations in this paragraph are from comments made to Browne in personal interviews, December 1990. Nonetheless, in federal affairs, Michigan governors have acted as leaders. See Marshall Kaplan and Sue O'Brien, *The Governors and the New Federalism* (Boulder C O: Westview Press, 1991).

22 "How States Share Federal Dollars," *Governing* 1 (June 1988): 56–57.

23 Ibid.

24 Information provided by the Michigan Department of Education, 1988.

25 A state survey of the seven-county southeast Michigan region saw a 44 percent increase in "chronic" or structural unemployment in the 1980s, a situation where workers were unable to find jobs after fifteen months of unemployment assistance.

26 Howard Tanner, Mercer H. Patriarche, and William J. Mullendore, *Shaping the World's Finest Freshwater Fishery* (Lansing: Michigan Department of Natural Resources, 1980).

27 These are direct expenditures in sportfishing. Indirect, multiplier expenditures as a result of sportfishing were $1.2 billion. Doug Jester, Michigan Department of

Natural Resources, and Ed Mahoney, Michigan State University, supplied these data.

1 Daniel J. Elazar and John Kincaid, "Covenant and Polity," *New Conversations* 4 (Fall 1979): 4–8; Daniel J. Elazar, "The Principles and Traditions Underlying State Constitutions," *Publius: The Journal of Federalism* 12 (Winter 1982): 11–25.

2 See the list of important claims in state constitutions for points of comparison in Elazar, "Principles and Traditions," pp.24–25.

3 See Charles Press and Kenneth VerBurg, *States and Communities in the Federal System,* 3d ed. (New York: HarperCollins, 1991), pp.95–96.

4 Willis F. Dunbar and George S. May, *Michigan: A History of the Wolverine State* (Grand Rapids MI: William B. Eerdmans, 1980), p.648.

5 Ibid, p.651.

6 For a detailed analysis of the changes made in the 1963 constitution in light of the 1908 constitution and its amendments, see Melvin Nord, "The Michigan Constitution of 1963," *Wayne Law Review* 10 (Winter 1964): 309–67.

7 The U.S. Supreme Court sanctioned the use of juries of less than twelve and as few as six in criminal proceedings. See *Williams v Florida,* 399 US 78 (1970). The court has also allowed use of non-unanimous verdicts in criminal cases in which a twelve-person jury is used, but six-member juries must render unanimous decisions. See *Apodaca v Oregon,* 406 US 404 (1972) and *Burch v Louisiana,* 441 US 130 (1979).

8 William J. Brennan, "State Constitutions and the Protection of Individual Rights," *Harvard Law Review* 90 (January 1977): 489–504.

9 *Sheridan Road Baptist Church v Department of Education,* 426 US 462 (1986).

10 See, for example, *People v Smith,* 420 Mich 1 (1984) (searches and seizures) or *People v Govea,* 421 Mich 462 (1984).

11 See, for example, *Maher v Roe,* 432 US 464 (1977) and *Harris v McCrae,* 448 US 297 (1980).

12 See *Right to Choose v Byrne,* 91 NJ 287 (1982) and *Committee to Defend Reproductive Rights v Unruh,* 29 Cal 3d 252 (1986).

13 Article IV, Section 12.

14 Article V, Section 28, as amended in 1978.

15 Article VIII, Section 3.

16 Article V, Section 19.

17 Article VI, Section 1.

18 Article VI, Section 25.

19 MCLA 168.474–168.478.

20 *Consumers Power Company v Attorney General,* 426 Mich 1 (1986).

21 Article XII, Section 2.

22 Article IX, Sections 25 through 34.

23 Dunbar and May, *Michigan,* p.114.

24 Congress passed the Ordinance of 1787 while sitting in New York City under the Articles of Confederation. After ratification of the Constitution, one of the first acts of Congress was to adopt the Ordinance and modify some of its terms to bring it into line with the new national government. See Acts of Congress, August 7, 1789, 1 U.S. Stat., Chapter VII, pp.50–53. See also Daniel J. Elazar, ed., "Land and Liberty in American Society: The Land Ordinance of 1785 and the Northwest Ordinance of 1787," *Publius: The Journal of Federalism* 18 (Fall 1988 – entire issue).

25 Thomas M. Cooley, *Michigan: A History of Governments* (Boston: Houghton Mifflin, 1885), pp.127, 130.

26 Michigan adopted a constitution in 1835 but did not formally begin as a state until January 26, 1837. Michigan argued that the Ordinance of 1787 guaranteed admission to the Union after satisfying the population requirement. Congress, however, was reluctant to admit Michigan until the longstanding border dispute with Ohio was settled, and admitted Michigan to the Union only after the state accepted an Ohio-Michigan boundary line drawn by Congress.

27 Dunbar and May, *Michigan,* p.245.

28 George N. Fuller, *Michigan: A Centennial History of the State and Its People* (Chicago: Lewis Publishing Co., 1939), p.245.

29 Ibid., pp.248–49.

30 Ibid., p.248; Cooley, *Michigan,* p.225.

31 F. Clever Bald, *Michigan in Four Centuries* (New York: Harper and Row, 1954), p.196.

32 Henry M. Campbell, *Outlines of the Political History of Michigan* (Detroit: Schober and Co., 1912).

33 Ibid., p.538.

34 Bald, *Michigan in Four Centuries.*

35 Cooley, *Michigan,* p.299.

36 Fuller, *Michigan,* p.327.

37 Cooley, *Michigan,* p.300.

38 Fuller, *Michigan,* p.326.

39 Ibid.

40 Dunbar and May, *Michigan,* p.368.

41 Ibid., p.329.

42 Ibid., p.332.

43 Fuller, *Michigan*, p.410.

44 W. A. Coutts, "Is a Provision for Initiative and Referendum Inconsistent with the Constitution of the United States?" *Michigan Law Review* 6 (February 1908): 305–17.

45 Campbell, *Outlines of the Political History*, p.23.

46 Article V, Section 1.

47 230 Mich 623, 203 N.W. 529: 1925.

48 240 Mich 584, 216 N.W. 450: 1927.

49 Article III, Section 8.

50 For greater detail, see Robert S. Friedman, *The Michigan Constitutional Convention and Administration Organization: A Case Study in the Politics of Constitution-Making* (Ann Arbor: Institute of Public Administration, University of Michigan, 1963); Albert L. Sturm, *Constitution-Making in Michigan, 1961–1962* (Ann Arbor: Institute of Public Administration, University of Michigan, 1963); Albert L. Sturm and Margaret Whitaker, *Implementing a New Constitution: The Michigan Experience* (Ann Arbor: Institute of Public Administration, University of Michigan, 1968).

CHAPTER FOUR

1 Michigan Constitution, Article V, Section 1.

2 Carolyn Stieber, *The Politics of Change in Michigan* (East Lansing: Michigan State University Press, 1970), p.76.

3 Much of this discussion stems from the index of gubernatorial powers designed by Joseph A. Schlesinger, "The Politics of the Executive," in Herbert Jacob and Kenneth Vines, eds., *Politics in the American States* (Boston: Little, Brown, 1965), pp.1220–31. For recent discussions see Keith J. Meuller, "Explaining Variation and Change in Gubernatorial Powers, 1960–1982," *Western Political Quarterly* 38 (September 1985): 424–31; Nelson C. Dometrius, "Changing Gubernatorial Power: The Measure vs. Reality," *Western Political Quarterly* 40 (June 1987): 319–34.

4 See chapter 8 for a detailed account of this campaign.

5 Article V, Section 17.

6 Willis F. Dunbar and George S. May, *Michigan: A History of the Wolverine State* (Grand Rapids MI: William B. Eerdmans, 1980), p.655.

7 E. Lee Bernick, "Gubernatorial Tools: Formal vs. Informal," *Journal of Politics* 41 (May 1979): 656–64.

8 For a more detailed account of this transition period, see Charles Press and Kenneth VerBurg, "Gubernatorial Transition in Michigan, 1982–1983," in Thad

Beyle, ed., *Gubernatorial Transitions: The 1982 Election* (Durham NC: Duke University Press, 1985), pp.212–35.

9 Charles Press and Kenneth VerBurg, *States and Communities in the Federal System*, 3d ed. (New York: HarperCollins, 1991), p.305.

10 G. Mennen Williams, *A Governor's Notes* (Ann Arbor: Institute of Public Affairs, University of Michigan, 1961), p.16.

11 George Weeks, *Detroit News*, February 11, 1989, p.B3.

12 *Detroit News Poll,* October 23–29, 1991. A poll taken at nearly the same time, by Market Opinion Research, showed the governor with a 44 percent approval rating, only 5 percent below that of June. Also, his approval rating in October was 9 percent higher than that for the state legislature, down 12 percent from June.

13 Stieber, *Politics of Change,* p.76. Also see Ferrel Heady and Robert Pealy, "The Michigan Department of Administration: A Case Study of the Politics of Administration," *Public Administration Review,* 2 (Spring 1956): 82–89.

14 Neal R. Peirce, *The Megastates of America* (New York: W. W. Norton, 1972), p.419.

15 G. Mennen Williams, quoted in Peter Kobrak, "Michigan," in Alan Rosenthal and Maureen Moakley, eds., *The Political Life of the American States* (New York: Praeger, 1984), pp.99–128.

16 Gerald O. Plas, *The Romney Riddle* (Detroit: Berwyn Publishers, 1967), pp.29–34.

17 Peirce, *Megastates of America,* p.420.

18 John Broder, "Milliken – The Governor, the Image, the Man," *Detroit News,* December 5, 1982, Michigan section, pp.19–28.

19 *Book of the States, 1988–1989* (Lexington KY: Council of State Governments, 1988), pp.116–17.

20 "Milliken Has Revenge in Veto Battle," *Detroit News,* October 2, 1977, p.A5. Milliken denounced the action and, according to this report, sought to humiliate legislators by maneuvering them into appearing to be unwilling to support a popular proposal to have the state police patrol freeways in Detroit.

21 Initiated legislation is not subject to gubernatorial veto.

22 Larry Sabato, *Goodbye to Goodtime Charlie: The American Governorship Transformed,* 2d ed. (Washington DC: Congressional Quarterly, 1983), p.61.

23 Personnel Division, Office of the Governor, March 1989.

24 Peirce, *Megastates of America,* p.425. Also see Kenneth VerBurg and Charles Press, "A Man of the Pros, Not the Pols," *Detroit News,* December 5, 1982, Michigan section, pp.36–48.

25 Rob Guiwitt, "The Governors' People," *Governing* 4 (March 1991): 26–31.

26 The governor appoints the directors to the Departments of Commerce, Labor, Li-

censing and Regulation, Management and Budget, Mental Health, Military Affairs, Public Health, Social Services, State Police, and Treasury.

27 Kobrak, "Michigan," p.105.

28 Stieber, *Politics of Change*, p. 99.

29 Charles Press et al., *Michigan Political Atlas* (East Lansing: Michigan State University, Center for Cartographic Research and Spatial Analysis, 1984).

30 For a look at more governors, see George Weeks, *Stewards of the State: The Governors of Michigan* (Ann Arbor: The Detroit News and Historical Society of Michigan, 1987).

31 See Williams, *A Governor's Notes*.

CHAPTER FIVE

1 E. Lee Bernick and Charles W. Wiggins, "Executive-Legislative Relations: The Governor's Role as Chief Legislator," in Eric B. Herzik and Brent W. Brown, eds., *Gubernatorial Leadership and State Policy* (Westport CT: Greenwood, 1991), pp.73–91.

2 Jeff McAlvey, personal interview with William P. Browne, July 1992.

3 John Burns, Citizens Conference on State Legislatures, *The Sometimes Governments: A Critical Study of the 50 American Legislatures* (New York: Bantam Books, 1971), pp.236–39. A recent study found legislators still plagued with problems in these areas; see Eugene W. Hickok Jr., *The Reform of State Legislatures and the Changing Character of Representation* (Washington DC: University Press of America, 1992).

4 Burns, *Sometimes Governments*, pp.52–53.

5 Gerald H. Stollman, *Michigan: State Legislators and Their Work* (Washington DC: University Press of America, 1978); Janet Miller Grenzke, *Influence, Change, and the Legislative Process* (Westport CT: Greenwood Press, 1982). See also Christopher J. Carl and Theodore M. Rusesky, *A Sesquicentennial Look at the Michigan Legislature* (Lansing: Michigan Legislative Council, 1987).

6 Charlie Cain and Roger Martin, "Who's Hot and Who's Not in Michigan Legislature," *Detroit News*, September 11, 1988, pp.1A, 14A–15A.

7 Burns, *Sometimes Governments*, pp.52–53. Michigan ranked third on this dimension.

8 "Michigan Lawmakers: 10 Best," *Detroit News*, September 11, 1988, p.14A.

9 Public Sector Consultants, *1991–92 Michigan Government Directory* (Lansing: Public Sector Consultants, 1991), p.88.

10 Personal interview with William P. Browne, February 1992. Additional quotes used in this chapter are from comments made to the authors.

11 Alan Ehrenhalt, "An Embattled Institution," *Governing* 5 (January 1992): 28–33.

12 This is unlike what was described in William K. Muir Jr., *Legislature: California's School for Politics* (Chicago: University of Chicago Press, 1982).

13 Bruce A. Rubenstein and Lawrence E. Ziewacz, *Three Bullets Sealed His Lips* (East Lansing: Michigan State University Press, 1987).

14 John H. Fenton, *Midwest Politics* (New York: Holt, Rinehart and Winston, 1966).

15 William P. Browne and Delbert J. Ringquist, "Sponsorship and Enactment: State Lawmakers and Aging Legislation, 1956–1978," *American Politics Quarterly* 13 (October 1985): 447–66; William P. Browne, "Policymaking in the American States: Examining Institutional Variables from a Subsystems Perspective," *American Politics Quarterly* 15 (January 1987): 47–86.

16 Legislator and other quotes used in this chapter are from comments made to the authors. See also Stollman, *Michigan,* on this point.

17 This description was used in Eugene Bardach, *The Implementation Game: What Happens After a Bill Becomes a Law* (Cambridge MA: MIT Press, 1977), p.297.

18 Close suburban seats, especially from Wayne County, often counted to swell the Detroit numbers on many votes.

19 In the senate in 1988, there were eleven noncommittee leadership positions for the majority party and eight for the minority. There were thirty-seven majority positions in the house and eight minority positions. Thus, 43 percent of all legislators were in leadership offices. That number changed in 1989 as the new Speaker revamped the rules determining positions.

20 Robert W. Becker, Frieda L. Foote, Mathias Lubega, and Stephen V. Monsma, "Correlates of Legislative Voting: Michigan House of Representatives, 1954–1961," *Midwest Journal of Political Science* 6 (November 1962): 384–96. This study was replicated in Christopher Lorenzen, "Comparisons of Legislative Voting: Michigan House of Representatives, 1954–1961 and 1984–1991" (M.A. thesis, Central Michigan University, 1992).

21 William P. Browne and Delbert J. Ringquist, "Michigan Interests: Diversity and Professionalism in a Partisan Environment," in Ronald J. Hrebenar and Clive S. Thomas, eds., *Interest Group Politics in the Midwestern States* (Ames: Iowa State University Press, 1993), pp.117–44.

22 Browne and Ringquist, "Sponsorship and Enactment." See also Stollman, *Michigan,* on committees. The gatekeeper role is quite important, as Alan Rosenthal suggests, because overall legislative performance can be judged on the basis of

committee efficiency. See Rosenthal, *Legislative Performance in the States* (New York: Free Press, 1974).

23 See Vincent A. Hauge and Spencer A. Hill, *Major Issues in Michigan Politics: A Study of Roll-Call Voting*, vols. 1 and 2 (Houghton MI: Political Press of Michigan, 1984 and 1986).

24 John Wahlke, Heinz Eulau, William Buchanan, and Leroy C. Ferguson identified legislative norms that emphasized interpersonal relations more than does the current Michigan emphasis on policymaking and its problems. See Wahlke et al., *The Legislative System* (New York: Wiley and Sons, 1962), pp. 141–69. Our analysis of norms results from what Richard F. Fenno Jr. would call interactive experience with legislators. Three of the authors who worked on this chapter spent time with the legislature over at least parts of the past three decades. We share an observation made by Kenneth A. Shepsle that legislative norms were encouraged when decisional resources were weak but then diminished as access to other sources of personal support grew. See Shepsle, "The Changing Textbook Congress," in John E. Chubb and Paul E. Peterson, eds., *Can the Government Govern?* (Washington DC: Brookings, 1989), p. 242.

25 Wahlke et al., *Legislative System*, pp. 146–47.

26 Karl A. Lamb, "Michigan Legislative Apportionment: Key to Constitutional Change," in Malcolm E. Jewell, ed., *The Politics of Reapportionment* (New York: Atherton Press, 1962); Karl A. Lamb, William J. Pierce, and John P. White, *Apportionment and Representative Institutions: The Michigan Experience* (Washington DC: Institute for Social Science Research, 1963).

27 *Baker v Carr*, 369 US 186 (1962).

28 *Reynolds v Simms*, 377 US 533 (1964).

29 *Marshall v Hare*, 378 US 561 (1964).

30 Bernard Apol, *Legislative Reapportionment in Michigan* (Lansing: Public Sector Consultants, 1987); see also Kathleen L. Barber, "Michigan," in Leroy Hardy, Alan Heslop, and Stuart Anderson, eds., *Reapportionment Politics: The History of Redistricting in the Fifty States* (Beverly Hills CA: Sage, 1981); William P. Browne and Delbert J. Ringquist, "Michigan," in Leroy Hardy, Alan Heslop, and George Blair, eds., *Redistricting in the 1980s* (Claremont CA: Rose Institute of State and Local Government, Claremont McKenna College, 1993).

31 A change in the 1980s, largely continued in 1992, saw the house plan favor Democrats while the senate plan, as accepted, favored Republicans; see table 8.

32 Fenton, *Midwest Politics*, pp. 11–43.

33 Charles Press and Kenneth VerBurg, *State and Community Governments in the Federal System*, 2d ed. (New York: Wiley, 1987), pp. 235–79.

34 Charles Press and Charles R. Adrian, "Why Our State Governments Are Sick," *Antioch Review* 24 (Summer 1964): 149–65.

35 Legislative Service Bureau, *Michigan Manual, 1991–1992* (Lansing: Legislative Service Bureau, 1991), pp.131–280.

36 James D. Barber found only a small group of "lawmakers" among the legislators whom he studied. Michigan today has a greater proportion of such individuals, although their lawmaker style varies. See Barber, *The Lawmakers: Recruitment and Adaption to Legislative Life* (New Haven CT: Yale University Press, 1965). He, however, also found many "reluctants" and "spectators" who did little.

37 Recent house and senate leaders have enhanced their influence by securing and then distributing funds from their own political action committees (PACs) to their loyalists. However, legislators expect to get funds, which limits leadership influence. In 1986, there were fourteen senate Republican PACs that distributed $461,762, five senate Democratic PACs that distributed $351,390, nine house Republican PACs that gave out $204,541, and six house Democratic PACs that provided $402,308. See David Waymire, "PAC Power in Lansing," a four-day series prepared by Booth Newspapers, Lansing Bureau (October 1988).

38 Jack R. Van Der Slik, "The Michigan Legislature in the Press of Time: 1953–1990," in Kenneth VerBurg, ed., *Forty Years of Change in Political Science: A Festschrift Honoring the Career of Charles Press* (East Lansing: Michigan Conference of Political Science, 1991).

39 Charles Cain and Jim Mitzelfeld, "Michigan Lawmakers: The Best and Worst," *Detroit News,* May 17, 1992, pp. 1A, 14A-15A.

40 House and Senate service office information. These data do not include part-time or Michigan Library personnel. Numbers are reported in rounded figures because staffing has become the forbidden subject of the legislature in the 1990s. No one wants to talk about the specifics of numbers or their organization, fearing voter backlash.

41 Nor are the staff viewed as the legislator's chief source of information. Both state agencies and interest groups were rated higher. See Richard McAnaw, *Science and the Legislative Process* (Lansing: The Michigan Legislature, Joint Committee of Science and Technology, 1978), p.9.

42 Grenzke, *Influence, Change, and Legislative Process.*

CHAPTER SIX

1 Most of the quotes used in this chapter were collected by William P. Browne in research for this book, 1991–92.

2 David Richey, "Damn the DNR," *Michigan Fisherman* 12 (February 1980): 17–20.

3 Interview comments from research by William P. Browne and Delbert J. Ringquist for chapter 9, 1986.

4 Board of Ethics, *The State Ethics Act: History of the Board, Rules and Decisions Abstracts* (Lansing: Michigan Department of Civil Service, Office of Policy and Public Affairs, March 1990).

5 Herbert Kaufman, "Emerging Conflicts in the Doctrines of Public Administration," *American Political Science Review* 50 (December 1956): 1057–73.

6 Willis F. Dunbar and George S. May, *Michigan: A History of the Wolverine State* (Grand Rapids MI: William B. Eerdmans, 1980).

7 Michigan Department of Civil Service, *Public Perceptions of State Employment in Michigan* (Lansing: Department of Civil Service, 1987; updated, 1992).

8 Ibid.

9 Michigan Employment Security Commission, *Occupational Employment Statistics for Michigan Federal, State and Local Government* (Detroit: Occupational Employment Statistics Unit, 1987; updated, 1992).

10 Neal Peirce and John Keefe, *The Great Lakes States of America* (New York: W. W. Norton, 1980).

11 Dunbar and May, *Michigan*.

12 Sidney Fine, *Frank Murphy: The New Deal Years* (Chicago: University of Chicago Press, 1970).

13 Frank Landers, *A Bureaucratic View of the Michigan State Government* (Marshall MI: The Marshall Press, 1987).

14 Robert Friedman, *The Michigan Constitutional Convention and Administrative Organization* (Ann Arbor: University of Michigan, 1963).

15 Ferrel Heady and Robert Pealy, "The Michigan Department of Administration: A Case Study of the Politics of Administration," *Public Administration Review* 2 (Spring 1956): 82–89.

16 U.S. Advisory Commission on Intergovernmental Relations, *The Question of State Government Capability* (Washington DC: ACIR, 1985).

17 Albert Sturm and Margaret Whitaker, *Implementing a New Constitution: The Michigan Experience* (Ann Arbor: University of Michigan Press, 1968).

18 Landers, *Bureaucratic View*.

19 Michigan Department of Civil Service, *Public Perceptions of State Employment in Michigan* (Lansing: Michigan Department of Civil Service, 1987).

20 Citizens Advisory Task Force on Civil Service, *Toward Improvement of Service to the Public* (Lansing: Citizens Advisory Task Force on Civil Service, July 1979).

21 Michigan Efficiency Task Force, *Implementation Progress Report* (Lansing: Michigan Efficiency Task Force, 1978).

22 Public Sector Consultants, *Michigan in Brief: An Issues Handbook for 1987–88* (Lansing: Public Sector Consultants, 1987).

23 Lee Sigelman, "The Quality of Administration: An Exploration in the American States," *Administration and Society* 8 (May 1976): 107–44.

24 Richard C. Elling, "Civil Service, Collective Bargaining and Personnel-Related Impediments to Effective State Management," *Review of Public Personnel Administration* 6 (Summer 1986): 73–93. Also see Elling, "Managing the States: Problems and Performance" (paper presented at the 1987 annual meeting of the American Political Science Association); Elling, "The Relationship among Bureau Chiefs, Legislative Committees and Interest Groups: A Multi-state Study" (paper presented at the 1983 meeting of the American Political Science Association); Elling, "Bureaucracy," in Virginia Gray, Herbert Jacob, and Robert B. Albritton, eds., *Politics in the American States: A Comparative Analysis,* 5th ed. (Glenview IL: Scott, Foresman/Little, Brown, 1990), pp.287–330; and Elling, *Public Management in the States: A Comparative Study of Administrative Performance and Politics* (Westport CT: Praeger, 1992).

25 Michigan Department of Civil Service, *Public Perceptions*.

26 Paul Courant, Edward Gramlich, and Daniel Rubenfeld, "Why Voters Support Tax Limitation Amendments: The Michigan Case," *National Tax Journal* 33 (March 1980): 1–20.

27 Gaye G. Benson, "Rational Actors and Administrative Rules: Legislative Veto in the State of Michigan: 1972–1984" (Ph.D. diss., Michigan State University, 1986).

28 Owen H. Porter, "Legislative Experts and Outsiders: The Two-Step Flow of Communication," *Journal of Politics* 36 (August 1974): 703–30.

29 Glenn Abney and Thomas Lauth, *The Politics of State and Local Administration* (Albany: State University of New York Press, 1986), p.43.

30 Martha Weinberg, *Managing the State* (Cambridge MA: MIT Press, 1977).

31 Brian W. Coyer and Donald Schwerin, "Bureaucratic Regulation and Farmer Protest in the Michigan PBB Contamination Case," *Rural Sociology* 46 (Winter 1981): 703–23.

32 Benson, "Rational Actors."

33 William P. Browne, "Variations in the Behavior and Style of State Lobbyists and Interest Groups," *Journal of Politics* 47 (May 1985): 450–68; and Browne, "Policymaking in the American States: Examining Institutional Variables from a Subsystems Perspective," *American Politics Quarterly* 15 (January 1987): 47–86.

34 Abney and Lauth, *Politics of State*, pp.101–2.

35 Elling, "The Relationship among Bureau Chiefs."

36 William T. Gormley, *The Politics of Public Utility Regulation* (Pittsburgh: University of Pittsburgh Press, 1983), p.148.

37 Kara Lynne Schmitt, "Licensing and Regulation: State versus the Federal Government," *Intergovernmental Perspective* 15 (Summer 1989): 33–35.

38 Stephen Frank, "State Supreme Courts and Administrative Agencies," *State Government* 51 (Spring 1978): 119–23.

39 Kirk Lindquist, "Budget Reduction Decisions in State Government: A Case Study of Michigan, 1979–1983" (Ph.D. diss., Michigan State University, 1985).

CHAPTER SEVEN

1 H. Ted Rubin, *The Courts: Fulcrum of the Justice System* (Pacific Palisades CA: Goodyear Publishing, 1976), p.47.

2 Robert L. Spurrier Jr., "The Trial Court Writ Small, Small Claims Adjudication in Oklahoma" (paper presented at the annual meeting of the Midwest Political Science Association, 1981).

3 Claims of lesser amounts are referred to the State Administrative Board.

4 Charles Joiner, "The Function of the Appellate System," in William F. Swindler, ed., *Justice in the States: Addresses and Papers of the National Conference on the Judiciary* (St. Paul MN: West Publishing, 1971), p.102.

5 Mary Cornelia Porter and G. Alan Tarr, "Introduction," in their *State Supreme Courts: Policymakers in the Federal System* (Westport CT: Greenwood Press, 1982), pp. xvi-iixx. See also, G. Alan Tarr and Mary Cornelia Porter, *State Supreme Courts in State and Nation* (New Haven CT: Yale University Press, 1988).

6 433 Mich 141, 445 N.W.2d 428 (August 1989).

7 *Trinova Corporation v Michigan Department of Treasury,* 111 S.Ct. 818 (1991).

8 *National Advisory Commission on Criminal Justice Standards and Goals of Courts* (Washington DC: Law Enforcement Assistance Administration, 1973), p.174.

9 Article VI, Section 25.

10 Article VI, Section 30.

11 "Ruling May Help Lawyer Skate Charges," *Detroit News,* September 14, 1992, p.1B.

12 Eric Freedman, "Michigan's High Court Gets an Appeal from Judges," *Detroit News,* October 21, 1988, p.5B.

13 *Judge of the 2nd District Court v Hillsdale County; Board of Commissioners of Cheboygan County v Cheboygan Circuit Judge* 423 Mich. 705 (1985).

14 G. Mennen Williams, "Full State Financing: The Price of Equal Justice," *Michigan Bar Journal* 64 (May 1985): 408–12.

15 Maurice Kelman, "A Tale of Two Parties," *Wayne Law Review* 19 (Winter 1973): 256.

16 *Committee for Constitutional Reform v Secretary of State,* 425 Mich 336 (1985). The Michigan Supreme Court rejected a challenge attacking this partisan method of nomination.

17 To confuse matters even more, sitting supreme court justices may simply renominate themselves by filing affidavits of candidacy with the secretary of state.

18 Kelman, "Tale of Two Parties," p.256.

19 Williams, "Full State Funding," p.408.

20 Larry L. Berg, Justin J. Green, John R. Schmidhauser, and Ronald S. Schneider, "The Consequences of Judicial Reform," *Western Political Quarterly* 28 (June 1975): 263–80.

21 Bradley Cannon, "The Impact of Formal Selection Processes on Characteristics of Judges Reconsidered," *Law and Society Review* 13 (May 1972): 570–93; Burton M. Atkins and Henry R. Slick, "Formal Judicial Recruitment and State Supreme Court Decisions," *American Politics Quarterly* 2 (October 1974): 427–49.

22 Brickley failed to gain the Republican nomination in the 1982 primary election.

23 Thomas Dye, *Politics in States and Communities,* 6th ed. (Englewood Cliffs NJ: Prentice Hall, 1986), p.213.

24 Dawson Bell, "Governor Courting a Legacy," *Detroit Free Press,* February 12, 1988, p.1A. Justice Williams noted that from 1963 to 1980, twenty-eight supreme court justices were elected and twenty-seven were first appointed; see G. Mennen Williams, "Selecting Michigan Justices," *Detroit College of Law Review* 4 (Winter 1983): 1497.

CHAPTER EIGHT

1 Daniel J. Elazar, *American Federalism: A View from the States,* 2d ed. (New York: Thomas Y. Crowell, 1972), p.126.

2 Willis F. Dunbar and George S. May, *Michigan: A History of the Wolverine State* (Grand Rapids MI: William B. Eerdmans, 1980), pp.215–60.

3 Ibid., pp.358–59.

4 Bruce A. Rubenstein and Lawerence E. Ziewacz, *Michigan: A History of the Great Lakes* (St. Louis MI: Forum Press, 1981), pp.119–82, 221–30. See this work for population patterns as well, pp.119–28, 221–30.

5 Ronald P. Formisano, *The Birth of Mass Political Parties: Michigan, 1827–1861*

(Princeton NJ: Princeton University Press, 1971), pp.15–31. This can be contrasted with patronage machines; see Harold F. Gosnell, *Machine Politics: Chicago Model* (Chicago: University of Chicago Press, 1937).

6 Dunbar and May, *Michigan*, pp.453–54.

7 Rubenstein and Ziewacz, *Michigan*, pp.187–92; James R. Shortridge, *The Middle West: Its Meaning in American Culture* (Lawrence: University Press of Kansas, 1989), p.110.

8 See Walter Dean Burnham on the states in *Critical Elections and the Mainspring of American Politics* (New York: W. W. Norton, 1970).

9 Dudley W. Buffa, *Union Power and American Democracy: The UAW and the Democratic Party, 1935–1972* (Ann Arbor: University of Michigan Press, 1984), pp.13–15.

10 This is not uncommon in the American states. See Austin Ranney, *Curing the Mischiefs of Faction: Party Reform in America* (Berkeley: University of California Press, 1975).

11 Michigan Democratic State Central Committee, *The Michigan Democratic Story, 1948–1954* (Lansing: Michigan Democratic Party, 1955). This labor and liberal intellectual alliance was not an easy one. To labor, issues of public policy were primarily bread-and-butter ones, and auto workers soon gained relatively high salaries, moving into the economic middle class. The intellectuals, however, were more idealistic and frequently found it hard to accept the labor movement of the 1950s and 1960s as one in need of philosophical defense. See also Robert L. Sawyer Jr., *The Democratic State Central Committee in Michigan, 1949–1959: A Study in the Rise of the New Politics and the New Political Leadership* (Ann Arbor: University of Michigan Press, 1960).

12 Dunbar and May, *Michigan*, especially pp.630–31.

13 Walter DeVries and V. Lance Tarrance, *The Ticket-Splitters: A New Force in American Politics* (Grand Rapids MI: William B. Eerdmans, 1972), pp.57–72.

14 Frank McNaughton, *Mennen Williams of Michigan: A Fighter for Progress* (New York: Oceana Publishing, 1960).

15 Buffa, *Union Power and American Democracy*, pp.64–68.

16 Daniel Angel, *William G. Milliken: A Touch of Steel* (New York: Public Affairs Press, 1974).

17 Douglas Crase, "Michigan Democrats in Disarray," *The Nation* 205 (March 11, 1960): 340–43.

18 Commission on Party Structure and Delegate Selection, *Mandate for Reform* (Washington DC: Democratic National Committee, 1970), p.4.

19 Edwin Chen, *PBB: An American Tragedy* (Englewood Cliffs NJ: Prentice Hall,

1979); Joyce Egginston, *The Poisoning of Michigan* (New York: W. W. Norton, 1980).

20 Don Albosta, interview with William P. Browne, 1980, as research on the national farm protest movement. See "Mobilizing and Activating Groups' Demands: The American Agriculture Movement," *Social Science Quarterly* 64 (March 1983): 19–34.

21 John H. Fenton, *Midwest Politics* (New York NY: Holt, Rinehart and Winston, 1966).

22 Buffa, *Union Power and American Democracy*, pp.27–48.

23 This went on in the same way that government action assisted union development. See Philip Ross, "The Role of Government in Union Growth," *Annals of the American Academy of Political and Social Science* 350 (November 1963): 74–85.

24 Jack Kroll, "Labor's Political Role," *Annals of the American Academy of Political and Social Science* 274 (March 1951): 118–22; Nicholas A. Masters, "The Politics of Union Endorsement of Candidates in the Detroit Area," *Midwest Journal of Political Science* 1 (August 1957): 135–50.

25 For information on COPE's founders, see Jacqueline Brophy, "The Merger of the AFL and the CIO in Michigan," *Michigan History* 50 (June 1966): 139–57.

26 Stephen B. Sarasohn and Vera H. Sarasohn, *Party Patterns in Michigan* (Detroit: Wayne State University Press, 1957), pp.33–45.

27 Timothy Conlan, Ann Martino, and Robert Dilger, "State Parties in the 1980s," *Intergovernmental Perspective* (Fall 1984): 12.

28 Ibid., p.13.

29 Cornelius P. Cotter, James L. Gibson, John F. Bibby, and Robert J. Huckshorn, *Party Organizations in American Politics* (New York: Praeger, 1984), pp.28–29.

30 Ibid., pp.52–53.

31 This information is based on a questionnaire mailed to all Michigan county chairs in 1986. The response rate was 94 percent. See Gregg W. Smith, "The Effect of Party Organizational Strength on Electoral Success" (paper presented at the 1987 annual meeting of the Midwest Political Science Association).

32 Ibid., p.23.

33 Ibid., pp.26–27.

34 See Gregg W. Smith, "Party Organizations and Voter Turnout: The 1988 Elections" (paper presented at the 1990 annual meeting of the American Political Science Association).

35 See David R. Mayhew, *Placing Parties in American Politics* (Princeton NJ: Princeton University Press, 1986). For an interesting commentary on Michigan

politics, see Samuel J. Eldersveld, *Political Parties: A Behavioral Analysis* (Chicago: Rand McNally, 1964).

36 These data were compiled from several sources by Gregg W. Smith and are based on the percentage of the presidential, congressional, and gubernatorial vote, and the percentage of the state legislature controlled by each party.

37 The expected vote is meant to measure the party identification of the electorate within the county. Its estimation is based on an analysis of votes for the two candidates from each party that run for the State Board of Education every two years. See Gregg W. Smith, "Effect of Party."

38 This finding should not have been too surprising. Detroit politics has long held bitter racial conflict. See B. J. Widick, *Detroit: City of Race and Class Violence* (Chicago: Quadrangle Books, 1972). Moreover, labor has never had hard-and-fast commitment from its members. See William Kornhauser, Harold Sheppard, and Albert J. Mayer, *When Labor Votes: A Study of Auto Workers* (New York: University Books, 1956).

CHAPTER NINE

1 Much of this chapter is the result of field research conducted by William P. Browne and Delbert J. Ringquist during the 1986 session of the legislature and then follow-up work in 1992. The material on PACs comes from John Klemanski's larger study of that subject.

2 Walter D. DeVries, "The Michigan Lobbyist: A Study in the Bases and Perceptions at Effectiveness" (Ph.D. diss., Michigan State University, 1960); William P. Browne and Delbert J. Ringquist, "Michigan Interests: Diversity and Professionalism in a Partisan Environment," in Ronald J. Hrebenar and Clive S. Thomas, eds., *Interest Group Politics in the Midwestern States* (Ames: Iowa State University Press, 1993), pp.117–44.

3 Daniel J. Elazar, *American Federalism: A View from the States,* 3d ed. (New York: Harper and Row, 1984).

4 Michigan's campaign finance law is similar to those of most other states, except in some details. Michigan requires disclosure of all contributions over $20. Those over $200 must also include the name, address, and occupation of the contributor. In contrast, Florida requires all contributions to be reported. North Carolina and Louisiana set reporting thresholds at $100 and $300 respectively. The range typical of most states is $25 to $100. Thus, Michigan's threshold limit is relatively low. Michigan's statute, however, is typical in that it also prohibits all cash contributions, a requirement that necessitates contributions by check, which would be traceable should a set of accounts be audited. Five reports are required during

election years; one in off years. Election-year reports must be filed before and after each primary and general election. An annual activity report is also required.

5 Browne and Ringquist, "Michigan Interests."

6 About one-fourth of the most current registrants were full-time public affairs employees even though not all of these were regulars. Some lobbying activity was a major part of the organizational responsibilities of the nonregulars.

7 Virginia Gray and David Lowery note considerable growth in the 1980s in Michigan interest groups. See Gray and Lowery, "The Diversity of State Interest Group Systems," *Political Research Quarterly* 46 (March 1993): 81–97; and Gray and Lowery, "The Density of State Interest Group Systems," *Journal of Politics* 55 (February 1993): 181–206.

8 On the regulars in various states, see Alan Rosenthal, *The Third House: Lobbyists and Lobbying in the States* (Washington DC: Congressional Quarterly Press, 1992).

9 The rankings are merged from our own 1986 survey and a 1987 mailed survey of all state legislators and lobbyists with long tenure. Response rates for our survey were 57 percent for legislators (83) and 35 percent for lobbyists (167). We also conducted extensive interviews with fifty of these policy activists.

10 William S. Ballenger, "Lobbyists in IMP Survey," *Inside Michigan Politics* 1 (November 2, 1987): 2–3; and Ballenger, "Multi-Client Firms 7 (and Muchmore) Top Lobbyist Survey," *Inside Michigan Politics* 7 (May 10, 1993): 1–3.

11 Bryan D. Jones and Lynn W. Bachelor, with Carter Wilson, *The Sustaining Hand: Community Leadership and Corporate Power* (Lawrence: University Press of Kansas, 1986; rev. ed., 1992).

12 For the pioneering study of Michigan PACs, see Richard McAnaw, "The Public Funding of Campaigns: The 1978 Michigan Experience," *Michigan Academician* 14 (Spring 1982): 403–14.

13 State of Michigan, Department of State, Elections Division, Campaign Finance Reporting Office, and various undated campaign finance summary reports.

14 John S. Klemanski, "Campaign Finance Reform, Election Activities, and State Political Party Organizations" (Ph.D. diss., Wayne State University, 1985).

15 Political action committees may contribute a minimum of $2,500 to primary and general election races for state representative seats; $4,500 to races for state senate seats; and $17,000 to gubernatorial races. In contrast, individuals may give only one-tenth these amounts to the respective races. Thus, while the act restricts direct campaign contributions from individuals, it does not limit their further financial participation through gifts to PACs or individual financial efforts on behalf of a candidate as long as the activity is entirely independent of a candidate's campaign committee.

16 Donald L. Correll, *Michigan's Gubernatorial Public Funding: Does It Work?* (Lansing: Michigan Department of State, 1984).

17 John S. Klemanski, "Campaign Contribution Strategies by PACs and Parties to Michigan Legislative Candidates, 1984," *Michigan Academician* 21 (Fall 1989): 221–33.

18 Common Cause in Michigan, "PACs and Michigan Legislative Races." Press release, October 27, 1986.

19 Many losing candidates raised and spent less than $500, thus exempting themselves from the reporting requirements.

20 William S. Ballenger, "PACs Increase Power in State Politics," *Inside Michigan Politics* 1 (September 4, 1987): 3–4.

21 Sarah McCally Morehouse, *State Politics, Parties, and Policy* (New York: Holt, Rinehart, and Winston, 1981). Also, for an analysis written at the peak of UAW power in the state, see J. David Greenstone, *Labor in American Politics* (New York: Alfred A. Knopf, 1969). He demonstrates how political context, as it changes from Michigan to California, affects auto union behavior.

22 Kenneth VerBurg and Charles Press, "He Was a Man of the Pros, Not the Pols," *Detroit News*, December 5, 1982, Michigan Section, pp. 36–48.

23 Browne and Ringquist, "Michigan Interests."

24 For an illustration, see Brian W. Coyer and Don S. Schwerin, "Bureaucratic Regulation and Farmer Protest in the Michigan PBB Contamination Case," *Rural Sociology* 46 (Winter 1981): 703–23.

25 Bryan D. Jones coined the descriptive term "bidirectional lobbying" to better illustrate the proactive nature of Michigan government in its interest-group politics. See Jones, "Government and Business: The Automobile Industry and the Public Sector in Michigan," *Political Geography Quarterly* 5 (October 1986): 369–84.

26 William P. Browne, "Variations in the Behavior and Style of State Lobbyists and Interest Groups," *Journal of Politics* 47 (May 1985): 450–68. Other aspects of these comparative state relationships are included in Browne, "Policymaking in the American States: Examining Institutional Variables from a Subsystem Perspective," *American Politics Quarterly* 15 (January 1987): 47–87; and Browne, "Some Social and Political Conditions of Issue Credibility: Legislative Agendas in the American States," *Polity* 20 (Winter 1987): 81–94.

27 The case was made interesting by disagreements as to whether the lobbyist saw the exchange of money as a bribe or as a legal honorarium.

28 Browne and Ringquist, "Michigan Interests"; Ballenger, "Lobbyists in IMP Survey."

29 L. Harmon Zeigler, "Interest Groups in the States," in Virginia Gray, Herbert Jacob, and Kenneth Vines, eds., *Politics in the American States,* 4th ed. (New York: Little, Brown, 1983), pp.97–131.

30 Sharon McGrayne, "Firms Budget Thousands to Influence State Officials," *Crain's Detroit Business,* November 1986, p.1; Mary Eurinoff, "Lobbying the Legislature," *Michigan Career Woman* 52 (August 1985): 16–20.

31 Thus, Public Sector Consultants was identified by reputation as among the most influential multiclient firms even though it identified no one as a lobbyist and it is noted for its research rather than for direct lobbying. Despite the firm's nonlobbyist self-image, its staff members are at least indirect advocates for specific policies that advantage its clients. Note also that the largest multiclient firm, Honigman and Associates, is not listed by reputation.

32 Janet Miller Grenzke, *Influence, Change, and the Legislative Process* (Westport CT: Greenwood Press, 1982); also see Joann Wilcox, "The Legislative Process: From a Lobbyist's Point of View," *Michigan Librarian* 42 (Winter 1976): 11–12.

33 Jeffrey Mirel, "The Politics of Professionalism: The Conflict over Teacher Licensure in Michigan," *Michigan Academician* 13 (Winter 1981): 317–35.

34 William S. Ballenger, quoted in Mark Hornbeck and Charlie Cain, "Legislators Can't Deliver on Key Issues," *Detroit News,* June 12, 1992, p.18.

35 For their helpful comments and suggestions to Charles Press, we thank Wes Thorp, manager of the House Press Room; Hugh McDiramid and Tim Jones of the *Detroit Free Press;* Eric Freeman of the *Detroit News;* Sarah Kellogg of UPI, Dale Atkins of AP, Rob Baykian of Great Lakes Media Group; Tom Greene, freelancer and former TV reporter; Paul Conn of Paul Conn and Associates and former staff of the House Democratic Communications Office; John Truscott, formerly of the House Republican News Office; and Scott Grigg of the Senate Republican Information Office.

36 Phill Brooks and Bob Gassaway, "Improving News Coverage," *State Legislatures* 11 (March 1985): 29–31.

37 Mary Tierney, "A Love-Hate Relationship," *State Legislatures* 10 (October 1984): 5–6; for an overview of relationships between politicians and journalists, see Charles Press and Kenneth VerBurg, *American Politicians and Journalists* (Glenview IL: Scott, Foresman/Little, Brown, 1988).

38 Dawson Bell and David Zeman, "Art of Milking Special Interests," *Detroit News and Free Press,* August 15, 1992, pp.1A, 8–9A. A typical defense was by Som Lisaius, "Pridnia Labels Articles 'Tabloid Reporting,'" *Manistee News Advocate,* August 18, 1992, p.1.

39 Bell and Zeman, "Art of Milking Special Interests," p.1A.

CHAPTER TEN

1 Willis F. Dunbar and George S. May, *Michigan: A History of the Wolverine State* (Grand Rapids MI: William B. Eerdmans, 1980), p.638. General taxes were added in 1933. Prior to that the state depended on property taxes. There were a few specific sales and use taxes that generated minimal revenue.

2 George H. Borts, "Regional Cycles of Manufacturing in the United States, 1914–1953," *The Journal of the American Statistical Association* 55 (March 1960): 151–211.

3 Roger L. Bowlby, "Michigan's Position in the Automobile Industry," *The Michigan Economic Record* 3 (January 1961): 8.

4 Alan Toffler, *The Third Wave* (New York: Bantam Books, 1980), p.14.

5 Harlen Cleveland, *Careers Tomorrow* (Bethesda MD: World Futurist Society, 1983), pp.126–31.

6 This view agrees with the convincing evidence of the legislature-sponsored Hudson Institute Report, *Michigan beyond 2000.*

7 Dennis R. Smith, "An Examination of the Taxation Bills Introduced into the Michigan State Legislature, 1981–1992" (M.S.A. thesis, Central Michigan University, 1993), pp.38–53.

8 Manufacturing jobs were counted differently before 1978 by Michigan statisticians, so comparisons vary somewhat. Computer workers employed by the auto industry in manufacturing, for example, are not listed as auto laborers. See Dunbar and May, *Michigan,* chapter 22, for early auto numbers and value.

9 Fredrick E. Terman, "Electronics and Education in the Midwest," *The Michigan Economic Record* 3 (January 1961): 8.

10 Jeffrey Mirel, *The Rise and Fall of an Urban School District: Detroit 1907–1989* (Ann Arbor: University of Michigan Press, 1993).

11 Robert Conot, *American Odyssey: A Unique History of America Told through the Life of a Great City* (New York: William Morrow, 1974).

12 John B. Rae, *American Automobile Manufacturers* (Philadelphia: Chilton Company, 1959); and Rae, *The American Automobile* (Chicago: University of Chicago Press, 1965).

13 Bryan D. Jones and Lynn W. Bacheler, *The Sustaining Hand: Community Leadership and Corporate Power,* 2d. ed. (Lawrence: University Press of Kansas, 1993).

14 Dunbar and May, *Michigan,* pp.610–30; Sidney Glazer, "The Michigan Labor Movement," *Michigan History* 29 (January–March 1945): 73–82.

15 Social welfare issues were also useful to union employees since they became prime beneficiaries during layoffs or when disabled.

16 Governor's Conference on the Future of Michigan Agriculture, *Competition, Survival, and Profitability* (Lansing: Michigan Department of Agriculture, 1985); updated 1991.

17 Mary Ahearn, Susan Bently, and Thomas Carlin, *Farming-Dependent Counties and the Financial Well-being of Farm Operator Households* (Washington DC: U.S. Department of Agriculture, Economic Research Service, August 1988).

18 U.S. Travel Data Center, Report on Michigan Tourism (Washington DC: U.S. Data Travel Center, 1988); Michigan Travel Bureau, *Michigan Travel Promotion 1990* (Lansing: Michigan Travel Bureau, 1991).

19 These estimates vary because state officials involved with tourism disagree among themselves as well as with the higher estimate of the U.S. Travel Data Center, which collects all the information. The variation is legitimate since jobs are defined differently as directly or indirectly involved in tourism or in some other service field. In some cases, officials also question whether positions really qualify as jobs, given low pay, short hours, and what is essentially supplemental income.

20 Corporation for Enterprise Development, *Making the Grade: The 1988 Report Card for the States* (Washington DC: Corporation for Enterprise Development, 1988).

21 Adoption of technology was not uniform within the Big Three, however. Firms varied in what they used, how successfully they adopted specifics, and their use of labor. GM and Ford provided an especially interesting contrast in the first wave of technology use.

22 David Osborne, *Laboratories of Democracy* (Cambridge MA: Harvard Business School Press, 1988), p.152.

23 Michigan Department of Commerce, *Path to Prosperity: Findings and Recommendations of the Task Force of Long-Term Economic Strategy for Michigan* (Lansing: Department of Commerce, 1984).

24 The fund was administered by a unique arrangement to avoid legislative or bureaucratic inertia and to still have partisan balance in appointing officials.

25 John Naisbett and the Naisbett Group, *The Year Ahead, 1986: Ten Powerful Trends Shaping Your Future* (New York: Warner Books, 1985); Osborne, *Laboratories of Democracy;* Corporation for Enterprise Development, *Making the Grade;* see also R. Scott Fosler, *The New Economic Role of American States* (New York: Oxford University Press, 1988).

26 Michigan Rural Development Partnership, *Rural Michigan: A Profile of Rural Michigan Today, a Strategy for Tomorrow* (Lansing: Department of Commerce, 1990).

27 Corporation for Enterprise Development, *The Development Report for the States* (Washington DC: Corporation for Enterprise Development, 1989).

28 Public Sector Consultants, *Michigan in Brief, 1988–89 Issues Handbook* (Lansing: Public Sector Consultants, 1988), p.178.

29 One indicator of this competitiveness has been the state's continued strength in patents, about 6 percent of domestic national registrations. See Patent and Trademark Office, Commissioner of Patents and Trademarks, *Annual Report, Fiscal Year, 1988* (Washington DC: U.S. Government Printing Office, 1989).

CHAPTER ELEVEN

1 The early literature on environmental problems, proposals, policies, and the movement that gave rise to Michigan environmentalism is extensive. A few of the works are Paul Ehrlich, Ann Ehrlich, and John Holdren, *Ecoscience: Population, Resources, and Environment* (San Francisco: W. H. Freeman, 1977); Barry Commoner, *The Closing Circle* (New York: Bantam, 1971); Garrett Hardin, *Exploring New Ethics for Survival: Voyage of the Spaceship Beagle* (New York: Viking Press, 1972); Murray Bookchin, *Toward an Ecological Society* (Montreal, Quebec: Rose Books, 1980); Dennis Meadows, *Alternatives to Growth I: A Search for a Sustainable Future* (Cambridge MA: Ballinger Books, 1977); and William Ophuls, *Ecology and the Politics of Scarcity* (San Francisco: W. H. Freeman, 1977).

2 Article IV, Section 52.

3 Michigan Environmental Protection Act of 1970 (House 1,11 3055, 75th Legislatures); MCLA 691.1201 et seq. (Supp. 1971).

4 Joseph L. Sax, *Defending the Environment: A Strategy for Citizen Action* (New York: Alfred A. Knopf, 1970). See also Elizabeth H. Haswell and Victoria S. Price, *State Environmental Management: Case Studies of Nine States* (New York: Praeger, 1973), pp.228–42.

5 See Joseph H. Thibodeau, "Michigan's Environmental Protection Act of 1970: Panacea or Pandora's Box," *Journal of Urban Law* 48 (April 1971): 579–605; Joseph L. Sax and Roger L. Conner, "Michigan's Environmental Protection Act of 1970: A Progress Report," *Michigan Law Review* 70 (May 1972): 1004–6; Joseph L. Sax and Joseph F. DiMento, "Environmental Citizens Suits: Three Years of Experience under the Michigan Environmental Protection Act," *Ecology Law Quarterly* 12 (Winter 1974): 271; Jeffrey K. Haynes, "Michigan's Environmental Protection Act in Its Sixth Year: Substantive Environmental Law from Citizens' Suits," *Journal of Urban Law* 53 (May 1976): 589–700; James M. Olson, "The MEPA: An Experiment That Works," *Michigan Bar Journal* 64 (February 1985):

181–85; Frank M. Olson, *Michigan Environmental Law* (Traverse City MI: Neahtawanda Press, 1985); Kevin T. Smith, ed., *Environmental Law in Michigan* (Ann Arbor: Institute of Continuing Legal Education, 1982); Joseph M. Polito, *Current Developments in Environmental Law* (Michigan Bar Association, 1980, 1985, 1987); and Joseph M. Polito, with Elizabeth Lowery, *Current Developments in Environmental Law* (Michigan Bar Association, 1986). These last four volumes by Joseph Polito were developed in each of the four years for the Michigan Bar Association law program.

6 *Ray v Mason County Drain Commissioner,* 393 Mich 294 (1975).

7 Speech by Michigan Governor William G. Milliken, Lansing, 1975.

8 Governor James J. Blanchard, *The Michigan Strategy: A Report to the People of Michigan and the Legislature* (Lansing: State of Michigan, 1987).

9 *Environmental Defense Fund v Director of the Department of Agriculture,* 11 Mich App 693 (1968).

10 *Organic Growers of Michigan v Michigan Department of Agriculture,* 10 ELR 20273 (1980).

11 Several accounts of this incident have been written (and cited in earlier chapters), and at least two films chronicle the events. See Joseph VanderMuelen, *An Outline of the Toxic Substances Control Act* (East Lansing: Michigan State University, Agricultural Experiment Station, 1983). A book not mentioned earlier is Frederick Halbert and Sandra Halbert, *Bitter Harvest* (Grand Rapids MI: William B. Eerdmans, 1978).

12 Smith, *Environmental Law in Michigan.*

13 Brian Wilson Coyer and Don S. Schwerin, "Bureaucratic Regulation and Farmer Protest in the Michigan PBB Case," *Rural Sociology* 46 (Winter 1981): 703–23.

14 Public Act 116, 1978; MCLA 286.181 et seq.; MSA 14.529 (101) et seq.

15 Joseph VanderMuelen and Greg Rosine, *Superfund: What's in It for Michigan?* (Lansing: Legislative Service Bureau and House Fiscal Agency, 1982). Also, see James A. Jarvis, "Toxic-Waste Management in Michigan: A New Policy Challenge," *Michigan Academician* 20 (1988): 303–15.

16 "Hazardous wastes" are defined in federal and state law. Generators of waste must determine if their waste material is so defined. Nuclear wastes, PBB, and PCB are not considered toxic. The term "solid waste" generally refers to trash, not infected with either hazardous or toxic substances.

17 Michigan Chemical Council, "Position Paper on Hazardous Waste Management" (Lansing: Michigan Chemical Council, 1985). Also, see MCC papers on "Community Right to Know," "Product Liability," and "Michigan Quality of Life Bond Issue."

18 "The Nuclear Waste Dilemma," *Detroit News,* March 9, 1992, p.6A.

19 Public Act 245, 1929; MCLA 323.1 et seq.; MSA 3.251 et seq.

20 Smith, *Environmental Law in Michigan*, p.238ff.

21 Council of Great Lakes Governors, Task Force on Toxic Substance Control Agreement, *A Report to the Governors of the Great Lake States*. (Chicago: Council of Great Lakes Governors, 1986).

22 Blanchard, *Michigan Strategy*.

CHAPTER TWELVE

1 These data come from the 1992 *Census of Governments*, vol.1, no.1 (Washington DC: U.S. Department of Commerce, Bureau of the Census, 1993).

2 Note that "district" does not imply, in the first instance, geographical area. Rather, it is a class of local government.

3 James Bryce, *The American Commonwealth* (reprint, New York: Macmillan, 1988).

4 Kenneth VerBurg, *Guide to Michigan County Government* (East Lansing: Michigan State University, 1987).

5 Article VII, Section 2.

6 Alexis de Tocqueville, "The American System of Townships," reprinted in Bruce Shinebrickner, ed., *State and Local Government*, (3d ed. Guilford CT: Duskin, 1987), p.14.

7 Kenneth VerBurg, *Managing the Modern Michigan Township* (East Lansing: Michigan State University, 1981).

8 John M. Beutler, "Townships, Towns, and Their State Associations" (M.A. thesis, Western Michigan University, 1980).

9 Joel Garreau, *Edge City: Life on the New Frontier* (New York: Doubleday, 1992).

10 Luther H. Gulick, *The Metropolitan Problem and American Ideas* (New York: Alfred A. Knopf, 1962), pp.132–36.

11 Article VII, Section 22.

12 Lincoln Steffens, *Shame of the Cities* (reprint, New York: Sangamore Press, 1957).

13 John F. Dillon, *Commentaries on the Law of Municipal Corporation*, 4th ed. (Boston: Little, Brown, 1890), p.145.

14 Article VII, Section 34.

15 Jefferson B. Fordham, "Home Rule – AMA Model," *National Municipal Review* 44 (March 1955): 137–42.

16 Article IX, Section 26.

17 Article IX, Section 30.

18 Article IX, Section 2.

19 Article IX, Section 4.

20 Often these are in competition with interests of the state police department.

21 Jeffrey Mirel, *The Rise and Fall of an Urban School System: Detroit, 1907–1981* (Ann Arbor: University of Michigan Press, 1993), pp.401–5.

22 Kenneth VerBurg, "Incorporation of the City of Wyoming, Michigan" (M.A. thesis, Michigan State University, 1960).

23 Kent Mathewson, ed., *The Regionalist Papers* (Detroit: The Metropolitan Fund, 1974).

24 *Report of the Governor's Special Commission on Local Government* (Lansing: State of Michigan, 1972).

25 *Detroit News*, October 10, 1992, p.1-B.

CHAPTER THIRTEEN

1 Floyd C. Fischer, *The Government of Michigan* (Boston: Allyn and Bacon, 1966), p.9.

2 DRI/McGraw-Hill, cited in "Where the Jobs Are Coming," *Governing* 5 (September 1992): 76.

3 Information provided by Robert Kleine, Public Sector Consultants, Lansing, 1992.

4 Public Sector Consultants, surveys on Michigan issues, Lansing, 1991–92.

5 Even the Senate Fiscal Agency, operating under Republican control, made this projection at the height of the proposal's campaign, just six weeks before the election.

6 For two studies of traditionalistic states where governors have emerged as catalysts for modernizing and industrializing their state, see Diane Blair, *Arkansas Politics and Government: Do the People Rule?* (Lincoln: University of Nebraska Press, 1988); and Dale Krane and Stephen D. Shaffer, *Mississippi Government and Politics: Modernizers versus Traditionalists* (Lincoln: University of Nebraska Press, 1992).

7 Marketing Research Group, surveys on gubernatorial popularity, Lansing, 1991–92. Engler's approval to disapproval rating was 51 to 40 percent in March and up to 54–39 in July. After the November election, it had fallen to 47–44 percent, according to surveys by Public Sector Consultants, 1992.

8 Bruce Catton, *Michigan: A Bicentennial History* (New York: W. W. Norton, 1985).

9 U.S. Department of Agriculture, Economic Research Service data, reported in *Rural Michigan: A Profile of Rural Michigan Today, A Strategy for Tomorrow* (Lansing: Department of Commerce, 1990).

10 Michigan can be compared to the trends noted by Christopher J. Bosso, "Into the

Third Wave: Environmental Activism in the 1990s" (paper prepared for the annual meeting of the American Political Science Association, 1992).

11 Steve Grooms, "The Enigma of the Lake Trout," *Trout* 33 (Spring 1992): 20–33, 44–49.

12 Ibid, p.45.

13 Allen Bronson Brierly, "Assessing State Environmental Policy Strategies: The Effects of Pollution Control Subsidies and Regulatory Standards on Economic Growth" (paper prepared for the annual meeting of the American Political Science Association, 1992).

14 See, for example, Sidney Fine, *Sit-Down: The General Motors Strike of 1936–37* (Ann Arbor: University of Michigan Press, 1969); National Advisory Commission on Civil Disorders, *Supplemental Studies* (Washington DC: U.S. Government Printing Office, 1968).

15 David R. Morgan, Robert E. English, and George G. Humphreys, *Oklahoma Politics and Policies* (Lincoln: University of Nebraska Press, 1992), p.208.

16 James Madison, Essay Number 10, *The Federalist Papers* (reprint, New York: New American Library, 1961), pp.77–84.

17 Public Sector Consultants, 1992.

18 Governor John Engler, personal interview with William P. Browne, January 1993.

About the Authors

JOHN B. ASHBY is a professor of political science at Northern Michigan University. His areas of academic interest are public law and state and local government.

DEBRA BRAND, a communications and computer network specialist with Dow Chemical, did graduate work in local government and also taught at Central Michigan University.

WILLIAM P. BROWNE, professor of political science at Central Michigan University, has written extensively on interest groups, public policymaking, and agricultural policy.

JOSEPH CEPURAN, associate professor of public administration, School of Education, University of Michigan–Dearborn, held previous positions in several research institutes publishing in welfare, urban, and other administrative areas.

RICHARD C. ELLING is an associate professor of political science and director of the Graduate Program in Public Administration, Wayne State University. His research and publications center on administrative and federalism problems of the state government.

SUSAN FINO, associate professor of political science, Wayne State University, has focused in her publications and teaching on national and state constitutions.

JAMES P. HILL is a professor and chair of the Department of Business Law and Regulation, Central Michigan University. A former U.S. Senate staffer, he does most of his work on environmental policy and is a Michigan National Resources Commission member.

ROBERT W. KAUFMAN is a professor of political science, Western Michigan University. His primary academic interest at present is environmental policy. His earlier work emphasized American national government.

LEO F. KENNEDY, Division Director, Legislative Research Division, Legislative Service Bureau, State of Michigan, is coordinating an oral history project through the bureau.

BERNARD W. KLEIN, professor emeritus of political science, University of Michigan–Dearborn, has also held administrative posts at that university, including that of acting chancellor, and at Wayne State, with the city of Detroit, and in state government.

JOHN S. KLEMANSKI is an associate professor of political science and MPA director, Oakland University. His research publications deal with campaign financing, state and local policymaking, and urban economic development.

PETER KOBRAK, professor and former director of public affairs and administration, Western Michigan University, previously worked for the governor of New York, the U.S. Department of Labor, and in Congress. His publications deal with various policy and administrative topics.

RICHARD MCANAW, professor of political science, Western Michigan University, publishes and teaches about state politics and the American legislature. He has done several projects with the Michigan legislature.

DAVID E. MURPHY is president of the Midwestern Higher Education Commission and was formerly an associate vice president of Central Michigan University and an education policy specialist with the Senate Fiscal Agency. His publications are in the area of public finance.

ALBERT F. PALM, associate professor and former director of the Center for Governmental Research, Central Michigan University, is a specialist and consultant in survey research and polling.

CHARLES PRESS, professor emeritus and former chair of the Department of Political Science, Michigan State University, has published extensively on numerous aspects of local, state, and national government. His most recent work looks at journalists.

DELBERT J. RINGQUIST, professor and chair of the Department of Political Science, Central Michigan University, has published on the American chief executive, state politics, and Africa.

THEODORE M. RUSESKY is a research analyst in the Michigan Legislative Research Division, Legislative Service Bureau.

NOELLE SCHIFFER, Membership Director, Engineering Society of Detroit, is a former state senate staffer and also teaches political science at Oakland Community College.

WILLIAM A. SEDERBURG is vice-president of Public Sector Consultants and former state senator and chair of the Michigan Senate Appropriations Committee. He has taught at several colleges and presently is president at Ferris State University.

JAMES D. SLACK, professor and MPA director, New Mexico State University, has published primarily on issues of personnel administration, including AIDS policy. He formerly directed a research institute in Michigan.

GREGG W. SMITH, assistant professor of political science at Gettysburg College, did his doctoral dissertation on Michigan politics.

KENNETH VERBURG is a professor of resource development and former associate dean of Continuing Education, Michigan State University. His numerous publications focus on state and local government, especially of Michigan. He also is a member of the State Boundary Commission.

DAVID S. VERWAY is a professor of finance at Wayne State University and research director at White/Calnan/White. He has edited several editions of the *Michigan Statistical Abstract* and has written numerous articles on the Michigan economy.

Index